EARLY CHILDHOOD EDUCATION
From Theory to Practice

EARLY CHILDHOOD EDUCATION
From Theory to Practice

DONALD L. PETERS
College of Human Development
The Pennsylvania State University

JOHN T. NEISWORTH
Department of Special Education
The Pennsylvania State University

THOMAS D. YAWKEY
Early Childhood Faculty
The Pennsylvania State University

with
D. Dudzinski, S. Willoughby-Herb, S. Golbeck, E. Klein, and E. Skinner

Brooks/Cole Publishing Company
Monterey, California

Brooks/Cole Publishing Company
A Division of Wadsworth, Inc.

Printed in the United States of America

10 9 8 7 6 5 4 3 2 1

Library of Congress Cataloging in Publication Data

Peters, Donald L.
  Early childhood education.

  Includes bibliographies and index.
  1. Education, Preschool—United States.   2. Handi-
capped children—Education (Preschool)—United States.
3. Mainstreaming in education—United States.
I. Neisworth, John T.   II. Yawkey, Thomas D.
III. Title.
LB1140.23.P48   1985   372'.21'0973   84-23026
ISBN 0-534-04680-0

Sponsoring Editor: Claire Verduin
Editorial Assistant: Pat Carnahan
Production: Stacey C. Sawyer, San Francisco
Manuscript Editor: Lyn Dupré
Permissions Editor: Carline Haga
Interior Design: Brenn Lea Pearson
Cover Design: Koney Eng
Cover Photo: © Jim Cronk
Interior Illustration: Robert N. Neisworth
Photo Researcher: Robert N. Neisworth
Photo Editor: Stacey C. Sawyer
Typesetting: G & S Typesetters, Austin, Texas
Printing and Binding: R. R. Donnelley & Sons Co., Crawfordsville, Indiana

PREFACE

*T*his book is written for the numerous people who are so dedicated to and who work so hard for young children and their families. It represents the culmination of more than ten years of collaborative efforts with our students. Throughout that period, we refined our theories of child development and learning, built bridges between theory and practice, and implemented high-quality programs for young children and their families. We also trained numerous student teachers, working professionals, graduate students, and parents in various aspects of theory, curriculum and program development, and adult-child interaction skills. Research and evaluation have been a continuous part of our activities.

We come from different backgrounds: special education, educational psychology, and child development and family relationships. We work for the same university but in three different departments at two colleges. Our commitments tend to be to different audiences and our professional allegiances to different organizations. Yet we are all very much a part of early childhood education, and early childhood education is very much a part of us.

Our separation within the university structure reflects, in part, the historical separation of the forms of early childhood education across different segments of the executive branch of government in the United States. That day-care programs usually are within the jurisdiction of the federal Department of Health and Human Services and state departments of welfare, whereas kindergartens and programs for handicapped children are generally controlled by departments of education, has more to do with these programs' history than with their current expression in society. Our separation is also, in part, an expression of the difficulties traditional university structures have with multidisciplinary fields. The tendency is to separate by academic field rather than to unite around common problem areas or interests. Luckily, students usually have the freedom to move across the artificial boundaries; indeed, we think they should be encouraged to do so. We have thus tried to provide a perspective in this book that is equally appropriate for students majoring in early childhood and kindergarten education, curriculum and instruction, child development, or special education. The book's content is equally applicable to nursery-school, day-care, Head Start, and early special-education programs—and to any other attempts to systematically use theory to design programs for normal or "mainstreamable" children during their early years.

The basic premise of this book is that practice should be *derived from* research and theory, not *rationalized by* it. It is this belief that has drawn the authors together; it is our message. We believe that programs built on theory and data can better optimize the development of children than can programs based on unvalidated rules of thumb, suppositions, or happenstance. We believe that a theoretical foundation makes consistency possible and that consistency in dealing with children is a real virtue. Understanding *why* one acts or should act in some way allows teaching to go beyond mere coping to thoughtful, planned activity—from mediocrity to excellence.

The fact that we use a theory-based approach does not mean that we believe any program, including those described herein, is a pure and precise prescription for action and organization. Rather, we think theory-derived programs are approximations—that is, alternative sets of operational definitions of theory as it is applied in practice. These operational formats and procedures are subject to evaluation—testing that will permit the refinement of both theory and practice. Format variation is possible and desirable but should be thoughtful, planned, structured, goal-oriented, and evaluated. In essence, we are advocating a systematic *theory of practice*.

We clearly do not intend to promote any one theory of child development and learning in this book. Indeed, the three main streams of educational thought are all represented to some degree. This evenhandedness was not difficult to achieve because the authors have different theoretical perspectives. However, we have given the most attention to two major approaches: cognitive-developmental and operant-learning theory. We believe that these two perspectives provide the basis for current innovations in early childhood education and that they also provide the clearest opportunities to demonstrate the relationship of theory and practice—our major message.

The opening section of the book, Chapters 1–4, places early childhood education within a historical and cultural context. The intent is to help you to know why things are as they are, not only to understand the present, but to also understand future possibilities. We all have a better sense of how things can change in the future if we know how they evolved. In this section, we look at the effects of economic, political, social, and technological change on programs and policies for early childhood socialization. We provide a framework for deriving practice from theory; this process of conceptual analysis presumably would hold no matter what theory of child development and learning is used as the starting point. We also discuss the extensive research in the field and the major findings that involve both program and policy.

Chapters 5 through 11 comprise an extensive presentation of operant behavior theory and the details of its implementation in the early childhood classroom. Chapters 12 through 15 provide a similarly detailed view of cognitive-developmental theory and its classroom applications. Chapter 16, an epilog, provides a recap of the materials and opinions presented in the book.

We have alotted roughly the same number of pages to the presentation of operant and cognitive-developmental theory, although the number of chapters devoted to the two sections are different. The intent is to allow the method of content presentation to be consistent with the principles of the theory being espoused—again to make our point that educational practice, including textbook writing, should be derived from research and theory.

In the years of our teaching and research, so many people have contributed to our ideas and understanding that it is impossible to list them all. They include our students who have helped over the years in the preparation of the manuscript: they are listed on the title page as our coauthors. These students have since developed their own careers in research and teaching in early childhood education. We are also grateful to our colleagues who have encouraged our work and expanded our understanding of both theory and practice and to the following reviewers, who provided helpful suggestions: Beverly Briggs, Kansas State University; Robert Rockwell, Southern Illinois University; Judith Washburn, California State University, Los Angeles; and Carol Wegley-Brown, University of Texas. Thanks also to Lori Amos for her invaluable assistance in reviewing and preparing portions of this text.

Finally, we wish to acknowledge the outstanding contribution of Arlette Manfull, who has been responsible both for manuscript typing and for keeping us well organized.

Donald L. Peters
John T. Neisworth
Thomas D. Yawkey

CONTENTS

PART THREE
_215_

COGNITIVE-DEVELOPMENTAL THEORY

PART ONE

EARLY CHILDHOOD EDUCATION

*E*arly childhood education has both a long history and a bright future. Since the beginnings of humankind there have been common understandings about the methods of socializing the young into society. Over the years, there have been differences about how best this socialization process might be accomplished, where and by whom it should be done, and what constitutes success. Some of the world's best thinkers, drawn from the fields of religion, philosophy and science, have directed their attention to understanding the processes involved and to writing prescriptions for their contemporaries. However, no one framework of beliefs and practices has ever been universally accepted. Now, as then, different points of view have enriched our understanding; current controversies have their roots in the past.

In the first four chapters we explore the origins and current manifestations of the diversity of ideas that surround early childhood education today. We examine early childhood education programs and policies by first taking a broad, cross-national view, asking why differences exist today even among industrialized western nations in the types of formal educational and child-care services they provide. We take a historical look at the origins of five major early childhood movements in the United States: the kindergarten, nursery-school, day-care, compensatory-education, and family-based program movements. Our intent is to show that, in a diverse society like that of the United States, there are many possible responses to the needs of early child care and education.

We then move on to an analysis of the belief systems, philosophies, and theories expressed in early childhood curriculum and program-content differences. Our basic beliefs about and understanding of child development and behavior influence decisions we make, both day to day as we work with children and as we design long-term programs and plan curricula. Systematic patterns of beliefs, usually termed *philosophies* or *theories*, emerge and continue to find vivid expression in early childhood programs. How theory becomes practice is the major concern of this book.

We place great reliance on the scientific method to inform our decisions at both the program and policy level. In Chapter 4, we turn to the burgeoning research literature of developmental psychology and education to look for the answers to some age-old questions: Is early childhood education effective? Does it make a difference? What is the best method for fostering the development of young children? Can we justify, through research, what we do with our children? The answers provided by scientific investigation are reassuring. Further, research provides us with some guidance to where we should go in the future.

The basic message of these first four chapters is that early childhood education is marked by diversity. It is full of the excitement of conflicting ideas and newly developing notions. One should enter this field with an open mind.

Chapter 1

Perspectives on Early Childhood Education

*E*arly childhood education has been part of human life for thousands of years. Each generation has been concerned with the socialization of its children with its norms, values, and attitudes. Each generation seeks to pass on its knowledge and technology. How best to do this has been the concern of some of the best thinkers throughout time. Philosophers such as Plato, Aristotle, Comenius, Locke, and Rousseau, and educators such as Pestalozzi and Froebel, addressed central questions of early education long before there were colleges of education or departments of psychology or child development.

Differences existed then, as they do now, about what, when, and how best to teach children. No one framework of beliefs or practices has ever been universally accepted. No single, overpowering theory has ever dominated to the point of totally squelching the opposition. Rather, there has been a continuous dynamic tension among conflicting ideas that has kept education from becoming stagnant and educators from becoming complacent. The result has been the evolution and testing of ideas, a process that has been markedly accelerated in recent years.

In this chapter, we set the stage for understanding what early childhood education is today and what it might be in the future. First, a broad definition of early childhood education is provided, one that both limits our view to the essentials and, at the same time, expands our horizons to the range of possibilities. Next, we place early childhood education within a historical and social context to see how our ideas are influenced by broad social, economic, political, and technological factors and how crucial early education is to the establishment and maintenance of society.

The socialization and education of young children has been the concern of many generations of adults in many societies.

A DEFINITION OF EARLY CHILDHOOD EDUCATION

To come to grips with the diversity of the field of early childhood education today, we need first to provide ourselves with a definition of early

3

childhood education—one that is sufficiently global to encompass past, present, and future possibilities. We have adopted the following:

> **Early childhood education** *is a programmatic effort in which an* **agent**, *operating within a* **context**, *uses some* **means**, *according to some* **plan**, *to bring about changes in the behavior of children between birth and age 8 [years] in terms of some definable* **criteria** *[Peters, 1977].*

Agents

The agents of change within early education, those who seek to foster and enhance the development of the young child, include many different kinds of people in many different relationships to the child. We usually think of the educators as professional teachers, but this is a very limited view. Even when we think of classroom- or center-based early childhood programs, our current notions of "professional teacher" do not apply. For example, many of the teachers of very young children have received little or no formal training in early childhood development and education. According to Zigler and Lang (1983), only

> *twenty-five percent of Head Start staff have professional training, such as the Child Development Associate credential or a bachelor's degree in early childhood education . . . [but] Head Start has a better trained staff than any other publicly supported program for [young] children with the exception of the public schools [p. 4].*

Data from a national survey of day-care programs within the United States provided confirmation of this situation (Ruopp, Travers, Glantz, & Coelen, 1979). The results of studies of countries other than the United States are similar.

The agents of change within early childhood education thus include professionals (usually but not exclusively teachers), paraprofessionals, grandparents, parents, siblings, peers, as well as other adults and children. Each of these many people brings to the situation different skills and a different background, not to mention a different personality.

Contexts

Each early childhood program is embedded in a physical, environmental, and historical context. The context of a program can be viewed as having many levels (Bronfenbrenner, 1979; Hildebrand, 1982), ranging from those that are close to those that are quite remote. For example, a particular nursery school operates within a physical environmental setting (such as the building structure, space, and playground facilities), for a particular group of neighborhood children, and with a particular group of teachers or agents. The school has its own particular purposes and history—all of these factors represent a "close-up" level. However, on a broader level, the fact that this nursery school exists at all is, in part, the result of the economic, social, and political substance of the nation as a whole, at a particular point in history—that is, a "remote" level. It would not have existed 200 years ago, and it might not exist 20 years from now—depending on a whole range of factors well beyond the control of the school's owner.

We shall come back to a more extensive discussion of contextual factors later in this chapter.

Means

The means employed within early education vary widely. They can be thought of as those factors that influence teaching and learning directly and those that do so indirectly. Direct means include such things as variations in the reliance on verbal interaction, the central importance of the educational materials provided, plus the timing, duration, and mode of presentation (for example, television or microcomputer), and a host of other possibilities, each designed to change directly the behavior of the child. These direct means are the primary focus of this book.

However, while focusing on direct means, we should not lose sight of the wide range of other alternatives for indirectly altering the environment (both physical and social) to bring about changes in children's learning and development. Indirect means include parent-education programs, community-development projects, health screening, nutritional supplements, and child-feeding programs. Such efforts are frequently tied to our direct early childhood education programs.

Plans

Included within plans are such things as sequences of learning, curriculum models, prescriptions for action, and intervention strategies. Each usually has a basis in some rationale, theory, or philosophy that dictates answers to questions such as:

1. Who will intervene?
2. When will they do it?
3. Where and under what conditions will it occur?
4. How will it be accomplished?
5. What are the goals of the effort?

Criteria

What we hope to accomplish with early childhood education is not always easy to say. Our choices reflect our values, hopes, and aspirations, both in-

Microcomputers: a new tool used in early childhood education.

dividually and as part of a larger society. We may have difficulty reaching consensus on such things. Still, as we shall see in the next section, at some important levels, agreement must and does exist.

Given our broad, introductory definition of early childhood education, you can certainly see a rich assortment of program possibilities. They range from giving a 2-year-old boy to his maternal uncle to be raised in the latter's tribe until puberty according to ancient tradition to introducing a 2-year-old girl to Disney software for the family's microcomputer. With such diversity possible, how do some types of early childhood programs and methods gain prevalence? The answer is explored in the next section.

BROAD DETERMINANTS OF EARLY CHILDHOOD EDUCATION POLICY AND PROGRAMS

Around the world and throughout time, the education of young children has varied greatly. Our definition of early childhood education suggests that not all possible alternatives exist or have been tried. Some have lost or gained popularity over time. To account for these variations, we need to look beyond the level of the specific individuals involved and their personal choices. Individual choices made by teachers can account for some differences in means that are seen from one day-care center to another. But they cannot account for a particular form of early childhood program's—for example day care's—rapid growth as an industry in the United States in the 1980s. To understand such phenomena, we need to look at what

Bronfenbrenner (1979) and others (Peters & Klein, 1981) have called *macrosystem factors*.

The macrosystem represents the overarching institutional patterns of culture or subculture as manifested in the economic, social, educational, legal, and political systems of a country. The macrosystem is a pervasive influence on the form and content of early childhood services.

The Form of Early Childhood Programs

When we speak of the *form* of early childhood programs, we are concerned with:

1. The *type* of services provided. Service types include formal programs such as kindergartens, health screening programs, and day-care centers as well as informal programs such as parent cooperative preschools and child-care arrangements. Also included are privately funded (through gifts, philanthropy, or fees) and publicly funded (through taxes) programs.

2. The *universality* of the services. The universality of a program form concerns its availability. Some programs are only for the poor or disadvantaged (Project Head Start), others are available to everyone within a geographical area (public kindergartens).

3. The *orientation* of the services. Some programs are oriented toward prevention of future problems (polio vaccination), some toward the amelioration of potentially dangerous or damaging situations (early intervention programs for the economically disadvantaged), some toward the remediation of already existing concerns (infant stimulation for the children of retarded mothers).

4. The *delivery system* of the services. Some programs are designed for delivery through the family unit (home visitor programs), some through centralized educational and social living arrangements (institutional and residential child-care facilities).

The Content of Early Childhood Programs

We use *content* to refer to what is delivered by some form of early childhood program. This includes such things as the specific services provided, the goals and objectives for children, and the curriculum. Content is usually based on some underlying theory of human nature that represents the world view of the people concerned; it represents what they consider important and how they interpret their world. Differences in world view have a major effect on what people do, whether in the early childhood classroom or elsewhere. Hence, much of the remainder of this book is directed specifically toward content issues.

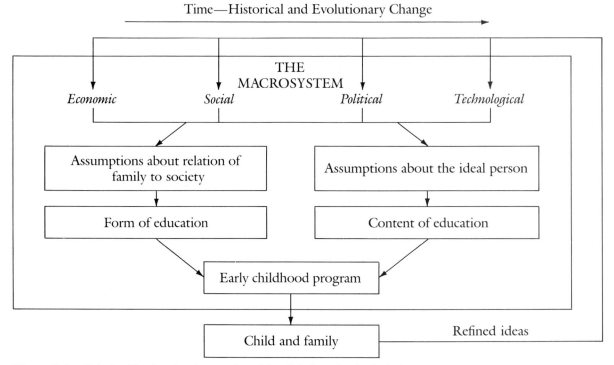

Figure 1-1   *Relationship of national economic, social, political, and technological structure to the general early education program (adapted from Peters and Klein [1981] with permission).*

FORM, CONTENT, AND NATIONAL POLICY

As we look around the world and across time, it is apparent that most people in most nations, in some general sense, have endorsed and fostered one or another theoretical position about early childhood. The common philosophical stance is reflected at all levels from the top government officials to the aide in the classroom. Within a single country or at a particular time, differences of opinion exist (we will discuss this further later), but at first blush it is the commonality that is most striking. What produces that commonality, that written or implied national policy?

To a very great degree, the commonalities, as well as the cross-national and historical differences, in the form and content of early education are a relatively direct reflection of macrosystem variations in the economic, social, and political systems of the country and the state of technology at the time (Peters, 1980). They reflect where a nation has been and where it aspires to go.

Figure 1-1 provides a quick look at what are indeed complex relationships. Put simply, the prevailing economic, social, and political beliefs of a

A country's needs, governmental system, and level of economic development determine the nature of its educational programs.

culture are translated into assumptions about the relationship of the family to society and about what the ideal person should be. These, in turn, are translated into the form and content of early childhood education. Successful early childhood education, then, presumably produces children who, when they grow up, will maintain the economic, social, and political order and cope with or further advance the technology.

The system seems self-serving and self-conserving; that is, it will help to maintain the status quo. In part that is true. It is a system that resists abrupt change, but it is also developmental because time (and hence historical and evolutionary change) is a constant factor in the equation. By the time the young children grow up, the social, economic, political, and technological worlds have changed somewhat; so they in turn design a different system than did their parents. Do not forget that the 5-year-old enrolled in an early education program in the 1980s will be having his or her influence on the economic, social, political, and technological world through 2050 and beyond. Let us turn now to a closer look at these relationships.

Economic Development

The distribution of wealth and the general level of economic development of a nation determine, to a great extent, the kinds and range of programs that are considered desirable and feasible (Robinson, Robinson, Darling, & Holm, 1979). A country with a large middle class and a relatively high standard of living for most of its citizens (such as Sweden, the United States, or Denmark) deals with an entirely different set of circumstances than does a country in which resources are grossly unevenly distributed, where there is mass poverty, and where there are real questions of survival. In the former, the number of program options is wider and the level of aspiration higher. In the latter, options are restricted by limited resources, and aspirations may be at quite a fundamental level. In India and Chile, for example, where the death rate of children ages 1 to 5 years is staggeringly high, survival and social responsibility become central concerns.

Differences also are found between nations that have a socialist economy and those that are organized around a free-enterprise system. The former generally encourage standardization of programs, available equally to all, which emphasizes cooperation and social responsibility. The latter permit diversification of programs, with differential accessibility, which stresses individualism and competition.

Social Orientation

Some societies, many of them with socialist economies, are oriented toward preventing social problems such as child abuse, unemployment, and mental illness. Such countries also tend to hold the prevailing belief that the child, from birth, is a member of the larger society, given during the formative years to the custody of the parents, whose civic duty it is to love the child and to bring up that child to be a public-spirited citizen and worker. The state retains the major responsibility for the child and has the obligation to assist the parents in executing their civic duty (Robinson & Robinson, 1972). This leads to efforts to provide programs that reach every child and family with a wide range of services considered to be their right and due.

Other societies, usually with a capitalist economy, hold the prevailing belief that the responsibility for child care is almost totally the family's and that the child "belongs to" the parents (Kadushin, 1978). It is assumed that most families should and will manage their responsibility without assistance. As such, social programs are provided only in cases of special need. Parents must prove themselves grossly inadequate before any governmental body intervenes. Public service programs are available only to those who are in an emergency and have proven eligibility (Kamerman & Kahn, 1976).

Political Organization and Orientation

In the creation and implementation of programs, countries differ widely in the degree to which there is centralized versus decentralized control. Some countries establish national goals and long-range plans to meet children's needs. Others leave priority setting to social and political happenstance. In some countries (the United States, Switzerland), planning, funding, and implementation are decentralized to the state or local level. In other countries (the Peoples Republic of China), the national government assumes full authority and responsibility (Robinson, Robinson, Darling, & Holm, 1979). Additionally, the relative power positions of professionals, parents, practitioners, and government officials vary widely (Peters, 1980). Where decentralization and division of power is common, there is less coordination among programs, parents have greater freedom in the selection of programs for their children, and there is a wider diversification of goals for children.

National Policy toward Early Education

Taken together, the economic, social, and political contexts affect both the *form* and *content* of early childhood education programs. Some examples will help to make the point.

The Soviet Union has a socialist economy, a social orientation that is preventative, and a highly centralized political structure. Within this system, it is clear that the child, from birth, is a member of the larger society and hence the responsibility of the state. For the state to meet its obligations and to ensure that future citizens will meet the needs of the economic, social, and political systems, a narrow and uniform array of programs has been established that provide health, nutrition, and education services to every child, and every child and family is expected to use these services. The educational programs that are a part of this larger delivery system are highly developed, and learning is not left to chance or to the competence of the individual teacher. Skilled specialists have developed and are continuously refining the one curriculum used by all preschool centers. Teachers receive detailed guidelines for implementing the program content.

The fostering and teaching of moral traits and positive social qualities is a primary responsibility of the Soviet preschool teacher. Several special teaching techniques have been developed to accomplish this goal. For example, games are central to the curriculum. The games involve several children working in a group. A collective or team spirit is fostered by having children within the group provide mutual aid. Children learn to support and discipline each other within this play group context. All competition is between groups rather than among individuals (Bronfenbrenner, 1970; Robinson et al., 1979). Children assume many responsibilities and duties of the classroom. They prepare and serve food, clear the tables, care for the animals and plants, do routine housework, and cultivate gardens; value is placed on this work. The program also heavily emphasizes love of country and respect for national heroes.

Other combinations of wealth, social policy, and politics, instead of creating a unified program, yield a diversified array of crisis intervention services, which may or may not be available to a child or a family when they are needed. In this case, it is typical to have health, nutrition, education, and social services viewed as separate systems operating independently of one another. Such is the case in Great Britain, Canada, and Israel where nursery schools and kindergartens are separate and distinct from day-care programs or child-health programs. Availability of services varies from locale to locale. Curricula are not centrally prescribed, and diversity is encouraged. Teachers have great individual autonomy. In such cases, it is not possible to describe the *one* program. Rather, we must talk about either the *modal* program, or the most typical program, or the most interesting program (as for example the new British infant school program, a very open, unstructured program that is practiced in only about 30 percent of Britain's infant schools), or the most innovative program (such as the Israeli kibbutz, a cooperative, intense, community living arrangement that affects only a small portion of the population; see Box 1-1) (Raben, 1982).

DEVELOPMENT OF FORM AND CONTENT IN THE UNITED STATES

In the United States, early childhood education has had a unique and particularly rich history. The economic, social, and political factors contributing to this history can be summarized as follows:

1. There has been sufficient economic wealth to provide the resources necessary to mount a large early childhood education effort.

2. Individual wealth is broadly but not evenly distributed. This has yielded several different segments of society, each relatively large, and

---

Box 1-1   *The Kibbutz**

The first kibbutz (Hebrew for *collective*) was founded in 1909 by seven young Zionist pioneers from Russia. A mixture of practicality and idealism determined their decision. They were influenced by the Russian novelist Leo Tolstoy's call for a return to nature and for a life of simple, selfless sharing with one's fellow humans and by Karl Marx's notions of socialist principles; the kibbutz's principal function, however, was and is economic, social, and physical survival in a hostile atmosphere.

Most kibbutzim in Israel today are rural communities. They usually have communal dining halls and meeting spaces. They rarely have less than 100 members. Marriage is the rule among couples who are usually given a small flat, whereas unmarried members generally share a room with someone else. In most kibbutzim, the children live in sepa-

rate communal houses until the age of 18 years; each group has its counselors and teachers who are responsible for the welfare of the children. Children of the kibbutz automatically become members on reaching the age of 18 or 21 years.

Although they account for only about 4 percent of the total Jewish population, Israel's kibbutzim have been held up as shining examples of social experimentation. These collective settlements occupy a special place in the political, social, economic, and national-defense scheme in Israel, and kibbutz members wield a governmental influence that far exceeds their number.

* Samuel, E. (Ed.). The kibbutz: past, present, future. *Keeping posted* 18(1972), 2–3.

Children playing at an Israeli kibbutz.

each with different needs, goals, and desires. The result has been a diversity in early childhood education programs.

3. The economic system is organized around competition. To succeed in a competitive economy, one has to "build a better mousetrap." Such competition in the early education field has produced a huge industry marked by innovation in programs, equipment, and materials.

4. The social structure is founded on beliefs in individualism and individual freedom. This has served both to diminish coordination and consolidation of efforts and to increase the diversity of individual program goals and content.

5. The social structure is crisis oriented and socially reactive. This has resulted in a concern for specific (rather than comprehensive) service delivery and the development of multiple single-purpose programs. It also has meant that programs come and go or are replaced as crises wax and wane.

6. The social system is built on the assumption that the parents hold principal responsibility for the child and that parental choice should be the primary determinant of what, when, and how children are taught. This has led to a wide diversity of opinion and a localization of control in early education.

7. The constitutional form of government has been designed to maintain a balance of power among the local, state, and federal levels of government. This has resulted in decentralized control and, hence, increased diversity of programs.

8. The governmental structure has separated responsibility for establishing and funding programs (legislative branch) from responsibility for implementing them (executive branch), which has provided opportunity both for the infusion of more new ideas and for flexibility in meeting new societal needs (crises) as they are identified.

9. The political process is an open one that permits professionals, parents, and special interest groups (frequently in the form of lobbies) all to influence decisions. This has led to a high level of responsiveness and innovation. Programs are conceived, developed, and implemented in an atmosphere of open discussion.

10. There is an underlying belief that science and technology are important contributors to the solution of problems (Peters, 1980).

All of these are important social-policy and program determinants. Taken together, they help to explain something of the diversity of early childhood education in the United States today. For example, the economic stratification of our society and the "reactive" nature of our social institutions help to explain why we have a nursery-school movement that basically serves children of middle-class or affluent parents while we have programs like Project Head Start for low-income children. Our assumptions about the relationships of children to parents and to the state explain our stress on parent involvement, and our belief in competition and the free market explains the wide range of curriculum models and materials available. Similarly, our belief in the value of science, and in the scientific method as a means of solving problems, accounts for our heavy emphasis on research and evaluation in early childhood education and for our conviction that every new technological advance has potential in the classroom. The rapid rise of the microcomputer in early childhood education is but the latest example of the results of this belief.

SUMMARY

In this chapter, we have provided a definition of early childhood education that focuses attention on the range of agents, means, and plans that can be considered part of our program efforts. We indicated that it is reasonable to go well beyond thinking of early childhood education as being professional teachers in a center- or school-based classroom with a group of children interacting verbally and with educational materials. The range of possibilities is far broader than that, but not all possibilities exist or survive. The form that early childhood services take in any particular place at any particular time, and the content of those services, is a function of broader macro-environmental cultural patterns manifested in the economic, political, and social system. Such factors as the economic development of a country, the organization of its economy, the orientation of its social system, and the openness of its political system all play a role in determining what people consider *desirable* (in terms of the relationship of families to the institutions of society and what is considered the ideal person for the society) and *feasible* (in terms of their resources). Within the United States, our economic, social, political, and technological beliefs have permitted the growth of a broadly diversified system, but it is "reactive" to problems and leaves out large numbers of people.

In the next chapter, we will take a historical look at the forms of early childhood education in the United States.

Review Questions

1. Using the introductory definition of early childhood education, describe at least three very different examples of early childhood programs.
2. Assume you are going to make a trip to the Far East to visit early childhood programs there. What kinds of questions might you want answered before you go? What sources might provide background reading?
3. List three economic, social, or political factors contributing to the history of early childhood education programs in the United States, and discuss what were their implications for the form and content of early education.
4. Discuss the implications for early childhood education of the social belief that children "belong to" their parents.
5. Go to the library and find articles or books describing early childhood programs in two different countries. List two characteristics of the political organization and orientation of those countries that have affected the form of the early childhood education programs developed. Explain how the two countries differ.

Suggested Activities

1. Ask several foreign or exchange students to visit your class to discuss what early childhood education is like in their country. Ask them to address issues such as their country's policy toward child care outside of the home, the availability of early childhood education programs, and the level of training of teachers.
2. Collect examples of unusual early childhood education programs from magazine and newspaper articles. Discuss what they have in common and where they differ.
3. Read several books on the economic, social, political, and technological changes that have occurred in the last 20 years in our society, and brainstorm about the implications of these changes for early education in the year 2000 and beyond (examples include: Toffler's *Future Shock* and *The Third Wave*, Naisbitt's *Megatrends*).
4. Ask several elderly persons in your community to discuss with you their early childhood years. How were they raised? What was the world like? What schooling or early child-care programs were available to them and their parents?

Suggested Readings

Fein, G., and Clarke-Stewart, A. *Day care in context.* New York: Wiley, 1973.

Strickland, C. E. Paths not taken: seminal models of early childhood education in Jacksonian America. In Spodek, B. (Ed.), *Handbook of research in early childhood education.* New York: Free Press, 1982.

Williams, C. R., and May, C. (Eds.). Early education: child and context. Special Issue, *Theory Into Practice* XX (2), Spring 1981 (Columbus: The Ohio State University).

Chapter 2	# *A Historical View of the Forms of Early Childhood Education in the United States*

*I*n this chapter, we examine how five somewhat different forms of early childhood education programs have evolved in the United States. We do so by regarding each program as a movement, with founders, purposes, and followers, each deriving from and reflecting changes in the basic economic, political, social, and technological structure of the dominant North American culture.

The five forms of early childhood education are the kindergarten, nursery-school, day-care, compensatory-education, and family-based program movements. The five are not independent of one another. They coexist and overlap at many points, both historically and currently. However, each has a uniqueness that helps us to understand the diversity of the early childhood education field today.

KINDERGARTEN MOVEMENT

The kindergarten movement represents the oldest and most widely established formal early childhood education movement in the United States. Its origins date back to the 1860s and the work of such people as Elizabeth Peabody and Susan Blow, who adopted the child-centered approach of Friedrich Froebel (1782–1852) of Germany. Of particular interest for understanding this form of early education is that as early as 1874 a department of kindergarten was established by the National Education Association (NEA). This move was followed by a significant NEA recommendation that the kindergarten program be included as a regular part of the public school enterprise.

Although private kindergartens continue to exist and flourish in some parts of the country, the notion that kindergarten is a rightful part of the publicly provided educational experience has won near universal favor. Today, most states provide financial support for public kindergartens and most communities provide such programs. Currently, over 3 million children are enrolled in such programs annually (Kadushin, 1978).

As part of the regular public education system, the programs are generally housed within public school facilities, and are taught by certified teachers. Although most are not academically oriented ("3R" subject matter), they focus on preparation for formal school learning. Most programs enroll 5-year-olds in a half-day program for eight to ten months per year. (The duration generally corresponds to the state-established length of the school year—approximately 180 days.) The programs are regulated by the federal, state, and local educational structure. Kindergartens seldom provide health, nutritional, or social services as a regular part of the program. Although in the early days of the kindergarten movement teachers were expected to spend their afternoons visiting pupils' homes or inviting mothers into the classroom for talks on health care and child rearing, current kindergartens seldom encourage more than a token form of parent involvement. As such, the kindergarten movement can be characterized as providing nearly universal, specific, formal educational services to an age-specific segment of U.S. children.

The earliest form of early childhood education in the United States dates back to the late 1800s.

NURSERY-SCHOOL MOVEMENT

Ties with Higher Education

From its beginning in the 1920s, the nursery-school movement in the United States has been closely related to the child-study and child-guidance movements. Indeed, many of the earliest programs were established by colleges or universities, or university-related research institutions, to permit the longitudinal study of child development and the training of early childhood personnel. Some of the earliest of these programs were founded at the Gesell Child Guidance Nursery at Yale University (about 1920), the Merrill-Palmer Institute (1920), Columbia Teachers College (1921), Bank Street College (1919), and the Iowa Child Welfare Research Station (1921) (Braun & Edwards, 1972). This close relationship between the nursery school and colleges and universities continues today, particularly with departments of child study and family-life education (usually part of home economics or human development).

Several features of the relationship between higher education and early childhood education are important for understanding the evolution and cohesiveness of the nursery-school movement. First, when the movement began in the United States, there was only a handful of people who had experience in the field. Their backgrounds were diverse, spanning many disciplines including education, nursing, nutrition, psychology, and social work. Their interests in the preschool child sprouted independently from their own professional contacts with children and families, but came together in their conviction concerning the importance of the preschool years for later development and their desire to know more about the processes involved in the course of development.

Being from an academic tradition and sharing a common focus of interest, this interdisciplinary group of pioneers held a conference in 1925 at Columbia Teachers College. Subsequently, they formed the National Committee on Nursery Schools (1926), the National Association for Nursery Education (1929, now called the National Association for the Education of Young Children), and the Society for Research in Child Development (1933). Each of these organizations has maintained a multidisciplinary tradition to the present.

Second, (although it played no part in the organization of European nursery schools) interest in child-development research was the motivation behind opening many of the experimental nursery schools in the United States. In 1923, the Laura Spelman Rockefeller Memorial Foundation be-

---

Box 2-1 What's New under the Sun? Old Thoughts about Early Intervention

Did you know that Friedrich Froebel (1782–1852) in *The Education of Man* (published in translation in 1912) anticipated current infant stimulation programs? His prescriptions include:

1. Children should never be left too long to themselves . . . without some external object to occupy them.

2. It is advisable to suspend in a line with the child's natural vision a swinging cage with a lively bird (or artificial birds cut from bright-colored paper). This secures occupation for the senses and the mind, profitable in many directions.

Comenius (1592–1670), the Moravian bishop, stated: "It is a property of all things becoming that they can easily be bent and formed as long as they are tender. . . . The young tree can be planted, replanted, trimmed, and bent to any shape; not so the grown."

His prescription for early intervention includes:

1. Begin early after the mind has been made ready

2. Proceed from the general to the particular

3. Do not force children to do anything but that to which they aspire according to their age and motivation

4. Everything must be related through sense impression

5. Everything must be applied immediately (from Ulich, 1950)

Arnold Gesell made clear the importance of the early childhood period. He stated it this way:

The preschool period is biologically the most important period in the development of an individual for the simple but sufficient reason that it comes first. Coming first in a dynamic sequence, it inevitably influences all subsequent development [Gesell, 1923].

And John Dewey, in 1897, wrote

I believe . . . the school life should grow gradually out of the home life; that it should take up and continue the activities with which the child is already familiar in the home. . . . I believe that education is the fundamental method of social progress and reform [Dewey, 1897].

gan supporting the fields of child study and parent education. These funds led to the rapid growth of the child-development field and fostered the dynamic interplay of research and practice.

Third, there was a continuous concern for the training of early childhood personnel. For example, the Merrill-Palmer Institute nursery school was founded by home economist Edna Noble White to provide a laboratory for training young women in child care. She believed that such courses should be made a part of the training of all young women because they come in contact with children in many capacities—as mothers, teachers, social workers.

Fourth, the role of the parent and the role of the nursery school were intimately bound together in the movement. Indeed, one of the earliest U.S. nursery schools was a parent cooperative initiated by a group of faculty wives at the University of Chicago in 1915. Education for parenthood was a central theme. Early childhood educators coming from social-work and home-economics backgrounds found working with parents a very natural part of the program. As early as 1922, some nursery schools were used as part of the treatment of preschoolers with behavior problems. The effort included both performing in-the-nursery-school therapy and teaching mothers to carry out therapy in the home—ideas that sound very modern today. The spawning of the parent cooperative effort swelled the ranks of nursery schools from 262 in 1930 to about 1700 in 1933 (Frank, 1962).

Hence, the nursery-school movement was founded in a set of traditions that included a multidisciplinary perspective, a close tie with research, an emphasis on personnel training, and a close alliance with parents. These traditions held even during the depression years when the nursery-school movement was first given national recognition and federal funding.

Public Funding but Private Control

Federal legislation and support were instrumental in establishing nursery schools throughout the country under the Works Progress Administration (WPA). The primary objective of the WPA schools was to give work to unemployed teachers, nurses, and other professionals while providing nutrition, protection, and an emotionally stable environment for 75,000 needy children from 2 to 5 years of age. Responsibility for program supervision and for staff training was left to the professionals and founders of the movement—the National Association for Nursery Education, the Association for Childhood Education, and the National Council on Parent Education. This maintained the integrity of the effort and ensured continuity in adherence to the underlying principles (Frank, 1962).

Therefore, the nursery school, as a 20th-century institution in the United States, was not bound by the same traditions of education as was the kinder-

For young children, play is the principal medium for learning.

garten movement. It was never incorporated into the public educational establishment. Rather, there has been continuity in the basic ideas of the movement and great freedom in their implementation.

Diversity of Form, Not Content

Today, over 1 million children are enrolled in nursery-school programs. Nursery schools can be found on the campuses of colleges and universities, in churches, in homes, shopping centers, and civic buildings. Some are publicly funded, some are commercial operations. Some require professional staffing and licensing, some do not. Some are exclusively parent cooperative ventures. Some accommodate 2- to 5-year-olds, some only one age group. Some operate on a half-day schedule, some for a full day. Some meet five days per week, others only two or three days. Some operate year round, others for only part of the year. In short, variations within this form of early childhood education are the rule rather than the exception.

Far less variation is found in the content of the educational programs provided, which take a child-centered approach. Following the foundational "whole child" approach of the genetic-maturationists such as Froebel and Gesell, nursery school programs tend to focus on basic socialization, the child's physical health needs, sensory-motor development, and emotional development. Play, both free and organized, is the principal medium for learning, and programs tend to establish an environment where the child is as free as possible from restraint and direction. Respect for and accommodation to individual differences is considered essential. Parent relations, including family-life education, also receives systematic attention in most programs that fall within the traditions of the movement.

As such, the nursery-school movement can be characterized as providing early social experience to basically middle-income children below age 5 years, as well as some parent education.

DAY-CARE MOVEMENT

Throughout its history, the purpose of day care most often has been described as a child-welfare service for the care and protection of children—a service focused on the children of "destitute widows and those with sick husbands" (Fein & Clarke-Stewart, 1973, p. 26). Indeed, the origins of the day-care movement in the United States lie in the combined traditions of preventive health care and "settlement house functionalism." Medical discoveries of the mid-19th century indicated the importance of sanitation to health, and the deplorable sanitation conditions of the poor were abundantly evident. The settlement-house movement arose in response to the needs of immigrant women employed in the sweatshops of early industry. These women were "bent under the double burden" of earning money to support their children while trying to care for their offspring. The incorporation of day nurseries within settlement houses was functional because it provided mothers with relief from their deplorable conditions while providing opportunity for improving children's health habits.

Conflict about Purpose

Right from the beginning, the U.S. day-care movement was embroiled in a battle of conflicting values. The needy mother was construed as a victim of a brutal system that provided no alternative. She had to work and leave her children unattended or she would not be able to feed them even the meager amount afforded by her pay. Yet,

> *She has no idea of how to economize money, time, or strength; she is largely ignorant of the needs of her little ones, and though she may wish them to be moral and decent, she has no idea how to train them to these ends [National Association of Day Nurseries, 1940, p. 5 as cited in Fein & Clarke-Stewart, 1973].*

The day nursery, then, could provide an alternative that would both provide relief for the mother and place the care of the child in the hands of those who were thought more qualified.

At about the same time, the battle was being fought for another alter-

Paris: Crêche de la Madeleine. Mealtime in a French day-care program.

native—public assistance. Social reformers campaigned for pension allowances for mothers. Grace Abbot, for example, argued that day nurseries were not a necessary part of child-welfare services and that the nation could well afford to support all mothers at home (Fein & Clarke-Stewart, 1973, p. 18). The first Mother's Pension Act was passed in 1911, and by 1919 public assistance was available to mothers in 39 states.

There was thus the conviction that the mother had the responsibility for child rearing and that it was in the best interest of society (and the child) to keep that responsibility with the mother and to keep the mother in the home.

Combined, the long-standing arguments might be summarized as:

1. *Pro:* The working mother needs relief in the form of alternative child-care arrangements.
   Con: Mothers should not work.
2. *Pro:* The best child-rearing environment is in the home with the mother.

Con: Some mothers do not know how to raise their children, and for the children of such mothers some alternative is desirable.

The same arguments are still heard, and uncertainty as to the purposes of day care continue.

World War II—Women Join the Workforce

With the advent of World War II and the passage of the Lanham Act the controversy was temporarily quieted. There was no alternative to a large number of women entering the work force. Child-care centers were mobilized on a large scale. For the day-care movement, this occurrence had enduring importance.

The World War II expansion of child-care centers introduced the concept of group care and guidance for young children to a wider community. Now day care could be experienced not just by the poor and the helpless, but by the middle class as well. This introduced a wider public to day care's potential value and provided reassurance that its effects were not noticeably detrimental.

With a different clientele, and with the experience and insight provided by early childhood educators who were enlisted in "the cause," greater effort was made to take day care out of the realm of custodial care and into the realm of child developmental programming and education. Teachers became more aware of the social and emotional needs of young children, whereas they had previously focused on only the child's physical health and safety. This made it possible to see the day-care experience enhancing the child rather than simply sustaining her or him.

The use of federally funded day-care programming on a large scale had been tested and would not be forgotten; it would be easier to obtain funding next time.

The Need Continues To Grow

After World War II, federal support for day-care centers was withdrawn on the assumption that women, no longer needed in war-related employment, would return to their roles of wives and mothers in their homes. During the last 40 years, that assumption has proven false.

The number of children and families served by day care in the United States is growing. Current estimates indicate that some 1.2 million children are enrolled in over 115,800 approved day-care centers and family day-care homes nationally (Hofferth, 1979). At the same time, more and more mothers are being employed outside the home. Estimates indicate that in 1980 there were over 14 million working mothers in the labor force who had children under the age of 18 years. Additionally, there were close to 3 million children under the age of 6 years who were from single-parent, female-headed families (Johnson, 1980). The economic and social viability of these families is frequently dependent on the availability of day-care and supporting services. In sum, many of the same social circumstances that precipitated the initial founding of the day-care movement still exist. Only now has the magnitude of the problem made it a major public concern (Caldwell & Freyer, 1982).

The resolution of the problem will not be easy. Although social attitudes concerning the role of women in society are changing, the underlying social, economic, and political issues that have been with the day-care movement since its start have not been totally resolved (Peters & Belsky, 1982). Congress, the President, and presumably people in the United States are still divided on whether there should be a national policy affirming the need for a national support system for all family units pursuing their child-rearing function or whether we should retain a crisis-oriented, reactive policy of assisting only those in the most dire need. Central to the debate are concerns of the family's responsibility for childrearing, the viability of the family in carrying out this responsibility, and the role of government in the process. There is some indication that this lingering tie with the welfare movement is changing and that day care is becoming part of a new, evolving personal service system (Kadushin, 1978).

Types of Day-Care Programs

Deriving as it does from a health and welfare tradition, one which involves both private philanthropy and public support, day care has evolved in several forms. Today not all day care is alike, nor is it all federally funded. Generally speaking, there are four major types of day-care programs: private for-profit, private nonprofit, public, and private industry (Peters & Belsky, 1982; Peters & Koppel, 1977).

Private For-Profit   The purpose of proprietary day care is to offer a service to families in the provision of child care while making a reasonable profit for the owner/operator or stockholders. Such programs, although usually requiring licensure and inspection by a state or local regulatory body, operate relatively independently and receive their income from fees paid directly by the parents. Fees are established by the competitive open market and usually exceed those that could be paid by low-income families. As such, the majority of the clientele tend to be middle-class, relatively affluent, two-worker families.

Proprietary programs vary in the range and quality of services they provide and the degree to which parents influence decisions concerning program, staffing, and the like. In general, such programs tend to be primarily child focused, providing few if any supplementary family health or social services. Many actually represent extended nursery-school programs (Peters & Belsky, 1982).

Private Nonprofit   Private nonprofit day-care providers are generally organizations of citizens incorporated under the nonprofit corporation laws of the particular state or governing unit. Many are affiliated with churches, educational institutions or humanitarian service organizations. Such organizations are usually dependent for their funds on some combination of private contributions and state or federal funds. They may be single-purpose agencies who provide child care and related services to selected categories of clientele, or they may be a component of a larger multiservice organization that provides a rich, coordinated array of health, welfare, and education services.

Private nonprofit agencies usually are governed and administered by a voluntary board of directors.

Public   Public day-care programs generally are under the auspices of state, county, or municipal governmental bodies. They receive their support almost exclusively from public funds and their services are delivered at no or reduced cost to the clientele. Eligibility requirements for the receipt of such services are set by regulation and generally result in an economically homogeneous, low-income clientele.

Private Industry   A small but growing number of day-care programs in the United States are operated by business, industry, or labor unions as a convenience or fringe benefit for their employees. They also serve as a means of attracting and enhancing the productivity of female workers. Occasionally, such programs are open to members of the larger community; they operate as private or nonprofit day-care programs.

Home versus Center Orientation

Actual day-care service delivery also varies in orientation. Three classifications may be made here as well. These include family day-care homes, extended day-care homes, and day-care centers. Generally accepted definitions of the three types are:

Family day-care home—an occupied residence in which day care is regularly provided for no more than six children from more than one unrelated family, including those of the caregiver.

Extended day-care home (minicenter)—any facility, including an occupied residence, in which day care is regularly provided for more than six but fewer than 13 children from more than one unrelated family.

Day-care center—any facility that regularly provides day care for 13 or more children who are unrelated to the caregiver.

Day-care centers are populated mostly by children aged 3 to 5 years.

Recipients of Day-Care Services

Day care in the United States enrolls children ranging in age from early infancy through adolescence. However, the vast majority of children served are in the preschool age range (3 to 5 years). Children below the age of 3 years are usually served in family day-care homes—although quality infant care may be provided in a day-care center (Caldwell & Freyer, 1982).

Day-care programs of the forms listed above may serve basically normal children (those without recognizable developmental problems), exceptional children (children with developmental disabilities, handicaps, or exceptionalities), or a combination of the two. Current emphasis is on individualized developmental programming and the integration or mainstreaming of exceptional children.

Depending on the age range and characteristics of the children served, programs differ markedly in the types of activities and supplementary services provided, staff/child ratios, and costs.

In general then, day-care programs serve a heterogeneous group of children (age, socioeconomic status, and ability) and their families, providing a range of services from custodial care through comprehensive developmental services.

COMPENSATORY-EDUCATION MOVEMENT

The compensatory early childhood education movement in the United States is in many ways the legitimate offspring of the three movements already discussed. It brings together the readiness-for-later-education orientation of the kindergarten movement with the child-study and parent-education orientation of the nursery-school movement, and couples both with the health-and-welfare orientation of the day-care movement. What is new about it, however, is that it represents a large scale, federally legislated and funded, systematic intervention into the lives of young children and their families with the explicit intention of accomplishing broad social goals—such as counteracting the destructive effects of poverty and optimizing human development (Peters, 1977).

Project Head Start

The compensatory-education movement had its beginnings in the 1960s and was both the product of political, economic, and social change within society and a reflection of increasing knowledge about child development (Peters, 1980; Zigler & Valentine, 1979). Perhaps most notable of the compensatory-education programs is Project Head Start. Project Head Start was launched in 1965—thus beginning what is probably the most remarkable experiment in child development in this country's history. It was the product of a political and social decision to use preschool enrichment as an antidote to poverty.

From the outset, seven broad objectives have guided the national Head Start program. These are

1. Improving children's health and physical abilities
2. Helping the emotional and social development of children by encouraging self-confidence, spontaneity, curiosity, and self-discipline
3. Improving children's mental processes and skills with particular attention to conceptual and verbal skills
4. Establishing patterns and expectations of success for children that will create a climate of confidence for their future learning efforts
5. Increasing children's capacity to relate positively to family members, while strengthening families' ability to relate positively to children and their problems

6. Developing in children and their families a responsible attitude toward society, and fostering constructive opportunities for society to work with the poor in solving their problems
7. Increasing the sense of dignity and self-worth of children and their families (Grotberg, 1969)

To accomplish these objectives, Head Start had to be a multidisciplinary program that was family oriented and center based.

Variations on Head Start

At its inception Head Start was primarily a one-shot intensive summer enrichment experiment, much like that provided by the traditional nursery school. During the more than 20 years of its history, Project Head Start has evolved and has also spawned a series of additional experimental early childhood education efforts. Summer programs were reduced in number in favor of full-year programs. The standard five-day-per-week, center-based classroom format has gradually given way to variations involving home teaching and flexible attendance. Locally designed program forms have been encouraged so that programs could better adapt to community needs. Child and Family Resource programs, by broadening the focus to entire families, provided continuity of service from the prenatal period through preschool. Home Start programs sought to involve the parents as those in the best position to help the child, and to train them to provide such help. Developmental continuity programs worked with the child and his or her family from infancy through the early school years. Project Follow-Through has revised the curricula and procedures of the early elementary grades of the public schools and has made parent involvement a part of the public-school program.

New programs following the Head Start model have been developed. The Handicapped Children's Early Education Program has established centers across the United States, for the first time bringing an early education program to thousands of young (infants to 6 years old) children with handicaps and developmental delays.

This First Chance network of demonstration and outreach projects now includes over 200 programs. About two-thirds of the programs were designed to develop and demonstrate methods and materials for use with preschoolers who display various handicapping conditions. The other one-third were devoted to "outreach"—that is, to training others in the use of new approaches and materials for exceptional youngsters. As a result, most states organized early special-education services.

The evolution of Head Start and similar federally funded programs over such a brief period of time has produced an extraordinarily rich set of options for comprehensive service delivery to young children and their families. Although the forms differ somewhat, the options have in common the capability of providing systematic social, educational, health, and nutritional services to large numbers of children. Several million children are now graduates of such programs.

As such, the compensatory early childhood education movement may be characterized as a federal- and state-supported, multidisciplinary, multi-service delivery system to low-income and handicapped children and their families.

Box 2-2   *Recommendations for a Head Start Program*

In 1964, after passage of the Economic Opportunities Act, a panel of experts was assembled in Washington, D.C. The panel was chaired by Dr. Robert Cooke of The Johns Hopkins University.

In part, that panel's recommendations, published on February 19, 1965, stated:

Improving the Opportunities and
Achievements of the Children of the Poor

1. There is considerable evidence that the early years of childhood are the most critical point in the poverty cycle. During these years the creation of learning patterns, emotional development and the formation of individual expectations and aspirations take place at a very rapid pace. For the child of poverty there are clearly observable deficiencies in the processes which lay the foundation for a pattern of failure—and thus a pattern of poverty—throughout the child's entire life.

2. Within recent years there has been experimentation and research designed to improve opportunities for the child of poverty. While much of this work is not yet complete there is adequate evidence to support the view that special programs can be devised for these four and five year olds which will improve both the child's opportunities and achievements.

3. It is clear that successful programs of this type must be comprehensive, involving activities generally associated with the fields of health, social services, and education. Similarly it is clear that the program must focus on the problems of child and parent and that these activities need to be carefully integrated with programs for the school years. During the early stages of any programs assisted by the Office of Economic Opportunity it would be pref-
erable to encourage comprehensive programs for fewer children than to attempt to reach vast numbers of children with limited programs [U.S. Department of Health, Education, and Welfare; Office of Child Development].

On March 18, 1965, the Office of Economic Opportunity, under the letterhead of the Executive Office of the President, issued the following statements:

The Office of Economic Opportunity will make major efforts to provide large numbers of young children of the poor with programs of high quality designed to meet the comprehensive health, education and welfare needs of these children and their families. . . . Full encouragement will be given to local communities to develop the kind of facilities which are most appropriate for, and most needed by, the children and families of the community, be they day care centers or centers of early childhood education. Desirable as it is that young children of the poor have preprimary educational experiences, the OEO does not assume that the needs of these children can be met only through a program of group experiences.

As further research and demonstration experience produces imaginative experiments and new knowledge, it is hoped that fresh designs will evolve for programs even better suited to enhance the developmental potentials of young children. It is hoped, too, that child development centers will be flexible and insightful, ready to modify their programs as they find out more about the lives of their children, the needs of their families, and the special characteristics of their own communities.

FAMILY-BASED PROGRAM MOVEMENT

Involvement of parents in their children's educational process was part of the nursery-school movement. Parent education was part of the role of the early kindergarten teacher. Federally funded day-care and compensatory-education programs have incorporated the concept of parent involvement. All of these efforts have been extensions of classroom programs for children. As a major thrust within early childhood education, however, the family-based program, conducted in the home with parents as the primary agents, is a relatively new phenomenon, dating back about two decades (Honig, 1982).

In those few years, quite a range of family-based programs have been developed and described in the literature. Some of these focus on teaching childrearing skills, others are directed to improving family communications. Many have been designed as extensions of the compensatory-education programs, and have as their goal making the parent (usually the mother) a home teacher; that is, they train parents to be teachers of their children in their own homes. The central goal of all such programs is to bring about enduring changes in what is happening in the home. Table 2-1 lists some typical objectives for family-based programs.

Within parent-as-teacher family-based programs, several program types

Table 2-1   Typical Objectives of Programs Seeking to Make Parents Home Teachers

Changes in Parental Behavior

1. Improved language skills used in interacting with their child; use of more elaborate, syntactically complex language, and more task-appropriate language, greater encouragement of children's verbalization
2. Greater responsiveness to and willingness to engage in cooperative play with the child
3. Greater awareness of the child's characteristics and ability to "read" the child's behavior
4. More appropriate selection and provision of play materials and more awareness of the learning potential of everyday household routines
5. Greater and more consistent use of positive disciplinary and motivational techniques

Changes in Children's Behavior

1. Immediate gains in intellectual development
2. Improved language development; increased syntactical complexity, improved questioning skills, greater knowledge of basic concepts, and higher rates of vocalization
3. Increased curiosity; more interest in novel objects, increased exploratory behavior
4. Improved ability to use parents as informational resources
5. Improved ability to play cooperatively with parents
6. Improved motivation for later or concurrent school learning

are prevalent. They may be classified as the home-visitation model, parent–group-meeting model, split-time model, media model, and combination models.

Home-Visitation Model

In this model, a home visitor makes recurring visits to work directly with the child, with the parent, or with the parent–child dyad. Frequently, the home visitor has preplanned prescriptive learning activities to be carried out with the child during the visit and others for the parent to do with the child between visits. Gordon (1971) pioneered the development of home-visitation programs, and there are now over 200 such programs in operation (Honig, 1982).

This parent has been provided with home-teaching activities.

Home visitation has the advantage of being relatively easily adapted to a wide range of environmental circumstances. It is particularly useful for children who are handicapped or live in isolated areas. The Wisconsin Portage Project (Shearer, 1979; Shearer & Shearer, 1972) and the High-Scope Parent-to-Parent Model (Evans, 1979) provide good examples. These programs include home teachers who provide parents with activities for their infants and preschoolers. The parents are taught how to conduct the activities and record data on their child's performance. Ideas for enriching the child's experiences and discoveries are drawn from resources that are at hand in the home. The home teacher meets the parents in their own territory where they are comfortable and where they are in charge.

In other programs, home visitors are also trained as generalists who provide consultation and suggestions in the areas of home management, nutrition, and health care in addition to providing training for parents as teachers of their children (Forrester, 1972).

Parent–Group-Meeting Model

A model that relies on parent–group-meetings has been used by a number of programs. Meetings and workshops conducted within group members' homes provide both emotional support and practical information about motivating children, making and using inexpensive home-learning materials, dealing with interpersonal problems within the family, and improving home-management skills (Levitt & Cohen, 1979; Peters, Burgess, & McConnell, 1979).

Split-Time Model

The split-time model is divided between and thus maximizes the advantages of the home-visit program and the group-care program (Karnes, Hodgins, Teska, & Kirk, 1969). The home-visit program extends the intervention effort to the home, brings about changes in the parent–child dyad, and provides emotional and informational support to the family. The group-care situation provides opportunities to work intensively with the child on specific developmental objectives, to bring the child to other professionals for diagnostic or remedial activities, and to foster social development by placing the child with other children. This model has become increasingly popular within Head Start, particularly in rural areas.

Media Model

Television programs have been used as an important component of some early-education programs that attempt to involve parents. Daily 30-minute televised lessons designed to encourage the desire to learn in young children have been used in the Home-Oriented Preschool Education program (HOPE) (Alford, 1972). Weekly home visits are made to deliver parent guides to the television activities and to provide materials that the parent and child can use together. Similarly, some programs have used "Sesame Street" as a resource for involving parents with their children's learning.

   Television and other media have been valuable teaching tools in such "remote control" programs; they have also been an important means of enlisting parents and focusing their interest on their preschool child's learning. Without parental involvement, television teaching may not produce enduring cognitive gains.

Combination or Omnibus Models

Some programs use a wide variety of techniques to carry out long-term intervention projects that encourage parental involvement from prenatal through school years. In one such program, the Family Development Research Program (Honig, 1982; Lally & Honig, 1975), nutritional, child-development, and child-care information is brought to pregnant women by paraprofessional home visitors. Once the child is born, eye–hand coordination, visual alerting, and vocalization are encouraged through special games taught to the family. The infant enters a developmental day-care program at 6 months of age. Parents continue to receive information about child development until the child is of school age. Particular attention is paid to selection of home visitors and to preservice and in-service training using a variety of techniques.

Key Elements of Effective Family-Based Programs

A number of elements go into making a successful family-based program. The most important of these are: (a) the structure of the learning situation; (b) the individualization of program activities; (c) the focus on the parent–child dyad; (d) the home visitor assuming a secondary role; (e) the motivation of the parents; and (f) the comprehensiveness of the family support system (Dudzinski & Peters, 1977).

Structure of the Learning Situation   Structure is having a goal or purpose to the learning situation, as when a specific interaction between parent and child is centered on a cognitively challenging task. For example, a father might read a book to his child and focus his questions on the colors in the pictures. The father could then extend the color concepts by asking the child such open-ended questions as "What else in this room is red?" or "What else can you think of that could be red?" In most programs, parents are encouraged to be warm and accepting of their children's ideas and to respond to them in a positive manner.

Structure does not refer to having a rigid curriculum and a fixed time each day when activities are done. In one program (Herron, 1972), each parent was allowed to ask the child only once each day if he or she wanted to do the activities. If the child refused, the parent could not force the child to do them or even ask again until the next day. However, parents were allowed to do the activities at any time at the child's request.

Individualization of Program Activities   Although there is structure and purpose to the learning situation, the goals, content, and methods are individualized to the present skill level of both the child and the parent. In a home-based program, success and progress are important if the welcome mat is to remain out and the parent is to continue in the program. As children come to each situation with different skill levels, so, too, do parents. Some will need more structure (and more patience); others will need less.

Focus on the Parent–Child Dyad   A crucial element for a successful intervention program is focusing on the parent–child dyad as an active, ongoing system. Not only does the child learn from the parent, but the parent learns from the child. Parent and child aim at developing an enduring interaction system so that once the intervention program ends, the parent can continue to modify strategies for dealing with the child as he or she grows and matures.

Several studies have shown that a home-based program must include more than just sending an expert into the home to tutor the child. Programs that focus only on the parent have little success. The New Orleans Parent–Child Development Center (Andrews, Blumenthal, Bache, & Weiner, 1975) compared two approaches to parent education. In the home-visit model, paraprofessional parent educators spent one and one-half hours per week teaching parents about child development. In the center-based model, parents spent six hours per week in the center learning about child development, but they also learned about home resources and were given opportunities to practice their new skills with their own

The parent is the primary teacher of the child.

child at the parent–child laboratory. In both models, there was minimal contact between children and professional educators, so all effects are assumed to have come through the parents. Parents in the center-based program became more accepting and responsive and talked more to their children. The children scored higher on standardized tests at 36 months of age than did children in the home-visit model, which dealt only with the parents' knowledge of child development.

Merely transporting a preschool curriculum or a parent-education class to the living room is not a successful way to carry out home-based intervention. Rather, many family-based programs have achieved success because they focused on the ongoing parent–child system. The thrust of the intervention has not been on educating individual members of the system, but on modifying the interactions between them.

Secondary Role of the Home Visitor   People from a variety of backgrounds—whether middle class and college educated, or poor, high school drop outs—have been effective home visitors. The main variable affecting success is the home visitor's ability to place on the parent the primary responsibility for the child's progress. The home visitor can act as a resource and a catalyst. She or he can help parents to see their own self-worth and their children's worth. The parents learn that they are the most important people in their children's lives and are their children's most effective teachers. While a parent is learning that she or he *can* make a difference, the home visitor can aid that parent in identifying and implementing the goals for the child. In this way, the parent gains the skills needed to maintain the program after the home visitor stops coming.

Parental Motivation   In effective programs, special attention is directed toward parent motivation. It is recognized that by far the great majority of parents are strongly motivated to be good ones. They want to succeed, and they welcome help and advice when it is provided in a friendly and constructive way. But many parents are under severe pressure from, for example, work or trying to make ends meet. Such parents need special encouragement, support, and reinforcement for their continued cooperation and participation in the program.

Family Support System   A final factor in successful programs is the degree to which they provide a complete family support system. The need for such a system varies with the population being served. For more advantaged parents, a small discussion group may be sufficient. Here parents can compare their problems and strategies for dealing with them and receive encouragement from others who have faced the same problems. This reinforcement can be very helpful and necessary for maintaining the parents' interest in the early stages of a program or in programs dealing with infants or with severely retarded or handicapped children (Robinson, M., 1975), because in these cases the parents cannot immediately see the results of their efforts.

A more comprehensive support system may be necessary for severely disadvantaged or disorganized families. This might include nutritional guidance, instruction in home-management skills, and referral to other social service agencies as well as some monetary relief to ease the burden of survival. For an intervention program that has the parent–child dyad as its focus to be effective, the parents must have the time to participate in program activities. This includes not only the time when the home visitor is present but the in-between times when they practice their new skills with their children. Karnes, for example, found that the children of working mothers did not benefit from a home-based program, presumably because those mothers who worked did not have enough time or energy to spend with their children (Karnes, Hodgins, Teska, & Badger, 1969).

Advantages of Family-Based Programs

There are a number of advantages of family-based programs:

1. There are many alternative approaches which may be tailored to fit the needs and the resources of the community and of the agency providing the services.

2. There is the possibility for earlier intervention without removing the child from the home.

3. Programs are family-centered, and the whole family benefits not only from the child's gains and the parents' behavioral changes but also from the enhanced confidence of the parent and the total family support provided.

4. More people can be serviced. The effects of such programs tend to spread. Parents use their skills with all their children, hence benefiting all. They also tend to share their new knowledge with friends and relatives, thereby potentially benefiting many more children.

5. Programs can be tailored to the individual child. This is especially important for children with severe handicaps or learning difficulties.

6. Children in rural or isolated areas can receive the benefits of the program.

7. Probably the most important reason for opting for a family-based program is that the gains made by the child tend to last—they do not wash out (Dudzinski & Peters, 1977).

Family-based programs will not always work. Disorganized families or parents who do not have the ability, time, energy, or will to participate will not benefit from a program that places on the parents the responsibility for promoting interactions with their children. Some parents need a legitimate reprieve from their responsibilities from time to time. Just providing them with new skills will not be enough to permit them to be "superparents" year after year. Nonetheless, the family-based program is a viable alternative for some parents and has unique advantages and real possibilities for meeting the needs of both child and parent.

SUMMARY

In this chapter, we have scanned the major forms of early childhood education in the United States. We have briefly traced the history and current expression of the kindergarten, nursery-school, day-care, compensatory-education, and home-based program movements. We indicated that the kindergarten movement is tied to public education, whereas the nursery school is closely allied with research, parent education, and a multidisciplinary perspective of child development. The day-care movement, with its ties to the child-welfare movement, has been identified with meeting the needs of the poor and of working women, although this seems to be changing. Four types of day care are most evident: private for-profit, private nonprofit, public, and private industry. These programs serve a heterogeneous group of children and their families, providing a range of services from custodial care through comprehensive developmental services. Compensatory education, an offspring of the three prior movements, represents a large-scale, federally legislated and funded effort at social intervention. Project Head Start, Project Follow-Through, and the Handicapped Children's Early Education Program are perhaps the best known examples. Family-based programs, newest of the early education movements, seek to make the parent (usually the mother) a home teacher of her or his own children. The central goal of such programs is to encourage enduring changes in the interactions in the home. Such programs, although sometimes effective, are not suitable for all children or all family situations.

Review Questions

1. Describe the nursery-school movement from its beginning until the present.
2. State and describe the six key elements that go into making a successful family-based program.
3. State the roles and responsibilities of a successful home visitor.
4. Outline briefly the "clientele" served by each of the early childhood education movements in the United States. How do they reflect the origins of the different movements?

Suggested Activities

1. Arrange to visit a day-care center, Head Start Program, kindergarten, and nursery school in your area. Discuss with the staff the purposes of the program, who the children are, and how the program is funded.
2. Check your local telephone directory yellow pages under such headings as nursery schools, day care, child care, schools, child and family services. Compile a list of the types of programs in your community.

3. Trace the governance and regulatory chain of command for several early childhood programs in your community. Which ones fall under education? Which under welfare? Try to plot the connections between them.

4. Discuss with local, state, and federal elected officials (legislators, senators) their attitudes toward kindergarten, day-care, nursery-school, compensatory-education, and family-based programs. Which programs do they believe warrant local, state, or federal support? For which programs is there current legislation pending? What are their views as to the role of government in early childhood care and education?

5. Compile a list of state and national professional organizations in the early childhood education field (for example, National Association for the Education of Young Children, National Head Start Association). Who belongs to these organizations? To which organization is a kindergarten teacher most likely to belong? A teacher in Head Start? A day-care center group supervisor? A home visitor? The owner and operator of a nursery school?

Suggested Readings

Berger, E. *Parents as partners in education*. St. Louis: Mosby, 1981.

Croft, D. *Parents and teachers: a resource book for home, school and community relations*. Belmont, Calif.: Wadsworth, 1979.

Evans, E. *Contemporary influences in early childhood education*, 2nd ed. New York: Holt, Rinehart & Winston, 1975.

Honig, A. *Parent involvement*. Washington, D.C.: National Association for the Education of Young Children, 1975.

Leichter, H. *Families and communities as educators*. New York: Teachers College Press, 1979.

Massoglia, E. *Early childhood education in the home*. Albany, N.Y.: Delmar, 1977.

Maybanks, S., and Bryee, M. *Home-based services for children and families*. Springfield, Ill.: Charles C Thomas, 1979.

NAEYC's first half century, 1926–1976. *Young children*, September 31 (1976), pp. 462–475.

Osborn, D. K. *Early childhood education in historical perspective*. Athens, Ga.: University of Georgia, Education Associates, 1975.

Chapter 3

Theory and Curriculum Development

*I*n the United States, rich *content variations* in early childhood education programs have emerged during the last two decades. These variations are evident no matter what form the programs have taken. This has resulted in what has been called the *models approach* to curriculum and program development (Evans, 1982). Underlying this approach is the assumption that practice should be derived from theory and research. Each model represents an approximate prescription for action and organization—an early childhood education plan—that has been deduced from a conceptually integrated body of knowledge about learning and development. In many ways, such early education model programs are operational representations of theory. In this chapter, a framework is provided for understanding the translation of theory to practice. We will present briefly the three major theoretical positions in early childhood education practice today. We then discuss the steps that are required to move sensibly and consistently from a basic theory of development and learning to the design of day-to-day classroom activities. Finally, we provide you with an opportunity to test your own beliefs.

DEVELOPMENTAL THEORY DERIVATIONS

Psychologist Lawrence Kohlberg has conceptualized three broad streams of educational thought that have come down from generation to generation and that are still discernible in practice today (Kohlberg, 1968). They are the maturationist-socialization stream, the cultural-training or behaviorist stream, and the cognitive-developmental or interactionist stream.

Maturationist-Socialization Stream

The maturationist-socialization view holds that what is most important to development is the inner *goods* within the child. Education should be designed to allow the child to "blossom" in a warm, supportive social environment. Naturally occurring, and virtually inevitable, maturational processes are at work. The educator need only establish a positive social-emotional classroom play environment. Focus is frequently placed upon affective and social development through dramatic play and creative activities. The child is free to explore many social roles and to express him- or herself in many different modes of activity. This stream of thought has its philosophical roots in the writings of Rousseau (1712–1778) and its psychological derivations from the works of Freud, Erikson, Gesell, and, more recently, Carl Rogers. It is currently implemented in traditional child-centered nursery schools in the United States, in the British infant school movement, and the Danish bornehaven, to name but a few.

B. F. Skinner, American behavioral psychologist.

Cultural-Training or Behaviorist Stream

According to the cultural-training or behaviorist stream of thought, the role of early education is preparation for later education and for integration into the mainstream of life. The obligation of early education is to teach preacademic skills, academic subject matter, moral knowledge, and the rules of culture in the most direct and efficient way. Based on the philosophy of John Locke (1632–1704) and propositions from American psychologists like Thorndike, Skinner, and Bandura, programs within this tradition strive to arrange optimal instructional environments by carefully specifying the behaviors deemed desirable; by employing structured, sequenced, high interest materials; by implementing systematic teaching strategies based on learning principles (for example, positive reinforcement, extinction); by ensuring controlled sequences for the child's behavior; and by providing salient models of desired behavior. Currently, models based on this set of assumptions and principles are found most frequently in compensatory-education programs (in the United States, Canada, and Israel, for example), in programs for developmentally delayed children, and in a wide variety of experimental settings. Many of the practices derivable from this stream of thought, although usually employed without the theory-associated labels, are found in teacher-centered kindergartens and day-care programs.

Cognitive-Developmental Stream

The cognitive-developmental view is based on the premise that the cognitive, social, and affective behavior education should emerge naturally from the interaction between the child and the environment under conditions in which such interaction is allowed and fostered. Development is seen as occurring in a fixed sequence of stages; within each stage, the

Jean Piaget, Swiss child-development theoretician.

child's manner of reasoning about and interacting with his or her environment will be qualitatively different. Transition from one stage to the next is not, however, inevitable. Indeed, although the impetus for the progression is internal to the child, the actual adaptation that occurs is dependent on the nature of the interactions with the environment. The educator has responsibility for setting the stage to ensure desirable and meaningful interactions for the child. What is desirable and meaningful depends upon the child's level of development at the time.

The principal theoretical contributors to the cognitive-developmental point of view have been the Swiss epistemologist Jean Piaget and the American psychologist and educator Jerome Bruner. Currently, programs reflecting this perspective are growing in number in both the United States and Canada. They are frequently associated with colleges or universities. Recent research suggests such programs are particularly beneficial to gifted children. Major elements from this theoretical stream have been at the heart of many of the recent innovations in early and elementary curricula.

All three major traditions of thought have survived and flourished within the rich panoply of U.S. early childhood education. The socialization stream was integral to the early kindergarten movement and has thrived within the nursery-school movement. The behaviorist stream was important to the second push of the kindergarten movement, has always been a part of the day-care movement, and is predominant in early programming for handicapped children. The cognitive-developmental stream is most discernible in the compensatory-education movement, although in that movement all three traditions have found strong followings. It is, in fact, in the compensatory-education movement where the newest phenomenon in U.S. early education is most visible: the *models approach* to the development of plans or curricula.

THE MODELS APPROACH

The models approach to curriculum and program development is based on the assumption that early childhood education practice should be a relatively direct derivation from child-development research and theory. According to this assumption our scientific knowledge in child development and learning is sufficiently well advanced that it provides a solid basis for intervening in the lives of children to optimize their development. Basing our activities on this knowledge will enable early childhood educators to be more effective than ever before. Further, the models approach presumes that early childhood education programs built on consistent theory and experimentation can attain more control over the outcomes of the process and be more efficient (cost-effective) while doing so. They should, therefore, be better than programs built upon tradition, unvalidated rules of thumb, philosophical suppositions, or happenstance. This, of course, reflects the underlying American valuing of technology and the scientific method.

Followers of the models approach do not assert that any one theory-derived program or curriculum is a pure and precise prescription for action or organization of early childhood programs. Rather, each model is seen as an approximation—just one of many possible attempts at the practical application of theory. The developers of such models recognize that current knowledge is not perfect, that their interpretations of the "facts" of child development research are fallible, and that their judgments of the correct applications will differ from those of others. That is why they are willing to and must subject their models to empirical testing and experimentation, which permit the refinement of both theory and practice.

Nor do most followers of the models approach assume there is necessarily a single true perspective on learning or development—although they have their favorites (Evans, 1982). The three traditions of educational thought all are represented by respectable and respected followings. Each group has derived early childhood methods and materials from its preferred theory. At one time, as part of its educational innovation program connected with Project Follow-Through, the federal government encouraged and funded 22 alternative educational plans or models (Goodwin & Driscoll, 1980).

In addition to rejecting the assumption that there is one best way to educate all children in all contexts, model curriculum builders assume that there may be some models that suit some children better than others. That is, there may be some optimal match between a particular type of program and a particular type of child. Seeking such matches is a major research objective as well as a very practical need.

It is also true that many educational practices have been *rationalized* by theory; that is, frequently instructional methods that seem to work can be explained reasonably well in terms of several different theories. Hence, different early education models have claimed the same or similar techniques to be derived from their own theory. The important point, however, is that each model has a consistent body of content and practice whether it is theory derived or theory rationalized. Even within the major traditions, differences exist, and often several different versions of implementations have resulted (Parker, 1974).

Within the scientific tradition, each model is subject to empirical validation. Experimental comparisons across theoretically derived models (and across theories) not only are called for but are considered essential. We will return to this topic later in the chapter.

Common to all efforts within the models approach is the conviction that early childhood education programming can and should be planned and evaluated thoughtfully.

Box 3-1   Try a Little History

To provide a bit of perspective on the three major streams of educational thought, think about the content of early childhood education. Match the following quotations with their authors: John Locke (1632–1704), Jean-Jacques Rousseau (1712–1778), and Friedrich Froebel (1782–1852). These quotations, taken from a variety of writings by the authors, were compiled by Robert Ulich in his book, *Three thousand years of educational wisdom*, in 1954—long before the current early education and compensatory-education movement and most of you were born. Although these quotations date back to the 18th century, they are clearly representative of the cultural transmission of behaviorist (Locke), cognitive-developmental (Rousseau), and maturationist-socialization (Froebel) points of view.

1. The only habit in which a child should indulge, is that of contracting none. . . . Prepare early for this enjoyment of liberty, and the exercise of his natural abilities, by leaving him in full possession of them unrestrained by artificial habits, and by putting him in a situation to be always master of himself, and to do whatever his resolution prompts him, as soon as he is able to form one [p. 392].

2. The grand motive, indeed the only one that is certain and effective, is present interest [p. 405].

3. Play is the highest phase of child-development—of human development at this period, for it is self-active representation of . . . inner necessity and impulse. Play at this time is not trivial, it is highly serious and of deep significance [p. 573].

4. Children are not to be taught by rules. . . . What you think necessary for them to do, settle in them by an indispensable practice, as often as the occasion returns: and, if it be possible, make occasions. This will beget habits in them, which,

being once established, operate of themselves easily and naturally, without the assistance of memory [p. 359].

5. Direct the attention of your pupil to the phænomena of nature, and you will soon awaken his curiosity; but to keep that curiosity alive, you must be in no haste to satisfy it. He should not learn, but invent the sciences [p. 408].

6. To stir up, to animate, to awaken, and to strengthen the pleasure and power of the human being to labour uninterruptedly at his own education, has become and always remained the fundamental principle and aim of my educational work [p. 525].

7. Humanity has its place in the order and constitution of things. . . . men should be considered as men, and children as children. Nature requires children to be children before they are men. . . . Childhood hath its manner of seeing, perceiving, and thinking, peculiar to itself; nor is there anything more absurd than our being anxious to substitute our own in its stead [p. 397].

8. Play-things, I think, children should have, and of divers sorts; but still to be in the custody of their tutors, or someone else, whereof a child should have in his power but one at once, and should not be suffered to have another, but when he restored that: this teaches them, betimes to be careful of not losing or spoiling the things they have; whereas plenty and variety, in their own keeping, makes them wanton and careless, and teaches them from the beginning to be squanderers and wasters [p. 372].

9. Education . . . originally and in its first principles, should necessarily be passive, following (only guarding and protecting

[the child], not prescriptive, categorical, interfering). . . . This should in no way be interpreted as a pretext for letting the child alone, giving him up wholly to his own so-called self-direction [p. 567].

10. I must here take the liberty to mind parents of this one thing . . . you must do nothing before him, which you would not have him imitate [p. 360].

11. Behold even the weed, . . . behold it in nature, in field or garden, and see how perfectly it conforms to law . . . what a pure inner life it shows. . . . Thus O Parents, could your children, too, unfold in beauty and develop in all-sided harmony [p. 555].

12. [Do not] check or discountenance any inquiries he shall make . . . but to answer all his questions, and explain the matters he desires to know, so as to make them intelligible to him [p. 363].

13. It has been made a matter of great importance, to find out the best method of teaching children to read; to this end cards and other implements have been invented, so various and numerous, that they made the nursery resemble the workshop of a printer. . . . A more certain method than any of these, and that which is nevertheless always neglected, is to excite in children a desire to learn. Give a child this desire . . . any method will then be sufficient [p. 405].

14. The rewards and punishments, things whereby we should keep children in order are quite another kind. . . . Esteem and disgrace are, of all others, the most powerful incentives. . . . If you can once get into children a love of credit, and an apprehension of shame . . . you have put into them the true principle, which will constantly work, and incline them to right [p. 358].

15. The child, the boy, man, indeed should know no other endeavor but to be at every stage of development wholly what this stage calls for. Then will each successive stage spring like a new shoot from a healthy bud, and, at each successive stage, he will with the same endeavor again accomplish the requirements of this stage: for only the adequate development of man at each preceding stage can effect and bring about adequate development at each succeeding stage [p. 567].

16. I imagine the minds of children as easily turned, this or that way as water itself. . . . The mind [should be] made obedient to discipline and pliant to reason, when at first it was most tender, most easy to be bowed [p. 356].

17. Content yourself, therefore, with presenting proper objects opportunely to his notice, and when you see they have sufficiently excited his curiosity, drop some leading laconic questions, which may put him in the way of discovering the truth [p. 409].

18. With the advancing development of the senses, there is developed in the child, simultaneously and symmetrically, the use of the body; of the limbs; and this, too, is a succession determined by their nature and the properties of corporeal objects [p. 570].

Answers

Locke: 4, 8, 10, 12, 14, 16
Rousseau: 1, 2, 5, 7, 13, 17
Froebel: 3, 6, 9, 11, 15, 18

From R. Ulich (Ed.). *Three thousand years of educational wisdom.* Cambridge, MA: Harvard University Press, 1954.

A FRAMEWORK FOR MODEL BUILDING

Not all components of theory are equally important for application. Indeed, some aspects of theory are only remotely relevant for day-to-day program planning for children. Some research findings are important for validating alternative explanations of behavior, but involve a degree of precision that is unattainable and unnecessary in the real world of the nursery school, day-care center, or Head Start Program. Other aspects of research and theory are much more directly relevant. How then does a program developer or teacher move from theory to practice?

Let us look at the process first at a fairly abstract level. Figure 3-1 provides a framework for viewing the relationship of theory and practice. According to this framework, potential derivations from theory include: program goals; program priorities; processes of learning, development, and teaching; and the criteria for evaluation.

Goals

Differences in theoretical perspectives are related to the presumed importance of some aspects of development to the total development of the child and the later development of the adult. Existing child-development and learning theories share some common assumptions. These include:

1. Early experience has an important relationship to later development
2. Growth and development can be modified through environmental intervention

Theories differ, however, in their other assumptions and the rigidity with which the assumptions are held. Different theories address their attention to different aspects of development (social versus cognitive development, physical development versus language acquisition). They often disagree about the processes that bring about changes in development and about the nature of the presumed interrelationships among different aspects of development.

For example, theories or partial theories that fall within the maturationist-socialization perspective have generally stressed the importance of socioemotional development. Whether attending to the psychosexual stages of development (for example, Freudian theory) or to the culturally imposed crises of development (for example, Eriksonian theory), the emphasis is on the personality development of the child. Satisfactory resolution of the conflicts and crises involved is essential if psychopathology is to be avoided. Failure to attain adequate resolution is assumed to interfere with social behavior and, to a lesser extent, intellectual development. However, such theories have generally not addressed the intellectual aspects of develop-

Theory → Theory Derivations → Theory Applications → Program Components → Program

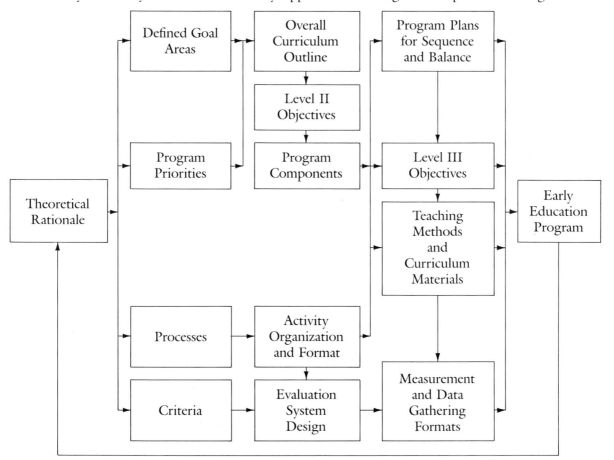

Figure 3-1   *The relationship of the components of theory and practice [reprinted from Peters (1977b) with permission]*

ment with any care. Similarly, failure to attain adequate resolution of early developmental conflicts is assumed to have a significant, although not unalterable, effect on adult personality.

Programs deriving from theories within the maturationist-socialization tradition stress socioemotional objectives and goals. Such programs emphasize the learning of inner controls of behavior and provide the child with opportunities to develop trust, autonomy, and initiative. Usually this is accomplished through an emphasis on free play and creative activities: activities that are child centered and relatively free of teacher direction.

By contrast, cognitive-developmental theory, although it also has a

Psychomotor development is a facilitator of environmental interaction and exploration.

stage-developmental perspective (indeed one that is even more firm in its assumptions), deals only peripherally with socioemotional development. Here attention is directed toward the developmental intellectual processes such as classification, memory, spatial relationships, and language. The development of the intellect is seen as a prerequisite for most aspects of socioemotional (or personality) development. Children's *understanding* of themselves, of their world and of the feedback the world provides to them determines their functioning in social situations; that is, intellectual processes determine what they *think* about themselves, hence how they will behave toward themselves and others. Psychomotor development is important both as an early vehicle for thought and as a facilitator of environmental interaction and exploration. Developmental sequences are fixed and early development is critical for later development.

Programs deriving from this perspective thus stress cognitive objectives. Motor exploration and manipulation are important, as is the notion that the child needs to discover for him- or herself the laws by which the physical world operates. Social rules and language are facilitators of exploration and the generation of knowledge.

Hence, the adoption of a particular theoretical position limits the scope of concern of the derived program model. It differentially focuses attention on the goal areas most central to the theoretical formulation and defines the sense of urgency surrounding these.

Program Priorities

All developmental theories set priorities for developmental concern. If a *stage* theory is adopted, then the hypothesized developmental sequence will suggest critical or sensitive periods, and specific concerns to be addressed at different stages of development. If the sequence of development is considered immutable, and if particular achievements of the stage must be accomplished if development is to proceed, then, obviously, aiding the child in accomplishing this step in development is of top priority. Where all aspects of development are considered to be interrelated, things become even more urgent.

An example from Piagetian theory is object constancy, the ability of a child—usually an infant of roughly 9 months—to understand that objects, including people, continue to exist when not within the scope of immediate apprehension (by one of the senses, such as sight or hearing). This understanding is essential to infant attachments, to their seeking of regularities in the physical world, and to their exploration of that world. Therefore, program developers have incorporated games and exercises in their infant programs that encourage the development of object constancy.

In contrast, non–stage-related theories such as Skinnerian operant theory are more flexible in their assumptions. Priorities derive from social demands, task analyses, or other analytical or empirical procedures used to determine which behaviors are prerequisite to the development of others. So, for example, the child must be able to hold a pencil, discriminate letters, and have a left-to-right orientation before writing his or her name.

Processes of Learning, Development, and Teaching

Psychological theories formulate different assumptions about children's development and learning (DeVries, 1974; Kohlberg, 1968). These assumptions are important for deriving program activities, materials, teacher–child interaction patterns, and the like. The theories of Freud, Piaget, and Skinner are vastly different, and programs derived from their formulations are correspondingly different in design and practice. The literature suggests at least ten dimensions on which the three theories differ and which lead to markedly different practices (Verma & Peters, 1975; Zimiles, 1982). Table 3-1 summarizes the assumptions of each theory.

Maturationist-socialization theorists combine the concerns of psychodynamic theory (Freud, 1935) and maturational theory (Gesell, 1923)

Table 3-1   Assumptions of Three Theories*

	Cognitive-Developmental Theory	Cultural-Training or Behaviorist Theory	Maturationist-Socialization Theory
Children	Active Qualitatively unlike adults in terms of thought	Active and passive Qualitatively like adults in terms of learning	Adaptive Qualitatively unlike adults in terms of emotions
Development	Occurs in surges Predetermined biological sequence modified by experience	Quantitative; gradual repertoire expansion Reciprocal operation of environment and child	Occurs in stages as a result of conflict resolution Predetermined, genetically programmed sequence in a supporting environment
Learning	Motivation from within Based on sensory education Stage dependent Based on massive experience of general type Process approach Irreversible (invariant)	Motivation from the environment Based on language, overt and covert verbal labeling Cumulative and continuous Based on specific training Product approach Reversible	Internal and external, based on conflict Based on social experience Progressive stages that may be reversible in adverse circumstances Natural unfolding Individual expression/process Reversible under adverse circumstances; premature demands may stagnate development

*Adapted from Verma and Peters (1975) and Elliott (1972).

into a genetic view of development that describes an uneven path of progress through qualitatively different stages of development associated with specific developmental tasks and the resolution of particular areas of emotional conflict (Zimiles, 1982). Of particular importance in this view is the provision of a supporting social environment, one that focuses not on the skills and knowledge that a child acquires, per se, but on how a child is strengthened psychologically (that is, builds ego strength, gains self-control, and learns to cope with his or her autonomy) as she or he progresses through the normal stages. Central to this theoretical approach is learning to control primitive and unacceptable impulses (Zimiles, 1982). The conflict is internal to the child, as is motivation to progress through the stages of development.

Piaget asserts that a child is active and intrinsically motivated, and passes through invariant stages of development as a result of general experience that taps all the child's senses in the exploration of his or her environment. The child, being in an early stage of development, behaves and learns differently than the adult. As such, the process of the child's interactions with the environment is more important than the content of her or his understanding at a particular point in time.

Behavior theory, however, portrays the child as both active *and* passive in relation to the contingent reinforcers provided by the environment. Children operate on the environment, and it operates on them. In the final analysis, however, the environment controls behavioral development. Children learn through specific experience, possibly mediated by verbal labeling and dependent on the outcomes of the action. Knowledge and skills are acquired in a cumulative fashion as the result of each discrete learning experience. The learning principles involved apply equally well to adults or children; the content of the child's repertoire of behavior is important in itself as a predictor of future learning.

Criteria for Evaluation

At the abstract level, the criteria for developmental change and learning, as derived from theory, are related to the scope and focus of the goals of development and the processes of development and learning (for example, process versus product). At a more concrete level, theory provides direction for specification of behavioral outcomes of importance, and, through theory-testing research, specific indices of theory-derived outcomes. For example, aspects of Piaget's cognitive-developmental theory have been tested in a large number of studies. These studies, including those conducted by Piaget and his colleagues, have produced a number of procedures for measurement of the child's developmental level in the understanding of concepts such as number, space, classification, seriation, and moral judgment. Such measures can be used as criteria in research or program-evaluation design. Similarly, psychodynamic theory has assisted the measurement of the achievement of goals such as fostering ego strength.

THEORY APPLICATIONS

Although theories form the basis for program development, they do not, in themselves, provide the means for application. Something more is necessary: the "how to" of program development, or what Fein and Schwartz (1982) have called a *theory of practice*. Through the use of this additional source of knowledge and skill, theory derivations can be: (1) organized and translated into curriculum outlines, specific objectives, practical program components, activities, and format; (2) used to establish an evaluation design and its associated measurement system. Finally, specifically defined program components and evaluation procedures are designed, given organization and temporal order, and placed into use. These last activities can be thought of as the "packaging" of the program.

We shall now look briefly at some parts of this translation process.

Overall Curriculum Outline

As indicated in Figure 3-1, the theoretical rationale for a particular program model provides both the goal areas of concern and some indication of their priority within the broad scheme of things. This level of derivation is broader, of longer range, and more visionary than is generally useful in determining day-to-day classroom activity. However, these goals can be translated into an overall curriculum outline. Cognitive-developmental theory, for example, organizes the development of thought processes under four general headings: logical knowledge, physical knowledge, social knowledge, and representational knowledge (Kamii, 1971). Therefore, these goal areas should become a central part of the overall curriculum. The theory also suggests the intimate and interactive relationship among psychomotor development, socioemotional development, and cognitive development. Psychomotor development is important, according to this theory, both for the exploration of the environment—through which the child discovers the underlying relations that are part of logical and physical knowledge—and for the early organization, storage, and retrieval of such knowledge. Similarly, interactions with other children and with adults are seen as important both to the recognition of the alternative points of view and to the development of representations, particularly language. Therefore, these two areas of development are also theoretically important within the curriculum outline. Hence, we end up with a listing that includes:

1. Psychomotor development
2. Socioemotional development
3. Logical knowledge
4. Physical knowledge
5. Social knowledge
6. Representational knowledge

Obviously, starting from different theoretical rationales, we would end up with different overall curriculum outlines. For example, within pre-schools based on the maturationist-socialization perspective, the broad areas for a curriculum outline would include:

1. Dependence on the teacher
2. Inner controls and sense of self
3. Social interaction
   a. Quantity
   b. Quality
4. Comfort in school (adjustment)
5. Achievement motivation and pride of mastery
6. Curiosity and exploration
7. Creativity

Note that in each case a careful derivation from theory would yield a far more detailed breakdown; we will do this in subsequent chapters.

Objectives

The statement of an objective is an attempt by the teacher or curriculum maker to clarify his or her own intent. It is, therefore, an important and fundamental part of planning. As the old saying goes, "If you don't know where you are going, you won't know when you get there" (or even if you are heading in the right direction). For an objective to be clear, the words chosen must convey the same meaning to all of the intended audience. Statements of objectives that can be interpreted differently by different people at different times provide little communication and no real direction.

Objectives can differ in their orientation, specificity, and temporal ordering (Bloom, Hastings, & Madaus, 1971).

Orientation   Essentially, there are three potential orientations for objectives.

1. *Subject matter*—those that detail the subject matter to be covered. Examples are: the alphabet, ordinal numbers, body parts, primary colors, the seasons, farm animals.
2. *Teacher attitudes, behavior, characteristics*—those that specify the teacher's actions, feelings, style. Examples are: to be accepting of children of all ability levels; to demonstrate the mixing of primary colors; to model the correct use of the word *please*; to have friendly interactions with each child.
3. *Child behavior*—those that specify the child's behavior or actions. Examples are: to write his first name; to share her toy with peers; to make positive self-statements; to answer the question correctly.

Within this text, we adopt and recommend (3), the child behavior orientation, as being the most fruitful in formulating objectives.

Specificity   Objectives differ in their level of specificity. Our theoretical rationale might indicate that a child with a positive self-concept is:

> *more himself, more loving, relaxed and brighter in his judgment, more activated and more activating. He is in free possession of a surplus of energy which permits him to forget failures quickly and to approach what seems desirable (even if it also seems uncertain and even dangerous) with undiminished and more accurate direction [Erikson, 1963, p. 246].*

Our goal statement, or level I objective might then read: "The child will have a positive self-concept." We can make this statement more specific by: (1) making a clear statement of what the child will be *doing* when he or she has achieved the goal; (2) indicating under what conditions we would expect to see the child doing it (Mager, 1962).

The above theoretical description includes several possible behaviors. Let's focus on exploration as an indicator of self-concept. We might then derive a statement such as:

> *Given a new and unfamiliar activity, the child will enter into the activity quickly and easily.*

To make the objective more precise we also would need to specify the level of performance we would find acceptable (Mager, 1962). This implies defining the words *quickly* and *easily*. Quickly, for example, could be defined as "without hesitation or prompting from the teacher." We also could specify that we expected such behavior always, most of the time, or at some other criterion level. Our level II objective would then read:

> *Given a new and unfamiliar activity, the child will enter into the activity without hesitation or prompting from the teacher.*

For day-to-day lesson planning or for purposes of daily evaluation, it might be necessary to provide an even greater level of specificity. This can be attained by directly relating the level II objectives to the materials and activities of the daily activity. For example,

> *Given the opportunity to participate with four other children in the preparation of pancakes, the child will enter into each step of the activity (assembling ingredients, measuring, mixing, cooking) without hesitation or prompting from the teacher.*

This would be one relatively specific objective relating to our goal of developing a positive self-concept. It would be only one indicator of that goal—there would need to be at least several others to satisfy the broad description presented by our theoretical rationale.

One objective of early child-
hood education: learning self-
help skills.

Temporal Ordering   Objectives also may be construed as falling into a temporal ordering. This ordering relates to the underlying validity assumptions (Suchman, 1967). An example will help to explain. Assume that one of our program goals (level I objective) is "The child shall assume responsibility for her or his own physical (traffic) safety." No one expects a child of 3 or 4 years to assume such responsibility (to do so would constitute child neglect). Rather, this constitutes our ultimate goal or long-term objective. It is somewhat more precise than "The child shall develop into a functioning, productive member of society," but not much so.

To attain our level I goal, a number of intermediate objectives have to be met. Figure 3-2 suggests the sequence that would be involved if we were working with a deaf child. Implied is the validity assumption that the immediate objectives relate to the attainment of the intermediate objectives, and the intermediate objectives are important to the attainment of the ultimate objective. Therefore, although on a day-to-day basis we teach for immediate objectives, the assumption is that over time children will attain intermediate objectives that are meaningful for some ultimate educational purpose. In this sense, objectives provide us with long-range direction.

In summary, our curriculum outline flows from the broad, long-range goal statements and theoretical priorities. In turn, through a process of refinement, specificity is added to produce short-term objectives based on child behaviors. The short-term objectives must be stated unambiguously, so that they are clear not only to the teacher or curriculum maker, but to others as well.

Figure 3-2 *Logical contingency of objective levels*

Program Core Components Once we have developed an overall curriculum outline, each part of which has specified level II objectives, we can derive program core components. For example, within a cognitive-developmental framework, our curriculum outline includes logical knowledge as one of its six emphases. Within that priority area, our program "core" might include the following (derived from Kamii & DeVries, 1977):

1. Logicomathematical knowledge
   a. Classification—the process of noticing similarities and differences and grouping things that are similar

b. Seriation—the process of comparing and coordinating differences

c. Number—the process of establishing equivalence

2. Spatiotemporal relations

a. Spatial reasoning—the process of ordering and relating things in physical space

b. Temporal reasoning—the process of ordering and relating things in time

Each of these core components is important within the logical knowledge portion of the cognitive-developmental curriculum. The program will need to be organized to provide learning opportunities in each component. Similar breakdowns can be developed for the other five areas mentioned in the cognitive-developmental curriculum outline and for the areas of the maturationist-socialization outline, although followers of the latter often believe it is not useful to do so (Zimiles, 1982). Details for both the cognitive-developmental and the operant curriculum core components are provided in subsequent sections of this text.

Activity Organization and Format

Up to now, we have dealt primarily with theory applications to curriculum content—that is, with *what* to teach. Now let us turn to theory application in the area of *how* to teach. We are still operating at a somewhat general level, but this time our discussion is not based on our knowledge about knowledge, but rather is based on our theory-derived knowledge of the processes of learning and development.

For example, cognitive-developmental theory suggests the following:

1. The child is an active learner; he or she learns by actively manipulating, experiencing, and interacting with his or her environment

2. The preoperational child thinks at a concrete level; the child develops concepts and representations through experience and work with actual objects and events

3. The child learns through *massed experience*; it is only through multiple experiences that the child incorporates concepts into his or her cognitive structure

4. The child learns when there is a discrepancy between the way she or he views or thinks things are and the way they are in the environment; just the right amount of cognitive conflict is necessary for learning to take place

Application of these theory-derived notions of the ingredients of learning suggests that:

1. Opportunities must be provided for the child to structure his or her own knowledge through direct manipulation of objects and events; that is, there should be many opportunities to manipulate, explore, and experiment with classroom materials
2. The activities and materials used in the classroom should be real objects and events—preferably ones common to the child's early world
3. A wide variety of activities and experiences should be incorporated in the program
4. Children should be able to initiate and choose from activities that represent multiple levels of difficulty and conflict

These are but a few of the principles that can be derived from cognitive-developmental theory and applied in developing activities and formats for teaching in the preschool classroom.

Similarly, operant theory indicates that certain principles should be followed. A few would include:

1. Desired behaviors can be achieved by moving through successively closer and more precise approximations
2. Learning can be facilitated by prompting a correct response
3. Reinforcement is most effective when it is contingent and is delivered promptly

Maturationist-socialization theorists would suggest these principles:

1. Coherence and depth of learning are achieved by choosing unifying, age-appropriate themes that can serve as a context for multiple avenues of exploration
2. Children should not be placed prematurely into learning situations for which they are not ready (readiness)
3. Classrooms should be organized to produce a free and relaxed atmosphere in which children are free to express themselves, question, exchange, and explore

There are many others, some of which are discussed in later chapters. Each is important for organizing the activity of the classroom and for guiding teacher behavior.

Evaluation System Design

Planning for evaluation is an important part of the design of any early childhood education program. As you can see in Figure 3-1, theory derivations contribute to the appropriate evaluation system design in two ways.

Has the program produced the desired results?

Outcomes   Theory provides the criteria for child development and learning. As indicated earlier, this is accomplished through the specification of outcomes of importance to the theory and, in some cases, by suggesting measures for those outcomes. This has been called *summative evaluation* or *outcome evaluation*. It focuses on the child's changes in learning and development. Although it is usually oriented toward end-of-program outcomes, it need not necessarily be so.

Implementation   Theory provides specification of the processes thought to be involved in learning and development. As these are translated into action (activity, organization, and format), it is important to determine whether the activities specified by theory are carried out. This has been called *formative evaluation* or *process evaluation*. The focus here is on determining whether the activity conditions of the program have been met.

An appropriate evaluation design will seek to answer these two questions:

1. Has the program been organized and implemented in a theoretically consistent and complete manner?
2. Has the program produced the child development and learning results desired?

PROGRAM COMPONENTS

We have now moved from theory, through the derivations from theory that have relevance to early childhood education practice, to the translation of theory derivations into application. Still required is the consolidation of theory application into program components useful on a day-to-day basis. This requires the addition of what might be called *reality factors*. For example, the needs of children—other than their educational needs—must be considered. Children need to be fed, toileted, dressed, exercised, and given rest, as well as educated. Although such activities may be integrated with the education and development program, they do not emanate from theory. By the same token, program materials can be produced or purchased. Choices will frequently depend as much on the availability of resources (both human and material) as on theory specifications. The kinds of theoretically consistent activities conducted will depend on the teacher/child ratio, the financial resources available, the ingenuity of personnel and parents, the physical settings, and a host of other factors. Variability is to be expected. Finally, the elaboration of the evaluation system design will depend upon the time and resources available. The use of highly sophisticated measurement systems and data gathering formats requires highly trained personnel who have sufficient time allocated to the execution of the plan. Where fewer resources are available, a less sophisticated design will have to be implemented.

Because much variability in such specifics of program planning is to be expected, most of the remainder of this book is devoted to such specifics and to the elaboration of alternatives.

BELIEFS TEST

Because it is clear that each person's beliefs are a critical factor in how he or she defines an early childhood program, it may be useful for you to do an exercise that will help to make explicit your own underlying "theory," your assumptions and beliefs. Read the directions for the Teacher Belief Inventory in Box 3-2 and record your answers on a sheet of paper. The scoring system for assessing your responses is presented in Table 3-2. After reading the remainder of this book, you may want to complete the inventory again.

SUMMARY

In this chapter, we have briefly reviewed three major streams of educational thought that have been used to produce current models of or content variations in early childhood education practice.

The maturationist-socialization stream, deriving from the works of Freud, Erikson, and Gesell, emphasizes the socioemotional development of children as they work through a stage-wise progression of internal conflict resolutions. This theoretical perspective is found in traditional child-centered nursery schools and in a number of open-education programs.

The cultural training or behaviorist stream emphasizes structured, sequenced teaching and is based on the works of Skinner, Thorndike, and Bandura. It is found in many compensatory-education programs.

The cognitive-developmental stream, based on the works of Piaget, emphasizes the stage-wise development of thought that results from the interaction of children with their environment. Many programs use part or all of this approach, and it has been particularly recommended for programs for the gifted.

Based on such theories, it is possible to move, step by step, from theory to practice. These steps include goal derivation, priority setting, defining processes of learning and development, and specifying criteria. From these, a translation is made into the form of overall curriculum outline, with several levels of objectives, and a specification of activities and formats.

You then tested your own beliefs as a first step toward thinking about the development of your own program.

Teacher Belief Inventory

This exercise will help you discover what you believe is good teaching. Each statement below describes a teacher practice—something a teacher might do in a preschool. Many different and opposing kinds of teacher practices are presented here. *There are no "right" or "wrong" answers to any of these questions.* People have legitimately different points of view. As you read these statements, you will find yourself agreeing with some, disagreeing with some, and uncertain about others. The best answer to each statement is your personal belief or opinion.

Answer every item by checking either Strongly AGREE, Moderately AGREE, Slightly AGREE, Slightly DISAGREE, Moderately DISAGREE, or Strongly DISAGREE.

1. Teacher uses ongoing activities to teach language rather than having a separate language training program.

:	:	:	:	:	:	:
Strongly AGREE	Moderately AGREE	Slightly AGREE	Slightly DISAGREE	Moderately DISAGREE	Strongly DISAGREE	

2. Language is used sparingly in instruction and always in a way matched to the child's level of readiness.

:	:	:	:	:	:	:
Strongly AGREE	Moderately AGREE	Slightly AGREE	Slightly DISAGREE	Moderately DISAGREE	Strongly DISAGREE	

3. Teacher is interested in how a child works and plays rather than what he or she produces.

:	:	:	:	:	:	:
Strongly AGREE	Moderately AGREE	Slightly AGREE	Slightly DISAGREE	Moderately DISAGREE	Strongly DISAGREE	

4. Teacher corrects child's answer or behavior to get adult-acceptable responses.

:	:	:	:	:	:	:
Strongly AGREE	Moderately AGREE	Slightly AGREE	Slightly DISAGREE	Moderately DISAGREE	Strongly DISAGREE	

5. Teacher helps or provides information to the child only when absolutely necessary.

:	:	:	:	:	:	:
Strongly AGREE	Moderately AGREE	Slightly AGREE	Slightly DISAGREE	Moderately DISAGREE	Strongly DISAGREE	

6. Teacher provides interpersonal support for children's exploration and never pushes children toward higher levels of achievement.

:	:	:	:	:	:	:
Strongly AGREE	Moderately AGREE	Slightly AGREE	Slightly DISAGREE	Moderately DISAGREE	Strongly DISAGREE	

7. The child's own interest and involvement in an activity is his or her reward; the teacher does not provide other rewards such as selective praise, privileges, or prizes.

:	:	:	:	:	:	:
Strongly AGREE	Moderately AGREE	Slightly AGREE	Slightly DISAGREE	Moderately DISAGREE	Strongly DISAGREE	

8. Teacher strongly encourages dramatic play as a means of solving emotional problems.

:	:	:	:	:	:	:
Strongly AGREE	Moderately AGREE	Slightly AGREE	Slightly DISAGREE	Moderately DISAGREE	Strongly DISAGREE	

9. Teacher adjusts language to child's level, or uses child's own words.

    :   :   :   :   :   :   :

Strongly AGREE	Moderately AGREE	Slightly AGREE	Slightly DISAGREE	Moderately DISAGREE	Strongly DISAGREE

10. Teacher is interested in activity or task completion.

Strongly AGREE	Moderately AGREE	Slightly AGREE	Slightly DISAGREE	Moderately DISAGREE	Strongly DISAGREE

11. Teacher acts as source of information by lecturing or explaining.

Strongly AGREE	Moderately AGREE	Slightly AGREE	Slightly DISAGREE	Moderately DISAGREE	Strongly DISAGREE

12. Teacher provides major segments of the day for free play.

Strongly AGREE	Moderately AGREE	Slightly AGREE	Slightly DISAGREE	Moderately DISAGREE	Strongly DISAGREE

13. Teacher permits child to use materials and equipment in ways he or she wants rather than the way they are designed to be used.

Strongly AGREE	Moderately AGREE	Slightly AGREE	Slightly DISAGREE	Moderately DISAGREE	Strongly DISAGREE

14. Teacher accepts child's answers and responses even if not correct.

Strongly AGREE	Moderately AGREE	Slightly AGREE	Slightly DISAGREE	Moderately DISAGREE	Strongly DISAGREE

15. Teacher structures each day depending on spontaneous choices of children.

Strongly AGREE	Moderately AGREE	Slightly AGREE	Slightly DISAGREE	Moderately DISAGREE	Strongly DISAGREE

16. Teacher prevents situations that cause uncertainty, doubt, or perplexity in child's mind.

Strongly AGREE	Moderately AGREE	Slightly AGREE	Slightly DISAGREE	Moderately DISAGREE	Strongly DISAGREE

17. Teacher teaches language and concepts through use of materials, games, or activities specially designed to teach language.

Strongly AGREE	Moderately AGREE	Slightly AGREE	Slightly DISAGREE	Moderately DISAGREE	Strongly DISAGREE

18. Teacher uses as rewards very selective praise, attention, recognition, privileges, grades, prizes, candies, or other rewards.

Strongly AGREE	Moderately AGREE	Slightly AGREE	Slightly DISAGREE	Moderately DISAGREE	Strongly DISAGREE

Box 3-2   (continued)

19. Teacher provides opportunities for cooperation and group work throughout the day.

:	:	:	:	:	:	:
Strongly AGREE	Moderately AGREE	Slightly AGREE	Slightly DISAGREE	Moderately DISAGREE	Strongly DISAGREE	

20. Teacher permits use of any sources of information or experience a child may want to have.

:	:	:	:	:	:	:
Strongly AGREE	Moderately AGREE	Slightly AGREE	Slightly DISAGREE	Moderately DISAGREE	Strongly DISAGREE	

21. Child initiates a task or activity.

:	:	:	:	:	:	:
Strongly AGREE	Moderately AGREE	Slightly AGREE	Slightly DISAGREE	Moderately DISAGREE	Strongly DISAGREE	

22. Teacher permits the child to leave an activity or task before finishing it.

:	:	:	:	:	:	:
Strongly AGREE	Moderately AGREE	Slightly AGREE	Slightly DISAGREE	Moderately DISAGREE	Strongly DISAGREE	

23. Teacher stresses using materials in prescribed ways.

:	:	:	:	:	:	:
Strongly AGREE	Moderately AGREE	Slightly AGREE	Slightly DISAGREE	Moderately DISAGREE	Strongly DISAGREE	

24. Teacher uses adult-level language with child, or requests child to use the teacher's words.

:	:	:	:	:	:	:
Strongly AGREE	Moderately AGREE	Slightly AGREE	Slightly DISAGREE	Moderately DISAGREE	Strongly DISAGREE	

25. Teacher is interested in the quality of final products, and in the child's ability to meet adult standards.

:	:	:	:	:	:	:
Strongly AGREE	Moderately AGREE	Slightly AGREE	Slightly DISAGREE	Moderately DISAGREE	Strongly DISAGREE	

26. Child is encouraged to follow teacher's set plan of activities.

:	:	:	:	:	:	:
Strongly AGREE	Moderately AGREE	Slightly AGREE	Slightly DISAGREE	Moderately DISAGREE	Strongly DISAGREE	

27. Teacher provides child with situations that make her or him experiment, explore, and solve problems on her or his own.

:	:	:	:	:	:	:
Strongly AGREE	Moderately AGREE	Slightly AGREE	Slightly DISAGREE	Moderately DISAGREE	Strongly DISAGREE	

28. Teacher initiates and/or directs activity appropriate to the child's level.

| : | : | : | : | : | : | : |
| Strongly AGREE | Moderately AGREE | Slightly AGREE | Slightly DISAGREE | Moderately DISAGREE | Strongly DISAGREE | |

29. Teacher changes child's behavior by using special activities, games, or equipment (such as earphone and tape recorder, magnetic tape readers) that allow for immediate correction of child's error.

| : | : | : | : | : | : | : |
| Strongly AGREE | Moderately AGREE | Slightly AGREE | Slightly DISAGREE | Moderately DISAGREE | Strongly DISAGREE | |

30. Teacher allows child to follow his or her own interests, but ensures that materials used are appropriate for child's developmental level.

| : | : | : | : | : | : | : |
| Strongly AGREE | Moderately AGREE | Slightly AGREE | Slightly DISAGREE | Moderately DISAGREE | Strongly DISAGREE | |

Table 3-2   Teacher Belief Inventory Scoring

1. Assign points as follows to your answers for each item.

Alternative	Points
Strongly Agree	6
Moderately Agree	5
Slightly Agree	4
Slightly Disagree	3
Moderately Disagree	2
Strongly Disagree	1

2. Sum your point scores for items 1, 3, 5, 7, 9, 13, 14, 20, 22, and 27. This sum represents your cognitive-developmental scale score.

3. Sum your point scores for items 4, 10, 11, 16, 17, 18, 23, 24, 25, and 29. This sum represents your cultural-training or behaviorist scale score.

4. Sum your scores for items 2, 6, 8, 12, 15, 19, 21, 26, 28, and 30. This sum represents your maturationist-socialization scale score.

5. Compare your three scores (subtract the lower from the higher in each case). If your scale score for one of the scales is 10 points higher than for the other, it may be taken to reflect your bias toward the theory represented by that scale. If the three scores do not differ by at least 10 points, you are not a strong adherent of any position. If none of the three scores differ, you have not yet firmed up your beliefs.

Review Questions

1. List the three streams of educational thought and briefly describe what each view emphasizes as important in education.
2. What are the common assumptions that all child development and learning theories hold to be true?
3. How do each of the three theories see child development? What key differences are noted in children's motivation?
4. What are three different sources from which objectives may be developed? What considerations are important in selecting one over the others? How do theories of child development contribute to the formulation of objectives for child education programs?

Suggested Activities

1. Discuss the implications of each quotation in Box 3-1 for early childhood education practice.
2. Seek in original sources quotations by B. F. Skinner, Erik Erikson, Jean Piaget, and other theorists, and put together a set of notable quotations for each of the three major streams of educational thought.
3. Visit several local nursery schools or day-care centers, gather any promotional materials they have, and discuss with the staff and director their program philosophy. Analyze the information gathered, and try to determine where each program might fit in the three major streams of educational thought.
4. Select some long-range goal of early education, and specify several intermediate objectives that would need to be accomplished for the goal to be achieved. Then take one of the intermediate objectives, and specify several immediate objectives that would have to be accomplished before the intermediate objective could be achieved.

Suggested Readings

Chou, S., and Elmore, P. *Early childhood information unit: resource manual and program descriptions*. New York: Educational Products Information Exchange, 1973.

Day, M. C., and Parker, R. K. *The preschool in action*, 2nd ed. Boston: Allyn & Bacon, 1977.

Hom, R., and Robinson, P. (Eds.). *Psychological processes in early education*. New York: Academic Press, 1977.

Range, D., Layton, J., and Roubinek, D. *Aspects of early childhood education: theory to research to practice*. New York: Academic Press, 1980.

Roberts, T. B. (Ed.). *Four psychologies applied to education*. New York: Wiley, 1975.

Does Early Childhood Education Make a Difference?

Chapter 4

*I*n the previous chapters, we discussed the major form and content variations in early childhood education programs. In Chapter 2, we covered the origins and historical development of the kindergarten, nursery-school, day-care, compensatory-education, and home-based program movements in the United States. In Chapter 3, we discussed the origin of curriculum ideas and their translation into early childhood education practice. These ideas were categorized as falling within the maturationist-socialization, behavioral, and cognitive-developmental streams of thought. We suggested that these theoretical belief systems are important to daily practice, but we did not provide much evidence of how or why. How do these variations in form and content affect children and their families, if at all? This is a complex question, leading to many others. In this chapter, we try to provide some not so commonly known information that might help to satisfy your curiosity.

A QUESTION OF FORM

In this section, we review briefly the research literature on the five major forms of early childhood education services discussed in Chapter 2. Our emphasis is on the most recent findings.

Kindergarten and Nursery School

Much of the research conducted before 1960 on the effects of early education experience addressed the question, "Does kindergarten or nursery school attendance make a difference?" Several good reviews (for example, Sears & Dowley, 1963) seem to suggest the best answer to the question is, "Maybe. . . . It depends." it is difficult to draw a clear yes or no answer

The child's emotional security has frequently been the concern of researchers of child care outside the home.

from this research, in part because of weaknesses in the research methodology used and in part because the kindergartens and nursery schools evaluated were too amorphous and nondescript to allow an interpretation of what they were or what they intended to accomplish. The general conclusion of this early research has been summarized by Sears and Dowley (1963) as follows:

> Finally, it should be mentioned that firm knowledge of the effect of teaching methods or roles cannot be gained without taking into account characteristics of the children toward whom the methods are directed. It is clear by now that a "method" cannot be abstracted from the interpersonal setting; methods are employed by teachers having certain characteristics and they are directed toward children with certain characteristics. Shorn of these factors, statements about a method must necessarily be stated in such tentative terms that they are of little value [p. 859].

Day Care

Because researchers are part of their culture and reflect the general values held by their society, including the basic assumptions about families and their child rearing responsibilities discussed in Chapter 1, the research on day care has had a unique negative quality (Peters, 1980). The great majority of research has focused on determining whether day care is *harmful* to children. This research has focused on five basic questions (adapted from Kagan, 1977):

1. Does day care *damage* the attachment between the infant and the mother?
2. Does day care *retard* cognitive development?
3. Does day care produce children who *lack* self-control, who are *overly* aggressive, or *overly* passive?
4. Does day care lead to *too great* a reliance on peers or to later *unsatisfactory* peer relationships?
5. Does day care *usurp* the mother's responsibility for the child?

The results of this research, although subject to major limitations (Belsky & Steinberg, 1978; Peters & Belsky, 1983), can be summarized as follows.

Intellectual Development   Overall, the research suggests that the day-care experience has neither positive nor adverse effects on the intellectual development of most children. Some evidence hints that for young economically disadvantaged children day care may attenuate declines in test scores usually found in such children after 18 months of age (Belsky & Steinberg,

1978) or may in some cases lead to some improvement in functioning (Fowler, 1977). We emphasize that the body of research, as a whole, does not indicate that day care improves cognitive functioning, only that day care has no adverse effects on intellectual development as measured by standardized tests.

Emotional Development   Historically, the mother–child bond has been of prime concern to those interested in the influence of early experience on emotional development. Psychodynamic theory and early research on institutionalized children (Bowlby, 1951; Goldfarb, 1943; Spitz, 1945) suggested that any arrangement that deprived the child of continuous access to the mother would damage maternal attachment and the child's emotional security. Because day care involves the daily separation of mother from child, researchers have been concerned whether child care outside the home does disrupt the child's emotional tie to his or her mother.

Children in day care, compared to children reared at home, interact more with peers.

Several reviews of the research literature make it clear that day care has little influence on the mother–child bond for most children. Only when the children are from extremely poor and deprived environments and are enrolled in unstable day-care arrangements do there seem to be any problems. Under such conditions, infants less than 1 year old will be more likely to develop a particular kind of disturbance in their relations with their primary attachment figure: they will be likely to avoid her. Even in such cases, the situation is not inevitable if the quality of maternal care is not compromised during those periods of the day when she is with the infant (Belsky & Steinberg, 1978).

Social Development   Social development is usually defined in terms of relations with peers and nonparental adults. On the basis of the available evidence, children in day care, when compared to age-matched cohorts reared at home, interact more with peers—in both positive and negative ways. Some evidence suggests, moreover, that children enrolled in day care for extended periods have displayed increased aggression toward peers and adults, and decreased cooperation with adults and involvement in educational activities once they entered school (Peters & Koppel, 1977).

However, as we indicated in Chapter 1, day-care programs are likely to reflect the values of the community at large. It is possible that this aggressiveness is characteristic of socialization in age-segregated peer groups in the United States generally and that the phenomenon may indeed be culture bound. Comparative studies of peer-group socialization in the United States, the Soviet Union, Israel, and other contemporary societies show that group upbringing can lead to a variety of consequences (Belsky & Steinberg, 1978). Ambron's (1979) suggestion that day-care staff are more permissive, more tolerant of disobedience and aggression, and less inclined to set behavior standards than parents lends credence to this conclusion.

Physical Development   Few studies have looked at the physical development of children in day care. Where data do exist, the focus is primarily on height and weight. The lack of evidence to the contrary probably suggests that there are no notable differences between home-reared children and those in day care. Evidence does indicate that the incidence of illness (infectious disease) is not significantly higher among children in group day care than it is among home-reared children (Loda, 1976).

Effects on Families   The availability and quality of child-care arrangements can have a major impact on the family unit that goes beyond the immediate effects on the child. Indeed, much of the public justification for the provision of day-care services has to do with the family (particularly the mother), not the child (Peters, 1980, Peters & Beker, 1975), and day care is generally considered a supplement to the family's child-rearing responsibilities.

This notion of supplementing the family role suggests the need for clear communication between the family and the day-care provider. Douglas Powell has conducted the most extensive examination of parent–caregiver communication (Powell, 1977, 1978, 1979, 1980), and his in-depth interviews of 212 parents and 89 caregivers in 12 metropolitan day-care centers in Detroit reveal that few efforts are made to coordinate children's socialization across contexts. Powell concludes on the basis of his work that "fragmentation and discontinuity" characterize the social world of children in day care.

Powell's detailed typology of parent–caregiver communication patterns, however, indicates that experiences across day care and home are not the same for all children. A small group of "interdependent" parents, Powell discovered, believe strongly that family information (on a wide variety of topics) should be shared with day-care workers. These parents practice what they preach, engaging in frequent communication with caregivers. "Independent" parents, in contrast, maintain a significant social distance between themselves and their children's caregivers, most probably because they conceive of family and day care as two separate rearing environments. Finally, a third group of "dependent" parents were identified who view the family–day-care relationship as a one-way street on which information flows only from day care to the home.

In addition to influencing the parent–child relationship, day care can support family functioning in other ways. Most significant in this regard may be its effect on the parents' relationship. Under two conditions day care may be a positive influence: when it frees a parent from the unsatisfying responsibilities of providing full-time child care, and when it enables a second parent in an economically stressed family to seek gainful employment. Because a harmonious relationship provides support for parents in their caregiving roles (Belsky, 1981), such effects of day care have the potential for positively influencing the mother–father relationship. Although men tend to be less enthusiastic, women report that their relationships are happier with day care (Hoffman, 1971). In one quasi-experimental study, it was found that employed mothers whose children were cared for in day-care centers were more satisfied in their relationships than both employed mothers with other forms of child care and unemployed (homemaker) mothers (Myers, 1972). The perceived quality of parent–child relations also has been found to be positively associated with work satisfaction in women, and work satisfaction has been found to relate positively to satisfaction with substitute child care (Harrell & Ridley, 1975). The child development literature also suggests that mother–child attachments do not differ for day-care children as compared to home-care children; it appears that, for some mothers at least, day care permits satisfaction in both the maternal role and the employment role but does not have a detrimental effect on the child.

Many employed mothers report satisfaction with day-care centers.

Center versus Home Day Care   The research just discussed focuses primarily on center-based day care. Center-based day care has received far more systematic attention by researchers than has family day care. Center-based programs tend to offer a wider variety of formal learning experiences, are usually licensed, and are most likely to employ at least some trained professionals and staff. However, variation within center programs can be great. Center group size and child/caregiver ratio are the characteristics of centers that have received the most empirical attention in efforts to understand how variations within programs affect children's experience. In an early observational study of 69 California preschool day-care programs, Prescott, Jones, and Kritchevsky (1967) found that when center population exceeded 60 children, more emphasis was placed on rules and routine guidance than when size ranged from 30 to 60 children. In fact, teachers placed twice as much emphasis on control in the large groups, which possibly accounts for the observation that in small centers children displayed more pleasure, wonder, and delight. Additional evidence from this study revealed that large centers were less flexible in their scheduling, offered children fewer opportunities to initiate and control activities, and had teachers who displayed less sensitivity to the individual needs of the children (Heinicke, Friedman, Prescott, Pancel, & Sale, 1973).

Most of these results have been replicated in a large-scale national study of 57 day-care centers in Atlanta, Detroit, and Seattle (hereafter referred to as the National Day Care, or NDC, study). Travers and Ruopp (1978) reported that for children 3 to 5 years of age, group size was the single most important determinant of the quality of children's experience. In groups of less than 15 to 18 children, caregivers were involved in more embellished caregiving (for example, questioning, responding, praising, comforting), less straight monitoring of children, and less interaction with other adults. And in these smaller groups, children were more actively involved in classroom activities (for example, considering and contemplating, contributing ideas, cooperating, persisting at tasks).

Interestingly, the NDC study found that child/caregiver ratio had little effect on the quality of *preschoolers'* (age 3 to 5 years) experience in day care, though it was an important determinant of *infants'* (age less than 3 years) experience. More overt distress was observed among infants as the number of children per caregiver increased. Additionally, in high-ratio (1 : 10 staff to children) infant and toddler programs, staff spent more time in management and control interactions and engaged less in informal teaching (Connell, Layzer, & Goodson, 1979; Travers & Ruopp, 1978).

Family day care constitutes the most used system of out-of-home care in this country, in terms of both the number of families using care and the number of children served. An estimated 1.3 million family day-care homes serve an estimated 2.4 million full-time (over 30 hours per week) pupils, 2.8 million part-time (10 to 29 hours per week) pupils, and 16.7 million occasional care (less than 10 hours per week) pupils. Over 50 percent of the full-time pupils in family day care are less than 6 years of age, with the greatest proportion of these children under 3. Family day care also represents the most prevalent mode of care for the 5 million school children between 6 and 13 years of age whose parents work (Fosburg, 1980).

Two generally cited strengths of family day care are: (1) the daily and close contact it affords children with mixed-age peers, and (2) its limited isolation from the noncaregiving world. Other advantages include more flexible hours, convenient location, and freedom afforded to parents in selecting caregivers with values similar to their own. For children without fathers, family day care frequently provides children with the man of the household to serve as a model.

Of course, family day care has its own unique disadvantages. As Steinberg and Green (1979) and Saunders and Keister (1972) suggest, family day care is, in some cases, unstable. Others have found that this is not always the case (Peters, 1972) and that the continuity or discontinuity between home and family day-care environments varies considerably (Long, Peters, & Garduque, 1984). Additionally, there is often little assurance that the provider has any formal training in child care, though most are experienced parents. More often than not, however, these caregivers lack the licensing *and* supervision that can help to assure quality care.

However, the findings of the National Consumer Study (Rodes & Moore, 1975) found that 72 percent of parents whose children were in family day-care homes were very satisfied with such care and 19 percent of parents whose children were in day-care centers would have preferred to have their children in family day-care homes. It seems reasonable to assume that the preferences represent a match between the parents' image of desirable child care and its actual availability.

Compensatory-Education Programs

Our best available research on the effects of early childhood education comes from studies of federally funded compensatory-education programs.

These programs have been subjected to close scrutiny since their beginnings in the early 1960s, in part because of the dependence on public funds and, hence, their accountability.

Bronfenbrenner (1975), after analyzing the data from a large number of studies, offered some conclusions that have been concurred with by others (Travers & Ruopp, 1978).

For center-based early intervention programs (children entering the program scored 90 or less on IQ tests):

1. Almost without exception, children showed substantial gains in IQ and other cognitive measures during the first year of the program, attaining or even exceeding the average for their age.

2. Cognitively structured curricula produced greater cognitive gains than play-oriented nursery programs.

3. Neither earlier entry into the program (from age 1 year) nor a longer period of enrollment (up to 5 years) resulted in greater or more enduring cognitive gains.

4. By the first or second year after completion of the program, sometimes while they were still in it, the children began to show a progressive decline in scores on standardized intelligence tests, and by the third or fourth year of follow-up had fallen back into the problem range of IQ scores in the lower 90s and below.

5. The period of sharpest decline occurred after the child's entry into regular school. Preliminary data from the Follow-Through program suggest that this decline may be offset by the continuation of intervention programs, including strong parent involvement, into the early grades.

6. The children who profited least from the program, and who showed the earliest and most rapid decline, were those who came from the most deprived social and economic backgrounds.

7. Results from a number of studies pointed to factors in and around the home as critical to the child's capacity to profit from group programs both in preschool and in the elementary grades.

At first glance, these findings seem disappointing in terms of cognitive gains (which, some people point out, is only one area of potential child care benefit and perhaps is not the most important one). However, more recent longitudinal analyses clearly paint a positive picture (Collins, 1983; Lazar & Darlington, 1982; Schweinhart & Weikart, 1980). A consortium of early childhood education program designers and developers have pooled their follow-up data on graduates of early intervention programs from the 1960s to the present. The results are impressive:

1. Infant and preschool early intervention programs improve the ability of low-income children to meet the minimum requirement of the schools

they enter. This is shown by the significantly *reduced* (when contrasted with comparable children without early education experience) percentage assigned to special education classes or held back in a grade.

2. Graduates demonstrate a significant increase in intellectual functioning during the critical elementary-school years.

3. As adolescents, graduates rate their own competence in school higher than comparable adolescents without the compensatory early education experience.

4. Graduates are less likely to drop out of school than are students without compensatory early education experience.

5. Graduates' parents were highly satisfied with the early-intervention programs and were sure that they were a very good thing for their children (Lazar, Hubbel, Murray, Rosche, & Royce, 1977).

These results indicate that graduates are more intellectually capable during the early years, are more confident and motivated in school, and, no doubt, are encouraged in school by their parents. The results are fewer special education placements and fewer children left back (and hence fewer drop outs later)—outcomes that are good for the individuals involved and that represent cost savings (human and dollar) for society.

Family-Based Interventions

Recent research on family-based programs has also been very encouraging (see Chapter 2). When the emphasis of a program is on the parent–child dyad (usually mother–child), the results seem to indicate that:

1. There are substantial and cumulative IQ gains that seem to endure after the programs are terminated.

2. Not only the child enrolled in the program benefits; the younger siblings do also.

3. Parent intervention influences the attitudes and behavior of the parents not only toward their children but in relation to themselves as competent people capable of improving their own lives (Bronfenbrenner, 1974).

These results seem to occur when parents learn to challenge their children cognitively and to develop mutual and enduring emotional attachments. Based on his analysis of this research, Bronfenbrenner (1975) has concluded:

> *The evidence indicates that the family is the most effective and economical system for fostering and sustaining the development of the child. The evidence indicates further that the involvement of the*

child's family as an active participant is critical to the success of any intervention program. Without such family involvement, any effects of intervention, at least in the cognitive sphere, appear to erode fairly rapidly once the program ends. In contrast, the involvement of the parents as partners in the enterprise provides an on-going system which can reinforce the effects of the program while it is in operation, and help to sustain them after the program ends [p. 54].

Conclusions on Form

The research seems to indicate that all forms of early childhood education have at least a salutory effect on children; that is, *any* early childhood education enrollment does no harm to children, and, in many cases, it can do some good. For children from warm, caring, and reasonably stimulating homes, early education seems to be an extension of the home environment, expanding the children's horizons somewhat and increasing opportunities for social interaction. For children from more disadvantaged home environments, compensatory programs, particularly those involving the parents, seem to produce positive effects on development and education both in the short and the long term.

A QUESTION OF CONTENT

In Chapter 3, we discussed content differences in early childhood programs based on different theories about development and learning.

When considering research on the comparison of different early education curriculum models or programs, two additional questions come to mind.

1. Are the programs actually different?
2. Do the program differences yield differences in development or learning for the children enrolled?

Few studies have attempted to answer both questions simultaneously. Therefore, we shall first look at the research on the two questions separately.

Program Differences

Several writers have traced the antecedents of current curriculum models in early education to their divergent philosophical bases in the writings of Locke, Rousseau, Hume, and Pestalozzi and through their psychological and behavioral theory foundations in the writings of Skinner, Watson,

Freud, and Piaget (Beller, 1973; DeVries, 1974; Kessen, 1965; Kohlberg, 1968; Peters, 1977). In general terms, most of these authors agree that, as discussed in Chapter 3, there are three major streams of thought: the maturationist-socialization stream, the cultural-training or behaviorist stream, and the cognitive-developmental or interactionist stream (Kohlberg, 1968).

Conceptually, at least, early education programs tend to derive from those three distinctive bodies of thought. Several analyses done of written materials produced by Head Start and Follow-Through programs confirm that, in writing at least, the programs (such as those of Bereiter & Engelmann, 1966; Gray & Klaus, 1965; Weikart, Deloria, Lawson, & Wiegerink, 1970; Montessori, Bank Street College, and others) differ in their basic features of theoretical foundation, program organization, and planned activities (Chou & Elmore, 1973; Gordon, 1972; Maccoby & Zellner, 1970; Parker, 1974). (Readers interested in substantial overviews of the nationally recognized program variations are referred to Chou & Elmore, 1973; Day & Parker, 1977; Evans, 1975; Ryan, 1974.)

Analyses based on written materials, curriculum guides, and the like are interesting, but the real question is "Do they differ in actual practice?"

Although there is a considerable amount of observational research in early childhood, and although the preschool is the most usual location for such research to be conducted (Gordon & Jester, 1973; Wright, 1960), few studies have attempted to determine whether actual classroom behavior is consistent with the theoretical foundation and organizational structure of specific programs (as derived from or prescribed by the model builders). Five studies are worth noting both because of what they found and how they approached the problems of defining the critical dimensions for observation.

Soar and Soar   In a study designed specifically to answer the two questions concerning program differences posed earlier, Soar and Soar (1972) selected and somewhat modified four existing observational instruments to analyze differences in the implementation of seven experimental programs in Project Follow-Through and two comparison "traditional" classrooms. Selection of the instruments was apparently based on their quality and prior use in the research literature.

Soar and Soar conclude that the evidence that programs are successful in creating differences in classroom behavior is strong. Although there were differences in success of implementation (a relatively wide disparity between teacher and child behaviors within different classes of the same model program), the Follow-Through programs could be differentiated on two major factors: free choice versus structured learning in groups, and teacher-directed activity versus pupil-selected activity. The clearest distinction was between the Bereiter-Engelmann program (behaviorist) and the

Education Development Corporation Program (maturationist). The latter is a program fashioned after the British infant school.

Verma and Peters   A different approach was taken by Verma and Peters (1975), who operated from the assumption that if the variables isolated for study were to have a potential effect on the children enrolled, they should be derived from developmental theory—the same theory as used to derive the early childhood education program. As such, a number of observational categories were deduced from an analysis of the two major theories currently influencing early education practice (behavior theory—Skinner; and cognitive-developmental theory—Piaget) without reference to the written materials of the program to be observed. Observations were collected over a six-week period from four different, well-implemented pre-school model programs. Included were a precision-teaching preacademic program (behaviorist), a cognitive-developmental program, a responsive-environment program, and a traditional program—the latter two most closely representing a maturationist-socialization perspective. The observational data located each program within the theoretical model predicted (Cohen, Peters, & Willis, 1976). Across programs, differences were found in such categories as teacher versus child initiation of activities, provision of contingent reinforcement, structuring of the environment, requiring completion of activities, and teacher provision of information.

Miller and Dyer   For purposes of comparing four different Head Start models, Miller and Dyer (1975) undertook three levels of analysis. Detailed descriptions were made of the models (conceptual analysis from written materials and conversations with the developers) and were organized under categories such as goals, content, methods, and techniques. From these, eight dimensions were derived (feedback, modeling and imitation, play, sensory stimulation, language, manipulation of materials, sequencing, and ecology) to differentiate the model programs conceptually. Because the programs to be studied were developed and implemented by others, those who were developers or who served as consultants to the program were asked both to participate in the conceptual analysis of their program *and* to rate (along the given dimensions) the success of the implementation. Finally, both in-class and video-tape observation schemes were used to analyze classroom practice.

Across the four programs studied, Bereiter-Engelmann (BE), DARCE (DAR), Montessori (MONT), and traditional (TRAD), the analysis indicated there were real and evident differences among the programs. The authors conclude:

> *There were two teacher-directed, fast paced, didactic treatments in a group format involving high amounts of positive reinforcement—one*

> (BE) characterized by requests for group performance, teacher modeling primarily verbal, more setting of academic standards and more error correction; the other (DAR) characterized by verbal instruction, requests for individual performance both verbal and role playing and by lower amounts of error correction.
>
> There were two child-centered, slower paced treatments in an individualized format, with one (MONT) characterized by more didactic teaching through giving information to individuals, low amounts of either positive or negative reinforcement, while children are conversing or manipulating material; the other (TRAD) characterized by low amounts of didactic teaching, teachers communicating primarily verbally through requests for individual performance which was largely elaboration and modification of social behavior, low amounts of positive reinforcement, but relatively high amounts of negative reinforcement, primarily for behavior control, while children were conversing and role playing (most imaginary games) [pp. 60–62].

The data indicate that, with few exceptions, the four programs in actual practice were congruent with the derived descriptions of the programs. Consultants also were for the most part satisfied with the level of implementation of their programs.

Stallings   Extensive research on seven Follow-Through model programs was conducted by Stallings (1975) and others at the Stanford Research Institute. They included two behaviorist models based on positive-reinforcement theory (from the University of Kansas and the University of Oregon), a model based primarily on cognitive-developmental theory (High/Scope Foundation—Weikart), an open-classroom model (Educational Development Center), and three other models that are more eclectic (Far West Laboratory—Responsive Environment; University of Arizona; and Bank Street College).

To study the degree of implementation of each program and the differences among them, they designed a *classroom observation instrument* (COI) to record classroom arrangements and activities. Because the observational scheme employed involved many variables, they had to choose a set of variables that were program relevant. To accomplish this: (1) a detailed model description of each program was prepared, (2) the model descriptions were reviewed and revised by the program developers, (3) variables that described representative elements of each sponsor's model were created from the codes used in the observation instrument, (4) each program developer identified those variables that were important to her or his model and those that were expected to occur more frequently in his or her model than in a conventional classroom, (5) a listing of 55 critical variables was formulated.

Child group size is one of the variables that differentiates model programs.

Observations were made in both first- and third-grade classrooms of five implementation sites for each of the seven models.

Stallings concluded that, with minor exceptions, the seven Follow-Through models were significantly different from conventional classrooms, the different classrooms of each model were highly similar to one another, and they could be correctly classified as to sponsor without prior knowledge on the basis of the critical variables. In all analyses, the two behavioral models tended to cluster apart from each other and from the other models. The important variables for differentiating among programs were those representing (1) adult reinforcement with tokens; (2) adult praise; (3) child group responses to adult academic commands, requests, or direct questions; (4) child group size (individual children, small group, large group); (5) the amount and variety of materials; and (6) the number and variety of activities during the day.

Bissell   Eight Head Start models were grouped into three categories on the basis of their primary orientation toward children's learning. Bissell (1971) chose the categories (1) preacademic—programs with heavy emphasis on systematic reinforcement, drills, or individualized program instruction; (2) cognitive-discovery—programs focused on the development of basic cognitive processes through planned and sequenced exploration and verbal labeling; and (3) discovery—programs that view learning as part of the normal growth process of the "whole" child; such programs emphasize free exploration and self-expression. The degree of implementation was assessed on the basis of sponsors', consultants', and teachers' appraisals of success. Again, the COI was used for classroom analysis.

At the beginning of the year, the degree of implementation was rated as low for 67 percent of the teachers, but by the end of the year the degree of implementation was rated as medium or high for 75 percent of the teachers. There were more ratings of high implementation in the preacademic programs and more ratings of low implementation in the discovery programs. Bissell suggested that the preacademic (cultural-transmission or behaviorist) models are more easily implemented because they provide discrete and highly specific preplanned components in their daily activities. In contrast, the cognitive-discovery and discovery models require the internalization of a theory to implement the model correctly by initiating and responding to materials in an insightful manner.

In the areas of primary importance to the models' programs, differences were most apparent and the children's experiences reflected the models' stated orientation. In areas of lesser importance to the models, the children's experiences were less distinctive. The preacademic programs were characterized by activities involving language and numbers. Puzzles and games that teach concepts such as sizes and shapes and social studies were most prevalent in cognitive-discovery programs. Expressive role-playing occurred most in the discovery programs.

Summary   In general, this line of research indicates that the various program models (1) may be successfully implemented in different sites, (2) differ from traditional classroom practice (both in the preschool and early elementary grades), and (3) are distinguishable from each other both conceptually and in practice.

The key variables for program differentiation are summarized in Table 4-1.

Given the disparate means for arriving at the different observational procedures employed, the age differences of the children in the classrooms studied (from 3 to 8 or 9 years), and the large number of programs and classrooms involved, the results are remarkably consistent. All five studies seem to indicate that despite the extensive theoretical rationales and "marketing" differences associated with the many nationally recognized models of early education, we are really dealing with only a few critical difference variables. These variables seem to define positions (and extremes) on a continuum from what has been called discovery learning versus didactic

Table 4-1   Empirically Derived Variables Important to Program Model Differentiation

Research Study	Summary Variables
Soar & Soar (1972)	Free choice vs. structured learning Teacher-directed activity vs. pupil-selected activity
Verma & Peters (1975)	Teacher- vs. child-initiated activities Provision of contingent reinforcement Structuring of the environment Requiring completion of activities Teacher provision of information
Miller & Dyer (1975)	Teacher direction Teacher provision of information (didactic teaching) Provision of positive or negative reinforcement Requests for group vs. individual performance Teacher modeling Setting of academic standards Error correction Manipulation of materials
Stallings (1975)	Adult reinforcement and praise Individual vs. group performance demands Group size Amount and variety of materials Number and variety of materials
Bissell (1971)	Preplanned, discrete academic activities Insightful teacher initiation and response

teaching (Peters, 1970) or child-centered versus teacher-centered programming (Beller, 1973).

Differential Program Effects

The research cited has been useful for determining actual program differences. It has been less useful in isolating cause-and-effect relationships between program activities and child outcomes. There are several reasons for this.

First, each curriculum model's activities are geared towards specific objectives and priorities derived from the body of knowledge on which the model is based. Commonality of objectives across models is not common and the differences reflect value judgments (Katz, 1974). Where outcome differences are found in specific objective-related areas, we have few empirical data to provide confidence that the differences are lasting or that they relate systematically to later important developmental outcomes.

Second, even in the few studies that have been well designed to minimize the confounding of specific teacher variables with program variables (for example, Miller & Dyer, 1975; Stallings, 1975) a number of nontheoretical implementation differences remain. These include the amount of actual schooling received by the child, the amount of inservice training and consultation received by the teachers, and the adequacy of physical facilities. In each of the studies cited, these remain at least partially confounded (Beller, 1973; Miller & Dyer, 1975; Stallings, 1975).

Third, and perhaps most important, the dimensions found to differentiate programs are themselves highly related in the models. For example, the amount of teacher-provided reinforcement is usually associated with the degree of teacher structuring and teacher modeling. As such, research involving comparisons of model programs in their totality cannot:

1. Isolate the independent effects of specific model variables on outcomes
2. Determine the most appropriate functional level for each model variable (as compared to nonfunctional levels that are either too high or too low)
3. Separate those variables that are truly important from those that are only window dressing

Still, based on the cumulative results of several studies, some tentative conclusions can be drawn. To discuss them we shall use the general framework of Bissell (1971) and Karnes, Hodgins, Teska, and Kirk (1969); that is, we have attempted to organize the programs along a broad, and certainly not perfect, dimension of discovery learning. Table 4-2 shows how we have placed certain programs.

Table 4-2   Program Placement in a Discovery Framework

Type of Program	*Examples*
Cultural transmission or behaviorist	Bereiter-Engelmann U. of Kansas U. of Arizona DARCE
Cognitive developmental	Compensatory Montessori Far West Lab High/Scope Foundation
Discovery or maturationist socialization	Bank Street College Educational Development Corporation Traditional child-centered

Cultural-Transmission or Behaviorist Programs   Our review suggests that academic programs foster number readiness (Karnes et al., 1969), arithmetic achievement (Miller & Dyer, 1975; Stallings, 1975), reading achievement (Stallings, 1975), some form of language and sentence production (Karnes et al., 1969; Miller & Dyer, 1975), task persistence (Stallings, 1975), and test-taking behaviors (Bissell, 1971). There is also some indication that such programs produce the largest initial IQ gains (Karnes et al., 1969; Miller & Dyer, 1975), though these do not seem to last (Beller, 1973; Miller & Dyer, 1975).

Preacademic programs do not foster, or may interfere with, the development of inventiveness and curiosity (Miller & Dyer, 1975), independence, cooperation, and flexible problem solving (Stallings, 1975).

Cognitive-Developmental Programs   The literature suggests that cognitive-discovery programs lead to higher levels of inventiveness and curiosity (Miller & Dyer, 1975), verbal expression and social interaction (Miller & Dyer, 1975; Peters & Stein, 1968), practice play (Beller, Zimmie, & Aitkin, 1971), and problem-solving ability (Stallings, 1975).

Discovery or Maturationist-Socialization Programs   Research indicates that discovery programs seem to produce children who score high on problem-solving and IQ measures and who take responsibility for their successes and failures (Stallings, 1975). Such children are independent of the teacher and cooperative in peer relations (Stallings, 1975). They engage in more complex symbolic play (Beller, Zimmie, & Aitkin, 1971), are highly creative (Dreyer & Rigler, 1969), and are able to monitor their own behavior (Bissell, 1971).

SUMMARY

It appears that the programs tend to produce what they set out to produce—at least in the short term; that is, different constellations of program variables produce different constellations of child outcome variables. The desirability of one set of child outcomes over another is a value judgment. Specific cause-and-effect relations are not definable from such research, and the studies add little to our knowledge of the developmental process. However, the results provide global information pertinent to decisions concerning educational practice.

The research literature does suggest that there are theoretically consistent program differences and that such differences are important to child outcomes. We turn now to a careful look at the two major, clearly defined alternatives: the behaviorist and cognitive-developmental model programs.

Review Questions

1. Write a concise statement, in terms that parents could understand, about the effects of day-care center attendance on children's development.
2. What key program factors does the research suggest affect the quality of experience children receive in a day-care program?
3. In what ways are early childhood compensatory-education programs effective? In the short term? In the long term?
4. Name four dimensions of program content that seem to be related to child outcomes for different curriculum models.
5. What do we mean when we say that different programs produce different outcomes, and that the choice of which one is best is a value judgment?

Suggested Activities

1. Find original articles or books on one of the curriculum models listed in Table 4-2. Prepare a summary of the program to share with other members of the class.
2. Visit a Montessori school in your community. Write your impressions of what is different about this program from others with which you are familiar.
3. Obtain catalogs from several early childhood education equipment and material suppliers.

Try to determine types of materials that might be found in the different program models listed in Table 4-2.

4. Role play the situation of a congressional or state legislative hearing to determine whether tax dollars should be used to support early childhood education. Try taking the role of: (a) an advocate for such spending; (b) a fiscally conservative legislator; (c) an advocate for more spending for the elderly. Role play as many points of view as might be brought to bear on the topic.
5. Write a newsletter summary of the research discussed in the chapter for parents of Head Start pupils.
6. Develop a brochure for parents who are trying to decide between sending their child to a day-care center or a family day-care home. Highlight the points they should consider, presenting arguments for and against both alternatives.

Suggested Readings

Abidin, R, (Ed.). *Parent education and intervention handbook*. Springfield, IL: Charles C Thomas, 1980.

Evans, E. *Contemporary influences in early childhood education*. New York: Holt, Rinehart & Winston, 1975.

Spodek, B. (Ed.). *Handbook of research in early childhood education*. New York: Free Press, 1982.

PART TWO

A BEHAVIORIST APPROACH TO EARLY CHILDHOOD EDUCATION

*S*cientists, and indeed most people, put together hunches or specula-
tions to understand events that have no clear observable causes. We
frequently supply our own minitheories regarding personal events. Why
did he (she) stop liking me? What might happen psychologically to a
youngster whose parents get divorced? How do children learn to share
instead of being selfish? Why do some children learn and remember
much better than others? Behaviorists as well as cognitive-developmen-
talists use theory to account for child learning and development. There
are, however, some major differences between behaviorists and other sci-
entists in the *kind* of theory building they do.

Behaviorists explain behavior in terms of actual, rather than fictitious,
circumstances. Observable and measurable factors such as amount, kind,
and timing of reinforcement are studied in detail to describe, predict, and
control behavior. There is no recourse to speculative mental processes or
hidden forces such as cognitive structure, ego strength, or curiosity drive.
Instead, behavior is explained as a result of real circumstances immediately preceding and following the behavior. Children exhibit "curiosity"
not because of a curiosity drive, but because exploratory and probing
behavior is shaped and maintained through environmental reinforcement.
Aggression is a behavior that can be strengthened or weakened, depending on the prevailing contingencies of reinforcement; it is not an expression of human nature or a frustrated drive. Likewise, learning, recall,
transfer, and other "mental" abilities are defined and explained in terms
of behavioral variables. The enormous advantage of behavior theory is
that it is composed of real variables that can be manipulated and measured to predict and control behavior.

In this section, we will examine some basic principles of behavior that
provide a perspective for explaining how behavioral development is controlled by the natural environment without systematic intervention. From
a behavioral perspective, child development is seen as much more predict-
able and subject to influence than was heretofore believed.

We will present behavioral assumptions regarding child development and the role of education. We will examine learning as comprising several components, each of which may require a separate teaching strategy. Finally, we will present some basic principles of behavior as they naturally operate without any special intervention.

After you have been introduced to basic behaviorist philosophy and principles, you will be given some detail on applying the behaviorist approach to a preschool program. Three aspects of programming are discussed: behavioral management, design of the curriculum, and teaching strategies and materials. These are key considerations in the operation of any program, regardless of theoretical orientation. You will see how a behavioral viewpoint can be translated into day-to-day practices for working with preschoolers.

The behavior management chapter will give you an overview of several strategies for establishing and maintaining motivation and order in the classroom. Although discipline and motivation are not precisely instructional matters, they are essential conditions for learning. The chapters on curriculum design and on strategies and materials for teaching are more directly addressed to the real job of the educator. They present ways to design the content and methods for teaching. Chapters 9, 10, and 11 discuss how the design of the learning environment, program management, and evaluation procedures are carried out from a behaviorist perspective.

As you read about the specific applications of a behaviorist approach, remember that the practices discussed are not necessarily universal features of all behaviorist programs, but reflect variations on a behaviorist theme. As we discussed in Chapter 2, there is no one-to-one correspondence between theory and application. However, the educational practices described here are consistent with principles of behavior theory and illustrate a high level of theory fidelity.

Behavior Theory and Principles *Chapter 5*

*S*cenes from Aldous Huxley's *Brave New World* (1958) depict the control of children's behavior and development with horrifying vividness. To train children to be manual workers rather than intellectuals, children are given colorful books while they are frightened with sudden loud noises and punished with spasm-producing electric shock.

Such procedures illustrate the deliberate and systematic (although technically imperfect) use of conditioning procedures. We may justifiably protest and recoil from such inhumane tactics, yet the life of any child is filled with innumerable events not totally unlike those pictured by Huxley. In fact, conditioning is as much a fact of life as is gravity. Children experience pleasant and unpleasant events as they interact with their expanding world. Their hands are slapped as they reach for "no-no's"; they touch excessively hot or cold objects and are naturally punished. They are scratched when they mishandle the household cat. Countless aversive outcomes accompany many behaviors. Likewise, many behaviors are accompanied by pleasant, rewarding events. While babbling, the child emits an approximation of "da-da," followed by a joyous parental reaction. When children reach for a colorful book, they frequently receive adult attention, cuddling, and other rewarding events. There are myriad episodes experienced by the child in which behaviors are encouraged or discouraged through rewarding or punishing outcomes. It would seem that the differences between Huxley's *Brave New World* and our good old world are not as great as would seem at first sight. There are, however, at least three fundamental differences: the intensity of punishment or rewards employed; the degree to which their use is intentional and systematic; and the objectives of such manipulation.

Four basic assumptions about child development and three fundamental principles of educational intervention that are derived from these assumptions are presented in this chapter. They form the philosophic base and the intervention format for a behavioral approach to early childhood education.

Chapter 5

BASIC ASSUMPTIONS AND
BEHAVIORAL RATIONALE FOR EARLY EDUCATION

Biological and Behavioral Development
Are Not Controlled by the Same Variables

Child development refers to changes over time in the *body* and *behavior* of the child. It is necessary to make this distinction because *bodily* (biological) development is, in part, governed by variables different from those controlling *behavioral* development.

Biological Development Biological development includes the essential and enduring changes in the anatomy and physiology of the child. There exists clear evidence that biological attributes are genetically based (Singer, 1978); that is, single or multiple combinations of genes control the presence and emergence of numerous bodily characteristics. Thus, in any discussion of physical attributes, genetic determinants usually are cited as being preeminent. This does not mean exclusive control by heredity, for it is known that even clearly gene-based characteristics can be altered in their expression by the environment. Extremes in nutrition, presence of drugs, or other departures from standard conditions can contribute to changes in even simple traits such as hair or eye color (Batshaw & Perret, 1981). These must be extreme conditions, however, and they act only to distort the otherwise certain expression of the genetic material. Thus, it appears that simple, nonmultiple gene traits are relatively immutable and are attributable, almost exclusively, to heredity (McKusick, 1976). Our *phylogenetic* characteristics (the traits common to the species) are certainly controlled by our heredity. The fact that we are born with two arms and two legs, five senses, and several basic organ systems is testimony to the constant and certain influence of the genetic heritage common to our species.

As biological characteristics become more complex, so does the hereditary base. In fact, most features of anatomy and physiology probably are the result of networks of genes acting in biochemical concert to bring about their expression. Generally speaking, the more genes involved in an attribute, the more variable is the resulting expression (phenotype); a greater range of expression is possible when more genes are involved. Further, polygenic traits are more susceptible to environmental variations, and this makes their range of expression even wider.

In sum, biological development is fundamentally governed by biological or genetic determinants that are influenced in their expression in varying degrees by factors in the environment (Dawkins, 1982).

Behavioral Development The behaviors acquired and displayed by the child can be attributed, from the behaviorist's perspective, almost exclusively to the environment. Of course, insofar as features of the body affect behavior, bodily characteristics must be credited with partially determining behavior. However, whereas biology provides the *enabling apparatus* for behavior, it does not *explain* behavioral development. For example, if a child trains as a gymnast, it is desirable that she or he possess certain bodily characteristics; extreme physical deviations may even rule out *any* gymnastics. Physical features are necessary for or conducive to, but not sufficient for, the acquisition of skills. Given fundamental physical features, behavioral development is controlled by environmental variables.

As a further example, excellence as a concert pianist is seen as the result of a variety of determinants. Critical enabling characteristics must be present: optimal finger length, motor coordination (itself perhaps mostly learned), auditory discrimination, recall, and perhaps dozens of other traits must interact with environmental circumstances that will shape them into behaviors leading to musical expertise. From a behaviorist's perspective, a concert pianist is made, not born; of course, certain enabling traits (raw materials) must be provided.

The behaviorist therefore is willing to work with almost any child to develop almost any competency. Emphasis is placed on improving the environment, selecting appropriate teaching practices and materials, and refining more precise behavioral technology. This would not be the case if preeminence were given to genetics and the immutability of talent and personality.

Numerous features of the environment are known to affect child behavior reliably. Behaviorists study these features and their effects, and then build intervention programs based on their findings.

Most Behavior is Learned

The behavior of a child can be divided into two types: species-wide and individual (Skinner, 1969). Species-wide (phylogenetic) behavior refers to those general actions that are common to all human beings. These characteristics are not unique to the individual; we all bend, reach, turn, blink, cough, jerk away from hot objects, and do other things that require no learning. However, much of our behavior *is* learned. The random species-wide activities of which infants are capable become molded and elaborated into specific learned behaviors that have direct uses for the child (ontogenetic behavior). The shaping of more general (phylogenetic) activities into specific (ontogenetic) useful behaviors is what we call *learning*. Learning, then, refers to *relatively permanent changes in behavior as a result of experience*. It is known that the kinds of experiences encountered by a child have a dramatic effect on learning (Box 5-1).

The Child and the Environment Are Partners in Learning

Dynamism   Chief within the vocabulary of the behaviorist is the term *operant*. This refers to any behavior that *operates* on the environment and is changed by the environment (Skinner, 1969). Note the dynamic nature of operant behavior: it alters the environment in some way and, reciprocally, the environment registers a change on the behavior.

The child's behavior, now altered by the environment, has a new capability to operate further on the situation. This continual and dynamic interaction certainly does not depict the child as passive. Those misinformed critics who discuss an operant position as mechanistic, passive, or puppetlike have missed the whole point of operant psychology (Skinner, 1974). The child's *behavioral repertoire* is (or should be) constantly expanding. Any change in the repertoire creates a new potential for action upon the environment. Early childhood educators who base their programs on a behavioral model have as one of their goals for children *behavior expansion*.

Interactionism   Here is an interesting question: Where does change originate—within the child or in the environment? This is much like the chicken–egg riddle. The solution may be that the point of origin of behavior is not to be found in either the child or the environment, but only in their *interaction*.

A sound *interactionist* position is not simply a statement that both constitution and environment are important. Both are available to influence each other in building and guiding the content, rate, and direction of development. By analogy, fermentation and catalysis are processes that require an interaction. No single variable can be credited as the "cause." Which is the "cause" of table salt ($NaCl$)—sodium or chlorine? Obviously, both are equally important, and salt is the result of their interaction, their effect on each other.

Learning and development thus result from the interaction of child characteristics (both biological and acquired) with environmental characteristics. Behaviorists focus their study on the identification and use of environmental variables to bring about child behavior expansion.

Box 5-1   *The Effect of Experience on Learning*

Give me a dozen healthy infants, well formed, and my own specified world to bring them up in and I'll guarantee to take any one at random and train him to become any type of specialist I might select—doctor, lawyer, artist, merchant, chief, and yes, even beggerman and thief, regardless of his talents, peculiarities, tendencies, abilities, vocations, and race of his ancestors.

Watson, J. B. *Behaviorism.* New York: Norton, 1925, p. 82.

Current and Accessible Variables Are Important

The behavioral early educator is not concerned with delving into the history of a child to find possible reasons (causes) for developmental or learning characteristics; this kind of historical investigation is typical of many other approaches (Neisworth & Smith, 1984). Instead, a behaviorist asks: What are the *present* variables that may be affecting a behavior? Examination of past conditions is usually speculative and correlational in nature. To illustrate, if a child is extremely anxious when left without his or her parents, we may speculate about the past causes. Even if we are able to point to some past event that may have created the child's anxiety, however, this past event is not accessible to manipulation. We cannot go back in time. What we *can* do is identify the present circumstances that seem necessary and sufficient to produce the child's anxiety, and then work at changing their effect. Thus, even though Billy may have lost his sight in an auto accident two years ago, we do not explain his current blindness in terms of that auto accident. Not all children in auto accidents become blind and not all blind children were in auto accidents. Rather, Billy is blind because of some *present* circumstance: a detached retina. We cannot return to the time and scene of the accident: it is not accessible. Citing a detached retina as the cause suggests possible intervention, such as retinal reattachment or perhaps some technological retinal replacement.

The same focus applies to positive aspects of child programming. Children who are happy and are learning at a rapid rate are doing so because of a *current* set of variables. Current variables are frequently accessible to manipulation—past events aren't.*

From their basic assumptions about how children grow and learn, behaviorists have derived educational principles that can be used to plan educational programs. We will present three basic guidelines that stress the importance of both child *and* environment in the learning process.

GUIDELINES FOR EDUCATIONAL INTERVENTION

Ability and Disability Do Not Reside within the Child

Problems in development are found in child–environment interactions. We cannot attribute cause to the child. Her or his problems are the effect of a less than optimal interaction with the world.

It is counterproductive to say that a child is not making progress because he or she is retarded or disturbed or has some other problem. We can nei-

---

*We acknowledge that identification of past events is important for future prevention; even here, however, clear specification of the current variables helps to direct attention to relevant past events.

ther credit nor blame the child for poor or excellent development. Likewise, we cannot blame or credit the environment alone for the child's development. What we must do is examine a child's current capabilities and then decide what goals and experiences would most help the child. Not all children can benefit from the same experiences, and not all experiences will benefit all children equally. *Experience*, however, is the keystone to learning. Children must experience environments that help move them along a developmental progression (Neisworth, Willoughby-Herb, Bagnato, Cartwright, & Laub, 1980).

Every Child Can Learn

In the past, many handicapped children were excluded from the public schools. At the nursery school level, handicapped children were not enrolled. After all, it was argued, children who are retarded, disturbed, or physically disabled simply cannot get along in the educational situation and, in fact, cannot be educated because of their limitations. Given this

Handicapped children in a German nursery school.

belief, it was not surprising that most handicapped children—deprived of any kind of early educational experience—did indeed show little improvement. The prevailing attitude was to be charitable to handicapped children but to expect little or no progress.

Every child's behavior can be improved through experience. Research clearly demonstrates that most handicapped children show startling progress if the right methods and materials are employed by people who know and care (Allen & Goetz, 1982). Head Start was one of the first programs to combine handicapped children with nonhandicapped children in early educational experiences. It is to the credit of Head Start that mainstreaming was attempted for years before the label *mainstreaming* existed. It is ironic that handicapped children have been excluded from early education programs, because it is this group that can benefit most from early intervention (Castro, White, & Taylor, 1983; Ramey & Bryant, 1982). A child can be experiencing significant problems in development and still be greatly helped by a good program.

Remember, the central goal of a behavioral program for children is behavioral expansion. Expansion can be both vertical and horizontal (Mori & Neisworth, 1983). When a given behavior is added to a child's repertoire, we refer to this as *vertical expansion*: a new behavior added to or built on existing behaviors. *Horizontal expansion* takes place when a new behavior is generalized across situations or circumstances. Usually, we strive for transfer (horizontal) as much as initial (vertical) expansion of learning.

Teaching Requires Environmental Arrangements

We have already stated that *learning* refers to changes in behavior and that behavior is changed through experience. Teachers must make decisions regarding what kinds of experiences a child will encounter while in school. We say that a child is "learning on his or her own," but what is learned, how fast it is learned, and how long it is remembered will depend on the materials available to the child and the consequences associated with the learning process. Some children will learn faster than others, so it becomes important to tailor the environment (materials and methods) to accommodate less-than-optimal child characteristics. No matter how open, unstructured, or "free" you would like a classroom to be, you must still make decisions about what is in the room, who is in the room, and what will happen or not happen to children on a given day. Research from Head Start and other programs clearly shows that progress in school-related readiness skills is best accomplished in programs that have high structure (Rhine, 1981). In highly structured preschool programs, the importance of teaching–learning arrangements becomes obvious. Many teachers who have been trained in behavioral techniques refer to themselves as *instructional engineers* or *educational arrangers*.

It is exciting to think that early childhood educators can approach their task with precision and effectiveness. The early childhood educator must, of course, care about children, but caring and loving are not enough to bring about learning. As much as dentists or physicians may care about their patients, caring is not a substitute for a well-placed filling in a cavity or an effective program to control high blood pressure.

Professionals must be armed with the methods and materials that make a difference for the clientele they serve. In the sections that follow, we will present some of the most basic principles that underly behavioral strategies for today's early childhood educator. If you agree with the assumptions on which these methods are based, the careful implementation of these procedures could put you a giant step ahead in your efforts to have an effect on the lives of the children for whom you care.

BASIC PRINCIPLES OF BEHAVIOR

Fortunately, just a few fundamental principles provide the foundation for an array of teaching techniques that are available to you. Once you understand the principles of behavior, you will be able to see why and how the various behavioral strategies (presented later in the book) are effective. You can create new strategies based on one or more principles, and thus add to the growing body of behaviorally based teaching methods.

Please note the distinction between *behavior principles* and *behavior technology*. From the behavioral perspective, teaching is a technology (Skinner, 1968). It is the application of techniques based on principles of learning derived from psychology, sociology, and related disciplines. The practice of medicine also is a technology, based on principles derived from biology, chemistry, and other relevant bodies of knowledge. Mechanical engineering is a technology built on principles from the science of physics. A behavioral approach to early childhood education is *the intentional, consistent, and systematic use of techniques that are derived from principles of behavior generated by the science of behavioral psychology.*

From this perspective, early childhood educators are responsible for applying strategies and may be considered to be behavioral engineers. Just as civil engineers design, oversee, and evaluate the construction of bridges, behavioral educators design educational programs, oversee the execution of programs, and evaluate their success. Teaching methods, or behavior technology, will be presented in greater detail in later chapters.

To give you an overview of the behavioral perspective, we begin with a description of the behavioral model. A model is a succinct way to summarize a perspective and a complex set of propositions. A three-component behavioral model is displayed in Figure 5-1. According to our model, behavior is sandwiched between antecedent and consequent events. The kind and quality of these events determine the future of the behavior. With the

Antecedents	$\rightarrow$	Behavior	$\rightarrow$	Consequences
Lights in auditorium are dimmed	$\rightarrow$	Audience becomes quiet	$\rightarrow$	Performance begins

Figure 5-1   *The ABC model of the behaviorist perspective. Behavior is sandwiched between antecedents and consequences and is shaped by both.*

right management of the environment, you can engineer behavior changes in directions deemed appropriate by the child, school, and society.

Our model emphasizes dynamic (not passive) interaction between the child and the learning environment: *operant* behavior. The influence of an operant behavior on the environment often produces changes that have powerful effects on the behavior. As educators, we can make sure that certain outcomes do or do not take place and, accordingly, begin to alter any given operant behavior. A behavioral or operant model has these attributes:

1. It is dynamic and ecological, emphasizing child–environment interaction.
2. It employs events before and after a behavior to explain and change the behavior.
3. It is optimistic regarding possible changes in child capabilities, because they are linked to environmental changes that are possible.

BEHAVIORAL OBJECTIVES

Rather than beginning with a discussion of antecedents, we shall begin by briefly considering behavioral objectives. It is the behavioral objective or target that must be specified before either antecedents or consequences can be designed; the behavioral engineer must first know what it is that is to be built or produced. In addition, it is simply easier to discuss the behavioral objectives first; the roles of antecedents and consequences thus will be clarified.

One of the first important questions for any early childhood educator is, "Who specifies goals for children?" Or, "Where do you get your objectives?" Some models have "built in" objectives; sometimes a model or theory not only suggests methods but also provides developmental objectives. This is not the case with a behavioral model. Primarily, a behavioral approach generates methods for *achieving* objectives but does not automatically produce teaching objectives. Teaching/learning objectives come from nontheoretical sources. *Society*—the culture of the child—specifies many educational goals. The *family* and the *child* can provide other, more personal objectives. Developmental norms and nonbehavioral theory offer objectives that are employed by many good early childhood education pro-

Cooperation is an important objective, and behavior techniques are powerful ways to enhance it.

grams. There are, however, two sources of objectives that are derived directly or indirectly from behavior theory: task (content) analysis, and learning (process) analysis.

Task or Content Analysis

Task analysis produces at least subordinate objectives. For example, given a goal of teaching proper eating manners at lunch time, the task can be analyzed into smaller units. Units of behavior dealing with use of the fork, spoon, cup, and napkin would be appropriate subdivisions of the main goal. Each subordinate task—for example, using a fork—can be broken down even further into steps such as picking up a fork, getting food on it, bringing it to one's mouth, and eating from the fork. Once a major goal is provided, by whatever source, task analysis is a crucial procedure for deriving smaller objectives that are instructionally manageable. The size of the units will depend on the child's needs and progress in learning (Snell & Smith, 1983a).

Learning or Process Analysis

Just as we can analyze the *content* of educational objectives into smaller units, the learning process itself can be broken into steps. Gagne (1974) has suggested that learning consists of eight phases. For our purposes, we have condensed these into six. When a child has a problem learning, it usually can be narrowed down to one of these six steps. Each of the steps can become a source for objectives. These objectives deal with the process of learning, the *how*, rather than with specific content, the *what*.

1. *Motivation* is the first phase of the learning process and must be present if children are to learn. Motivation refers to the child's approach to and involvement in a learning activity.

2. Perhaps the toughest job of all is for the teacher to arrange for *attention*. Children must learn to look at, listen to, and otherwise focus on those aspects of the teaching–learning situation that are relevant.

3. We must help the child to *acquire* the material that we teach.

4. *Retention* is a crucial part of learning and teaching. What good is it to teach a skill if it is forgotten the next day or week?

5. *Generalization* is also important. New capabilities should be useful across different situations. Never expect transfer of learning to be automatic (Stokes & Baer, 1977). Transfer of learning must be taught so that learning will not be tied to the training environment.

6. A child may know something but be unable to demonstrate the knowledge. Educators must try to arrange circumstances to encourage optimal *performance* of learning. This is especially important for children who are shy or whose style is otherwise cramped by environmental circumstances. Teachers can appreciate the distinction between what children can do and what they actually do when a supervisor is present. (This environmental circumstance can certainly cramp performance!) Teaching for performance is especially important when children are to be in a testing situation. We want psychological and achievement tests to portray accurately what the child has learned. (Performance problems are really a special case of problems in generalization but are so prominent that they are dealt with separately here.)

Early educators are responsible for identifying, selecting, and organizing instructional and developmental objectives. Educators who use the behavioral model have access to a number of powerful teaching methods, but are not automatically provided with objectives.

ANTECEDENTS: CIRCUMSTANCES THAT SET THE OCCASION FOR LEARNING

Much of behavior is obviously triggered by environmental events. We use the words *signal* and *prompt* to refer to stimuli that set the occasion for a behavior. In working with young children, the behaviorist not only uses existing signals or prompts, but builds new ones appropriate to an instructional target.

Stimulus Control

Because of the influence of differential reinforcement (reinforcement of behavior under some conditions but not others), various arrangements in your environment come to control your behavior. If you munch while watching television, a turned-on television can soon become a stimulus not only for viewing but also for eating. After some "training," you will reliably engage in food gathering and consumption in front of the television—even if you ate not long ago or do not really want to eat. We call a stimulus that sets the occasion for a behavior a *discriminative stimulus* (S^D) for that behavior. *Signal*, *prompt*, or *cue* all refer to an event that sets the occasion for a behavior, and are roughly equivalent to an S^D.

It is not surprising to learn that overweight people frequently eat in a variety of circumstances (including while watching television). They eat while reading, talking on the phone, relaxing in bed, and so on. In other words, these people are under the control of many (and some inappropriate) S^Ds for eating. One of the first steps in behavioral weight control therapy is to have the overweight person begin to eat only under appropriate circumstances (Craighead, Brownell, & Horan, 1981). For example, an individual can be advised to eat whenever he or she wishes, but only at the table, even if it is just a cookie. In this way, the table becomes the chief S^D for eating, and other circumstances begin to lose their control over eating.

Another example may prove helpful in understanding the important role of discriminative (antecedent) stimuli. If you practice behaviors while in bed that compete with sleeping, you may find going to sleep, even when you want to, a difficult matter. For example, many people read in bed. The bed may become an S^D for reading, in addition to or rather than for sleeping. Depending on the degree of control of the bed for reading behavior, individuals may begin to experience great difficulty in falling asleep. On the other hand, reading in bed may be a technique employed by the individual in falling asleep. Holding a book and reading it may come to set the occasion for sleep even out of bed. If this is the case, people will find that reading causes them to become drowsy and they will not read very effectively.

The behaviors of arguing and nagging are, unfortunately, often practiced around the dining room table when the family is gathered for the evening meal. If this occurs with some frequency, fussing begins to be signalled by the event of sitting around the dining room table together. You can see how vicious this can become. People may not have the slightest intention of being unpleasant to each other; however, because of the stimulus control of the circumstances, they will begin reminding, nagging, and in other ways irritating each other simply because this is a behavior that has been established in this setting. Generally, one should not practice behaviors that are inappropriate for a given setting, because there is always the danger that the setting will begin to prompt these behaviors (see Box 5-2).

There are many obvious educational applications of the principle of stimulus control (Allen & Goetz, 1982; Neisworth et al., 1980). Children should not practice behaviors at their desks or tables or in their chairs that are considered inappropriate for those settings. As an example, it is not a good idea to have children learn to take naps at their desks or tables; the desks may begin to be a prompt for sleeping rather than for attention to instructional activities. The college student who falls asleep at her or his desk is in trouble. The desk has mixed control; it is an S^D not only for studying course work but also for falling asleep.

Of greater instructional relevance are the prompts and cues we employ with children to carry out the teaching/learning process. The specific materials, verbal instructions, and suggestions the teacher provides are all examples of prompts that are intended to influence the behavior of the child. The extent to which these stimuli influence the child's behavior in the intended ways depends on many factors, chiefly on the prior learning history of the child. A large cartoon of a bumble bee might be an S^D for the behavior of saying "bee" or "bumble bee." If this cartoon is held up in front of a child, and the child says "bird," we can draw two plausible conclusions. First, our cartoon is not an S^D for saying the word "bee." Second, saying "bird" does seem to be under the control of the cartoon of a bee. A "no smoking" sign may be an S^D for smoking for some people. Obviously, in their learning history, "no smoking" signs have not achieved the intended control. Control is achieved when appropriate behavior is *differentially* reinforced in the presence of signals.

The same problem of stimulus control is often apparent in reading difficulties. If the letter "b" is presented to a child and the child says "dee" rather than "bee," we know that we have a case of inappropriate stimulus

---

Box 5-2   *Donald Quits Smoking*

After twenty years of smoking cigarettes, Don decided he would get serious about quitting. He had tried many times—usually "cold turkey"—with no success. This time, Don turned to a friend who was a behaviorist, a special education teacher who used behavior modification with her students. She told him that smoking behavior was *situational*, and that his smoking was triggered by a variety of situations. Treatment should involve *deprogramming* smoking behavior in each situation. Here are the suggested steps that Don followed:

1. First, he made notes for a week on *where* and *how many* cigarettes he smoked.

2. Next, he practiced *not smoking* in the situation where he smoked least: the bathroom.

3. After a week of not smoking in the bathroom, he added sitting in his car to the taboo smoking situation list. By this time, he didn't even think about smoking in the bathroom—that situation had lost its power to trigger smoking.

4. Don proceeded through his list of all eleven situations. As he conquered each situation, his refraining from smoking became more and more reinforced. After three months of this program, he had succeeded: he no longer smoked in any situation.

control: the instructional task becomes one of correcting the stimulus control of the letter "b" so that it does set the occasion for the response of saying "bee." You can consider antecedent arrangements as a large part of the work of the teacher. Your task involves proper selection of stimuli, proper training of children so that the stimuli will have their intended influences, and proper use of such stimuli once established.

Stimulus Generalization and Discrimination

When a behavior is indeed under the control of a given stimulus or a narrow range of stimuli, we say that stimulus control has been achieved. Frequently, however, a behavior that is learned in the presence of a particular stimulus arrangement is emitted under other circumstances where stimuli are present that were not part of the original training situation. We refer to this as *stimulus generalization*. When a child says "bee" when shown the letter "d" or "b" we have a clear instance of undesirable stimulus generalization. The "b" and "d" are similar and unfortunately the same response may be occasioned by both. Instances of stimulus generalization are most frequent with young children where discriminative control of many familiar stimuli has not been achieved. A child may have been taught to say the word "dog" when in the presence of a dog but also refer to cats, cows, and other animals as "dog." It can be embarrassing to many parents when a child refers to strange men as "da-da." This is an instance of stimulus generalization that most parents wish to correct quickly!

Neither stimulus generalization nor stimulus discrimination is to be preferred; it depends on the intended objectives. We wish the boisterous, hyperactive behavior appropriate on the playground to be set off by the playground and not by the classroom; that is, we would hope that the playground is the S^D for active play and that generalization to the classroom does not take place. Similarly, we want to train children that when they sense bladder tension (an S^D for urinating), they should use a toilet or urinal. We want the restroom to be the appropriate S^D for elimination; stimulus generalization in this regard can be most inappropriate and annoying (Box 5-3). You will find in your work with young children that establishing appropriate stimulus control will be one of your most important jobs. After you teach a given behavior in a particular instructional circumstance, your next job will be to check for appropriate and inappropriate instances of stimulus generalization. For example, you will want both a picture of a dog and a real dog to set the occasion for the child to say "dog." If your pictures of animals are not too different from the live ones, you may be able to get much desirable stimulus generalization. This is fortunate, because it is difficult to bring many live animals and other real objects into the classroom. You cannot, however, count on automatic stimulus generalization. Frequently, you will have to take children on field trips where they can have real objects pointed out by you.

Unplanned and frequent unwanted stimulus generalization does take place. When you observe children generalizing in inappropriate ways behaviors that you have taught, your job becomes one of *discrimination training*, which involves the use of *differential reinforcement*.

Prompting

Behaviorally oriented teachers often construct S^{D}s to facilitate learning (Alberto & Troutman, 1982; Allen & Goetz, 1982). Discriminative stimuli that are used by preschool teachers can be divided into four categories: verbal, concrete, symbolic, and manual. *Verbal* prompts are spoken instructions or suggestions given to children to set the occasion for certain behaviors. This type of stimulus control will be relied on by many educators later in the child's life. *Concrete* or actual objects can be used to prompt language and other behaviors of children. Showing children a pencil, chair, or book and demonstrating (modeling) how to use these objects are attempts to have the objects gain stimulus control over appropriate corresponding behaviors.

A teacher with whom we have worked made excellent use of some of the concrete objects in her room to gain stimulus control over some troublesome behaviors. She used verbal prompting to instruct the children to get out of their seats and sit on the rug any time they wished to chat with each other. Additionally, she intermittently reinforced working and paying attention while the children were in their seats. After a short period children were quite attentive when they were in their seats and were appropriately playful while on the rug. She never demanded instructional attention and compliance to her when they were on the rug, but she always required and reinforced these behaviors when the children were in their seats. Other teachers have used lights-on and lights-off in the classroom as prompts for attention or inattention.

Symbolic (abstract) prompts use written, drawn, or other representa-

---

Box 5-3 Fasten Your Seatbelt!

There are bedsheets and diapers that are equipped with moisture detectors and buzzers so that an "early warning signal" can send a child to the potty before much wetting takes place. Eighteen-month-old Herman learned quickly to stop wetting his pants with this special help. Even when wearing regular pants, he remained dry. However, there was a complication worth remembering. After one week of wearing his special pants at the preschool and one week of no wetting in regular pants, Herman's mother came to pick him up as usual in her stationwagon. After Herman climbed into his carseat, his mother closed all the doors and switched on the key. All seatbelts were not fastened and a buzzer sounded. Herman exclaimed "Potty! Potty!" His mother did not know what to do; she decided to drive home. Herman "regressed" and wet his pants. Here was an instance of undesirable generalization!

tional material to set the occasion for behavior. A picture of a cow can often be relied on to set the occasion for the response "cow." The character string "c-o-w," however, is quite symbolic and differs considerably from a picture of a cow; this is often a point of difficulty. It becomes the job of the teacher to equate pictures and words so that symbols acquire the same stimulus control as their corresponding objects.

Manual prompts involve the use of the teacher's hands in guiding a child's behavior. Examples include holding the student's lips together to facilitate an "mm" sound, guiding someone's golf swing or tennis racquet clutch, and physically assisting a person to work with various tools.

Young children usually can learn quickly to call objects by their name. An instructional objective is to add more sophisticated prompts, or to expand stimulus control. After a new behavior has been taught, ask yourself what other prompts might be appropriate. (It can be especially important to make sure that handicapped children's skills are not prompted solely by developmentally primitive prompts.) Always try to add prompts that are developmentally more sophisticated.

Techniques Involving Prompting

Adding Prompts   We want children to learn progressively more appropriate behaviors to more appropriate prompts. Notice that the behaviorist educator is not only interested in expanding but also in altering the prompts. Not only should the child learn to say words such as "house," "dog," "car," "toy," and "food" more distinctly—she or he should learn to say them under more sophisticated and varied prompts. Whereas initially the prompt for saying "car" may have been the actual sight of a car, we also want a model, picture, and symbol (printed word) for a car to be a signal for saying "car."

Antecedent prompt	Behavior	Consequence
1. Actual car	Says "car"	Reinforcement such as
2. Model of a car		praise, obtaining
3. Picture of a car		desired event, etc.
4. Printed word: "car"		

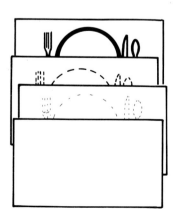

Subtracting and Differentiating Prompts   Sometimes, the task is not one of adding prompts for a behavior, but of removing inappropriate prompts. We want our question, "What is your name?" to be a prompt for Billy to reply "Billy." However, we do not want him to say "Billy" when asked where he lives, how he is getting along, or what is his age.

We can remove a prompt for a behavior by making sure that the behavior is not reinforced in the presence of that prompt. We also should be certain the behavior *is* reinforced in the presence of the appropriate prompt.

Baby Dori says "da-da" when she sees a male police officer, the mail carrier, or her father. It is fine for Dori to say "da-da" to her father, to a model or picture of him, or to her father's printed name, but it is not fine for her to respond this way to other men. How can we remove the control of these unwanted prompts? First, we must not reinforce Dori's saying "da-da" to other men and, second, we must reinforce her saying "da-da" to her father. This *differential reinforcement* will result in the behavior (saying "da-da") being under the exclusive control of the appropriate prompt. We must differentiate one prompt from another and remove the influence of one or more prompts.

Fading Prompts   When we shift to more appropriate prompts, we often use a procedure called "fading." This refers to the gradual reduction of a prompt so that another prompt can gain control. Prompts may be faded in their intensity, magnitude, frequency, or duration (Neisworth et al., 1980b). When actors learn their lines, they usually rely on their script at first. Gradually, they try to say their lines while glancing at the script less frequently. The script as a prompt is faded in frequency and duration of use. A clever technique for teaching children how to put on boots employs fading. When you teach a child to put the left boot on the left foot, put colored tape on the left boot and shoe (or leg). Gradually reduce the size of the tapes until the behavior is under the control of less contrived, more subtle stimuli such as shape of boot and location of foot.

A dramatic example of fading is available in research on teaching word–object pairs (Corey & Shamow, 1972; Dorry & Zeaman, 1975). Assume you wish to teach preschool children how to read the words referring to ten different objects. Conventional flash cards pair a picture of the object with the word on one side, and have just the word on the other side. When both picture and word are presented together, the child can easily guess what the word is by looking at the picture. The trouble with this procedure, however, is that the child relies too heavily on the picture for a prompt. Shifting to the word as a controlling prompt is slow. Frequently, children are unable to recognize the word whenever the pictorial prompt is removed suddenly. A less abrupt procedure involves gradually fading the picture so that the word gains progressively more control over the child's attention. Tissue paper can be used to fade the intensity of the picture. Successively more tissue can be placed over the picture until only the word can be seen. With the gradual fading of the picture, the child does not experience any sudden removal of help, and the shift from picture to word is smooth and successful.

Timing of Prompts   Prompts always must come *before* the behavior they are to control. When teachers repeat a prompt *after* an inappropriate behavior to correct it, they are often only nagging, reminding, and frequently actually reinforcing an unwanted behavior. When a prompt occurs at the

These children are learning words through use of pictures. The picture is gradually faded until the printed word alone serves to prompt the correct verbal behavior.

wrong point in a sequence of behavior, it is often more of a problem than a help. As an example, assume you wish to teach Henry to hang up his coat as soon as he comes in the door. An appropriate prompt might be to say, "Henry, please hang up your coat right away" as Henry enters the room.

Now consider what happens when you supply the prompt *after* the appropriate point in the behavior sequence. You see Henry's coat on the sofa and *then* give your instruction. At this point, however, the instruction is not a prompt so much as it is a nag. *Timing* in presenting prompts (and reinforcers) is all important. If a prompt is to be helpful, it must appear at the correct point in a behavior sequence (Neisworth et al., 1980). You might decide that Henry needs practice and ask him to repeat the whole sequence of behavior: coming in the door, removing his coat, going straight to the closet with it. Repeating a correct chain of behaviors is often the best way to establish a correct sequence (Box 5-4). Note that repetition of an incorrect or undesirable sequence also will establish it. Thus, if you tell Henry to hang up his coat after the appropriate point in the behavior sequence, he will learn this ill-placed prompt. Henry will probably continue to throw his coat on the sofa until he hears the command to hang it up. Precision prompting is an indispensable skill of the behavioral early childhood educator. Analyze your use of prompts and employ prompts at the right time and place.

Modeling

It is well known that children often imitate the behaviors presented (modeled) to them. There is extensive literature on the effects of models, the characteristics of a good model, and how to facilitate the modeling effect (LeBlanc, 1982; Ross, 1981). From a behaviorist point of view, a model is a prompt, as are other educational materials. Demonstration and modeling of activities is one of the best techniques for teaching children the steps in some more complex behaviors; politeness, courtesy, proper eating, and many other socially relevant behaviors are best taught through appropriate modeling. Teachers definitely should be aware that children learn through modeling whether it is a planned part of the curriculum or not. Teachers must provide modeling prompts that correspond with their verbal prompts. Teachers who verbally prompt children to settle their problems in polite, civilized ways and then use physical punishment to settle conflicts with children are providing inappropriate and conflicting models. Unfortunately, we often see parents hitting children while shouting "Stop hitting each other." Behaviorist teachers try to avoid great discrepancies between their verbal prompts and their modeling. Children often try to imitate significant others; parents, teachers, relatives, and friends can exert a powerful influence on a child's behavioral development. Parents and teachers need to "practice what they teach."

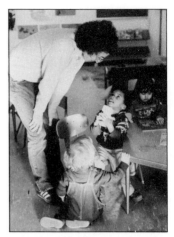

Children learn through modeling, whether it is a planned part of the curriculum or not, such as when teachers verbally prompt children to settle problems in polite ways.

Box 5-4 Let's Take It from the Top

Jenny kept leaving her keys in the ignition of her car when she arrived home. Her first reminder (prompt) that she had forgotten her keys was the key hook in her hallway. Often, Jenny would go back outside to retrieve her keys. Finally, she got an idea to practice the correct chain of behaviors: go back outside, get in the car again, drive around the block, pull in the driveway, remove the keys, proceed to the house, and then place the key on its hook. By rehearsing this sequence three times each time she forgot her keys, Jenny repaired her faulty chain as well as strengthening her positive self-confidence.

CONSEQUENCES: EVENTS THAT CONTROL BEHAVIOR

The development of practically any behavior depends on its consequences (Skinner, 1974). Once you understand and take seriously this basic principle, you will see how powerfully the environment influences the direction and rate of learning. Of course, not all consequences effect learning in the same way. Some events that happen during or immediately after a learning effort have little influence. Other events, however, can have a profound influence in building the strength of a new behavior. Table 5-1 indicates the different ways events exert their effects. Some consequences have the effect of weakening or reducing learning. Generally speaking, behaviors that are followed by favorable events survive and become more dominant. Behaviors accompanied by unfavorable subsequent events become weak and often disappear. The effect of the environment on behavior operates much as Darwin's principle of *natural selection* does, and this similarity has been discussed by B. F. Skinner (1974b).

A child's behavior is developed by the environment chiefly through contingencies of reinforcement (Bijou & Baer, 1978; Skinner, 1969). *Reinforcement* refers to increasing the probability of behavior through the effect of favorable subsequent events. When events after a behavior strengthen the behavior, we refer to them as reinforcing events, or reinforcers. The process of building behavior through the immediate application of favorable events is called reinforcement. Reinforcement can be *positive* or *negative*, depending on whether an event strengthens a behavior by its *addition* or by its *removal*.

Unfavorable events that occur after a behavior serve to weaken or eliminate the behavior. Extinction and punishment can weaken behaviors. *Extinction* refers to the lack of reinforcement for a behavior. *Punishment* always involves either the active addition of an aversive event right after a behavior (positive punishment) or the removal of a favorable event (negative punishment).

REINFORCEMENT

Strengthening Behaviors

As mentioned, reinforcement strengthens a behavior through favorable subsequent events. A favorable event may involve the presentation of some variable, such as getting praise, money, points, or extra leisure time (positive reinforcement). In contrast, another sort of favorable event is one that involves the *removal* of some variable, such as getting out of unpleasant work, escaping an argument, getting rid of your headache, or avoiding an inferior grade in a course (negative reinforcement). Both kinds of reinforcement act to build or strengthen a behavior.

Table 5-1   Effects of Consequences on Behavior

If immediately after a behavior you . . .	and the effect is to . . .	the process is called . . .
Add an event or item	Strengthen the behavior	Positive reinforcement
	Weaken the behavior	Positive punishment
Remove an event or item	Strengthen the behavior	Negative reinforcement
	Weaken the behavior	Negative punishment
Withhold an event or item that has functioned as a reinforcer	Weaken the behavior	Extinction

Positive Reinforcement   Certain events delivered immediately after a behavior have the effect of building or strengthening that behavior; they are called *positive reinforcers*. You cannot know if a consequence is a positive reinforcer until you can observe the effect that consequence has on the behavior. The effect on the behavior, further, cannot be just momentary but must have some durability. All animals tend to repeat those things that result in success. So it is with children—any behavior they emit that is followed by any positive change in their world will tend to be repeated more and more often. A good example is when parents reinforce a baby's accidental utterances of "da-da." Unfortunately, many parents and teachers unwittingly also reinforce highly undesirable behavioral trends in children. As an example, children may shriek when something displeases them or when they are hungry. Parents rush to the screaming child, providing a positive event. This may get rid of the shrieking for the moment, but the result is strengthening of shrieking behavior. There are, of course, times when the parent may decide that it is appropriate to reinforce shrieking; the infant has few means of communication other than crying. The point, however, is that parents and teachers should be aware of who is reinforcing whom for what.

Teachers of young children have hundreds of opportunities daily to reinforce developmentally appropriate behavior; the devilish other side of the coin is that there are also hundreds of opportunities accidentally to reinforce inappropriate and developmentally destructive behavior.

Negative Reinforcement   Teachers and parents who learn to use positive reinforcement often overlook the role of negative reinforcement. Remember that behavior also is strengthened if it is followed by the reduction or elimination of an aversive event. Thus, when you scratch yourself, you reduce an itching sensation. Scratching is negatively reinforced. Assume a child is crying and you pick her up in your arms to quiet her. Picking her up is negatively reinforcing to you, because you enjoy the reduction in crying; removal of an aversive noise reinforces picking-up behavior. At the same time, the child's crying behavior is apt to be positively reinforced; the consequence is being picked up. Often, one behavior is positively reinforced while another is negatively reinforced. Be aware of accidental negative reinforcement. People frequently act to reduce annoyances, sometimes positively reinforcing these annoying behaviors. Giving a cookie to a crying child to quiet him is an example: giving a cookie to the child will negatively reinforce your behavior because it eliminates the crying. The child's annoying behavior, however, will be positively reinforced with the cookie. Note that the child may be quiet temporarily (to get the cookie) but is actually learning to cry to get a cookie.

Use negative reinforcement to benefit children and yourself. Remove annoying events contingent on the development of constructive behaviors.

Weakening Behaviors

Often our first concern is to get rid of some behaviors that interfere with learning. Screaming, running around the room, fighting, daydreaming, and many other behaviors can be weakened to permit more rapid reinforcement of constructive behaviors. We will discuss four principles briefly: extinction, positive punishment, negative punishment, and preempting.

Extinction   Withholding reinforcement for a behavior that previously has been reinforced is *extinction*. Frequently, teachers and parents will realize that they have been inadvertently reinforcing an unwanted behavior. Perhaps their mere attention to the behavior was supporting it. When this attention is withdrawn, the behavior is *on extinction* and usually will begin to disappear (Box 5-5). Extinction is a useful technique. It is simple, does not involve punishment (in the usual sense), and is part of the differential reinforcement procedure (Ferster & Culbertson, 1982).

There are some teachers who find it difficult to ignore (not reinforce) unwanted behavior. Extinction requires a certain kind of patience or passive resistance that can tax a harried preschool teacher. Another problem with extinction is that the behavior on extinction usually gets worse before it gets better. That is, if an unwanted behavior that has been reinforced suddenly receives no reinforcement, an increase in this behavior often occurs before the behavior weakens. During this period of increase, an inadvertent reinforcement can strengthen the new higher intensity of the behavior. Extinction can be quite effective, but you must use it carefully.

Punishment   *Punishment* refers to weakening a behavior through the presence of an event right after the behavior. There are two kinds of punishment, positive and negative, depending on whether an event occurs or is removed. The most familiar punishment is getting spanked for some misdeed. The spanking is an event after the misdeed. If the spanking is aversive enough and if it follows right after the inappropriate behavior, it will act to weaken the behavior. Spanking is an example of *positive punishment*. It is positive in the sense that it is *added* right after the behavior. We can scold, spank, or add other aversive events after a behavior.

Negative punishment refers to weakening a behavior by the *removal* of something. Taking away a child's allowance for swearing is an example of negative punishment. *Response cost* is used to describe this form of negative punishment where there is a charge for behavior. A speeding ticket (response cost) is an all too familiar example of negative punishment. You can probably think of many other examples: removal of privileges, taking away a dessert, no television for the night, and going to bed early can be effective in weakening behavior when used properly.

Most behaviorists do not advocate the use of positive punishment to weaken behaviors of children except when all other techniques fail (Ross, 1981). Extinction and negative punishment are usually sufficient, especially when used with a good program of positive reinforcement for appropriate behavior.

Preempting   Arranging circumstances so that an unwanted behavior is not likely to occur is called *preempting*. Keeping breakables out of reach, using partitions to cut down distractions, and general good sense about the physical environment can preempt many problems, obviating the need for punishment. Good room design and student grouping can significantly reduce unwanted behaviors in the classroom.

Box 5-5   Crying at Naptime—Behavior Strategies to the Rescue!

Billy cried throughout naptime. No amount of comforting and reassurances from the teacher seemed to help. Of course, Billy became quiet *while* he was being attended to, but resumed crying when left to take his nap.

On the advice of a (behaviorist) friend, the teacher rearranged the room so that he could smile at and praise Billy for the brief moments when he was quiet. Crying was ignored. Billy earned a bonus when he completed the whole naptime without crying. Other napping children were also given tokens. In four days, the problem was gone and Billy was proud about what a good naptaker he was. The differential reinforcement (smiling and praise) for napping and extinction (ignoring) of crying coupled with modeling (tokens for napping children) accomplished in four days what had been an increasing problem over the preceding two months.

VARIABLES RELATED TO THE EFFECTIVENESS OF CONSEQUENCES

There are many ways to categorize reinforcers; only several basic variables will be discussed here. They are those that seem most related to the educational applications of reinforcement.

Reinforcement Must Immediately Follow Behavior

Behavior is influenced by the consequences that *immediately* follow it. No matter how positive an event may be, it cannot strengthen a behavior unless it follows immediately. If a positive event is delayed, it will reinforce whatever behavior is occurring when it is finally delivered. Strike while the iron is hot!

Reinforcement Schedules

There is much research on the effects of the *schedule or pattern of reinforcement* (Ferster & Skinner, 1957; Bijou & Baer, 1978). We will mention a few major conclusions.

Continuous Reinforcement   Reinforcement may be delivered after every instance of a given behavior. This is known as *continuous reinforcement* (CRF) and is one of the best schedules for building a new or weak behavior. Make liberal use of positive reinforcement in the beginning stages of a desired behavior's development.

Fixed-Ratio Reinforcement   A schedule of reinforcement may not be continuous, but still may be quite liberal and "rich." Every second, third, fourth, fifth (or any defined number) behavior can be reinforced. When reinforcement is contingent on every so many behaviors, this is a *fixed-ratio* (FR) *schedule*. On an FR 10 schedule, reinforcement occurs after every tenth time the behavior occurs. You can see that the CRF schedule is actually a special instance of a fixed-ratio schedule: it is FR 1. Teachers often use FR schedules when they want children to perform a behavior a number of times before getting reinforcement. Sally might have to produce three completed papers before she can bring them to the teacher (FR 3). Sometimes children must earn 10 points to buy a particular privilege (FR 10), or must bring materials to school twice in order to get a prize (FR 2).

Variable-Ratio Reinforcement   Frequently, a *variable-ratio* (VR) *schedule* operates: a behavior is reinforced every so many times *on the average*. On a VR 6 schedule, for example, a behavior is not reinforced every sixth time it

occurs, but *on the average* six behaviors are needed for every reinforcing event. Playing poker is a good example of *intermittent* or variable-ratio reinforcement. If there are six players about equally skilled, you will win one out of every six hands in the long run. However, you cannot predict which hand you will win (this would require an FR schedule). When a behavior is on a VR schedule, the behavior can become quite durable even in the face of prolonged lack of reinforcement.

New behavior is most easily built on a CRF or liberal FR schedule, but behavioral persistence is built on a VR schedule. Many persistent behaviors you can think of are the result of VR schedules. Playing bingo, betting on the horses, using a slot machine, and other forms of gambling all use VR schedules. Often, intense and persistent child behaviors are the product of VR schedules. Nagging to stay up late usually is not rewarded, but every now and then it is. The schedule might be VR 30, but the child learns that sometimes (although unpredictably) nagging will have a payoff. Crying, fighting, begging, sulking, and lying are examples of persistent undesirable behaviors that often are maintained through VR schedules. Of course, desirable persistent behavior also is developed on VR schedules of reinforcement. Volunteering in class, exploring the environment, and persisting at a task are all examples of developmentally important behaviors that are based on VR schedules.

Fixed-Interval Reinforcement   We have discussed fixed and variable schedules in reference to the number of behaviors needed for reinforcement. Sometimes, however, reinforcement is contingent on the passage of time, rather than the frequency of behavior. Birthdays and holidays usually are reinforcing events that come only at fixed times. Story time, snack time, and recess are all examples of reinforcers that usually are more linked to the passage of time than to the exhibition of behavior. Behavior that is on this sort of FI schedule comes to be quite time-specific. Children will become quiet and "good" right before recess. Best behavior is exhibited right before Christmas or a birthday. This "cramming" of behavior right at the end of an interval is to be expected when reinforcement is delivered only at the end of the interval.

Consider your own behavior as you wait for a bus. If the bus arrives on the hour and the half hour, it is not likely that you will look for the bus at ten minutes after the hour. Such visual scanning simply is not reinforced. As the interval draws to a close, however, the frequency of your scanning will rise sharply. There will be a pile of scanning responses right near the end of the interval—at half past the hour—and the behavior will be reinforced—the bus will arrive.

Now consider what happens to children's behavior when it is on a fixed-interval schedule. If you want a certain behavior to occur only at a given time, then it is appropriate to use a fixed-interval schedule of reinforcement. As an example, you may want children to clean up their areas and put away toys only at a certain time in the late morning. You can follow cleanup time with some reinforcing event such as story or snack time.

In the home, parents may use FI reinforcement to establish many desirable routines. Children may be required to wash, brush their teeth, and get their pajamas on in time for a bedtime story. Of course, we do not want children to put their pajamas on earlier in the day or more frequently. Thus, an FR schedule would not make sense. We do not want to reinforce the frequency of putting on pajamas, but the time for it. Whenever the *time* for a behavior is the important consideration, the use of an FI schedule of reinforcement may be the best procedure.

Variable-Interval Reinforcement   A variable-interval (VI) schedule operates whenever behavior is reinforced at the end of a time interval, *and that interval is unpredictable*. Waiting for an elevator is an example of behavior that is reinforced on a VI schedule. It matters neither how many times we push the button nor how much time elapses: the elevator arrives on an unpredictable schedule. Similarly, dialing to get through to a phone number that has been busy will be reinforced on a variable-interval schedule—success depends neither on the number of times you try nor on the passage of a specific amount of time, but on some variable interval (see Table 5-2 for a summary of schedules of reinforcement).

Intrinsic Reinforcement

Reinforcers should, when possible, be a *natural outcome* of the behavior being learned. Enjoyment from reading, keeping your hands warm by remembering to wear your mittens, and relaxing when you get your work done are all instances of natural or intrinsic reinforcers. Unfortunately, the natural outcomes often do not work initially. The reinforcer may not be immediate enough or of sufficient magnitude. Ideally, reinforcement should be as relevant to the behavior as possible and be as *normal* or usual as possible. Awarding tokens for remembering to wear mittens is neither relevant to mitten wearing nor normal. Being paid by prizes to learn how to read is also not relevant or normal. But sometimes contrived reinforcers are needed to get a behavior established. After all, we do not deny a person the use of crutches if she or he needs them. As teachers, you will have to decide what behaviors must be built or modified through what procedures. You may find that many behaviors require that you use highly contrived arrangements. Later, as a behavior becomes more reliable, you may alter the reinforcer to a less contrived one.

Use of contrived interim reinforcers can greatly facilitate the learning of a behavior. The trade-off, however, is that this will later require further effort to graduate to consequences more typically provided by society. Perhaps the best advice is to use the least contrived reinforcer that will get the

Table 5-2   Examples of Four Schedules of Reinforcement

Schedule	Example of a Behavior target	Example of a Reinforcer
Variable Ratio (VR) (reinforcer presented unpredictably but, on the average, a certain number of times)	Raises hand to volunteer	Called on every 4th time, on the average (VR 4:1)
	Attempts to join group of children	Accepted by group about every other time (VR 2:1)
Fixed Interval (FI) (reinforcer presented at the end of a definite amount of time)	Plays cooperatively at water table for 15 minutes	Praise and permission to do preferred activity (FI 15 min)
	Spends all morning without crying	Given page of "Scratch 'n Sniff" stickers (FI 3 hr)
Variable Interval (VI) (reinforcer presented unpredictably but on the average after a certain amount of time)	Waits to get help to put on boots	Teacher's aide comes to child after 5 minutes on the average (VI 5)
	Sits attentively during a play	Told that he/she will get extra dessert after 15 min of attention on the average

results you need (Snell & Smith, 1983b). Always strive for *results* and then alter procedures until they involve more typical consequences.

Differential Reinforcement

In the natural environment, some behaviors survive and others do not. The reason for this selection process is *differential reinforcement*. Several variations of a behavior may be emitted by a child, but only one may be reinforced. The one that is reinforced will survive; the others will undergo extinction. As an illustration, children are born with a potential for making a wide range of vocalizations, including French nasal sounds, German gutturals, and Spanish trills. Soon, however, speech sounds are differentially reinforced and children become more proficient in some sounds and lose skill in others.

Differential reinforcement takes place when consistent reinforcement follows one behavior and not its alternative *or* when a behavior is reinforced under one set of stimuli but not another (Alberto & Troutman,

1982). We reinforce crossing the street when the light is green and do not reinforce crossing when the light is red. When a child is presented with french fries, use of a fork or fingers is reinforced but use of a spoon is not. If a teacher wants soft music to become a discriminative stimulus for quiet work, then appropriate behavior must be reinforced when soft music is on and not be reinforced when the music is not on. The fastest way to establish an effective S^D is to use differential reinforcement. Whenever a particular stimulus is to be a signal for a particular behavior, training should involve reinforcement of the behavior when the signal is present, and withholding of reinforcement for the behavior when the signal is absent (Box 5-6).

Remember, you can encourage one behavior over others by reinforcing the one and not the others. Reinforce honesty, not dishonesty; volunteering, not passive attendance; nonviolent disputing, not fighting; cooperation, not strife. You must decide which behavior is to be strengthened and which competing behaviors are to be weakened. Differential reinforcement is an effective method for achieving your goal.

The right behavior may be present at sufficient strength but may not be manifested under the right conditions. Crossing the street may be a well-established behavior, but it may occur when the light is red. Again, differential reinforcement will be effective in pairing the behavior to the appropriate signal circumstances.

Signal present $\rightarrow$ Behavior followed by reinforcement
Signal absent $\rightarrow$ Behavior followed by no reinforcement

If the pattern of differential reinforcement depicted here is followed, soon the target behavior will no longer be emitted when the signal is not present.

Box 5-6   *The Television Thumbsucker*

Four-year-old Martha seemed to be unable to watch television without sucking her thumb. Her parents became increasingly concerned and tried several ways to stop her behavior. Nagging did no good (it usually does not); sending little Martha to her room only caused a great emotional upheaval and actually resulted in increased thumbsucking. Offering her a favorite cereal or dessert if she did not suck her thumb did not work. Martha's parents attended a parents' workshop on child behavior management and decided to try behavior modification. They understood that watching the television was a prompt as well as a reinforcer for thumbsucking. They came up with an ingenious solution: a long cord with an in-line switch was used so that the television could be turned on or off remotely. Unknown to Martha, her parents observed her and turned off the television whenever she began to place her thumb in her mouth; they turned it back on when she refrained from thumbsucking and sat still for a moment. Technically, this procedure involved differential reinforcement for behavior incompatible with thumbsucking. It worked effectively and rapidly. Soon, the television was no longer a prompt for thumbsucking.

Differential reinforcement has application not only to management of behavior but also to instructional problems. Letter discriminations can be established through consistent use of differential reinforcement. Consider the following example:

> Seeing the letter "b" (signal on) → saying "bee" (behavior) → teacher praise (reinforcement)

> Seeing some other letter (signal off) → saying "bee" (inappropriate behavior) → no praise

After repeated differential reinforcement, the child will stop saying "bee" to any letter other than "b." Usually, we do not have to program so carefully; many signals become established by the natural differential reinforcement that takes place without additional planning. Whenever there is a problem in discrimination, however, deliberate differential reinforcement can come to the rescue.

SUMMARY

This chapter has presented the rationale and basic principles that underlie a behaviorist approach to early childhood education. Given these basics, you should be able to read the subsequent chapters on program design and delivery and see how they are built from a behaviorist's perspective.

Behaviorists view a *person* as a composite of biological and behavioral characteristics. Mentalistic explanations of behavior such as "drive," "will," "ego strength," and the like are rejected in favor of external variables such as antecedent and consequent events. Observation and recording of behavior can reveal and assess the contingent relationships between an individual's behavior and events in the environment.

Educators and therapists who embrace a behavioral philosophy assert that ability and disability are functions of experience, that all children can learn, and that good teaching involves good behavioral engineering.

Through appropriate application of the principles underlying reinforcement and prompting, teachers and parents can bring about behavior expansion, developmental progress, and the eventual goal of individuals who engineer their own circumstances to produce their own destinies.

Review Questions

1. Name six assumptions concerning development and learning that compose the philosophic base for behaviorist early childhood education.

2. Describe the basic behavioral model; explain each of the three parts and show their interrelationships.

3. List the major sources of objectives for curricula in a behaviorist program.

4. Explain the role of antecedent stimuli in controlling behavior.
5. Explain the role of various consequences in controlling behavior.

Suggested Activities

1. Debate the soundness and ethics of behavioral preschool programs. List major points of pro and con positions. Try to determine your position. Are you in favor of or opposed to a behavioral approach to early education?
2. Conduct a survey among students and faculty regarding their position on a behavioral approach to preschool programs. Present your findings in class.
3. Name two behaviors of your own that you can see are controlled by your environmental circumstances. State how you could increase or decrease each one by manipulation of antecedents and consequences.

Suggested Readings

Alberto, P. A., and Troutman, A. C. *Applied behavior analysis for teachers*. Columbus, Ohio: Charles E. Merrill, 1982.

Bijou, S. W., and Baer, D. M. *Behavior analysis of child development*. Englewood Cliffs, N.J.: Prentice-Hall, 1978.

Evans, E. D. *Contemporary influences in early childhood education*. New York: Holt, Rinehart & Winston, 1975.

Miller, L. K. *Principles of everyday behavior analysis*. Monterey, Calif.: Brooks/Cole, 1980.

Skinner, B. F. *Beyond freedom and dignity*. New York: Knopf, 1971.

Skinner, B. F. *About behaviorism*. New York: Knopf, 1974.

Applications of a Behaviorist Approach to Child Management

*B*ehavior management procedures are useful in the day-to-day orchestration of children's behavior. Unfortunately, *behavior management* has come to mean managing inappropriate behaviors to many people. However, behavior management techniques are equally useful in precluding behavior problems. In this chapter, you will find examples of how prompting, reinforcement, and various techniques to weaken behavior can be used to prevent or remove behavior problems. In developmentally integrated (handicapped with nonhandicapped) preschool settings, in which some children may have behavior problems, it is especially important that teachers be skilled in using such techniques.

Before describing specific techniques we mention two general rules for behavior management that are applicable across situations.

Consistency is perhaps the most important guideline in using the various behavioral techniques. For example, if you are using praise to establish a new behavior, you must initially use it consistently. A continuous schedule of reinforcement establishes new behaviors quickly (see Chapter 5). When rules (prompts) and consequences are initially inconsistent, the behavior desired will not be developed or will be shown only on a hit-or-miss basis. Consistency of technique across situations and staff members is important (Alberto & Troutman, 1982). For example, teachers should use management procedures during snack and recess just as they do during lessons and circle time. We realize that absolute consistency is probably not possible, but be as consistent as is feasible.

Learning through modeling refers to the concept that children are learning about management procedures in the way the procedures are being taught (Axelrod, 1983). Children will often deal with others in ways that mimic their teacher's behavior. "Do as I say, not as I do" does not usually work with young children. Actions speak louder than words. Additionally, children often learn by what adults offer to them as reinforcers. We emphasize natural, positive management techniques and, where necessary, the careful use of punishment.

Social interaction is an important objective as well as a powerful reinforcer.

TECHNIQUES FOR AVOIDING PROBLEM BEHAVIORS

Teachers can prevent the occurrence of many behavior problems in the classroom by following these practices:

Be Prepared

Always be completely *prepared* for the day's activities and lessons. Problems often occur when children have nothing to do or are waiting for teachers to direct them. In fact, it is best to be overprepared in activities and lessons because there are times when planned activities or objectives cannot be used or are not successful. Indexed resource files containing clear directions can also be used for sudden and necessary activity substitutions.

Observe Behavior

Be constantly *observant* of children's behaviors, being careful to reward appropriate and desirable behaviors. This, of course, makes sense from the perspective of behavior theory. It is often difficult to reinforce the behavior of children who have behavior problems because they may act inappropriately most of the time. It becomes a challenge for the teacher to catch them being good. These are the very children, however, whose infrequent or weak appropriate behaviors require the most frequent reinforcement. Teachers might prompt themselves to be sure to reinforce desirable behaviors by wearing wrist counters that can be used to count the frequency of reinforcing certain child behaviors. Often, too, teachers can avert behavior problems by meeting children who typically engage in inappropriate behaviors at the doorway in the morning or by giving them great amounts of reinforcement and attention before they have an opportunity to do something inappropriate. In this way, these children begin their school day being rewarded for appropriate behaviors.

Determine Reinforcers

Observe closely to determine what events are *reinforcers* for each child. (Remember that reinforcer specificity is important.) Write down these reinforcers and use them when teaching. If a teacher notices that one child really enjoys a certain toy she or he can use that toy during lessons either as part of the lesson content (recognizing colors or shapes on the toy) or as an activity to follow some behavior being taught to the child (after independent toileting). Remember that children's reinforcer preferences might change from day to day, so attempt to make reinforcer observations daily.

Many teachers use the *Premack principle* to maintain child motivation and to preempt problems. Basically, premacking involves sequencing child activities so that less preferred activities are followed by more preferred ones. Eating your spinach and then your ice cream or doing less preferred work before more preferred show-and-tell activities are examples of the Premack principle (Box 6-1).

Teach Constantly

Be as *instructive* as possible during school hours. Teach constantly, not just during scheduled lessons. When you walk across the room, note which children are engaging in desirable behaviors. Pat, tickle, or wink at these children as you pass. You can spontaneously reinforce many good behaviors while you are on the fly. If you are forced to do some work unrelated to your teaching (such as filling out a form), tell nearby children what you are doing and allow them to observe you if they wish. You can model many behaviors that children will imitate.

Use Intrinsic Reinforcement

Use *task-imbedded reinforcers* as much as possible. Many tasks include aspects that automatically reward children's involvement in them. Putting puzzle pieces together, connecting the dots to develop a picture, and dialing a phone all illustrate built-in or task-imbedded reinforcement. When planning direct instructional lessons or activities, choose content and activities that are already reinforcing. Behavior problems are less likely to occur when the content or manner of activities is reinforcing. Lesson plans for teaching counting might have children counting objects that are reinforc-

---

Box 6-1   Food for Thought

When you are studying material of low interest and feel like stopping to have a snack, do you:

1. Stop immediately and have the snack (as a reinforcer for studying)?

2. Deny yourself the snack because it interferes with studying?

3. Set a goal, such as finishing the chapter, then have the snack?

Choice (1) is not desirable; what is being reinforced is not studying but the decision to quit.

(2) is not preferred; the material being studied has little intrinsic or task-imbedded reinforcement and some reinforcement probably is needed to maintain study.

(3) is a good strategy; the snack you are going to have anyway is used to reinforce task persistence, goal setting, and self-management, which result in better grades.

ing for them to handle—for example, coins, buttons on the teacher's shirt, pieces of candy, buttons on a tape recorder. Or have the children count in a manner that is reinforcing to them—roaring numbers like a lion, squeaking numbers like a mouse, or whispering numbers.

Establish Prompts

Help children to discriminate that certain behaviors are being expected of them by using *prompts* for these behaviors. There are times when teachers want children to listen, to sit down, or to look at certain objects. When standardized prompts are used and when reinforcement is delivered following those prompts, children will learn quickly to engage in these behaviors at the teacher's request. When teachers want children to be quiet and listen, for example, they might say "listen" and quickly put a finger to the mouth as if to say "shh." Children who get quiet and listen should immediately be rewarded and told that they are "really watching the teacher" or that they "sure know what to do when the teacher says 'listen.'" Saying "listen" is an example of a standard prompt. It can be used at snack time for announcements about food, at circle time for stories, or at lesson time for verbal instructions.

Minimize Rules

Have as few rules and "don'ts" as possible. Remember that you must always have consequences for breaking rules. Initially children often "test" the importance of rules by breaking them. When there are too many rules there are two possible dangers: children will break rules and you will have to use a high frequency of punishing consequences, or children will break rules and you will allow the behaviors to go unpunished because you do not want to be highly punitive. If you must have as many as five classroom rules, it might be best to choose only three at the beginning. As children comply easily with those three, add the other two.

Preempt Inappropriate Behavior

Preempt problem behavior by rearranging the environment so that the inappropriate behavior is less likely to occur again. Remove conditions that prompt or allow the behavior to occur. With these environmental facilitators removed, you can begin to build new, appropriate, incompatible behaviors. After these new behaviors are established, the environmental conditions can be restored slowly to their original state without recurrence of the problem behavior. Such a strategy was used in a classrom where several aggressive children frequently threw wooden blocks at each other. The teacher immediately removed the blocks and began to build positive interactive behaviors in these children. When the children learned to play cooperatively, the blocks occasionally were brought back to the class. Initially, the teacher demonstrated some fun block play activities (other than throwing), and the blocks were used only for a short, supervised time. Gradually, the blocks were kept in the room for longer periods. Meanwhile, appropriate play was rewarded. The teacher marveled at the children's buildings and roadways. Eventually, the blocks were again standard equipment in that classroom but were not used as weapons.

Other environmental manipulations teachers can use to preempt problem behaviors are:

1. Arrange seating patterns so that children who distract one another are not seated together.
2. Remove and then gradually reintroduce objects that frighten children.
3. Remove and then gradually reintroduce any objects that are not properly used.
4. Do not give a full portion of materials to children who tarry on the way to activities.
5. Make children who do not eat their food at mealtime wait until the next meal to eat.

Aggressive children often throw things at each other; such behavior can be preempted.

Natural consequences can be effective, but you may choose not to use them. When a child takes a toy away from another child, the second child may hit the culprit. The action is likely to continue back and forth. The loser of the battle will be punished by natural consequences; however, the winner will be rewarded for his or her aggression. The latter result may not be a desirable educational objective, so for this type of behavior problem natural consequences might have harmful outcomes.

Using natural punishing outcomes to reduce a behavior problem is a useful strategy under two conditions. First, the natural outcome must not be *dangerous*. We would not want to teach children to refrain from putting items in electric outlets by letting them experience the natural shock. Second, natural punishers usually work only if they are *immediate*. The natural outcome of drinking too much alcohol may be a hangover the next morning, but this punishment is too delayed to have much influence, even with intelligent adults. Generally, the more remote the consequence (even if it is deadly), the less influence it has on current behavior. The link between cigarette smoking and heart and lung disease is well established, yet this knowledge has little control value for most smokers; the consequence is too remote. In contrast, everyone quickly learns to avoid touching hot objects because of the immediacy of the consequences.

Figure 6-1   *Sample token charts*

Contrive Powerful Reinforcers

Use a powerful, *contrived consequence* to reward appropriate behaviors and the absence of problem behaviors (Snell, 1983). Even very young children can participate successfully in simple token economies or contingency contracts. Teachers often find timers useful for these arrangements. When the timer rings, if the child is engaging in appropriate behaviors or is not engaging in the problem behaviors, she or he receives a reward. DRI is a related procedure and simply refers to the *differential reinforcement* of behavior that is *incompatible* with the unwanted one.

Teachers should depict concretely the contingency arrangements for young children. Tokens, such as poker chips or coupons, can be given out as concrete reinforcers, but they are easily lost or traded. A more easily used token system is a picture or chart that can be filled in by the teacher or child as appropriate behavior occurs. The balloons and gum machine in Figure 6-1 are examples of token charts.

A child might wear a chart on his or her clothing if the problem behavior occurs continually throughout the day. When the timer rings and the child is behaving appropriately, the teacher fills in a spot on, for example, a giraffe chart. When the giraffe's spots are all filled, the child can trade the giraffe for an item selected from an array of rewards. A more detailed discussion on setting up token economies can be found in the books and materials listed as supplementary reading at the end of this chapter (see, for example, Ayllon & McKittrick, 1982). Such contrived management procedures, however, are seldom needed at the preschool level unless the children do not respond to standard motivation.

Contracts are agreements between the teacher and child (Hall & Hall, 1982; Box 6-2). The child agrees to engage in a certain behavior (one incompatible with the problem behavior) and the teacher agrees to give the child a certain reward. These contracts can be depicted on a contract board that specifies the agreed-upon behavior and the reward. Children often enjoy signing these contracts with the teacher. As shown in Figure 6-2, the pictures of teacher, student, behavior, and reward can be attached to a flannel board. The cards for signing names are placed under the agreed upon behaviors. Notice the timer at the upper right corner. After the teacher and child agree on the behavior and reward, the teacher sets the timer for a specified period of time. When the timer rings, the teacher and child meet at the contract board and decide whether the reward should be delivered.

DRO refers to the differential reinforcement of *other* behavior; that is, you reinforce whatever a child is doing, as long as the specific unwanted behavior does not occur (Alberto & Troutman, 1982). Usually, a time interval is decided on. At the end of the interval, reinforcement is presented if the undesirable behavior has not been emitted by the child.

Box 6-2   A Contract

"What a very nice school this is!" observed Nat, in a burst of admiration.

"It's an odd one," laughed Mrs. Bhaer; "but you see we don't believe in making children miserable by too many rules, and too much study. I forbade nightgown parties at first; but, bless you, it was of no use. I could no more keep those boys in their beds, than so many jacks in the box. So I made an agreement with them: I was to allow a 15-minute pillow-fight, every Saturday night; and they promised to go properly to bed, every other night. I tried it, and it worked well. If they don't keep their word, no frolic; if they do, I just turn the glasses round, put the lamps in safe places, and let them rampage as much as they like." . . . A few slight accidents occurred, but nobody minded, and gave and took sound thwacks with perfect good humor, while pillows flew like big snow flakes, till Mrs. Bhaer looked at her watch, and called out—

"Time is up boys. Into bed, every man Jack, or pay the forfeit!"

"What is the forfeit?" asked Nat, sitting up in his eagerness to know what happened to those wretches who disobeyed this most peculiar, but public-spirited schoolma'am.

"Lose their fun next time," answered Mrs. Bhaer. "I give them five minutes to settle down, then put out the lights, and expect order. They are honorable lads, and they keep their word."

That was evident, for the battle ended as abruptly as it began—a parting shot or two, a final cheer, as Demi fired the seventh pillow at the retiring foe, a few challenges for next time, then order prevailed; and nothing but an occasional giggle, or a suppressed whisper, broke the quiet which followed the Saturday-night frolic, as Mother Bhaer kissed her new boy, and left him to happy dreams of life at Plumfield.

From: Alcott, L. M. *Little men: life at Plumfield with Jo's boys.* Boston: Roberts Brothers, 1871, pp. 17–18.

Figure 6-2   *Sample contract*

When Bill plays pleasantly (no crying) until the timer rings, Mr. Brown reads to him.

Use Careful Interaction

In addition to these general classroom rules, be careful about directing children's behaviors as you interact with them throughout the day. Do not, for example, tell children they *must* finish their lunch unless you have a plan of action if they do not. Otherwise, children learn that there is no consequence for ignoring your directions. The children may then ignore your verbal directions at other times. Require children to do or not to do something only when that behavior is an important objective and when you have planned a consequence.

TECHNIQUES FOR MANAGING EXISTING PROBLEM BEHAVIORS

Earlier you read about behavioral principles that underly behavior change techniques as well as some theoretical and ethical issues and guidelines for their use. In accordance with that discussion, the specific techniques suggested here are listed in hierarchical order with the mildest, least controversial techniques described first. Teachers can deal with many behavior problems easily by using these mild techniques (Box 6-3).

Before considering the use of punishment, collect *baseline* data on the problem behavior (Axelrod, 1983). Baseline data give you valuable information for selecting the behavior target. After collecting five days' of simple frequency data, you know the current level of the problem so you can evaluate the effectiveness of the behavior-reduction program. While collecting data, note any frequently occurring patterns, such as events that often precede or follow the problem behavior, or time of occurrence of the problem behavior. These observations also can be useful in deciding which procedures to use. For example, while counting how many times a child throws food at the table, you might notice that other children laugh each time the food is thrown. The other children are a likely source of reinforcement. Choose a technique such as preventing the behavior from occurring or removing the other children, rather than simply ignoring or punishing the food throwing.

Box 6-3   *Application of Behavior Management Teaching Strategies to Child Behavior*

Try your skill at answering these questions for the four problem situations described below:

1. What is the problem behavior(s)?
2. What is controlling the behavior?
3. What is the target behavior or objective for behavior change?
4. What is the procedure for changing the behavior?

Situation 1: Jerry

Jerry is 5 years old and is attending a preschool. Each morning, when he arrives with his mother or father, he resists coming into the classroom. He hangs back and pulls against his parents to avoid coming in. Once in the room, he retreats to the corner where the coats are hung and stands with his head against the wall and often cries there.

Situation 2: Stephany

Stephany is a 4-year-old preschooler who likes to bring toys in from home and carries them from place to place in the preschool. When teachers take the toys away so that Stephany can attend during small group instruction, Stephany pouts or whines or cries, and this inappropriate behavior will often last the entire lesson.

Situation 3: Jeffrey

Jeffrey is a 4-year-old boy with limited language. On his first day of school, he came in with both parents, dropped to the floor, and began to bang his head on the floor violently.

When picked up by his mother, he began to scream and pull at her arm. When released, he ran from place to place throwing materials in the air and to the floor. When restrained, he began to bite his hand.

Situation 4: Hirum

Hirum is a 3-year-old preschooler who does not talk. He says nothing to anyone except his mother, and he whispers to her. Once his mother leaves the classroom in the morning, Hirum does not utter a word until his mother picks him up. This includes requests to go to the bathroom, for food, for anything. He does comply with any request not requiring him to speak. When his mother asks him at home why he does not talk at school, he says "don't have to."

Be consistent in using ignoring as an extinction technique.

In addition to collecting data, try to identify a positive behavior that is incompatible with the problem behavior (Kazdin, 1980). Prompt and reinforce this incompatible behavior as frequently as possible. Use this technique to accompany any other behavior-weakening procedures, so that you build positive behaviors while weakening inappropriate ones. Be patient in building these incompatible behaviors. Many children who engage in inappropriate social behaviors with other children (biting, hitting) seldom engage in *appropriate* social interactions. The teacher's problem is not just to reinforce appropriate social behaviors but to *teach* the child to engage in some desirable social interactions. A good rule is: Always teach the child what to *do*, as well as what not to do. After making the baseline observations of the problem behavior, choose from the following strategies for managing inappropriate behaviors:

Extinction

Use *extinction* when you can identify and control the reinforcers that are maintaining the behavior (Hall & Hall, 1980a). Extinction is particularly appropriate to use for problem behaviors that have been encouraged inadvertently by extra teacher attention—whether positive or negative.

For extinction to be effective, the behavior to be reduced must be *clearly specified*. For example, if Lila frequently interrupts other children while they are speaking during lesson time, the behavior *in the classroom* or *during lesson time* is the problem. The same behavior on the playground or in the bus may be tolerable.

Record the behavior accurately. Collect a day or two of information on how often Lila does interrupt (see Chapter 12 for more details on observing and recording). Be *consistent* in using ignoring. If a behavior is ignored sometimes but occasionally accidentally reinforced, it may become even more persistent. Remember that intermittent positive reinforcement is extremely effective. We continue spending money at restaurants where meals are occasionally outstanding, but are usually not worth it.

Expect the unwanted behavior to increase before it diminishes. Any behavior that has been reinforced will tend to intensify in the absence of that reinforcement. This behavioral inflation sometimes succeeds in gaining attention and, thus, is reinforced—making the problem worse and worse. A frustrated father remarked, "When I put Mickey to bed and he yammers, I ignore him because I don't want to encourage it. But sometimes he goes on for so long or gets so sad or loud that I just have to say something to him. Doesn't he understand that he had better stop it? It's driving me crazy!" Unfortunately, Mickey's father is unwittingly reinforcing his son's crying on a VI schedule and is thus ensuring the endurance of the behavior. He must ignore it *consistently*, or not use this method. Teachers who have difficulty using extinction may be better able to ignore behaviors if they can engage in something else while ignoring the behavior. Attending to other children, working on a project, checking papers, writing notes, or reading a book can help ease the pain of carrying out extinction.

Finally, remember to pay attention to other desirable behaviors while you are ignoring the unwanted one.

Intrinsic Aversive Reinforcers

Allow *natural punishing consequences* to occur. This is often a successful and appropriate strategy. It is most effective when the consequences are fairly immediate and pose no danger. When young children protest having to wear mittens outside on winter days, the teacher can say, "If you do not wear mittens, your hands will get cold," then allow the children to go outside without mittens. When the children's hands become cold the teacher can again state the rule and give the children their mittens. The consequence in this example is not immediate, yet the short verbalization can provide a connection between the behavior and its consequence. Other examples of using natural punishing consequences are:

- Children who mangle their paper cup at snack time now cannot be served second helpings.
- Children who pop their balloon now have no balloon.
- Children who eat their clay now have none for sculpting.

Punishment

Use *punishment* only when other techniques are not successful. As you begin to use punishment, also begin to collect data on the frequency of punishment. If intense crying is associated with the procedure, also collect data on this behavior. Parents might be upset to see their child cry when the child is required to sit in the "time out" chair. Such parents are calmed, however, to know that the teacher, too, is concerned and can report the extent of crying each day. Of course, parents are even more satisfied when the teacher can report that the crying is decreasing. As you read about punishment techniques, remember these guidelines:

1. Punish the behavior quickly and consistently.
2. While you are engaged in a punishment intervention, give the child extra attention for appropriate behaviors.
3. Be brief and matter-of-fact in stating the reason for punishment. Do not let the child involve you in a verbal encounter—state the reason for punishment only once.
4. Make sure the "punishment" you choose is severe enough to be truly punishing. If the punishing event is too mild, the child

may accommodate to it, thus requiring progressively more severe punishment. It is better to begin with an effective aversive consequence.

5. Precede the punishing consequence with some signal, so that the signal itself will subsequently act as a punisher. The signal might be a word or motion, but will act as a threat or prelude that will inhibit behavior. This technique will spare both the teacher and child from the actual, more aversive punishment.

6. If you must use a physical punishment, choose one that the other children are not likely to model. If the teacher does not want children to hit each other, then the teacher should not hit children.

Negative Punishment   *Negative punishment* refers to the weakening of a behavior through the *removal* of some event after a behavior. *Response cost* (a type of negative punishment) is similar to a fine. Something gets taken away as a result of inappropriate behavior. If a child is looking at a book and begins to eat it, the book is taken away and the child is not permitted to look at books for a period of time. The cost of that child's behavior is that the book privilege is taken away. In other situations, the child may lose some forthcoming privilege rather than an immediate one. After spattering paint about the art corner, a child might be told that she or he will not be permitted to go outside for the picnic later. Remember the following guidelines:

1. Be sure that you verbally link the behavior and its consequence both when the behavior occurs and when the negative punishment is administered. The contingency should be stated firmly and briefly.

2. If a child is operating under a token economy or a point system, the response cost can be the removal of tokens or points. It is important to state explicitly rules for losing points. Make sure that points are not lost too frequently, or children may not be as motivated to earn points.

3. Be sure to reinforce desirable behavior.

Technically, *time out* refers to a situation in which the child is removed from sources of reinforcement (Hall & Hall, 1980b). This is not entirely possible unless you have a time-out booth, but this is not necessary for most preschool or public school situations. Teachers can use a modified time-out arrangement. A special chair set off in a quiet corner of the room is appropriate. When children engage in inappropriate behaviors, the teacher simply states the contingency, "You hit someone; you must sit in the green chair." Quick and consistent time out can effectively reduce or eliminate many troublesome behaviors. The time-out period need not be long; three to five minutes is usually adequate. Time out must not be used to get rid of the child, but to weaken specific behavior.

Be aware that when the child is permitted to leave time out, the behaviors he or she is engaging in at that time are negatively reinforced. So if a child is sobbing or pouting, those behaviors get reinforced. If you wait until children are behaving more pleasantly and then allow them to leave time out, the pleasant behaviors are reinforced.

Positive Punishment   The child is positively punished by the *application* of some aversive event. Some behaviors can be punished by *disapproval* (Van Houten, 1980). Examples of this are frowning and statements of disapproval. Of course these mild forms of punishment will be successful only if they are infrequently used and if the person who punishes is usually very reinforcing. Disapproval is quite punishing to some children, and its effects should be considered individually.

Overcorrection involves having the child perform some restitution or correction for an inappropriate behavior (Azrin & Besalel, 1980). The compensatory behavior is performed several times or for a long period of time. As an example, a child who has thrown paint on a table is required to wash *all* the tables in the room. The point of overcorrection is to have the child take responsibility for his or her own mistakes. Be certain that the overcorrection task required of the child is connected with the mistake. Requiring a rude child to say and do polite things is overcorrection, whereas depriving that child of recess is not.

Physical punishment may never be needed. If you use it, carry it out with caution. Each of the punishment guidelines should be followed carefully and data should be recorded.

Establish a signal for punishment that can be used for all children and situations. Counting from one to ten is an example of such a conditional aversive stimulus. If a child has refused to comply with an important rule,

---

Box 6-4   *The Hyperseat*

Behaviorists do not advocate teaching children to be still and quiet as an educational objective—a corpse can be still. However, frequently staying seated or being in one place is prerequisite to learning, especially during group lesson time. Five-year-old Malcomb seemed unable to stay in his seat, even when he was scolded and "fined." A bit of technology guided by behavior principles achieved what several months of harassment and frustration could not. A child-size chair was equipped with a timer affixed under the seat. A spring-loaded mechanism was attached to one leg of the chair so that the timer turned on when someone sat down and off when there was no weight on the seat. Now the teacher was able to play "beat the clock" with Malcomb. At first, she set her own timer for five minutes and Malcomb's timer for four minutes. She told Malcomb he could run around the room if his bell went off before hers—and it did. Gradually, she increased the required time, but in an unpredictable (variable interval) fashion. After two weeks, Malcomb was able to stay seated not only in the hyperseat, but in other chairs and on the floor (generalization). Of course, the happy teacher was delighted to provide occasional praise (intermittent social reinforcement) for Malcomb's success.

the teacher can say the child's name, state the rule, and count to ten. If the child has not complied by the count of ten, the teacher must use the planned physical punishment. A signal must be used only once or it will become a meaningless threat. When aversive signals are consistently used, children learn to comply immediately to avoid receiving the physical punishment. When a teacher uses the same signal for all punishments, the entire class quickly learns the significance of that stimulus.

One must carefully choose the form of the physical punishment. As was mentioned earlier, teachers should not model behaviors they do not wish children to practice. It is sometimes convenient and unobtrusive to choose a form of physical punishment that is related to the inappropriate behavior. The child who fails to hold hands and who wanders from the group during a field trip can be punished by the teacher holding his or her hand *very* firmly and tightly for a period of time. A child who hits or otherwise hurts classmates can be restrained *firmly*. These types of physical punishments are less likely to be modeled by the other children.

Remember that parents should be consulted about the use of physical punishment.

SUMMARY

This chapter presented a number of techniques for managing children's behaviors in a preschool setting. The techniques are based on basic behavior principles. Throughout the discussion, emphasis was placed on a positive approach to managing behaviors. Harsher techniques such as physical punishment should be used only as a last resort.

Remember that behavioral management and instruction are two different jobs of the educator; management often is a necessary prerequisite to real teaching. Reducing behavior problems, preventing them, and providing motivation for constructive behavior can go a long way toward establishing a setting for an effective early childhood education program.

Review Questions

1. State and describe five techniques for avoiding problem behaviors in a classroom.
2. Describe a situation in which extinction is an appropriate technique.
3. Give an example of a natural punishing consequence.
4. Describe an example of preempting a behavior problem.
5. List seven guidelines for using punishment.

Suggested Activities

If you have access to a preschool class, try these activities:

1. Make up a list of classroom rules for guiding the children's behaviors. Keep your list as short as possible. Write it in terms that children could understand. List the rules in order of importance for teaching.
2. Observe two or three children closely and make

lists of behaviors that you think should be reinforced, punished, or extinguished.

3. Observe the entire class for three minutes. Write down all the appropriate behaviors you observe. Try this several times to see if you can catch more children being good each time.

If you do not have access to a preschool class, try these activities:

4. Describe two common behavior problems of preschool children and tell how you could prevent them from occurring.
5. List three behaviors incompatible with throwing food at the table.
6. Describe some intrinsic reinforcers that you could use when teaching children to name colors.

Suggested Readings

Ayllon, T., and McKittrick, S. M. *How to set up a token economy*. Lawrence, Kans.: H & H Enterprises, 1982.

Azrin, N. H., and Besalel, V. A. *How to use overcorrection*. Lawrence, Kans.: H & H Enterprises, 1980.

Azrin, N. H., and Besalel, V. A. *How to use positive practice*. Lawrence, Kans.: H & H Enterprises, 1981.

Hall, R. V., and Hall, M. C. *How to use planned ignoring (extinction)*. Lawrence, Kans.: H & H Enterprises, 1980.

Hall, R. V., and Hall, M. C. *How to negotiate a behavioral contract*. Lawrence, Kans.: H & H Enterprises, 1982.

Jones, V. F., and Jones, L. S. *Responsible classroom discipline: creating positive learning environments and solving problems*. Boston: Allyn & Bacon, 1981.

Kazdin, A. E. *Behavior modification in applied settings*. Homewood, Ill.: Dorsey Press, 1980.

Kazdin, A. E. The token economy: A decade later. *Journal of Applied Behavior Analysis*, 15:431–445, 1982.

Millman, H. L., Schaefer, L. E., and Cohen, J. J. *Therapies for school behavior problems: a handbook of practical interventions*. San Francisco: Jossey-Bass, 1981.

Striefel, S. *How to teach through modeling and imitation*. Lawrence, Kans.: H & H Enterprises, 1981.

Van Houten, R. *Learning through feedback: a systematic approach for improving academic performance*. New York: Human Sciences Press, 1980.

Chapter 7

The Curriculum and Materials

*A*s noted earlier, operant theory has more to say about the structure and sequence of the curriculum than it does about the content. Operant procedures can be used successfully to teach any content if vague educational and developmental goals can be converted into observable behaviors and events. Therefore, the main thrust of this chapter is to provide suggestions for the design and selection of the curriculum and materials. Considerations are given to: (1) selection of curricular objectives, (2) content objectives, (3) principles for sequencing the curriculum, (4) guidelines for the selection of curricula, and (5) uses for a well-designed curriculum.

Operant technology is suited to the teaching of any preschool curricular content. The theory does not prescribe goals for education. Nevertheless, the design and selection of a curriculum is an important first step in setting up a preschool program and, thus, deserves discussion from a behaviorist perspective.

DESIGN AND SELECTION OF CURRICULA

Developmentally Balanced Curricula

First, consider the scope of the curricular objectives. Teachers and programs using operant methodologies typically enjoy success in meeting their objectives (Allen & Goetz, 1982). Critics do not usually assert that behavioral programs have failed to teach, but that certain areas have been neglected. For example, if the entire preschool program were based on a successful reading, math, and language series, we could predict success in these areas but not necessarily in gross motor behaviors, social skills, or personality characteristics. Our commitment to educate the whole child becomes most important as teachers select educational objectives. Yet, looking through preschool advertisements in local directories, one can see programs boasting of emphasis on particular aspects of a child's development—academic preschools, social interaction preschools, gymnastic preschools. Sometimes high-powered materials and pressures heavily tilt a program. The popularity of DISTAR (reading: Engelmann & Bruner, 1969; arithmetic: Engelmann & Carnine, 1969; language: Engelmann, Osborn, & Engelmann, 1969), for example, makes it possible for preschools to offer successful programs that emphasize reading, math, or language development. As noteworthy as these goals are, it does not make behavioral sense to employ a lopsided curriculum, to neglect other areas of the child's development. Behaviors are not independent of one another; expansion of the child's repertoire proceeds both through building new skills in specific areas (vertical expansion) and through elaboration and relatedness to other skills (horizontal expansion) (Mori & Neisworth, 1983). Accordingly, an optimal curriculum must be built on a broad base of objectives that come from multiple sources that are developmentally and socially sound. There are several major sources for objectives.

Will she go down by herself? Independence is an important teaching goal.

Sources for Objectives

Societal Demands   Society expects our children to develop certain capabilities at certain ages. Behaviorists do not believe that the acquisition of skills must necessarily await the attainment of a given chronological age (LeBlanc, 1982). Nevertheless, what society *expects* children to achieve at various ages provides a rich source of objectives for teachers.

Societal sources for objectives are articulated by various educational and child development authorities. There are many spokespersons who state that the schools are either too structured or too permissive, are teaching too many frills and not enough basics or are too narrowly sticking to the three R's and not providing enough instruction in life's more meaningful aspects. Whatever your point of view, you can find a number of objectives by listening to experts and critics of education.

Although the culture as a whole does provide a broad array of objectives, the child's more immediate social situation provides a great number of teaching goals. The subculture of the child and the parents, especially, are direct and important sources for selecting preschool objectives. In fact, recent law (PL 94-142) requires the involvement of parents of handicapped youngsters in the formulation of individual educational plans (IEPs).

Child-specific Needs   Certainly, the child can be considered as a source for educational objectives. Observing a child and asking what he or she would like to learn can often lead to many objectives that may otherwise be neglected. Behaviorists do not generally believe that a curriculum or program should be child-centered, that it should be dictated by the wishes of the child. Nevertheless, involvement of children in their own program is essential and provides input to complement the educator's program for the child. The *ultimate* goal of a good preschool program is to have children select or design their own educational objectives and participate in their own repertoire expansion (Mori & Neisworth, 1983). Of course, this is one of the goals of education—independence—but it is certainly not what we start with. Working towards establishing an independent, self-governing individual is one of the most valuable teaching goals an educator can hold. The process of teaching children how to contribute to their own goal planning can, itself, generate many objectives.

Child Development Research   Much research with young children has produced solid information concerning what children do, and when they seem able to do it. Numerous tests of development use "developmental landmarks" to assess the capabilities of children at various ages (Bagnato & Neisworth, 1981). From these sources, we generally know what 1-year-olds, 2-year-olds, and so on can do. Note that the findings do not tell us what children *should* do or *could* do—just what they actually do. Such developmental norms are valuable sources of objectives. We want our children to demonstrate capabilities at or before appropriate ages, pass developmental tests, and so on. Building a curriculum around the items found in developmental assessment tools may be teaching to the test. If done in a general rather than specific way, however, a curriculum that borrows from developmental norms is sure to contain objectives important to the child, because it includes developmental landmark capabilities.

Developmental theory also provides many possible objectives for the preschool. Piagetian theory, for example, offers many measures of child development that can be translated into instructional goals (Furth & Wachs, 1975) (see Chapter 13).

Goal Analysis   Society, the child, and developmental theory do not always provide sufficiently specific objectives for instruction. Before goals can be an effective part of a behavioral curriculum, they must be stated in terms of observable, attainable, and measurable objectives. Often, goals and objectives must be analyzed into smaller, more specific instructional units that then lend themselves to lesson planning. Creativity, delayed gratification, cooperation, and task persistence are all worthy objectives but must be analyzed into attainable behaviors before they can be considered useful in a behaviorally oriented curriculum. Content and process analyses constitute the fourth major source for a well-designed curriculum.

Balancing the Curriculum   A well-rounded curriculum would use objectives from all four of these sources. Educational and developmental goals derived from the four sources are listed in Table 7-1.

A fruitful approach to a well-balanced curriculum would be to first list broad areas of child development (for example, cognitive, affective, and psychomotor) and then to generate objectives under each of these that reflect the sources mentioned (society, the child, child development research, and goal analyses). The HICOMP curriculum (Willoughby-Herb & Neisworth, 1983) was developed in this fashion by the HICOMP Project at the Pennsylvania State University. This curriculum is divided into four domains: communication, self-care, motor skills, and problem solving. Each broad area is further divided into subdomains representing the child, society, research, and content and process analysis as sources. The four domains and their subdomains are shown in Table 7-2.

Excellent preschool curricula are available and can save your time and

Table 7-1   Four Sources of Objectives

Sources	*Focus of Objectives*
Society (what parents, communities, etc. tell us)	• Social conventions: e.g., saying "please," using a fork • Toilet training and other independence skills taught by given age • Values
The child (what the children and their behaviors tell us)	• Normal developmental tasks: e.g., hopping, skipping, speaking in complete sentences • Content chosen because of children's interest: e.g., caring for gerbils, living in a circus
Child development research (what the experts tell us)	• Skills known to be prerequisite to reading: e.g., left-to-right eye movement, sounds of letters • Scientific method (observing, recording, etc.)
Goal analysis (what a break-down of larger objectives and steps in learning tell us)	• Separate components of a task are taught separately, then put together to form a more complex behavior • Problems in any phase of learning are detected and specialized techniques used

Table 7-2   Four Domains of Developmental Objectives as Organized Within the HICOMP Curriculum

Communication	*Own Care*	*Motor Skills*	*Problem Solving*
Language-related play	Health, safety, and personal cleanliness	Fine motor control (skilled movements)	Attention
Self-expression			Imitation
Language responding	Self-competence	Mouth and jaw control	Recall
Imitation related to language	Meeting social conventions and values	Gross motor control (fundamental movements)	Concept formation
Language-related attention	Appropriate and proportioned affective reactions		Grouping Sequencing Application of principles Creativity

(Adapted from Willoughby-Herb, S., and Neisworth, J., 1983.)

energy. These curricula have been developed over a number of years with considerable funding and expert consultation. Take advantage of the work that has been done for you.

Curricula Should Accommodate Child Variance

A curriculum should include skills that are appropriate to children's developmental level or behavioral repertoire. Although you may have a well-developed curriculum for a class of normal 3 to 5 year olds, you might have some children for whom some lower-level objectives are appropriate—for example, toilet training, speaking in two-word sentences, following group norms. Therefore, you should either choose a curriculum that covers a broad developmental span or make accommodations and additions within your current curriculum (Allen, 1981; Cook & Armbruster, 1983).

Accommodating delayed, accelerated, and "different" children is becoming increasingly important with the national trend to mainstream handicapped youngsters in regular preschool settings. There is a great deal of research indicating that exceptional preschoolers are best served by integration with nonhandicapped children as early as possible (Allen, 1980; Guralnick, 1978). Curricular adaptations are needed when the enrolled children display significant variance from the norm.

MAINTENANCE AND GENERALIZATION

Children may perform a given behavior once during lesson time. However, we cannot assume that the child will reliably perform that behavior. Children differ in their recall. It is important to state curricular objectives that lead the teacher to teach for and check on behavior *maintenance*. A further consideration is to examine the usefulness of the objectives to be taught. Useful objectives, such as hand washing, can be practiced outside of school and hence might need less maintenance effort on the part of the teacher. Consider these two objectives:

- *Acquisition objective*: The child washes and dries hands after toileting whenever the teacher says, "Time to wash hands."
- *Maintenance objective*: The child reliably washes hands after toileting, with no verbal prompt.

Maintenance objectives are aimed at helping children develop automatic behavior patterns. Often children do not develop reliable behaviors unless behavior maintenance objectives are taught with behavior acquisition objectives. Curricula that use a spiral design act to maintain what has been taught; they repeat objectives with increasing complexity (Bagnato & Neisworth, 1981).

This little girl is sharing some news with her classmates — an example of generalized behavior.

Include the *transfer* of behavior as an objective. It is important that children learn to generalize learned behavior to other settings (see Chapter 8).

We teach preschool children to give their name and address when asked. In our classrooms, it is usually a teacher who asks, "What is your name? Where do you live?" Yet we teach this in the hope that if children become lost in a department store, they will answer correctly to a clerk or store detective. The children's correct performance requires that the behavior be generalized from the teacher as a questioner to the clerk as a questioner. As many frantic parents have discovered, such transfers do not necessarily occur. If we want children to practice a given behavior with a variety of persons, then our curricular objective should include generalization. Children with learning problems often have special difficulty in both maintaining and transferring behaviors (Hundert, 1981; Rabin-Bickelman & Marholin, 1978; Rose, Koorland, & Epstein, 1982).

A final point concerning transfer objectives is that there are several situations in which we expect behaviors to transfer—from one person to another (in the case of the lost child), from one setting to another (in another teacher's classroom), and from one person to a group situation (sharing "news" with the whole class as opposed to just the teacher). Below is an acquisition, maintenance, and transfer objective for a problem-solving skill:

- *Acquisition objective*: When shown a cardboard traffic light, the child starts or stops appropriately 100% of the time when shown the words "walk" or "don't walk."
- *Maintenance objective*: During classroom games using the cardboard traffic light, the child reliably stops or starts appropriately on seeing the words "walk" or "don't walk."
- *Transfer objective*: On field trips into town the child reliably stops or starts appropriately when seeing the words "walk" or "don't walk" on actual traffic lights.

Sequencing Curricula

Now that we have discussed the desirable content for a curriculum we need to know how to arrange this content. The operant approach suggests some ways to sequence curriculum objectives.

Maximize the Learner's Chances of Success   *Errorless learning* means maximizing the student's chance of success (Etzel & LeBlanc, 1979). When we are concerned that each new learning experience lead to positive results, we can structure the curriculum so that new units begin with review, and so that we move from simple to complex learning, from concrete to abstract experiences, from rote to problem-solving methods, and from the familiar to the unfamiliar.

Teach Prerequisite Behaviors First   An operant view of the many complex behaviors we teach children is that these behaviors can be broken down and arranged in a hierarchy of difficulty (Allen & Goetz, 1982). The curriculum should reflect hierarchies within subject areas. The teacher proceeds through these hierarchies rather than waiting for children to arrive at stages of development. Table 7-3 shows a segment from a hierarchy of skills within a problem-solving curriculum.

Incorporate Intermittent Reviews   We have all read the high-school or college textbook where subject matter was divided into discrete units and no carryover was required from one to the other. We study for the unit test on electricity, and then promptly forget all that information as we move to the unit on sound. The cycle continues: we successfully complete a general science course and remember practically nothing.

Viewing this situation from an operant point of view, we see ourselves being reinforced for remembering facts and concepts about electricity only while that unit is being taught. We are not asked to recall anything about

Table 7-3 A Sample Hierarchy of Behaviors

Imitation of Visual Events

1. Imitates a sequence of two simple motor behaviors involving own body (for example, pats head, touches nose)
2. Imitates a sequence of two behaviors involving limb and object (for example, pounds with hammer, throws ball)
3. Imitates a sequence of two behaviors where one involves a discrimination problem (for example, throws ball, touches the *red* triangle)
4. Imitates a sequence of three behaviors involving own body (for example, pats head, touches toes, raises arm)

electricity as we move on to other units. Those facts and concepts are put on extinction, because they are no longer relevant to an impending test, in-class discussion, or other daily activity. We may be asked to recall them on achievement tests, but often we have forgotten them.

What does this have to do with planning a preschool curriculum? We must structure our teaching and curricula so that preschool children do not have the opportunity to practice the learn-and-then-forget sequence. The curriculum can include review and integration of curricular objectives in several ways. Require monthly reviews of all or of samples of behaviors learned. Evaluate curricular objectives. Use the maintenance objectives in the previous sections.

Record Keeping

A well-designed curriculum should contain inclusive objectives and be properly sequenced from least difficult to more difficult learning tasks (Bagnato & Neisworth, 1981). A list of the sequenced curricular objectives for a given class should be included in each child's folder. The curricular sequence can then be used to provide:

1. A record of where the child is in the program,
2. A basis for progress reports and parent conferences,
3. Information on the child's rate of learning new skills and on his or her maintenance and transfer skills,
4. A foundation for lesson planning.

Several preschool curricula include a record-keeping system, usually objective attainment forms. As a child shows mastery of given objectives, these are checked and dated. Progress charts on all or at least selected (troublesome) objectives are instructionally useful and are helpful when communicating with parents. Table 7-4 is a sample form.

Table 7-4   Curriculum-based Developmental Checklist on Andy

Objective Number	General Objective	Pretest	Date Begun	Date Ended
M—2—1	Fundamental movement (gross motor)			
M—2—1.1	Stoops and recovers	+		
M—2—1.2	Starts and stops walking without falling	+		
M—2—1.3	Climbs into chair, turns around to sit	+		
M—2—1.4	Runs stiffly, sometimes falls	+		
M—2—1.5	Crawls up stairs unassisted	+		
M—2—1.6	Walks up stairs if one hand is held	±	9/15	10/26
M—2—1.7	Walks sideways	−	9/15	
M—2—1.8	Walks down stairs if one hand is held	±	9/17	10/30
M—2—1.9	Squats in play for 2–3 minutes	+		
M—2—1.10	Walks backward	±	9/17	
M—2—1.11	Walks up and down stairs holding rail, both feet on each step	±	9/22	11/10
M—2—1.12	Kicks large (stationary) ball	±	9/22	11/3
M—2—1.13	Jumps off floor, both feet	±	9/24	12/21
M—2—1.14	Tries to stand on one foot	−	9/24	12/21
M—2—2	Skilled movement or visual-motor or fine-motor			
M—2—2.1	Stacks two objects	−	9/26	
M—2—2.2	Puts 5–6 cubes (e.g.) in container	±	9/26	1/8
M—2—2.3	Helps turn pages of book	−	9/26	12/4
M—2—2.4	Puts very small object into narrow container	+		
M—2—2.5	Makes random marks on paper with crayon held in fist	±	9/30	11/12

Teacher–Curriculum Compatibility

No matter how good the curriculum is, it will not provide the basis for an effective program if it is not acceptable to the teacher and related staff. The teacher may consider the amount of effort and time required to manage a curriculum excessive, and may use the curriculum only grudgingly. More important, the curriculum should be consistent with the teacher's viewpoint and instructional skills (Allen, 1981; Bagnato & Neisworth, 1981). Requiring a behavioral teacher to use a Piagetian curriculum (or vice versa) is asking for trouble. Thus, some very pragmatic considerations may override other factors.

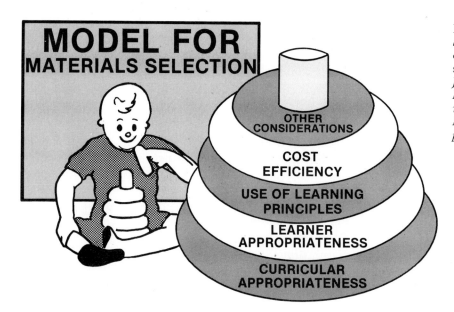

Figure 7-1   *Model for materials selection (adapted from* Individualized education for preschool exceptional children, *J. T. Neisworth, S. J. Willoughby-Herb, S. J. Bagnato, C. A. Cartwright, and K. Laub. Rockville, Md.: Aspen Systems, 1980, p. 112)*

GUIDELINES FOR THE DESIGN AND SELECTION OF MATERIALS

Select materials for the classroom with care. Study samples of the materials if possible. Advertising for instructional materials can be both helpful and confusing. Be sure the advertised use of each material is realistic for the children who will be using it. The strategies recommended for use of the materials should be related to the principles of behavior change, including combinations of modeling, prompting, shaping, chaining, behavior rehearsal, and questioning. The proliferation of instructional materials may seem overwhelming, but there are some useful considerations that can make choosing them easier. A useful four-step model is shown in Figure 7-1.

Curricular Appropriateness

The most fundamental consideration is whether the materials are appropriate. Instructional materials should be useful in teaching the curriculum. Assuming a comprehensive curriculum is used, materials should be selected on the basis of their relevance to curricular objectives. Some materials are useful for more than one curricular area, whereas others are somewhat specific. A good pull toy, for example, is useful in teaching both motor and social objectives. Because of limited budgets, wise teachers usually choose materials that are helpful across several curricular areas. Your final selection of materials, however, should allow you to carry out the whole curriculum.

Learner Appropriateness

If children do not like the materials selected, teachers are forced to employ contrived and extrinsic incentives or revert to aversive means to force children to use them. Compelling children to learn is foolish. If children do not enjoy the learning activity itself, they will not be learning how to learn. Instead, they will be learning to go through certain paces to get a reward or avoid punishment. Behaviorists emphasize reinforcement and know that the best reinforcers are integral to the task. We do not wish to train children to learn only under the narrow conditions of school-arranged reward or punishment. Enjoyable materials that are eagerly sought by the children make learning easier, more generalizable, and more enduring.

Children, like adults, rapidly develop behaviors that successfully avoid aversive circumstances. The bored or hostile child will play hooky or at least daydream in order to escape the school-imposed conditions. It is antithetical to a behaviorist approach to select materials that are not of high interest. Many teachers encourage their children to help them select materials.

Finally, certain learners may have atypical characteristics and require special materials. A visually impaired child can benefit from materials that promote learning through other senses.

Use of Learning Principles

Materials should be tools for behaviorally based instructional strategies; they should promote *shaping*, *reinforcement*, *discrimination*, *learning*, and *generalization*. Materials should provide or permit immediate feedback (reinforcement) so that errors are not repeated (Box 7-1). They should provide for an easy-to-difficult sequencing. Prompts should be effective and easily faded. Peer learning or self-instruction is often possible when materials meet these requirements.

Cost Efficiency

The last consideration—and, unfortunately, it can be the decisive one—is cost efficiency. Budgets in preschools often are limited, and good learning materials often are expensive. The durability and flexibility of the materials chosen can often justify the high initial cost. In some cases, teacher- or parent-made substitutes can be fabricated at low cost. Be sure to check the talents of all those involved in the preschool.

Other Considerations

When you choose materials, ask yourself:

1. Are the materials nonsexist and nonracist? Note pictures: they are often a clue to the tone of the material and can depict stereotypes.
2. Can the materials be used independently? Is that use safe? Can they be used by a small independent group of children?
3. Do the teacher's guides suggest further uses of the materials? Are the objectives clearly stated?
4. Are the materials punishing in any way? For example, a poorly designed sequence of activities may punish a child by causing frustration if the child cannot complete the task.
5. Will children be actively involved in the use of the materials? Do the materials make noise, light, sound? Are children involved in many sensory areas—visual, aural, tactile?
6. Do you, as the teacher, enjoy having the materials in the classroom? Your enthusiasm, or lack of it, can heighten or diminish the usefulness of any materials.

Using the guidelines discussed, a materials evaluation form can be constructed. An example using a rating scale is shown in Table 7-5.

Box 7-1 Self-Correctional Materials: Maria and the Golden Beads

Maria Montessori is rightly thought of as a pioneer in the field of early childhood education. Her method was one of the first consistent attempts to develop a program to address educational problems encountered by young children. As the children in her schools progressed, she began to question the effectiveness of regular school education, believing that if "unteachable" children could progress successfully through her program, much more could be done for "normal" children. She designed what she believed to be the proper environment for learning: an environment that was responsive to the child's needs. One of the characteristics of this environment was the didactic materials used there. Based on the theories of Seguin, these materials were designed to promote sensory discrimination and to develop ideas of form, size, color, weight, temperature, and texture. These were radical materials in their day, but in one respect they are amazingly contemporary. They were among the first materials designed to be self-correctional, to provide immediate feedback to the child who is playing with them. Errors or successes are evident to the child, so that the child can correct mistakes, and the probability for error is low. As a result, these materials can be used only correctly or incorrectly: the brown stair can be built only one way, the Golden Beads work only one way. Thus, children do not need the teacher to tell them how successful they have been; the feedback is immediate and corrections can be made independently.

Table 7-5   Materials Evaluation Form

Rate the material on a 1-to-5 scale on each dimension, with 1 being low, 5 being high					
	1	2	3	4	5
1. Does the teacher's guide suggest objectives?					
2. Are the objectives task-analyzed?					

3. Are any of these strategies used in the materials or suggested methods?
   a. modeling
   b. prompting
   c. shaping
   d. chaining
   e. behavioral rehearsal					

4. Do the materials provide task-imbedded reinforcers?					
5. Would the materials contribute to curricular balance with the materials you already have?					
6. Can the materials be used independently? By small groups?					
7. Do the materials provide immediate feedback?					
8. Are the materials punishing in any way?					
9. Are materials nonsexist and nonracist?					
10. Do durability and efficiency outweigh costs?					
11. Is a useful teacher's guide included?					

SOME EXEMPLARY CURRICULA AND MATERIALS

Bagnato and Neisworth (1981) used a comprehensive evaluation form and checklist to examine five widely used preschool curricula. Among those five were the Learning Accomplishment Profile (LAP) (Sanford, 1978), the HICOMP curriculum (Willoughby-Herb & Neisworth, 1983), and the Portage Project Curriculum (Shearer & Shearer, 1972). All these curricula have a strong theoretical and conceptual basis and are based on experimental and applied research. They employ a developmental task approach and sequence the tasks. Data on the development of the curriculum and effectiveness studies are available for all three curricula, either as part of the package or from the project directors. All three programs are applicable to normal and developmentally delayed children. They can be used with minimal restructuring of existing facilities in the classroom. The Portage is especially designed for home use. Teacher training is required for all three, but demonstrations or a good workshop are quite sufficient. All

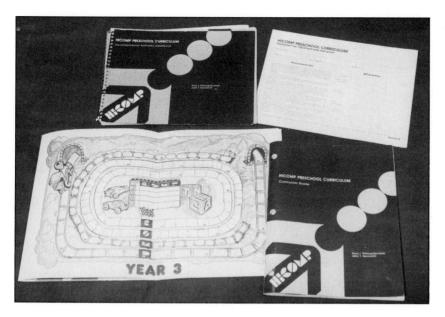

HICOMP preschool curriculum.

of the programs include a system for assessing entry skills. Linking the curricula with a norm-referenced test is recommended to place children in the curricula. In all three, a method of organizing progress is provided, such as graphs or color-coded cards. There is space in all three formats for comments, suggestions, activities, and materials. This can be helpful in program development at a later date for a child, and can suggest modifications or slight alterations useful in given situations. Directions for use, as well as a materials listing and optional or supplementary activities, are also included. They are all durable and logically organized, and the language used is clear and comprehensible.

All three of the curricula goal statements as well as specific objectives were formulated to meet the requirements of PL 94-142, which guarantees the programs' usefulness for both normal and developmentally delayed populations. The behaviors required are stated and defined objectively—materials are specified for each activity. Criteria for mastery of each lesson are set by the teacher or parent based on the child's own situation. Pre- and post-test procedures are set, so that a reliable check of progress is possible. The teaching procedures are written specifically to ensure that the objectives will be taught. In all three, structured program modifications are available for students who are having problems, although none of them has procedures supplied for working with children who have specific handicapping conditions. Maintenance can be documented in all three programs, but there are no planned strategies provided for documentation of generalization. HICOMP provides a detailed discussion of instructional (behavioral) procedures; it also has suggestions for practicing acquired skills in other activities. All of these curricula are useful in either an individual or a group setting. Both parents and teachers can use these programs; the optimum program is coordinated between home and school.

The Portage curriculum differs from the others in that it was designed mainly as a home-based program. Parental involvement is vital to the program's effectiveness.

SUMMARY

A well-balanced curriculum is crucial; behavioral development can quickly become uneven when certain areas are encouraged while others are neglected. To achieve balance, objectives should be derived from broad developmental areas as well as from society, the child, child development research, and goal analysis. A curriculum also should include objectives relating to deficits of individual children, and to the maintenance and transfer of tasks. Content should be sequenced for success. Hierarchical arrangement of tasks according to prerequisites, and intermittent reviews also are important. Individual curriculum sequences can be used for program planning and record keeping. Finally, certain pragmatic factors such as teacher preference and school budget must be considered when selecting the curriculum.

Box 7-2   *The DISTAR Program*

Direct **I**nstructional **S**ystems for **T**eaching **A**rithmetic and **R**eading (Science Research Associates, 1969, 1972, 1975, 1976, 1977), more commonly known as DISTAR, is often used in special classrooms but is just as appropriate for many preacademic and academic settings.

DISTAR incorporates many behavioral principles for direct instruction. The program breaks down its major goal (teaching language, reading, or arithmetic) into smaller subgoals or sequential teaching steps (task analysis). It is highly structured and moves from simple, basic material to more complex skills (shaping). Teacher directions and actions are precisely specified, and hand signals (prompts) encourage student responses and pacing. The lessons move very quickly, lasting approximately 10 minutes, and contain abundant reinforcement from

the teacher. Peer models and teacher modeling are used. Printed prompts are used and then faded in later lessons in the sequence. Mastery tests are used approximately every fifth lesson. The teacher's manual gives suggestions for remediation of problems. The program is designed to be used in small groups, with the entire group participating at all times. Workbook material and repeated drills are used to supplement the lessons.

DISTAR programs are available for math and reading and are exemplars of behaviorally based instruction. Research on the longer-term effects of preschool instruction shows that the direct instruction model (employed by DISTAR) yields superior child progress in language, reading, and arithmetic by the end of the third grade (Becker, 1978).

Review Questions

1. Describe two approaches to choosing objectives for a well-balanced curriculum.
2. What are the three main sources of curricular objectives? Give an example of each.
3. Give an example of behavior maintenance. What technique could you use to encourage maintenance?
4. Give an example of behavior transfer or generalization. How would you encourage generalization? How would you discourage it?
5. List three principles you would follow in sequencing curricular objectives.
6. Given the following breakdown of the task of counting objects up to 3, sequence the parts into a performance hierarchy by using the principles listed in your answer to (5).
   a. Touches objects one at a time as teacher counts
   b. Counts by rote from 1 to 3
   c. Counts by rote from 1 to 2
   d. Coordinates counting and touching objects up to 3
   e. When asked "How many are there?" answers with the last number spoken
   f. Counts objects one at a time as teacher touches them
7. List and describe the four major considerations in choosing materials for use in the classroom.

Suggested Activities

1. Write one developmental/behavioral objective appropriate for a 4-year-old child in each of the four basic developmental domains: communication, social/emotional, motor, and cognitive.
2. Devise a rating scale that you could use for evaluating published curricula. Then use your scale to evaluate at least two curricula. Share your conclusions with your classmates.
3. Choose a task that you would teach a preschooler and write acquisition, maintenance, and transfer objectives for that task.
4. Assume that you are in a teaching situation in which you have no written curriculum. Choose one broad curricular area (for example, cognitive skills) and construct a one- or two-year curricular sequence. Remember to use the sequencing principles and to balance the sources of content.
5. Examine several curricular materials and assess their appropriateness for use in a preschool setting. Specify the criteria you use.

Suggested Readings

Bagnato, S. J., and Neisworth, J. T. *Linking developmental assessment and curricula: prescriptions for early intervention.* Rockville, Md.: Aspen Systems, 1981.

Cook, R. E., and Armbruster, V. B. *Adapting early childhood curricula—suggestions for meeting special needs.* St. Louis, Mo.: C. V. Mosby, 1983.

Hodges, W. L., McCordless, B. R., and Spicker, H. H. *Diagnostic teaching for preschool children.* Arlington, Va.: The Council for Exceptional Children, 1971.

Lerner, J., Mardell-Czudnowski, C., and Goldenberg, D. *Special education for the early childhood years.* Englewood Cliffs, N.J.: Prentice-Hall, 1981.

Safford, P. L. *Teaching young children with special needs.* St. Louis, Mo.: C. V. Mosby, 1978.

Chapter 8

Strategies for Teaching the Curriculum

In Chapter 6 you read about operant-based strategies for managing child behaviors. In this chapter, we focus on *instruction* rather than management. How can we teach specific curricular objectives? Techniques and examples are presented for analyzing tasks, teaching tasks, giving corrective feedback, choosing appropriate reinforcers, choosing appropriate materials, and teaching for generalization and maintenance.

TASK ANALYSIS

Often curricular objectives must be broken down into smaller tasks before being taught. Teachers can make learning easier by teaching complex tasks one step at a time (Neisworth et al., 1980; Rowbury, 1982). This is especially important when you attempt to teach an objective to children who are developmentally younger than the age at which children typically acquire the objective. Teaching a 2-year-old to tie shoes and teaching a retarded 5-year-old how to spell his or her name are instances that usually require analysis of objectives into simple steps. Here are some suggestions to locate task components within the tasks you are analyzing:

1. What *concepts* must children know in order to complete the task?
2. What kinds of *attentional* skills must they have?
3. What kinds of *physical movements* are necessary?
4. What behavior *sequences* must children perform?

Here is a task analysis for table setting that specifies these four components:

1. *Concepts*: left and right; recognizes plate, knife, fork, spoon; recognizes that the fork belongs to the left and the knife and spoon to the right; recognizes that the spoon goes to the right of the knife; recognizes that the water glass goes to the right and the napkin to the left of the plate.

2. *Attention*: attends to the areas surrounding the place settings, attends to left and right positions relative to the plate or silverware.
3. *Physical movements*: lays plates on table carefully, places silverware down with handles at bottom; places silverware proper distance from plate and each other.
4. *Sequence*: places plates first; says "fork left"; places fork; says "knife by plate"; places knife; says "spoon by knife"; places spoon.

Note that in the sequence for setting the table, there are verbal directions to oneself—for example, says "fork left." In tasks where self-instruction will assist a child in performing a task, you should place the instructions at the proper points in the sequence.

Of course, not all tasks must be analyzed. Children learn many complex behaviors through simple imitation. However, it is easier for children to learn difficult tasks that are analyzed and broken into small steps for teaching. The individual task components of the task analysis may be sequenced in a variety of ways—from simple to complex, from familiar to less familiar (Box 8-1). Sometimes there are prerequisite component tasks and these are taught first. Sometimes the task itself has a necessary sequence (as in tying shoes) and this dictates the order.

Box 8-1   *Putting Mittens On*

Chain

Skill:
In this program, the child, a boy called S, learns to grasp one mitten, insert his hand, and adjust his thumb while he pulls the mitten on. This skill is an extension of pulling but requires fine motor coordination to insert and adjust his hand and thumb.

Entry Behaviors:
1. S *brings his hands together* in front of him. Frequently, S pulls his mittens off (pulling off: mittens) before he pulls them on because the removal requires little adjustment (simple grasp and pull) and less thumb control (for positioning the thumb).
2. S *grasps the mittens*, one hand on each mitten, and retains each while gently pulling. Or, adapt to allow use of adaptive equipment or materials that enable S to secure the mitten.

Objective:
S pulls his mittens onto his hands with his thumbs properly adjusted without assistance. S must initi-

ate his response within five seconds of the command and respond correctly four out of five trials. One mitten = one trial.

Cycle:
None specified.

Follow Up:
Continue to have S put on his mittens. Establish routines so that he learns to put them on at appropriate times without your command. Combine this with other tasks so that S performs all tasks for getting ready to go outside. For example, S puts on his coat (putting on shirt), hat (putting hat on), and mittens. When S puts on his mittens, repeat the word *mittens*, and emphasize it to expand S's vocabulary. As S develops more control over his finger movements, teach him to put on gloves.

Tawney, J. W., Knapp, D. S., O'Reilly, C. D., and Pratt, S. S. *Programmed environments curriculum*. Columbus, Oh.: Charles E. Merrill, 1979.

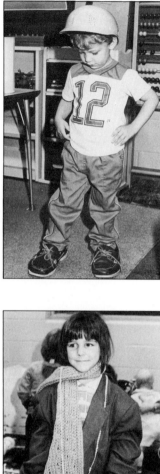

Children often imitate people important to them.

TEACHING TASKS

After you have selected appropriate teaching objectives from the curriculum and have task-analyzed them where necessary, you are ready to choose strategies for teaching the target behaviors. We will describe five operant techniques for teaching new behaviors. These methods are quite versatile; they can be used in teaching any curricular area or at any developmental level. The techniques, of course, are based on basic principles of behavior.

Modeling

Modeling is a technique in which the teacher or another individual demonstrates the behavior to be learned (Ross, 1981). This is a kind of prompting.

Modeling can be an effective way of teaching specific skills and sequences of skills, especially with children who do not have much problem paying attention (Alberto & Troutman, 1982). We all know of good and bad models to whom children are exposed, and sometimes we inadvertently model behaviors that we do not want children to imitate. Cigarette smoking, swearing, and getting angry are typical behaviors that adults all too often demonstrate for children.

To increase the effectiveness of modeling, several guidelines or tips follow:

1. The individual who models the behavior should be someone who is admired by the child, or with whom the child can readily identify. Often the teacher is an ideal model, assuming he or she is liked by the child. Peer models can be extremely effective in teaching many skills such as toileting, handwriting, riding a bus, eating at the table with others. Even 2-year-olds will spontaneously imitate behavior exhibited by peers (Box 8-2) (Apolloni & Tremblay, 1978). Follow-the-leader is clearly a game based on children's interest in and capability of imitation. The practice of mainstreaming is partly based on the assumption that peer imitation will help to normalize the handicapped. Advertisers are well aware that children imitate other children: children are usually employed to promote toys, cereal, clothing, and so on.

2. Clear verbal instructions accompanying the demonstration can facilitate imitation, especially when the task is complex (Smith & Lovitt, 1976). Modeling also is of great benefit to children who are learning by self-instruction (Bornstein & Queuillon, 1976). Diagrams, cartoons, pictures, and films or videotapes can illustrate or demonstrate behaviors.

3. The demonstration should be provided from the child's perspective. In showing a youngster how to tie shoes, teachers can work from behind the child to achieve the right perspective. Also, care must be taken to

avoid obscuring parts of the demonstration (Cooper, LeBlanc, & Etzel, 1968).

4. Provide encouragement and rewards for the model. Modeling often has a greater effect when the observer sees the model receiving reinforcement for the target behavior (Striefel, 1981).

5. Reinforce the observer for imitating the model. Remember that imitation may not at first be complete or correct. Reinforce any approximation; begin shaping the imitation.

Songs and finger plays can be taught step by step through modeling one section at a time. In a long task, it is important to maintain the children's attention on the model. Reinforce watching and listening.

Many physical or mechanical skills can be taught by peer modeling. Children can watch slightly more skilled peers climb on various apparatus before attempting to climb on it themselves. The influence of a more sophisticated peer is especially important for handicapped children, who can improve developmentally simply by being around more advanced models (Alberto & Troutman, 1982).

Problem-solving skills such as working jigsaw puzzles can be taught by modeling. For example, if the teacher states, "I usually look for the corners first," as she or he puts puzzles together, the child may later imitate that strategy.

Prompting

Prompts can assist children to display the right behavior at the right time. Prompts can be visual, tactual, or physical. When children respond appropriately to a prompt, they should be reinforced. When behavior is rewarded in the presence of selected cues, those cues become reliable prompts for the behavior. Often, teachers will use exaggerated and contrived prompts initially to trigger a behavior, then gradually alter or fade the prompt so that it becomes more natural (Box 8-3).

Box 8-2 Potty Modeling

Mikey was 2 years old but did not use the potty yet. His parents tried bribery, commanding him to use the potty, and just waiting it out. Nothing worked until one Sunday when friends came over for dinner. They brought Johnny *and* his potty, which he recently had learned to use. They put his potty next to Mikey's. When Johnny used his potty, Mikey ran over to his own potty and used it with no prompting or fuss. Peer modeling can be a powerful teaching tool.

We provide some examples of the different kinds of prompts useful with preschoolers. General guidelines for their use are included.

Visual Prompts   *Visual prompts* are stimuli that help children to respond correctly. They can be pictorial (photos, cartoons, diagrams) and involve color or color-coding (Goetz, 1982), or can be other nonverbal cues such as hand signals or facial expressions.

Most teachers are familiar with the procedure of presenting a picture of an object next to a corresponding word to be learned. A drawing of a house next to the printed word "house" will prompt the child to say "house" when the printed word itself does not yet have the prompting capability. Ideally, the pictorial prompt should be faded so that the printed word itself will independently prompt the correct verbal response. When children have difficulty in recognizing their names on the bulletin board or locker, their photos can be initially paired with their names.

Draw children's attention to a particular part of a word by writing the letters in bolder print such that the letters stand out. Prompt children to put their clothes away into particular drawers by having pictures of the correct clothing on the outside of the drawer; to walk to the cafeteria by placing feet outlines that direct them there; to complete a puzzle by having the pieces outlined in the frame. Figures 8-1 through 8-4 are examples of visual prompts.

Auditory Prompts   Verbal instructions are the most common form of verbal prompting, but any spoken or sounded signal can function as an *auditory prompt*. As adults, we learn to behave in certain ways when presented with even subtle auditory prompts. The lecturer clears his or her throat

---

Box 8-3   *Guidelines for the Use of Prompts*

1. Prompt only when necessary. Overprompting is a waste of teacher effort and restricts the child's independence.

2. Choose prompts that are easily faded if they are highly contrived. Placing a piece of colored tape on the left boot and the left pant leg is a prompt that can be faded by making the tape smaller and smaller. Having the whole left boot be a different color would make fading more difficult.

3. Fade prompts by making them progressively smaller, presenting them less frequently, or gradually blending them into context.

4. Choose a prompt that focuses on the significant aspect of the task that is critical for proper discrimination (criterion-related prompting).

5. Deliver prompts in a way that minimizes teacher intrusiveness. The *signal* should be the prompt, rather than teacher presence. Try to present prompts from the child's perspective rather than from your own.

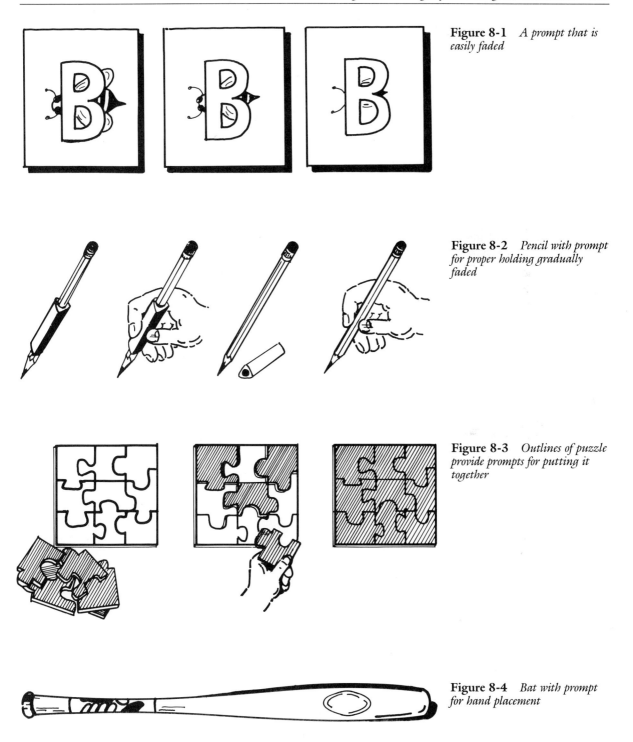

Figure 8-1   *A prompt that is easily faded*

Figure 8-2   *Pencil with prompt for proper holding gradually faded*

Figure 8-3   *Outlines of puzzle provide prompts for putting it together*

Figure 8-4   *Bat with prompt for hand placement*

This boy is rapidly learning to tie his shoes because his teacher is able to provide immediate and consistent feedback and reinforcement.

to prompt our attention; the announcement "Now hear this," cues us to pay close attention to what follows; the bell of the telephone cues us to answer it.

Questioning is a special type of verbal prompt. After children have mastered skills, teachers can encourage them to use these skills merely by asking them questions. After children have learned color names, you can teach for maintenance and generalization of the use of color names by frequently questioning the child about colors. In these cases no contrived prompts are needed to assist children in answering correctly. This prompt is a stimulus to get children to practice a behavior they have already acquired.

To prompt neat pouring of juice into a cup, say "Hold the pitcher steady with your other hand." To help children brush teeth correctly, say "Up and down." Play recorded music every day to signal clean-up time or playground time. Reinforce compliance. Tap on the table or a bell to signal story time. Some teachers find it most useful to establish prompts for both management and instructional activities. The use of such prompts relieves the teacher of always having to use spoken commands or announcements. Prompt children to follow directions by emphasizing critical words.

Physical Prompts   Manual or *physical prompts* involve touching or physically guiding children to assist them to perform some motor behavior. Teaching a child to turn book pages, cut with scissors, walk up steps, or brush teeth are occasions that frequently require manual prompting. In using manual prompting, it is usually best to prompt only the necessary parts of a behavior sequence. If the child needs help in cutting around corners with scissors, it would be a mistake to physically prompt other parts of the cutting activity. Do manual prompting from behind the child so that he or she is looking at the task and not at you.

To prompt letter and word writing, use a stencil cut-out. To prompt children to make the "m" sound, press the child's lips together. Guide a child's face and hand washing by holding the child's hand and taking the hand through the proper motions. Teach a child to count objects one at a time by requiring the child to touch each object as she or he counts.

Criterion-Related Prompts   *Criterion-related prompting* (Goetz, 1982) deserves special mention. It is frequently helpful to point out aspects of a stimulus that will help the child recognize or discriminate correctly. Freddie has trouble discriminating "ship" from "shop." One solution is to color-code the "i" in ship, so that Freddie will discriminate the words correctly. But this prompt cannot be easily faded or altered to become the final criterion. A better procedure might be to point out how the "i" in "ship" is like a smoke stack; the "i" might even be drawn to look like a small smoke stack and then gradually converted to just the letter "i." This procedure permits meaningful prompting that lends itself to naturalization.

Shaping

Successive approximation or *shaping* is useful in teaching entirely new behaviors or behaviors that ought to operate at a certain frequency or intensity. If a child can already button, the teacher might shape independent buttoning by first requiring the child to button the bottom button, then bottom two, then three, and so on. In teaching children to eat balanced meals, teachers can initially require that children taste each food, then eat two bites of each, and so on.

The main mission of shaping is to reinforce any improvements in a behavior. Sometimes very small steps must be rewarded, and then reward withheld until improvement occurs. A *shifting criterion* for reinforcement is used so that what once earned reward no longer does, but just a little better does (Alberto & Troutman, 1982). Teachers cannot always predetermine when reinforcement should be delivered, but must watch closely and deliver reward appropriately. This is a "clinical" or technical skill that takes practice.

If you want a student to participate in an activity for the full 15 minutes, set up a graduated sequence of 3 minutes, 5 minutes, 8 minutes, 10 minutes, and then finally 15 minutes. To help the student say, "More juice, please," try "Juice," "Juice, please," "More juice, please." If you want children to brush their teeth on their own, give children a toothbrush with toothpaste already on it and help them brush bottom teeth; then give toothbrush with toothpaste, but have them brush all teeth on their own; and finally have them put toothpaste on toothbrush and brush teeth without your assistance. To help a child sequence a story that uses four pictures, have the child sequence a two-picture story, then a three-picture story, and finally a four-picture story.

Chaining

The *chaining* technique is useful for teaching sequenced tasks, such as table-setting procedures or handwriting. Behavior chains can be taught either backwards or forwards. Many people advocate using backward chaining with nonverbal children or ones who have severe learning problems (Alberto & Troutman, 1982). More verbal children can be taught sequences using forward chaining accompanied by verbal directions. The table-setting objective that was previously task analyzed could be taught through chaining. In backward chaining, the instructor would do all steps up to spoon placement, which the child would do. Next the instructor would perform all except the last two steps, and so on. In teaching this same task using forward chaining, the instructor would request that the child place the plate, then the instructor would complete the task or continue to prompt the child to complete each subsequent step in the task.

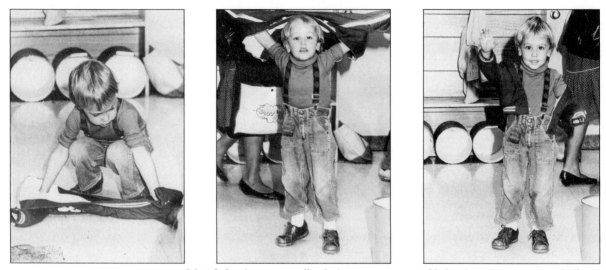

Most behaviors are really chains or sequences of behaviors. Putting on a jacket is analyzed into three steps to make learning easy for this 2-year-old.

Most behavior is part of a chain or sequence. When children learn to do anything in order, they are learning a chain. Putting on a sweater, using the toilet, washing hands, and putting away toys are typical sequences taught in the preschool. When a chain is analyzed into its components, each part can be taught and practiced separately and then integrated into a smooth flow. Table 8-1 summarizes the relationship of learner characteristics to teaching strategies.

Behavior Rehearsal

Children can practice a behavior under contrived conditions (Malott, Tillema, & Glenn, 1978). During this *behavior rehearsal*, teachers have an opportunity to reinforce appropriate behaviors and to provide necessary prompts. As children become skilled at behaviors in contrived rehearsal, they are encouraged to practice the behavior in real-life settings.

Role-playing is a special type of behavior rehearsal. Roles can be interchanged and the role-play used as a stimulus situation for discussions or for practicing appropriate behaviors.

Teach proper responses to traffic signals by using a traffic light for behavior rehearsal in the classroom. Teach appropriate telephone answering by using a toy telephone in the classroom. Teach children to hold hands during field trips by having "pretend" field trips around the classroom. Teach children to substitute an appropriate behavior for an inappropriate

Table 8-1 Relationship of Learner Characteristics and Teaching Strategies

	Prompting	*Modeling*	*Shaping*	*Chaining*	*Discrimination Training*
Task Characteristics	Tasks for which shaping alone would be too time consuming; e.g., handwriting Tasks in which it is important to start, stop, and change behaviors to certain signals	Tasks in which unique performances are not required Behaviors for which the natural environment provides many models; e.g., speaking, social customs	Tasks involving honing of skills; e.g., aiming at targets, learning speech Tasks involving fine motor coordination; e.g., drawing	Tasks involving several steps; e.g., a complicated art activity Sequences of behaviors that must be performed quickly and in precise sequences; e.g., reciting phone number	Tasks involving attaching labels to concepts; e.g., color names, numbers Tasks in which two or more stimuli are so similar as to result in confusion; e.g., differentiating among similar plants
Learner Characteristics	Learners who do not readily attempt new behaviors Learners who have difficulty focusing on critical stimuli Learners who may have problems in attention	Learners who have acquired generalized imitative skills Learners who enjoy identifying with others—peers, television personalities, etc. Learners who have good attention and observation skills	Learners who lack imitative behaviors Learners who are resistant to acquiring the behavior; e.g., a child who does not want to go to school Learners who are dependent on immediate reinforcement	Learners who are not able to imitate sequences Learners who cannot follow sequenced verbal directions	Learners who currently confuse two stimuli; e.g., red and purple Learners who often overgeneralize; e.g., who call all teachers by the same name

one by role-playing first being angry and then going to a quiet corner to look at a book.

Use Several Strategies

Attempt some balance in your use of the strategies described. Remember that children are not only learning curricular content but are also acquiring strategies for learning. You would not want to teach all tasks through modeling, or children might not learn to learn in other ways. For example, such children may wait to hear another person's responses before answering questions. If teachers are versatile in instructional methods, their students will be more flexible in learning.

GIVING CORRECTIVE FEEDBACK

Even though you have done a thorough task analysis and chosen an appropriate strategy for teaching an objective, children may make mistakes in performance. At these times the teacher must provide corrective feedback, to let the child know that the behavior is incorrect and to teach the correct behavior. Follow these guidelines in giving corrective feedback:

1. Do not punish the incorrect response when the child is honestly attempting to respond correctly.
2. If possible, stop the incorrect response as soon as it begins. There is no benefit in having the child practice an incorrect behavior. Sometimes inadvertent reinforcement occurs and strengthens incorrect behavior.
3. After stopping the response, model the correct behavior and emphasize prompts if necessary.
4. Lead the child through the correct behavior, reinforcing it until the response is acquired.
5. Go back to the beginning of the task and repeat. This will strengthen the correct chain of events.
6. Reinforce upon completion of the task.

Using these guidelines you could correct children who do not hang up their coats in this way:

1. Stop children who begin to throw down their coats.
2. Say, "In this room we hang up our coats like this" and show the child how to hang up the coat.
3. Ask children to hang up their coats a few times until you are sure they can do it.
4. Ask children to put their coats on, go back out of the room, come inside, and hang up their coats. (Require going through the whole chain of behavior; otherwise your prompt may become a necessary link in it.)
5. Reinforce after the coats are hung up.

USING APPROPRIATE REINFORCEMENT

Reinforcement techniques can be contrived or natural; we can now separate the latter into task-imbedded and intrinsic reinforcers. In planning lessons you should choose the reinforcement techniques that are most appropriate for individual children and their skills in specific tasks. Behaviors, not children, have different levels of optimal reinforcement. A given child might typically operate best with "self" or "intrinsic" reinforcement but might still require highly contrived reinforcement to establish certain behaviors. We will examine the three reinforcement categories.

Contrived Reinforcers

Some reinforcers are not typically related to a behavior and are not an integral part of the task. Examples of *contrived reinforcers* are tokens, primary reinforcers (food), *premacked* (low-then-high preference) activities, and unusually high rates of social reinforcement. These kinds of reinforcers frequently are needed for difficult tasks or for children who are experiencing unusual difficulty in learning. Contrived reinforcers, however, should be used only when necessary and for as brief a time as necessary, so that the child will not be made dependent on reinforcers that are not normally available.

One interesting type of contrived reinforcer is one that combines a generalization prompt with the reinforcement. An example of this is pinning a zebra's picture to a child who has learned to say "zebra." The picture is a reinforcer, but it also prompts others to ask the child, "What's that?" This gives the child many additional opportunities to practice the word and thus generalize the skill.

Task-Imbedded Reinforcers

Task-imbedded reinforcers occur naturally as a consequence of children's participation in a task (Robinson, C. C., & Robinson, J. H., 1983; Snell, 1983). Some tasks are reinforcing for certain children. Many children love to use the vacuum cleaner; vacuuming their bedroom rug would be reinforcing in itself. This task requires no arranged reinforcer.

In other cases, teachers can build reinforcement into the task. Tasks can be made reinforcing when the teacher uses high-interest content. The meaning of the labels "loud" and "soft" can be taught in the context of a zoo. Children can pretend to be loud- and soft-spoken lions, bears, or birds. Tasks can be made reinforcing because of the manner of their presentation. Some days the teacher can dress up like an old "granny" to read stories; reading sounds can "appear" on the flannel board when children say magic words; pictures for labeling can be hidden around the room. Naturally occurring social reinforcers are also task-imbedded reinforcers; the task itself brings about the reinforcement.

Intrinsic Reinforcers

The highest level reinforcers are *intrinsic reinforcers* (Box 8-4). They are the typical self-reinforcers, such as being happy to do something independently, being pleased at the completion of a long or difficult task, enjoying certain task areas (for example, arithmetic), or enjoying challenging tasks.

Teachers can plan to move children to this level of reinforcement. They can put task-imbedded reinforcers on progressively longer intermittent schedules. They can pair social or other reinforcers with performance-related statements such as, "You completed a really difficult puzzle." Gradually these statements can be replaced by asking the child to comment on the difficulty of the task and with statements such as, "Aren't you proud of yourself?" Teacher attention can be faded gradually so that the teacher only occasionally approaches the child who is learning and makes statements such as, "I bet you like writing the letters," or "You sure are a hard worker."

TEACHING FOR GENERALIZATION AND MAINTENANCE

"Thus, it is not the learner who is dull, learning disabled, concretized, or immature, because all learners are alike in this: no one learns a generalized lesson *unless a generalized lesson is taught*" (Baer, 1981, p. 1–2). For a long time, educators operated on the notion that a well-taught skill would stay with the child, and would automatically be exhibited under diverse, appropriate circumstances.

It seems that many teachers simply train and hope (Stokes & Baer, 1977); that is, they teach a skill thoroughly and hope that it will spread to appropriate other settings. When children do not exhibit the desired generalization, these teachers use further drill or admonishments to try to promote generalization.

But what can be said of Matthew who is polite and skillful while eating at the nursery school but becomes obnoxious in restaurants (no generalization across settings)? Or Kim who seems to articulate well with her speech therapist but with no one else (no generalization across persons)? Or John who learns to tie his shoes on Tuesday but cannot do it on Thursday (no generalization across time)? And what about the three children who did

---

Box 8-4　*Is Positive Reinforcement Really Bribery?*

Offering a reward for illegal, unethical, or otherwise inappropriate acts *is* bribery. In contrast, giving rewards for personally or socially important accomplishments is not. Reward after a behavior strengthens that behavior; it may indeed be unethical *not* to provide reward immediately after any sign of developmental progress.

Of course, the type of reward must be modified as the behavior progresses. Behaviorists suggest using the highest-level reinforcers that are effective at the time. Reinforcers are ranked from most primitive or basic (primary) to most advanced or abstract (secondary) as follows:

1. Food, drink, touch
2. Tangibles (toys, desired objects)
3. Tokens (money, stars)
4. Social approval
5. Task-imbedded
6. Intrinsic (self-approval)

not seem to learn what the other six youngsters did about picking up litter (no generalization across children)? These are all *instructional* problems. To "teach" means to establish a skill not only for the *here and now*, but also for the *there and then*.

Behaviorists are not amazed that learning often is tied to specific circumstances. Much learning is under stimulus control; that is, behavior is controlled by the circumstances prevailing during training and reinforcement. Something must be done to transfer learning beyond the constraints of the training situation (Miller, L. K., 1980). Strategies can be implemented to encourage the use of skills across *situations* (school, home), *people* (teacher, parent, most adults), and *time* (today, next week).

Guidelines for Promoting Generalization

There are a number of tactics for enhancing generalization (Stokes & Baer, 1977); basic approaches of practical use in the preschool are presented here.

Teach in the Child's Context   Instruction done within the child's own settings minimizes generalization problems. The social and physical stimuli encountered in the actual situation often are hard to duplicate; it often makes more sense to do the teaching in situations where we want the behavioral skills to be practiced. Teaching children how to wait for a bus, how to go to the corner store, how to wait in line at a fast-food restaurant, and what to say when lost on the street or in a store, are all examples where the real situation may be the optimal training situation. Field trips and use of the neighborhood as an instructional setting are good ways to maximize generalization.

Simulate the Child's Context   Often it is not feasible to do training in the child's context. Considerations such as instructional time, safety, or other factors may rule out on-site training. Instead, many teachers try to approximate the real setting by bringing stimuli from the child's context into the classroom. Bus riding can be taught in the classroom with a simulated bus stop, complete with a bench, bus stop sign, and other people waiting. A simulated store can be arranged where the children must wait in line, make requests, and pay for items. Placing a sofa, lamp, and rug in the corner of the preschool where children can practice reading is yet another instance of simulating the "target context" so that skills are not so situation-specific.

Design simulations to capture much of the variety inherent in the real situation, and thus prepare the child to exhibit new skills appropriately.

Include Aspects of the Training Setting in the Child's Context   Sometimes certain features of the preschool instructional situation can be intro-

When children read books in a school environment similar to that at home, they are more likely to transfer the behavior to the home setting.

duced into the child's other settings. Having a little school desk at home may help transfer in-school behavior to the home. High-interest books, games, toys, and other materials found in the preschool can be taken home for continued practice and can help transfer training to the home situation.

Normalize the Training Procedure   Contrived prompts and reinforcers are sometimes called for to establish a skill. With some children, much urging (prompting), simplification of what is to be learned (task analysis), and encouragement (high rates of contrived and social reinforcement) are needed. We wish to maximize the chances that a skill will survive and flourish in situations beyond the preschool. Therefore, we must gradually alter the training contingencies so that they match normal contingencies. That is, training and reinforcements must be changed to approach normal conditions.

Use a Full Range of Examples   If a collie is repeatedly used as an example of a dog, many children may fail to identify other breeds as "dogs." To teach for generalization, examples of various breeds should be used, thus expanding the category. For a behaviorist, concept teaching does not involve manipulation of cognitive events or mental reorganization. Teaching a concept refers to prompting and reinforcing the same response (in this case "dog") to a *class* of stimuli (dogs differing in specifics but sharing common properties). By varying the illustrations used, you encourage effective generalization across specific instances (abstractions or inductions).

Here are some final suggestions to assist you in arranging for generalization of newly learned skills:

1. Play games that require children to *practice* skills they have already learned. The game format provides a task-imbedded reinforcer as well as a different situation in which to practice the skills. The more a behavior can be practiced in appropriate different settings, the less situation-specific the behavior will be.

2. Place *cues* on the child or in the room that will prompt others to reinforce or request the newly acquired behavior.

3. Give the child a *prompt* that will help her or him remember to practice the behavior. For example, make a red wristband that says "right" to remind the child to practice left–right discrimination.

4. *Vary the reinforcement* so that the child can reinforce him- or herself for the behavior, even in other situations. The child can place an X on a card when she or he puts away toys.

5. *Alternate reinforcement* so that the behavior is not dependent on constant reinforcement.

6. *Vary the conditions* (prompts, teachers, areas) during training so that the behavior is not under specific stimulus control.

SUMMARY

The behaviorist early educator is an engineer who specifies the target (instructional objective) and then manipulates antecedents and consequences until the target behavior is established, generalized, and maintained. Several strategies and guidelines are available to accomplish this. Consistent use of behavior modification strategies can contribute to a highly effective program for early childhood development.

Fundamental strategies for early educators include task analysis, modeling, prompting, shaping, chaining, and behavior rehearsal. Behavioral teachers are careful to use reinforcement techniques that are matched to the task demands and that are developmentally appropriate. Contrived, task-imbedded, and intrinsic reinforcers might all be employed with the same child, depending on task difficulty. Teaching programs include not only initial learning, but generalization (transfer) and maintenance (recall).

To promote child competence beyond the usual educational settings, teachers can use the child's own house and neighborhood, simulate natural circumstances, establish prompts that can be placed within the child's setting, progressively use more typically occurring prompts and reinforcers, and provide a wide range of illustrations and exercises to make learning more comprehensive.

Review Questions

1. State the four categories of skills that teachers should identify when analyzing tasks.
2. Name and give examples of the six strategies given for teaching tasks. Write a specific program for teaching six tasks, using each of these strategies once.
3. State the guidelines for giving corrective feedback. Give an example of the steps you would take to correct an inappropriate response.
4. Describe contrived, task-imbedded, and intrinsic reinforcers. Assuming that you are teaching a child to write his or her name, tell how you could use contrived, task-imbedded, and intrinsic reinforcers as the child learns and then becomes competent at the task.
5. List at least four techniques for teaching for generalization. Give five ways you could help generalize this behavior: finding circles and triangles in the environment.

Suggested Activities

1. Try to model a relatively complex behavior (for example, putting toothpaste on a toothbrush) for a 3-year-old child. Note how it may be important to demonstrate the behavior slowly and from the child's perspective.
2. Teach a young child to draw an animal. Use visual and manual prompts and contrived and imbedded reinforcers. Take note of any difficulties and attempt to refine your procedures.
3. Identify a troublesome behavior of a preschooler and design a program to change the behavior. After observation, determine antecedents and consequences that may be responsible and change these. Specify the behavior principles or procedures involved.
4. Show a youngster how to discriminate a left from a right shoe by placing a colored piece of tape on the left shoe and left pant leg or sock. After each successful trial, reduce the size of the pieces of tape. Eventually, you should be able to eliminate the tape and the child will continue to correctly discriminate right and left shoes.
5. Help a teacher or parent to design ways to generalize a newly learned behavior. Use at least three of the five ways discussed in this chapter.

Suggested Readings

Baer, D. M. *How to plan for generalization*. Lawrence, Kans.: H & H Enterprises, 1984.

Bagnato, S. J., and Neisworth, J. T. *Linking developmental assessment and curricula*. Rockville, Md.: Aspen Systems, 1981.

Fallen, N. H., and Umansky, W. *Young children with special needs*, 2nd ed. Columbus, Oh.: Charles E. Merrill, 1985.

Hall, R. V., and Hall, M. C. *How to select reinforcers*. Lawrence, Kans.: H & H Enterprises, 1980.

Kazdin, A., and Esveldt-Dawson, K. *How to maintain behavior*. Lawrence, Kans.: H & H Enterprises, 1981.

Lerner, J., Mardell-Czudnowski, C., and Goldenberg, D. *Special education for the early childhood years*. Englewood Cliffs, N.J.: Prentice-Hall, 1981.

Neisworth, J. T., Willoughby-Herb, S. J., Bagnato, S. J., Cartwright, C. A., and Laub, K. W. *Individualized education for preschool exceptional children*. Rockville, Md.: Aspen Systems, 1980.

Striefel, S. *How to teach through modeling and imitation*. Lawrence, Kans.: H & H Enterprises, 1981.

Willoughby-Herb, S. J., and Neisworth, J. T. Strategies for promoting accomplishment of the HICOMP developmental activities. In Willoughby-Herb, S. J., and Neisworth, J. T. (Eds.), *HICOMP preschool curriculum* (pp. 5–19). Columbus, Oh.: Charles E. Merrill, 1983.

Willoughby-Herb, S. J., and Neisworth, J. T. Using consequences to build skill. In Willoughby-Herb, S. J., and Neisworth, J. T. (Eds.), *HICOMP preschool curriculum*. Columbus, Oh.: Charles E. Merrill, 1983.

Chapter 9

Designing the Learning Environment

*M*any people view behavior modification as something that someone does to someone else. This is indeed the case when, for example, the teacher prompts and reinforces selected child behavior. But personal behaviors and social interactions do not operate in a vacuum. Adults as well as children are influenced by the physical settings in which they behave.

This chapter considers some relatively stable aspects of child space, such as lighting, sound, temperature, and color. We focus on the factors that can be readily manipulated by the teacher, such as room layout and the design of activity areas. Especially pertinent is the use of behavior principles for organizing the environment to help maximize three major goals: safety, learning, and teaching.

For a long time, early childhood educators have emphasized the need for a special child-tailored environment (Marion, 1981). That is, regardless of theoretical orientation, there are certain considerations common to any child-care space. Child-sized furnishings, safety arrangements, and sanitation facilities must be provided in any program. Furnishings and arrangements, however, can reflect the theoretical position of the teacher. The placement and accessibility of learning materials, grouping of children, availability of reinforcers, prompts for learning, and places for progress recording are considerations dictated to some extent by the teacher's approach to early childhood education. We shall first turn our attention to keeping the educational environment as safe as possible. High standards in this regard are dictated more by our immediate and practical concerns for the child than by theory. As you proceed through the chapter, however, you will see how tactics for maximizing learning and teaching are strongly influenced by theory.

MAXIMIZING SAFETY, COMFORT, AND CONVENIENCE

Preschool teachers (operant and otherwise) are typically aware of common safety considerations for classrooms and equipment. They look for equip-

Comfort, safety, and convenience make play equipment inviting!

ment with rounded edges, nontoxic paints, and so on. However, as more preschools integrate handicapped and nonhandicapped children, teachers must become even more cautious as they select and arrange the environment. Children should always be within the teacher's range of vision. This is especially important for children with locomotor or speech problems who cannot call or go to the teacher for assistance. Walking areas must be cleared and wide enough for children with locomotor problems, especially those who use devices such as walkers or wheelchairs. When developmentally delayed children are placed in preschools, teachers must be careful about choosing which materials are easily available. Sharp or tiny objects are potential hazards for some children. All equipment and activities must be evaluated for safety based on information about individual children's developmental skills. Safety must come first, even if learning opportunities are thereby reduced.

Comfort and convenience for both children and teachers comprise a number of considerations. Aside from furnishing adequate illumination, lighting can help to "tilt" activities in the educational setting. Brighter illumination in the reading or other preacademic areas can facilitate these activities; softer levels may be concordant with other activities. Tasks requiring concentration should have low noise levels and be adjacent to other quiet activities. Sound from other activities can either directly jam intended communication or indirectly distract attention if it is of high interest.

Avoid extremes of room temperature. Generally, more aggressive behavior can be expected under oppressively hot conditions (Baron & Lawton, 1972; Griffitt & Veitch, 1971). Teachers as well as children can become cranky, less cooperative, and listless. Cooler temperatures, somewhere between 65° and 70° F, seem better for concentration and learning.

Use common sense in selecting colors in the classroom. Cheerful colors are better than drab and dreary colors in settings where child alertness is desired. Intense colors should be avoided unless used to focus attention. Colors can be employed to designate specific activity areas and to color-code placement of materials.

Practices That Maximize Safety

The following guidelines are practical suggestions that come from both common sense and behavioral theory. You need not follow all these guidelines, but adherence to the intent of these suggestions will help you to develop an effective preschool environment.

1. To improve visual accessibility, tall bookshelves and other obstructions can be moved to the walls, and low (2 to 3 ft) moveable structures (pegboards) can be used to divide activity areas. Such room dividers do not

block the view between teachers and children yet are high enough to prevent distraction from tasks.

2. To keep walkways clear and wide enough, use masking tape strips to outline them. Instruct children to keep these areas clear while they play. This is an example of using a contrived prompt to facilitate appropriate behavior.

3. Where funds are available, carpeted and noncarpeted areas can also be used to define play areas versus walkways. Use colors, lighting, or other means to provide contrast in the environment and help children to discriminate one area from another. Additionally, sharply defined areas provide distinctive settings for different activities.

4. Materials that could be dangerous for less mature children can be kept in specially color-coded containers. Yellow containers, for example, could be used to denote *use with caution*. Scissors and other sharp or small objects could be kept in closed yellow containers. Children can be required to ask to use any object in a yellow container. A quick glance will show a teacher whether yellow containers are in use in an area in which children are playing freely.

MAXIMIZING LEARNING

Facilities and Arrangements

Room furnishings and arrangements can enhance or discourage learning activities (Bailey & Wolery, 1984; Marion, 1981; Rogers-Warren, 1982; Titus, 1975). Although story time can take place almost anywhere, it is more likely to be successful where comfortable seating (or carpeting) and teacher–child eye contact are available. Sometimes, fixed features of the situation define the roles of people in that situation. The stage, podium or lectern, fixed seating, cafeteria counter, and basketball hoop all invite certain behaviors and discourage others. A room with many manipulable items, dials to turn, and keyboards to press is not one where children should be expected to be still and keep their hands to themselves. Certain seating arrangements are more conducive to conversation and active participation. Cooperation among preschoolers can be enhanced when arrangements requiring two-children operation (for example, a seesaw) are present (Titus, 1975). Seating arrangements can have an effect on social behavior in the preschool. Using one large area rug, as opposed to individual mats, has been found to decrease attending and increase disruptive activity (Krantz & Risley, 1977). Toys and materials for child use can be stored on open shelves, rather than in toy boxes or bins; this seems to increase the time children spend using these items (Montes & Risley, 1975).

Principles for Room Design

You can see that many aspects of the classroom physical setting help or hinder educational objectives. To provide some order, we can turn to the two fundamental behavior principles of *stimulus control* and *reinforcement*. As used here, *stimulus control* refers to the use of physical *prompts* for a particular behavior or activity. For example, a study area should include items such as a desk and books, which serve as cues for study behavior. Such an area should not include a television or bed; these objects are cues for other behaviors. Stimulus control can be implemented in a preschool room by dividing the room into various learning areas. Examples of these areas might include math, science, graphics, and reading rooms, bathroom, group area, and individual learning booths. The math area might be decorated with numbers and seriated objects, which serve as prompts for counting and other math activities. A group room would include a free play area for noisy activities, such as playing cars, running, and jumping. Color-coding further facilitates stimulus control. Remember that a stimulus becomes a prompt for behavior when behavior is reinforced in the presence of the prompt—and not in its absence. The behavioral teacher, then, must be alert to reward the right behavior in the right place.

Areas should be highly discriminable from each other (Rogers-Warren, 1982). Learning materials and activities ought to be readily available to children. The environment should provide opportunities for independent as well as other-directed learning. Because of the significance of transfer and maintenance as well as the acquisition of learning, the environment should provide many and varied opportunities for children to practice skills they are learning. Finally, if the preschool itself is to be a positive stimulus, it should be arranged and furnished so that it prompts specific and general behavior that is developmentally constructive (Glass, Christiansen, & Christiansen, 1982).

Besides prompting, the environment also reinforces, or acts as a consequence to, children's learning. A boring, sterile classroom will not reinforce active involvement. Keep the environment full of invitations to learn. The preschool must be a land of opportunity. Materials can be chosen or altered so that children receive immediate feedback for their involvement. The teacher's availability can be structured into areas and activities in which children need more immediate reinforcement for appropriate behaviors. Reinforcers can be built into activity areas and materials (Snell, 1983).

The layout of the room should facilitate the use of contingency management through the Premack principle (Premack, 1965). Separate learning areas permit flexible sequencing for child activities. Children might be permitted to move from a less- to a more-preferred area after completing some work in the first area. Use of the Premack principle in this fashion can result in highly effective behavior sequences. If Joy does not like to go to the reading area, she can be encouraged to attend by allowing her to go to a desirable area following completion of her assigned reading activity. To use contingency management, you must know reinforcers for each child. These will include a wide variety of activities and items desirable to young children, such as snacks, painting, games, and toys. Another activity area, such as the math room, might be a high-preference activity for a child and also could be used for contracting. Joy may visit the math room (high-preference area) *after* spending some time in the reading room (low-preference area). In brief, children can be encouraged to engage in low-preference learning activities by the use of contingency management (Hall & Hall, 1982) (Box 9-1).

Maximize Learning Through Prompting

Because behavior is triggered by environmental circumstances, the behaviorist teacher gives much consideration to the display of materials and use of signals for appropriate behavior (Alberto & Troutman, 1982; Allen & Goetz, 1982). The following suggestions focus on the use of cues for prompting learning.

Have some materials placed out on tables and in various activity areas each morning to prompt children to interact in those areas. Like the good shopkeeper, you must attract customers.

Arrange materials neatly and in an interesting manner so that they are readily in sight and stand out as visual prompts. Do not overcrowd shelves used by children. Keep additional materials in storage areas and periodically exchange these for materials already placed out in the room. Instructional materials can be displayed to attract involvement, the way display windows in stores attract customers.

Plan the arrangement of learning centers within the classroom so that activities in adjacent areas do not interfere with each other. Do not place

---

Box 9-1   Children's Territoriality

Many children become attached to specific locations within the preschool. They may even personalize these areas and treat them as their own. Peers tend to recognize and accept a given child's space as long as it is consistent with that child's status in the group.

When "territoriality" occurs, these tips may be useful:

1. Make sure the preschool includes special spaces for children to go when needed.

2. Do not permit aggressive or other antisocial behavior to succeed in dominating prime locations.

3. Avoid letting children withdraw for too long—arrange conditions for more active involvement.

4. Consider allowing children to claim or share spaces contingent on progress (Titus, 1978).

It's a good idea to place some materials out on tables to attract customers!

the reading room next to the piano. The library area would be more compatibly placed near a quiet game area.

Choose furniture and storage spaces that are child-sized so that children can select materials and activities independently and also can return them to their places. Store equipment on shallow shelves; it is difficult for young children to see or reach far behind other objects. Child-sized equipment prompts children to be autonomous rather than dependent.

Put up posters or photographs in a learning area that depict children engaging in appropriate activities. For example, near the blocks post pictures showing children using the blocks in an appropriate activity. Posters can be used, like advertisements, to prompt intended behavior.

To assist children in the transfer of behaviors to environments other than the preschool, you might arrange some areas in the room to resemble other settings. One corner might be furnished like a living room; another could be furnished like a regular schoolroom. Children can be encouraged to learn and practice behaviors that are especially appropriate in these settings. Group lessons, where sitting in seats and raising hands are emphasized, can be taught in the schoolroom setting. Social and conversational skills can be taught in the living room setting. Teaching children to look at books in a simulated living room setting will enhance the chances that they will use books in their own living rooms.

Certain standard visual and auditory prompts can be used throughout the various learning centers to maximize their effectiveness. For example, use a color sequence: green (start), yellow (proceed with the task), and red (stop). These color prompts can be used in a fine motor area with writing materials. Children learn that in tracing letters they start on the green dots, continue on the yellow, and stop on the red. These same color prompts can be used in the practical skills area in which materials to be used for shoe polishing are placed in green, yellow, and red boxes. The students reach first into the green box for the polish and application cloth; then reach into the yellow box for the wiping cloth; then into the red box for the buffing cloth. In the motor area, obstacle courses could be similarly color-coded to direct children through the course. The use of such standard prompts increases the children's independence and accuracy in completing many activities.

Learning centers themselves prompt children to engage in certain behaviors. Young children often are very creative in their use of materials and at times may have notions quite different from the teacher's plans for use of materials. For example, a teacher might put out pencils and papers that have dotted alphabet letters for tracing. A child, however, might make a paper airplane. If you have selected printing as an objective, you would be wise to have special cues to communicate the purpose of your materials. Have one small table that is used just for learning to write letters, numbers, shapes, or names. If children begin to do other activities there, take them to another area. The children can be further cued if you use a special kind or color of paper and pencil for writing. Other kinds of prompts can also be built into learning centers. Children's work can be posted there. Pictures of appropriate activities can be posted and arrows can be used to point out important materials.

When many aspects of the classroom environment remain constant, children learn to recall rules, locations, sequences, and so on. For example, children can more easily learn to put equipment and materials away if these things have regular, well-designed storage spaces. Pictures, labels, outlines, or words help children learn where objects belong.

Keep the classroom arrangement uncluttered and serene enough that when new equipment or activities are introduced, children will quickly be aware of them. Promote incidental learning and curiosity.

Changing the room arrangements can help children to learn to accommodate to new settings—a particularly useful strategy when preparing children for transition to kindergarten or first grade (Fowler, 1982). Especially near the end of the school year, begin to rearrange areas and routines. If you know in what setting the child will be placed, simulate the arrangement and thus reduce its unfamiliarity to the child.

Maximize Learning Through Reinforcement

To enhance the reinforcement value of school areas and activities that are not already attractive, pair them with prompts and reinforcers that are attractive.

During initial parent–teacher meetings, ask about the children's favorite toys and activities. Parents often volunteer to lend some of these toys to the classroom, or you might reserve a small sum from your budget to buy a few of these toys. For example, the presence of Sesame Street puppets in the creative dramatics area often makes such activities more reinforcing. Purchasing a favorite record or two for rhythmic activities makes the latter more reinforcing. Serving some favorite snacks for the first few days of school makes coming to the table more reinforcing. Decorating the bathroom walls with favorite television, cartoon, or book characters makes going into the bathroom more reinforcing.

Selecting materials that provide immediate feedback enables children to be reinforced for correctness without the teacher's presence. Many of the materials designed for Montessori classrooms are self-corrective (Montessori, 1965).

When self-corrective materials are not available, you can sometimes alter materials so that children can determine the correctness of their performance. A simple technique is to code the backs of any materials to be sorted, for example pictures of creatures that are to be sorted into piles of humans and nonhumans. The backs of all cards depicting humans could have an **X** on them; the backs of the others could be blank. When children are finished sorting according to the pictures, they can then turn them over to check correctness themselves.

Children's behavior can be reinforced by *humor*, especially of the silly, slapstick type. Teachers can occasionally put humorous posters on walls of learning centers to reinforce looking at the posters. (If you use posters to prompt certain behaviors, you would want to reinforce the behavior of looking at the posters.) In the music area, for example, you could hang a poster that shows one of the children riding round and round on the record player (and hope that the children will laugh rather than try to take a ride). Finding items in unusual places also is humorous to many children. Finding the teacher's shoes in the play stove would reinforce children for playing in the learning-center kitchen.

Finally, *social reinforcement* is powerful for most children. The classroom should be arranged so that the teachers can readily see children as they engage in activities and can easily get to them to deliver reinforcement (Hall & Hall, 1980).

MAXIMIZING TEACHING

The Role of the Behavioral Teacher

One of the most significant factors in differentiating an operant-based program from other programs is the role of the teacher. This role is of particular significance in room design. The teacher within an operant model is the engineer of the environment. She or he is responsible for structuring a fa-

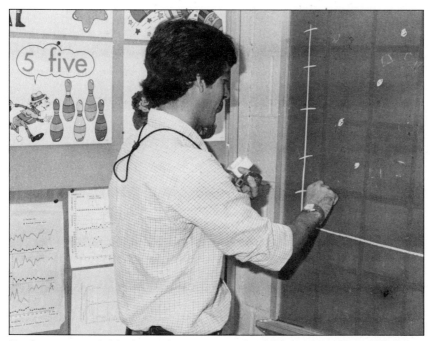

In the operant model, the teacher arranges the children's learning conditions and the contingencies of reinforcement.

vorable situation for the acquisition, maintenance, and generalization of target behaviors and for minimizing incompatible behaviors (Cooper & Holt, 1982; LeBlanc, 1982). This can be contrasted with the traditional didactic role in which the teacher is the intermediary between the student and the learning environment. In the traditional model, the teacher acts as the primary stimulus or dispenser of ideas and information. This is reflected in the layout of the room. The teacher usually is placed in the front of the room, gives instructions to groups of students, and is the source of knowledge. It is difficult to adapt this model to individual child performance levels. The teacher in the operant model, in contrast, arranges the learning conditions and contingencies of reinforcement so that children interact more directly with the learning environment. Rather than standing *between* the child and the learning environment, the behavioral teacher stands aside and orchestrates or arranges for learning (Brabner, 1970).

The classroom environment can facilitate the teacher's various roles: observer, instructor, behavior model, reinforcer, evaluator, and parent consultant. When various teacher materials are organized, labeled, and placed in convenient locations, teachers are more efficient in performing their varied roles. A behavioral preschool is, above all, organized. Teachers must have clear objectives, materials, and settings. When children and their activities are constantly within view, teachers have more opportunity to observe and to intervene for instructional purposes. When children can see the teacher, the teacher has greater opportunity to instruct through modeling of appropriate behaviors.

Maximize Opportunities to Teach

Store teaching materials (timers, counters, stopwatches, data sheets, lesson plan booklets, and curricular charts for direction during teaching) in a convenient location for use during the day. These items should be labeled and should be available only to the staff.

Teachers may need prompts for their teaching behaviors just as children may need prompts for their learning behaviors. During free activity and recess it is more difficult to teach appropriate behaviors than during more structured lessons. To remedy this, teachers might post small notes to themselves in various activity centers. Once or twice per month, discuss some appropriate targets for each child during free activity in specific learning centers (such as those for fine motor skills, creative dramatics, art). Write these targets on a card in a small notebook and place it in the appropriate learning centers. During free play or recess, refer to these notes and help direct the child's activities so that the child is continually learning. Your notes might look like Table 9-1.

Sometimes you will be interested in emphasizing certain behavior changes at all times and in all learning centers. In Table 9-1, this seems to be the case with Peter, who has social targets listed for both areas. At other times, you will want to encourage children to use newly acquired behaviors in various situations.

During lessons, prompt yourself to reinforce or ignore behaviors not part of the lesson content. At the top of each lesson plan, write two or

Table 9-1   Reminder Notes on Teaching Objectives

Arts and Crafts Area	
Children	Behaviors to Encourage
Gretchen, John	Using scissors to cut slits
Peter	Sharing materials
Edith, Carol	Working with minimal social reinforcement
Anne, Steve	Using various shapes in their drawings

Gross Motor Area	
Children	Behaviors to Encourage
Gretchen	Using variety in building structures
John	Climbing without fright
Peter	Respecting other children's structures
Joe, John, Mary	Reading words on toy traffic signs

three reminders such as reinforce Karen's smiling, or reinforce Anne's coming quickly to sit down, or keep Henry busy so that he attends; then reinforce attention.

You can often do incidental teaching by allowing students to observe some of your work behaviors (Bandura, 1977) (Box 9-2). Children can learn many important behaviors through observation—for example, patience, neatness, responsibility, persistence, child care. Teachers are among the few adults that many children have an opportunity to observe in a work role. By placing your desk or work area within the children's view, you can demonstrate behaviors such as neatness, organization, and persistence. Of course, you will not spend long periods of time at your desk during school hours. However, do some brief work there periodically. Also take care of simple first aid problems at your desk rather than in a closed-off area; demonstrate behaviors such as cleanliness, patience, and concern and sympathy for others, in addition to simple first aid procedures. Sometimes the effectiveness of observational learning is enhanced when actions are accompanied by verbalizations. When you clean a child's cut with a disinfectant, say, "Now I am cleaning the cut so it will not get infected."

Sometimes teachers can be too quick to prompt or provide reinforcement. A child may merely grunt or turn toward a desired object instead of approximating a verbal request. Reinforcement of this primitive behavior (when the child is capable of a more developmentally advanced behavior) is not desirable. Simply wait for the more advanced request, then reinforce. If necessary, supply a prompt—the most minimal prompt that might work. When Zelda wants a drink and can approximate a verbal request, do not reinforce a simple grunt or wave of the hand. If waiting for a better behavior does not work, try a minimal prompt such as, "What do you want?" If necessary, model the correct response.

Box 9-2   *Practice What You Preach*

You could not argue with Ms. Willoughby's concern for the messiness of the preschool. For whatever reason, at least seven of the twelve children were stubbornly opposed to cleaning up or keeping the room organized. This situation cried out for arranging a contingency between cleanup and some privilege. Ms. Willoughby decided to use a token economy, awarding a special token to children who did keep order. The "stubborn children," however, still did not clean up. Finally, she asked one of the messiest children, Manuel, what it would take to get him to shape up. "Clean up your own desk for a token," replied Manuel. The teacher's desk was messy, indeed. She even complained about it to the children. Ms. Willoughby took Manuel's advice seriously: she put herself on a contingency program to maintain an orderly desk. She earned a coffee break only after she received a token from a special "committee" of children who decided if her desk was acceptable. When she participated in (modeled) her own system, every child cooperated.

SUMMARY

Discriminative stimuli (prompts) are important for setting the occasion for specific activities or for making the activities more pleasant. Coding of materials, distinctive arrangements, posters, arrows, and other markings help provide the clarity and structure needed for a smooth-running program. All children can benefit from the structure typical of a behavioral preschool program.

Reinforcers, both natural and contrived, are basic to a behavioral approach. That learning itself be reinforcing is our goal as educators, but it is not always the reality we face. Whenever situations and activities are not themselves reinforcing, they can be made so with proper behavioral engi-

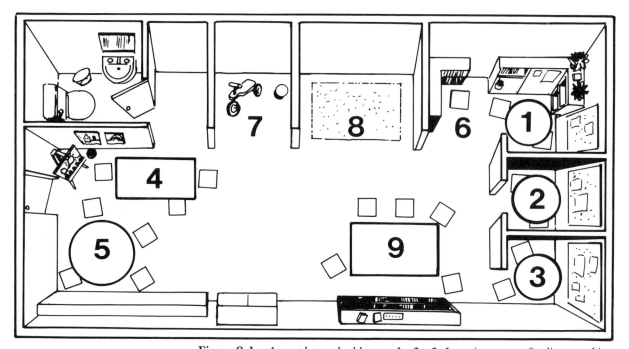

Figure 9-1   *A sample preschool layout. 1., 2., 3. Learning centers for direct teaching of new skills. One is used for teaching language and arithmetical skills, one for manipulative and fine motor skills, and the other for a variety of other skills. One-to-one and small group intensive instruction can be carried out in these areas. 4. The arts and crafts area, which is placed near the bathroom area for ease of cleanup. 5. The creative dramatics area is placed near the arts and crafts area because some materials may be useful in both areas. 6. The library area is placed near the preacademic learning centers because it is relatively quiet and activities in it will not interfere with instruction. 7. The motor area is placed where there is plenty of space and separation from quieter areas. 8. This area usually is kept clear and can be used for group activities such as parades or dances. 9. Manipulative, fine motor activities are located here.*

Figure 9-2   *A sample shelf arrangement in the manipulative skills area. 1. (puzzles) Sign containing label and stylized drawing of puzzles serves as location prompt. 2. (pegboards) Outlines of pegboards on bottom of shelf used for location prompt. 3. (varies) Curtain covers this space and the word "surprise" is placed on top. This is to prompt the children to be curious and to reinforce them for approaching the manipulative skills area. 4. (beads for stringing) These are placed in bright yellow closed containers to signal to teachers to reward children for careful use of the materials and to watch carefully so that the children do not try to eat the beads.*

neering. Pairing with known reinforcers can turn neutral or even unpleasant activities into happy ones.

Modeling is a powerful tool in the preschool. Teachers must be aware that they are "teaching" even when they do not intend to. Children will imitate the teacher, especially if he or she is a reinforcing agent.

Teachers also need some prompts. They can use notes and reminders to help them remember what behaviors are to be encouraged for each child.

Room preparation requires work and detailed consideration, but the time and energy will be well spent. A well-structured setting will permit a smoothly operating program that is a joy to children and teachers. Figures 9-1, 9-2, and 9-3 illustrate the environments discussed in this chapter.

Review Questions

1. State the three major objectives for organizing the classroom environment.
2. What are some safety considerations in designing a classroom environment that includes some handicapped children?
3. Give three examples of how classroom structure can act as a prompt for learning.
4. Give two examples of how the classroom structure can act as a reinforcer for learning.
5. For each of the three objectives you listed in your answer to (1), give two specific examples of strategies for arranging the classroom to meet those objectives.

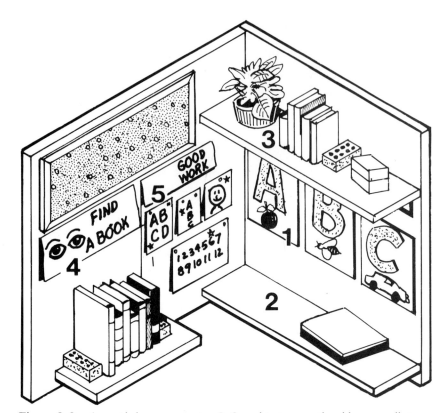

Figure 9-3   *A sample language center. 1. Sound posters are placed low on walls to prompt children to trace sandpaper letters and to make the sounds that go with the letters. 2. Low shelves for storage of language materials allow children to use and replace materials independently. 3. High shelf for storage of materials to be used by teacher. 4. This low bulletin board contains a poster directing children to find a book. The eye drawing is a prompt that can be used in other situations where children are asked to find things. 5. This low bulletin board has especially good work posted on it. Again, there is a standard prompt on the board (the smiling face and the words "good work") so that even nonreaders can understand the message.*

Suggested Activities

If you have access to a preschool classroom, try these activities:

1. Arrange materials on a table in the manipulative skills or art area. Try to lay out the materials in interesting ways (for example, try partially assembled constructions, partially painted pictures, paper arrows or footprints pointing to certain materials). Observe children to determine which of these techniques are effective in prompting them to engage in the activities. Can you draw any conclusions?

2. Arrange one shelf of materials. Be sure to include a way to prompt children to the proper location of the materials. Place materials so that children will be able to use them readily and so that they will use appropriate safety precautions.

3. Interview five children and their parents to de-

termine what events and activities are reinforcing to those children. Use this information to structure a certain area of the room (for example, the library area) so that those children will be reinforced when they approach and interact with that area. Observe the children's behaviors in that area both before and after your intervention. Can you see a difference? How do *other* children respond to the new arrangement?

Suggested Readings

Bandura, A., and Walten, R. H. *Social learning and personality development*. New York: Holt, Rinehart & Winston, 1963.

Guralnick, M. J. Integrated preschool as educational and therapeutic environments: concepts, design, and analysis. In Guralnick, M. J. (Ed.), *Early intervention and the integration of handicapped and nonhandicapped children*. Baltimore: University Park Press, 1978.

Herbert-Jackson, E., O'Brien, M., Porterfield, J., and Risley, T. R. *The infant center: a complete guide to organizing and managing infant day care*. Baltimore: University Park Press, 1977.

Hewett, F. M., and Taylor, F. D. *The emotionally disturbed child in the classroom: the orchestration of success*. Boston: Allyn & Bacon, 1980.

Hildebrand, V. Setting the stage. In *Introduction to early childhood education*, 2nd ed. New York: Macmillan, 1976.

Hoffman, M., Banet, B., and Weikart, D. P. *Young children in action*. Ypsilanti, Mich.: The High/Scope Press, 1983.

Kritchevsky, S., Prescott, E., and Walling, L. *Planning environments for young children: physical space*, 2nd. ed. Washington, D.C.: National Association for the Education of Young Children, 1977.

Rogers-Warren, A. K. Behavioral ecology in classrooms for young handicapped children. *Topics in Early Childhood Special Education 2*(1), 21–32, 1982.

Titus, R. Assessing the physical environment. In Neisworth, J., and Smith, R. (Eds.), *Evaluating educational environments*. Columbus, Oh.: Charles E. Merrill, 1979.

| Chapter 10 | *Program Management* |

Skill in coordinating a program is especially important in an operant pre-school because of the emphasis on arranging the child's environment so that it has consistent and direct influences on behavior. The program direction should be managed with precision so that each child's curricular objectives are met, progress is recorded, and consistency is maintained among the staff. In addition, home and school education should be coordinated as much as possible. In this section, six major aspects of program management are discussed: planning teaching schedules, planning teaching content, keeping progress records, coordinating the staff, integrating handicapped children in the classroom, and working with parents.

PLANNING TEACHING SCHEDULES

At the beginning of each school year, teachers usually plan a daily, weekly, and year-long schedule. This long-range planning ensures that curricular objectives are met within each year. It is best to begin by planning a workable daily schedule. A teacher might first divide the children's attendance into blocks of time, such as:

1. Greetings and adjustments at the beginning and end of each session
2. Direct instruction for learning of curricular objectives
3. Open activity center practice for maintenance and generalization of skills and information
4. Necessary activities, such as toileting, snack, outside play
5. Whole group activities, such as music, circle time

How much time is allotted to each of these activities depends on the individual teaching situation. Teachers will have to consider the ages of their children, their children's independence in self-care areas such as toileting and eating, and schedules imposed by their school (such as assigned recess times and availability of staff). A general daily schedule might look like this:

1. 9:00–9:10 A.M.   Greetings
2. 9:10–9:45
   a. Direct instruction (during which children are taught curricular objectives on a one-to-one or small group basis) *and*
   b. Activity centers (in which children practice curricular objectives to enhance maintenance and generalization)
3. 9:45–10:00   Outside recess (another opportunity to practice new learning)
4. 10:00–10:20   Toileting and snack
5. 10:20–10:40   Circle time
6. 10:40–11:15
   a. Direct instruction *and*
   b. Activity centers
7. 11:15–11:30   Cleanup and dismissal

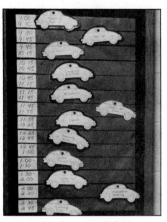

Example of a posted daily schedule.

Using this general schedule, your next step is to determine where the curriculum fits into the schedule. Obviously, in the sample schedule, the time segments (2) and (6) have been set aside for direct instruction of curricular objectives. Now, more specifically, you must decide *which* children receive *what* instruction at these times. In making these assignments, you must remember to provide a *balanced* curricular program for each child. For the following example, which is a more specific description of the previous schedule, assume that there are three teachers or assistants and 25 to 30 children. Also assume that the curriculum has four major domains—motor skills, social and self-help skills, language skills, and problem-solving or cognitive skills. The sample schedule segments (2) and (6) are expanded as follows:

	Teacher 1	*Teacher 2*	*Teacher 3*
9:10–9:45 A.M.	Direct instruction for problem-solving skills	Direct instruction for motor skills	Activity centers management
10:40–11:15 A.M.	Direct instruction for social and self-help skills	Activity centers management	Direct instruction for language skills

This schedule provides instruction in all four curricular areas each day; hence, it maintains a curricular balance. In classrooms where there is a less optimal teacher–pupil ratio, the four areas of curriculum may have to be taught over a two-day period; for example, problem-solving and motor skills could be taught on odd-numbered days, and the other two areas taught on even-numbered days.

At this point, we have a workable schedule that includes time allotted for *acquisition* of objectives in each major curricular area. Now the schedule must be further specified to include time allotted for the *maintenance and generalization* of curricular objectives. Looking back to the previous schedule, note that segments (2) and (6) include assignment of a teacher to activity centers. Activities such as crafts, dramatic play, and various manipulative games can be offered in the centers. The content of the activities can be planned so that children are encouraged to use the skills and knowledge they are learning during direct instruction. In addition to using these two time periods for generalization and maintenance, circle time, snack time, and playground or recess time can also be used for these purposes. Now we have a schedule that includes time segments for acquisition, maintenance, and transfer of curricular objectives. (In the section on staff coordination, more specific suggestions will be given for planning activity centers to include transfer and maintenance objectives.)

Once the daily schedule has been decided on, the teacher must plan for its successful implementation. Here the teacher can use behavioral techniques such as prompting and reinforcement. Getting the staff and the children to remember the daily schedule and to move quickly from one schedule segment to another often requires engineering. Auditory prompts, such as a bell or rhythm instrument, can be used to tell children and teachers that it is time to move on to the next activity. The same prompt can be used for all activity changes, and specific sounds can signal specific activities. Visual prompts can also be used to signal activity changes. For example, in the schedule you read earlier, children have circle time after snack. They can be taught to wait for a visual prompt (for example, the circle-time rug being laid down) to leave the snack tables. Reinforcers can be built into the schedule through Premacking; that is, less preferred activities can be scheduled before more preferred ones. Difficult activities might be scheduled before snack time, for example. Sometimes, the teacher will Premack staff duties. Messy art activities might be planned as the last event on Friday. Even though it may take the staff an extra 20 minutes to clean up from the activity, the work is followed by a restful weekend!

Next, the teacher can plan the yearly schedule, assigning times to intermittently occurring events such as units of study for weekly or monthly themes, parent newsletters, conferences, open houses, plays, and field trips. Scheduling these events in advance provides sufficient time for adequate preparation, rather than forcing the teacher to shoot from the hip.

PLANNING FOR TEACHING CONTENT

Curricular objectives themselves have been discussed in Chapter 7. The current discussion concerns only how to plan direct lessons for the acquisition of curricular objectives. Lessons must be planned each week for all children and in all major areas of the curriculum. Lesson planning is a critical aspect of the preschool program, and one that requires a significant amount of teacher time—probably three to five hours weekly. (For a handicapped preschooler, an individual educational plan [IEP] is not only important, it is required by law.)

An efficient method for managing lesson planning is to group children according to level of ability in a given skill, to mark each group's status within a list of curricular objectives, and to write out the group's lesson plans one week at a time. If there are four major curricular areas, four lesson plans are written for each group of children each week. Tables 10-1 through 10-4 show sample lesson plans for a group of five children, ages 2 to 3 years. Notice that there is one plan for each major curricular area and that each plan has five to ten objectives. Each plan is used in full or in part for the entire week.

Under the objective category, the teacher lists the several behavioral objectives being taught. These objectives are either written by the teacher or taken from a comprehensive list of curricular objectives. Next to each objective are written the material, teaching strategy to be used, planned consequences, and finally the method used to evaluate acquisition of the objective. The lesson plan should be detailed.

Table 10-1   Lesson Plan 1—Motor Skills

Objectives	Setting	Strategy	Consequence	Evaluation Method
1. Jumps from bottom step with feet together	Motor area with three children, one teacher	*Modeling*—teachers and peers	*Continued reinforcer*—wearing a "froggie" picture for the morning	Check if child can do correctly three times in a row
2. Walks on a line on the floor that is 5 feet long	Motor area with three children, one teacher	*Verbal prompt*—"Remember to put your foot back on the line"	*Task-imbedded*—children pretend to be tight-rope walkers	Count number of times a foot lands off the line
3. Stands on one foot momentarily without falling over	Motor area with three children, one teacher	*Physical prompt*—allow children on one foot to touch you then fade prompt	*Task-related feedback*—tell how many seconds children stand on one foot	Record number of seconds children can stand on one foot
4. Draws a circle	At a table with three children, one teacher	*Tactual prompt*—cardboard form for tracing	*Differential reinforcement*—hang up one drawn particularly well for each child	Record task as complete when child can draw circle without prompt
5. Cuts paper with scissors—makes one cut from edge of paper	At a table with three children, one teacher	*Verbal prompt*—"Hold the paper straight, open your scissors, snip"	*Task-imbedded reinforcer*—using scissors	Record the ratio of cuts to trials

Table 10-2 Lesson Plan 2—Language Skills

Objectives	Setting	Strategy	Consequence	Evaluation Method
1. Joins in with rhyme—"Twinkle, Twinkle, Little Star"	Small circle of children, language area	*Visual and auditory prompts*—emphasize your own voice and enunciation	*Social reinforcement*—clap for children who participate	Record frequency of participation over five trials
2. Uses short, compound sentences	Small circle of children, language area	*Limitation*—show pictures and say "I see a boy and he is running"	*Task-related feedback*—"You said a really long sentence"	Record which children use compound sentences over a five-day period
3. Follows two-step directions involving nearby objects	Small circle of children, language area	*Verbal prompt*—simply repeat directions twice, then have child repeat them	*Social reinforcement*—getting to help you give the next child direction	Record which steps of directions are followed
4. Imitates sentences of six words	Small circle of children, language area	*Verbal prompt*—emphasize words that are hardest to recall	*Social reinforcement*—handshake	Record trials correct out of five attempts
5. Looks at pictured objects as teacher reads about them	Small circle of children, language area	*Questioning*—after reading about certain objects, ask children to point to them, or ask visually related questions, such as "What is the cat wearing?"	*Task-related reinforcement*—"You sure are watching those pictures"	Record pictures found for every five requests

KEEPING PROGRESS RECORDS

Throughout the year, the teacher keeps two kinds of progress records for children. First, the teacher maintains records of each child's progress through the curricular objectives. This is easiest to do by placing a copy of the curriculum in each child's folder. Each week the teacher can scan the child's curricular list, check off objectives that are accomplished, and select new ones. In this way, the teacher can at any time report what each child has accomplished, what is presently being learned, and what is targeted for learning next.

In addition to curricular records, teachers should keep records of any specific behavior change projects. It is not feasible, of course, to maintain data on every objective taught to every child. However, it is important to record some behaviors with precision.

Daily or other regular data recording can provide specific information as

Table 10-3   Lesson Plan 3—Self-Help/Social Skills

Objectives	Setting	Strategy	Consequence	Evaluation Method
1. Engages contentedly in play with others	Small group, manipulative area	*Verbal prompt*— "Marcia and Patty take turns nicely"; "Marcia is sure having fun"	*Social reinforcement*—play with children who are playing well together	Record time spent playing happily
2. Zips large zipper independently (use oversized zippers fastened to frames)	Small group, manipulative area	*Physical prompt*—place hand over child's	*Natural*—zipping being completed	Check names of children who can zip with no prompts
3. Enjoys completing difficult tasks	Small group, manipulative area	*Modeling*—bring a difficult task to table, say it is hard to do, work on it, tell how happy you are when task completed	*Social reinforcement*—compliment children who complete difficult puzzles	Record names of children who complete tasks and smile, show someone their work, or compliment themselves
4. Uses teacher's pen carefully and returns it when finished	Manipulative area; 1st a small group lesson and then throughout that day	*Behavior rehearsal*—show magic marker, demonstrate proper use and cap replacement; let each child practice using pen and tell them they may borrow it any time that day	*Privilege*—if pen is used correctly, children receive a "borrowing" card that entitles them to use the pen again	Note which children maintain their "borrowing" cards throughout the day
5. Identifies some common vegetables when asked to name foods that are good for one's skin	Small group, manipulative area	*Visual prompt*—flannel board pictures used to prompt naming of vegetables *Verbal prompt*—"remember, vegetables are good for your skin"	*Reinforcer with maintenance prompt*—children get to wear vegetable pins that say, "Ask me to name some foods that are good for my skin"	Place check marks on badges for correct answers

to how quickly a child learns specific objectives, how effective certain teaching techniques are, and how much punishment or extinction is needed to affect needed changes (Alberto & Troutman, 1982). These data should be stored in children's individual folders.

You may have noticed that data from standardized tests have not been mentioned here. The teacher is interested in keeping records of a child's curricular progress *within* the preschool program, not progress on stan-

Table 10-4   Lesson Plan 4—Problem-Solving Skills

Objectives	Setting	Strategy	Consequence	Evaluation Method
1. Attends during group lessons for 5–10 minutes	Group story circle, reading area	*Verbal prompts—* positive earshotting	*Social reinforcement—*call on or sit close to children who are attending	Check those who attend for the full activity time
2. Imitates two motor behaviors in sequence	Small group, chairs in corner of room	*Verbal prompts—* say, "*First* clap hands, *then* stand up" while you model the behaviors	*Contrived reinforcement—*children who imitate correctly get a monkey picture to wear	Record correct performances out of two sequences
3. Recalls four new animal names from previous day	Small group, chairs in corner of room	*Questioning—* show pictures and ask, "Do you remember what this animal is called?"	*Contrived reinforcement with maintenance prompt—*child is given a booklet (containing pictures of those animals) to take home if all names are recalled	Check names of children who were able to recall all names—reteach other children and "test" next day
4. Names primary-colored objects when asked	Small group, chairs in corner of room	*Verbal prompt—* prompt children by beginning sound of the color name, if necessary	*Task-imbedded—*children "fish" for objects and can put ones correctly identified in "fishing baskets"	Record rate of correct unprompted responses
5. Repeats words "thick" and "thin" when shown appropriate objects	Small group, chairs in corner of room	*Modeling—*emphasize label as you name it	*Contrived reinforcement—*getting to hold the object after correctly repeating the word	Check words that are repeated correctly two times

dardized tests. These, however, may be administered and used as another basis for progress measurement. Sometimes, for example, funding agencies ask for children's status on norm-based tests; these provide some comparison with children in other programs.

COORDINATING THE STAFF

The head teacher must be prepared to specify the various teacher tasks, teach staff members to perform their assigned duties, and make sure that all staff members are familiar with each child's curricular program.

Staff Training

In teaching the curriculum, there are two types of responsibilities that staff members perform. They might be asked to conduct activities in the learning centers while others are involved in direct instruction. The head teacher might ask one staff member to assist in teaching the acquisition of curricular objectives. That staff person might be asked not only to teach the lesson, but also to plan subsequent ones. It might be wise to ask each person to teach only one or two curricular areas so that she or he becomes familiar with those curricular domains. At the beginning of the school year, the head teacher might plan the lessons, while asking the staff member to implement the lessons. Later, staff are asked to take over responsibility for planning more and more of the lessons. For example, they would first be asked to plan just the consequences, then the consequences and evaluation, then consequences, evaluation, and strategies, and so on. Eventually, they could take over all responsibilities for teaching two curricular areas, including the record keeping. Another staff member might be assigned to manage the learning centers. This person's eventual assignment could be to plan, manage, evaluate, and supervise the cleanup after the activities in the learning center.

Staff members may or may not have been trained for teaching young children. The head teacher might have to teach the staff how to interact with children, how to teach objectives, and how to manage problem behaviors. The head teacher can facilitate staff training by modeling important strategies and behaviors before asking others to do them, by shaping the "demands" on the staff, and by providing feedback and reinforcement for progressively improved staff performance. Some new staff members may not know what to do with children when no particular planned activity is underway. The head teacher can list possible activities and post them in the various learning centers to prompt the staff. A prompt in the fine motor skills area might include:

1. Ask questions about: color, length, shape, weight
2. See if children can imitate: patterns, sequences, specific verbal labels
3. Reinforce: persistence, returning equipment, attempting challenging but appropriate tasks

These prompts can be changed weekly or on some other schedule so that the staff becomes flexible in their interaction with children.

Staff Consistency

We have been discussing how the head teacher can train the staff in various skill areas. Another important element of staff coordination involves achiev-

It's obvious that these day-care staff members enjoy their work.

ing *consistency* across staff members and program segments in what is taught to each child. That is, when children are involved in free play, group circle time, learning center activities, and so on, the adult supervisors should know what behaviors to encourage and ignore in individual children. Remember that it is at these times that the newly acquired curricular objectives are maintained and generalized. One way to achieve consistency is to have weekly staff meetings in which children's progress is discussed. Activities for the learning centers can be planned at this time so that they are appropriate for the maintenance and generalization of children's skills. Another way to promote consistency is to place weekly prompts in each learning or activity center. These prompts can be brief statements of recently learned objectives that might be generalized to activities in that area. For example, if one group of children has learned to name shapes (circle, square, triangle) during direct instruction in the problem-solving curriculum, their teacher might post these prompts in other learning centers:

Center	Prompt
1. library	recognizes circle, shapes in books
2. motor	recognizes circle, block shapes
3. fine motor skills	constructs circular designs
4. arts and crafts	traces circles

These prompts for teachers might be posted on small bulletin boards, be hung from a ceiling mobile, or be written on a small cardboard square in a learning center. Prompts can also be placed on children after direct instruction to encourage other staff to ask them to practice the new learning. As an example, newly learned reading sounds and questions (ask me to say

"Hickory, dickory, dock") can be pinned on children's shirts. Again, it is the head teacher's responsibility to reinforce staff collaboration in following these prompts.

INTEGRATING HANDICAPPED CHILDREN

Many preschool programs have now broadened their scopes to include handicapped children. Recent legislation (PL 94-142) mandates that all children with handicaps, including preschoolers, be provided with individually prescribed education. Many states have begun preschools for handicapped youngsters, and Project Head Start and other facilities are integrating handicapped children more than ever. Behavioral technology, when properly applied, can benefit all children, handicapped and nonhandicapped.

The Normalization Principle

In a behavioral program, instructional methods need not be changed for the inclusion of exceptional children. This practice of using the same educational techniques with all children is not only practical and successful, but also desirable in terms of the normalization principle. Wolfensberger (1972, p. 28) has defined the normalization principle: "Utilization of means which are as culturally normative as possible, in order to establish and/or maintain personal behaviors and characteristics which are as culturally normative as possible." This principle has gained wide support in guiding programs for exceptional children. In fact, the practice of mainstreaming young exceptional children into regular preschool programs is a partial result of educators applying the normalization principle in program planning for these children.

Even after exceptional children are placed in regular educational programs, teachers should apply the normalization principle in planning programs. Looking again at Wolfensberger's principle, notice that it relates to two educational decisions: (1) the means used for teaching (that is, the instructional methodologies) and (2) the behaviors taught (that is, the curriculum). Both the procedures and objectives should be as culturally normative as possible. Remember that it has been suggested throughout our discussion of the behavioral approach that the curriculum and the methods used in a behavioral program are applicable and appropriate for all children.

Practical Considerations

The kinds of program accommodations that teachers may need to make when their classrooms become mainstreamed do not involve the instructional model; instead they reflect some practical considerations. Teachers must expect more than the usual number of children to exhibit learning or behavior problems. Many of the basic teaching skills (for example, analyzing tasks, making decisions about appropriate consequences) are especially critical in planning and conducting successful programs for these children.

Teachers who have a child with a sensory deficit may need to reassess room arrangement, behavior prompts, materials, and methods with respect to the deficit. For example, if a partially sighted child is in the program, visual prompts might be made larger and more intense. Visual prompts might also be paired with tactile or olfactory ones. The teacher might choose some materials for the classroom that combine visual with other modalities (record and book sets) or ones that provide nonvisual learning strategies (sand table, rhythm instruments). The teacher will need to combine visual strategies (modeling a behavior) with other less visual strategies. Teachers might verbally describe the behavior being modeled, or provide manual prompts. These kinds of program accommodations, however, do not suggest the use of unusual methods for the exceptional child. These same methods also are often used with normal children in the class.

Teachers usually should provide more structured situations to teach certain behaviors to exceptional children (LeBlanc, 1982). These children may not be as skilled at incidental learning and, therefore, may require more structured learning activities to progress through the curriculum. In cases where this requires significantly more teacher time, teachers might involve children in teaching each other or in correcting one another's work. Children can be encouraged to help one another and to cooperate— valuable lessons in themselves.

The presence of some exceptional children in a preschool program emphasizes the importance of certain socialization objectives. Teachers need to observe and direct children's modeling of peer behavior. There is the possibility that nonhandicapped children will begin to imitate the less desirable behaviors of some handicapped youngsters. It is important that children differentially imitate more mature behaviors. Teachers can influence the direction of modeling by differential reinforcement of positive modeling and by requesting children to model behaviors for others during the day.

Another socialization objective that might become critical in a mainstreamed preschool program is behaving with fairness or consideration toward individual differences. Children in such a program have an opportunity to learn to play and work successfully with peers who are dissimilar to themselves. Although most people would agree that this is a worthwhile objective, children may not have opportunities to learn these cooperative, considerate behaviors in a segregated setting. A mainstreamed setting enhances social learning opportunities for all the children.

WORKING WITH PARENTS

Early childhood education includes parents by its nature. Childrearing and education are overlapping enterprises; parents and teachers can pull together with or against each other. Not only do parents usually want to be central, but it is their legal right to help determine their child's future. Working with parents can be an added burden or an enormous help to an early childhood program. Skillful inclusion of parents can bring all closer together for the benefit of the child; productive parent involvement is a must.

Many parents become enthusiastic as they learn about effective strategies that solve child problems. This teacher is helping a parent to design a potty training program.

Reasons for Parent Involvement

There are a number of reasons for encouraging parents to participate in their child's educational program. One reason, obviously, is that parents are such an influential part of the child's world. Any gains made in the classroom are limited without a stimulating environment at home, where the child spends the greatest portion of time (Rutherford & Edgar, 1979). A review of child development literature provides ample evidence that early enrichment programs, both at home and in the school, contribute greatly to the achievement of higher levels of performance by participating children (Berger, 1981). Not only do children enrolled in the preschool benefit by parent participation, but siblings at home gain when parents are better informed and more active in educational efforts (Bronfenbrenner, 1975; Karnes & Teska, 1980).

A second reason for parent involvement is that many parents request help in training their children. It is not uncommon to hear the following: "I'm not a teacher. I don't have much training for childrearing. How can I help my child?" In addition, parents often request assistance for a specific problem, such as temper tantrums or difficulty in toilet training. The teacher is often the best person to offer guidance.

Ethical concerns are a third reason for the participation of parents in their child's program. One controversial question is: "Who should decide on the child's educational and developmental goals?" Obviously, the child is often too young to make such decisions. The teacher can avoid functioning as an absolute dictator of goals by soliciting the input and participation of parents, and by selecting goals that meet ethical standards, are realistic, and are (eventually, if not immediately) useful to the child (Krasner & Krasner, 1972).

The fourth reason for parent involvement is to promote the generalization of school-acquired behaviors to other settings (Touchette, 1978). We know that target behaviors can be established and that undesirable behaviors can be terminated or weakened in a behavioral preschool setting. However, a complaint heard from parents is: "My child behaves so well at school. Why not at home?" If the parents are taught to employ the effective child management techniques being used at school, and if teachers learn about the home setting and parental concerns, a coordinated home–school program can be established to improve behavioral consistency. This will be reinforcing for the parents to continue their child in the program and to participate in it themselves.

Finally, a fifth practical reason for parent involvement in a program is that parents can be employed as teachers' aides to help fill personnel needs. Most parents have a great deal to contribute because they bring to the classroom their knowledge, skills, and intense interest in child-care activities. There always is a demand for qualified personnel, and who can execute the job better than a concerned parent skilled in positive techniques?

Parent Conferences and Progress Reporting

Conducting parent conferences and writing progress reports are skills a teacher must acquire (Kroth & Simpson, 1977). In most programs, parent conferences and reports are completed on a regular basis and contribute to a total educational plan in several ways:

1. General information is given to families concerning program objectives and techniques
2. Specific information is given about the child's progress through the program objectives
3. Information is given about how parents can enhance their child's opportunities to learn in the home setting
4. Opportunity is provided for parents to make suggestions concerning appropriate educational objectives for their child

Parent conferences and progress reports will be discussed in terms of tasks that the teacher should perform *before*, *during*, and *after* the conference or report.

Before   Preparation for a parent conference or report should not be a last minute endeavor. To prepare themselves and parents for reports and conferences, teachers should:

1. Keep *continuous records* (checklists) of the child's progress through the curriculum. On *any* day (not only progress report day), the teacher should know each child's location within the curriculum.
2. Send periodic *newsletters* to parents to familiarize them with the planned school activities (units of study, field trips). In this way, skills and knowledge can be practiced at home as well as in school. For example, if parents know that their children are learning animal names, they can use and request these names when interacting at home. This, in turn, increases the chance that behaviors will be generalized and maintained.
3. Write frequent *notes* or make *phone calls* concerning a child's accomplishments. When parents are informed about the child's accomplish-

ments on the very day they occur (rather than three months later on parent conference day), they can commend the child for the current accomplishments or activities.

During   Two important aspects of the conference or report are the *manner* of communication and the *content* of the communication.

In writing reports or conducting conferences, the teacher should use language appropriate to the language and experiential background of the family. The teacher must demonstrate a respect for the parents' concerns, empathy in listening to their problems, and encouragement of their participation in educational planning.

Teachers ought to have an outline of content distinctive to each child's program. However, the following broad topics should be included:

1. *General information* concerning curriculum, materials, procedures, and evaluation. This is not a necessary part of each conference or report, but should be explained at least once a year.

2. *Specific information* about how parents can enhance their child's school achievement. Include specific techniques and content that parents might use: help parents to be teachers. Following good didactic principles, do not try to teach more than one principle (technique) to parents at a time—on one progress report, emphasize the use of immediate reinforcement; on the next, emphasize shaping.

3. Specific information as to the child's *progress* through the curriculum. Include not only *what* the child has learned, but *how* she or he has learned it (rate of learning, problems encountered, effective methodology).

4. Request and accept *parental input* for the program. In this way, parents help teachers to be "parents" of their child. In a written progress report, the teacher should include a telephone number where he or she may be reached, as well as stating times when he or she is available for further discussion. A detachable comment slip or questionnaire also can be supplied to the parents.

One final point: parents often approach these communications with predetermined notions of what they expect or want to hear. For example, a parent may wish to hear that "John's only problem is a speech defect. When that is corrected, he will be fine." Teachers may be subtly led into making such statements, because parents will naturally reinforce the teacher who says what they want to hear. Although maintenance of parent–teacher rapport is important, the teacher should not be tempted to make unjustified statements just to make parents happy. Be accurate and honest in discussing child problems.

After   Just as it is important to record efforts and accomplishments with children, it is important to record progress made with parents. For example, when it is time to contact the parent for a second report or conference, you will want to know what happened during the first one without having to rely on your memory. Of course, written reports may be photocopied and kept on file. However, it is effective to maintain folders that contain brief checklists of interactions as well as copies of written reports. Categories you might include are:

1. General management skills communicated to parent
2. Target behaviors parents were asked to practice with their children
3. Goals parents have requested you to execute
4. Comments concerning parents' "affect" behaviors toward the child and program

The steps included in this section may appear to require great effort. But after you organize such things as a curriculum, conference outlines, and

---

Box 10-1   Tips for Successful Parent Conferences

1. Give parents sufficient notice of when and where the conference will occur and schedule the time for the conference when it is the most convenient for the parent to attend.

2. Make sure to invite both parents, if it is a two-parent family.

3. Try to send a reminder or call the parents to remind them of the place and time of the appointment.

4. Prepare ahead by collecting records, tests, papers, workbooks, art materials, notebooks, and other records dealing with the child's progress for the time period to be discussed.

5. Make arrangements for a place for the parents to wait if they arrive early for the appointment. This area should be stocked with reading materials and/or displays to occupy parents while they wait. If possible, also arrange for some type of refreshment, such as coffee or tea, to be available.

6. Provide child care if at all possible.

7. Make the room for the conference bright and attractive and remove any physical barriers (such as a desk) from between yourself and the parent.

8. Welcome parents with a friendly greeting and make sure you use their correct full name. Do not assume that their last name is the same as their child's.

9. Begin on a positive note and keep the remainder of the conference evenly balanced between discussing the child's strengths and weaknesses. Be sure to keep to the subject at hand—the child and his or her progress in the program.

10. Ask questions about the child and show genuine interest. Keep the lines of communication open by avoiding jargon and by encouraging the parent to express opinions, disagree, and ask for clarification if anything is unclear to him or her.

11. Have clear objectives for the conference. At the end of the conference summarize what has been discussed to be sure that these objectives have been sufficiently discussed and conclusions formed about the next steps to be taken in the program.

12. Begin and end on time. If another appointment is needed, be sure to schedule it before the parent leaves or, if that is not possible, in the next week after the initial appointment.

Summarized from E. H. Berger, *Parents as partners in education*, C. V. Mosby, St. Louis: 1981.

communications checksheets, you can conduct parent conferences and reports that are meaningful for both teacher and parent. Box 10-1 provides other tips for successful conferences.

Often parents request training in the behavioral procedures used in the preschool. Teachers can find strong allies in parents who seek and accept some basic training in behavior techniques.

A Parent Training Program

What should a parent training program include? First of all, an explanation of basic behavior principles should be provided (see, for example, Becker, 1971; Patterson, 1976; Smith & Smith, 1976). It is important that this material be presented in a simplified manner complete with numerous examples. The principles to be covered include:

1. Most behavior is learned and, therefore, can be changed.
2. We can increase the occurrence of certain behaviors through positive reinforcement.
3. We can decrease the occurrence of selected behaviors through extinction, time out, and punishment.
4. We can be more effective in our teaching and discipline if we are deliberate about our methods—that is, if we provide immediate and consistent feedback on a predetermined schedule.

Following the explanation of these principles, training can be provided in the use of strategies for *behavior management at home* (see Miller, 1975). This program should include the following strategies:

1. Shaping behavior
2. Premack principle
3. Use of contracting and points
4. Token economy
5. Schedules of reinforcement
   a. To establish, reinforce every time
   b. To maintain, reinforce intermittently
6. Reinforce behavior incompatible with undesirable behaviors
7. Use rules to help the children know what is expected of them, and also to aid parents in being consistent

After exposure to the basic principles and strategies for their use, parents can be provided with steps or guidelines for setting up a home program (Redd & Sleator, 1978). These steps can include:

1. Identify the target behavior.
2. Take a baseline record of the occurrence of the behavior (parents should be given training on identifying behaviors and observing and counting the duration or frequency of the specific behavior; practice sessions should be included).

The maintenance of effective levels of attention is only one important behavior that can be established by reinforcement techniques.

3. Decide which consequences to use—strengthening or weakening.
4. Determine reinforcers.
5. Keep records to evaluate the program; if no progress is made, modify the program.

The final consideration is *how* parents should be instructed. A number of strategies can be used to train parents (Berger, 1981). Group meetings allow parents to exchange ideas and assist each other in goal setting and decision planning. Role-playing sessions with the instructor and one or several parents also are good training methods. In addition, the instructor can model different child management techniques. Homework exercises, too, can be used in training. They should include data collection activities to be reviewed periodically. Feedback and monitoring systems may be used in conjunction with the homework. Telephone calls or mailing in results are simple ways to monitor learning.

Direct training and feedback can be provided to the parents who work in the classroom. Active participation in the classroom is desirable for several reasons. First, the parents will be working with other children, not just their own. Therefore, it will be easier for them to be objective as they will be less directly and emotionally involved. Secondly, stimulus control will be already set up in the classroom. What occurs there may provide a model for some parents to follow at home.

These strategies for teaching parents do not, of course, represent a conclusive list of training procedures. The teacher must modify and devise methods specific to the parents to be trained. Ideally, the teacher should view the family as being as individual, distinctive, and deserving of respect as each child. No training or communication techniques can replace genuine mutual understanding and information exchange. When the family and teachers are *partners* in helping the child, behavioral techniques offer an approach and skills that provide consistent, powerful, and accountable results. Box 10-2 emphasizes parents' needs for guidance and help in childrearing.

SUMMARY

Management of a behaviorally based preschool may seem laborious and time consuming to someone not familiar with behavior technology. The need for precision in selecting objectives, arranging settings and consequences, and recording progress will dissuade some people from adopting a behavioral model. There is a trade-off in most things we do (or fail to do). Time and effort invested in adequate program management pays off eventually in demonstrable child progress, anxiety-free teachers, cooperative parents, and a great feeling of professional expertise.

The main management duties include planning teaching schedules; selecting learning objectives, strategies, and settings; coordinating staff and recording progress; and encouraging parent involvement.

The scope of parent involvement usually is up to the teacher, but all par-

---

Box 10-2   All Parents Can Use Some Help

Bob was delighted—exuberant—that he finished writing the final chapter of his new book on behavior modification. He called his coauthor to exclaim "It's done!" During his long-distance conversation, Andy, his 2-year-old son, burst into the kitchen (where the phone is located) yammering about his broken balloon. "Quiet!" said Daddy. More yammering. "Please be quiet or leave—I'm on the telephone." Andy then broke into a full cry. Desperate, Daddy grabbed a large chocolate chip cookie out of the jar and thrust it into Andy's mouth to shut him up. Andy stopped crying, quietly munched his cookie, and Daddy finished his conversation on the telephone. As any behaviorist should know, however, giving a cookie for inappropriate behavior may be momentarily effective—but will probably actually strengthen the unwanted behavior. Behaviorists are parents too, and parents are often so close to the problem that they cannot assess their own behavior objectively.

ents should be encouraged to contribute and participate in their child's program—and to be partners in the enterprise of early education.

As much as possible, the head teacher should practice application of behavior principles not only with the children, but also with the staff (including him- or herself). Good prompts and reinforcers for teachers are important in maintaining staff persistence and professional zeal. Behavior is the result of interaction with the environment—including the social environment. When teachers are happy, well prepared, and expert, children grow within a superior social context.

Review Questions

1. Tell how you can use prompts to facilitate following a daily schedule.
2. Tell how you can build reinforcement into a daily or weekly schedule.
3. Name and explain the five parts of the lesson plan format given in Tables 10-1 to 10-4.
4. List several ways to enhance generalization and maintenance of new learning; include possibilities in the school and the home.
5. State several circumstances that call for individualized data collection.
6. Discuss why standardized child assessment instruments may not be sensitive measures of child progress within a particular program.
7. Explain two ways to improve staff training and interstaff consistency.
8. Explain what is meant by *normalization* and why it is important to both handicapped and nonhandicapped children.
9. Cite several methods that the teacher can use to facilitate developmental integration. How can a blind 4-year-old child be meaningfully integrated into a regular preschool?
10. Name five reasons to encourage parent involvement in the preschool program.
11. Provide two suggestions for enhancing a parent conference before, during, or after the conference.
12. State three strategies for maximizing parent instruction.
13. Construct two daily schedules—one for a class with a high teacher–pupil ratio and one for a class with a low teacher–pupil ratio.
14. Refer to the lesson plans in Tables 10-1 to 10-4. For two of the plans:
    a. Describe some learning center activities that would provide opportunities for children to generalize and maintain those skills.
    b. Write prompts that might be posted in two specified learning centers to encourage teachers to practice those skills with children.
15. Write a progress report for an actual or fictitious child, using the criteria provided in this chapter.
16. Design a format for a classroom newsletter. What content will you include? How might you use operant procedures to keep parents interested in the newsletter?
17. Make a list of educational materials that might be especially appropriate for:
    a. Children with visual deficits
    b. Children with auditory deficits
    c. Children with mobility deficits
18. Collect catalogs of companies who sell educational products for exceptional children, and identify what materials might be useful for teaching in the home by the parents.
19. Describe how you would help parents to eliminate some troublesome child behavior, such as not picking up toys before bedtime.

Suggested Activities

1. Role play a parent–teacher conference. Include a child progress report and parent reactions.
2. Write a note to a parent suggesting how a child might be encouraged to name colors at home.
3. Go through a toy catalog or toy store and identify four toys that would be appropriate for teaching a new skill in the language, social, motor, and "cognitive" areas of development.
4. Visit two different preschools and take note of the schedules and activities. Analyze the two schedules and decide which one makes more "behavioral sense." Redesign either schedule to maximize child learning and staff functioning.

Suggested Readings

Cook, R. E., and Armbruster, V. A. *Adapting early childhood curricula: Suggestions for meeting special needs.* St. Louis: Mosby, 1982.

Glass, R. M., Christiansen, J., and Christiansen, J. L. *Teaching exceptional students in the regular classroom.* Boston: Little, Brown, 1982.

Kurtz, P. D. A systematic supervisory procedure for child care training. *Child Care Quarterly* 5, 9–18, 1976.

Madle, R. A. Behaviorally based staff performance management. *Topics in Early Childhood Special Education 2*(1), 73–83, 1982.

Neisworth, J. T. (Ed.). Managing the preschool environment. *Topics in Early Childhood Special Education 2*(1), 1982 (entire issue).

Neisworth, J. T., Willoughby-Herb, S. J., Bagnato, S. J., Cartwright, C. A., and Laub, K. W. Keeping up the good work. In Neisworth, J. T., Willoughby-Herb, S. J., Bagnato, S. J., Cartwright, C. A., and Laub, K. W. (Eds.), *Individualized education for preschool exceptional children.* Germantown, Md.: Aspen Systems, 1980.

Neisworth, J. T., Willoughby-Herb, S. J., Bagnato, S. J., Cartwright, C. A., and Laub, K. W. Putting it all together. In Neisworth, J. T., Willoughby-Herb, S. J., Bagnato, S. J., Cartwright, C. A., and Laub, K. W. (Eds.), *Individualized education for preschool exceptional children.* Germantown, Md.: Aspen Systems, 1980.

Chapter 11

Evaluation Procedures

*P*reschool programs use evaluation to answer many different questions. Some programs are interested in improving children's academic skills, and they use standardized or criterion-based measures to evaluate the effectiveness of their program. Other programs base their criteria for success on participation of children and parents. These programs could use student attendance and parent involvement as evaluative indices. The evaluation questions educators ask reflect the goals of their programs. Hence, in behavioral programs, an emphasis is placed on precise measures of child *behavior change* to guide program operations. Teachers are encouraged to record child behavior frequently enough to determine how it is affected by environmental arrangements, such as particular teaching materials and methods. Teachers receive immediate feedback concerning instructional practices and can make changes when necessary; in this way, educators make their day-to-day programming sensitive to child progress.

This chapter illustrates some basic approaches to collecting specific kinds of behavior-change and progress data. We discuss reasons for data collection, ways to specify behaviors for observation, basic techniques and tools for data collection, and some general guidelines for collecting data as you teach.

No science or technology can go very far without some accepted system of measurement. Behaviorists base instructional decisions on data that reflect the influence of consequences, prompts, and other environmental arrangements and materials. Data collection is not only integral to a behavioral program, it is essential.

REASONS FOR PRECISE DATA COLLECTION

As you teach you will encounter situations in which you will need to collect specific information on behaviors rather than just checking whether the child has learned curricular objectives. Naturally, you will not be able to collect specific data (beyond the curricular checklist) on each curricular objective for each child—that would be a laborious if not an impossible task! There are, however, some occasions on which a teacher should collect more precise data:

1. When the child is engaging in inappropriate behaviors that you wish to reduce; when education becomes therapeutic, greater precision in measurement is required both to guide and to document change
2. When you are uncertain as to the seriousness of inappropriate behavior and need more information to compare the behavior with norms or to assess the extent of the problem
3. When you are using a new instructional setting, consequence, method or material and want to evaluate its effectiveness
4. When you believe a child's behavior is quite deviant from normal (for example, you think a child is abnormally fast in concept acquisition)
5. When you want to give the child immediate feedback on his or her own behavior to motivate the child toward achievement
6. When you must describe a child's functioning (for example, to the parent, another teacher, or a psychologist); precise data are important in supporting your work with the child

PINPOINTING BEHAVIORS

When you have decided to collect data on child behavior, you must define the behavior exactly. One way to check the precision of your behavioral definition is to try observing for instances of that behavior. See if you can easily identify instances of the behavior you have described. Perhaps you will need to add further specifications. When observing how long a child cries, you will see after a few observations that you need to specify in your definition whether to count sobs, whines, or sniffles. Another way to check on the precision of your definitions is to ask another staff member to observe instances of the behavior. Ask that person what difficulties arise in recognizing instances. It is surprising how confusing specifications that are not clear and easily countable can be.

There are several observable aspects of most behaviors. You should decide which aspect you want to observe. Many behaviors result in an *end product* and you may merely want to observe that product. Painting, working puzzles, dressing, writing, and cleaning up all are behaviors that have end products. Therefore, you could observe aspects such as number of colors used, percentages of puzzle pieces correctly placed, number of buttons done up, number of letters correctly written, or number of toys put in place.

At other times, you may be interested in the behavior *process* rather than the end product. In observing a given behavioral process you might choose to observe the frequency (how many times the behavior occurs), the intensity or magnitude (with what strength the behavior occurs), the duration (for how long the behavior occurs), or the latency (how much time passes between the stimulus for the behavior and the occurrence of the behavior). Samples of these types of behaviors are listed below.

Measured Aspect of the Behavior	*Observed Behavior*
1. Frequency	Number of times child asks questions during snack
2. Intensity or magnitude	Volume of water and other fluid a child drinks during preschool hours
3. Duration	Number of minutes child plays independently with blocks
4. Latency	Number of minutes it takes child to arrive in classroom after teacher rings recess bell

Often, parents and even school psychologists and other professionals may offer vague statements regarding a child's strengths and weaknesses. "Betty is hyperactive," "Douglas doesn't pay attention," and "Molly doesn't socialize enough" are statements of problem areas but not specifications of behaviors. It is usually possible to identify the behavioral subcomponents of such global characteristics. Consider the following illustration how a global statement was *behavioralized*, thus permitting measurement of the problem and detection of change. Betty, a 5-year-old girl, was enrolled in the preschool at mid-year. Betty was a "hyperactive child," according to her parents. In fact, Betty was scheduled to begin taking medication for her problem. The pediatrician asked that the preschool staff "size up" Betty's behavior in the preschool to verify the parents' concern. How do you assess "hyperactivity" and how do you evaluate its relevance to teaching or learning?

First, it was necessary to behavioralize "hyperactivity" so that clearly observable and measurable behaviors could be monitored. After discussion with the pediatrician, "hyperactivity" was defined as consisting of several dimensions. Each of these dimensions was then defined in terms of what behaviors to look for:

1. *Attention span* was assessed by measuring the percentage of on-task behavior in four learning areas of the preschool. These were reading, numbers, language, and science. Thirty daily observations of 15 seconds each were conducted in each area over a seven-week period. For the first ten days of observation, two observers independently recorded on-task behavior to determine whether the measure was indeed objective and reliable. Using the procedure of dividing the number of times the observers agreed by the number of total observations each made, an average inter-observer agreement of 92 percent was calculated. The

high agreement indicated the specifications were exact enough, and further observations were conducted by a single observer.

2. The dimension of *impulsivity* was translated into two measures. The first of these was shifts of interest as reflected in movements from one learning area to another. The second was the total number of minutes spent in each learning area for each week.

3. The last measure was *auditory memory*.

4. Simultaneous with observation of Betty, the same measures were taken on two children of the same age and sex who appeared normal in all respects (controls).

Comparison of Betty's behavior with the two control children revealed that she did *not* show any significant difference from the other children; in other words, Betty was not hyperactive in our setting, using children who were considered perfectly normal as referants (Neisworth, Kurtz, Ross, & Madle, 1976). Because of these measurements, Betty was not given inappropriate medication, she did well in the preschool, and her parents were pleased to learn that there was no basis to consider her to be hyperactive.

GENERAL GUIDELINES FOR DATA COLLECTION

If you have not had experience teaching in a behavioral preschool, the notion of recording specific data on child behaviors might appear to be a real nuisance. Of course, collecting data frequently does add an extra dimension to the teacher's role. Collecting data is one of those tasks that is difficult to do initially but that becomes much easier with practice. You will eventually find it to be naturally reinforcing because you will be getting direct feedback on your success as a teacher. It is quite rewarding to see graphs that depict problem behaviors decreasing and depictions of appropriate behaviors increasing. As you begin to share these kinds of data with other teachers, parents, and supervisors, you probably will get some additional social reinforcement for your effective teaching. You will begin to view teaching and data collection as inseparable, rewarding activities.

What if the data show lack of success? This information also is useful. We can learn both from success and from failure. When you find that a technique is unsuccessful in a particular situation, you can try others until you find one that is effective. Even if you must ask for help from a consultant, you will have specific data for describing the problem. Each time you solve a difficult teaching problem, you gain more teaching competency.

Because it is difficult to begin recording behavior, we will offer some suggestions to help you become more efficient in your evaluations:

1. Make some *standard data forms* and mimeograph several copies so that each new data collection project will not require constructing new data forms. As you read this chapter, you will see some examples of data

Standard data forms

forms that would be useful in your classroom. Some types of information for which you should allot spaces on these forms are:

a. Child's name
b. Date
c. Observer
d. Behavior in question
e. Technique being used to change the behavior (when appropriate)

2. When you collect data, try to *record your observations directly on the final record sheet* rather than first writing the information on scrap paper and then transferring it to the recording form. Keep the individual behavior recording forms either in the area where they are being used or with the lesson plans with which they are used.

3. When you *arrange your classroom*, design a section of the teacher's space to be used for data collection materials. Here you can store graph paper, various recording forms, clipboards, counters, timers, and stopwatches.

4. Be certain to record data for *adequate time periods* before using it for evaluative purposes. It is generally considered that five days of data give an adequate depiction of the current state of a behavior when no particular intervention is being used. Therefore, a five-day baseline period usually is satisfactory.

   When you are measuring the effect of an intervention, you may need to collect more than five days of data. For example, you should measure the effectiveness of some programmed materials for months before making a decision. This is usually the case when you are making an evaluation of an end product. A phonetic approach to beginning reading may have fewer end product results (number of words child can read) than a word recognition approach during the beginning phases of teaching. After a few months, however, the phonetics method may result in more words read. The length of observation time should be decided separately for each intervention; be careful to give your interventions an adequate trial period before deciding that they are not effective.

5. You can extend the scope of your observations by becoming a *skilled behavior sampler*. You need not watch a child the whole day if you are interested in his or her social behaviors. You could spend just five minutes each day recording that child's behavior during snack, for example, and use a stopwatch to record the time spent talking with other persons. Over a period of several days, this would provide good data on interaction. You might also sample behaviors during certain events. If you are interested in how well some children remember to identify their numbers, you could record their responses for just the first question you ask them each day; this way, the recording interrupts your teaching only at the beginning of the lesson. Events also could be longer units, such as snack time, recess, and free play.

   Momentary time sampling often is useful in recording high-frequency behaviors such as thumbsucking, attention during a lesson, or sitting in a chair during snack time. At snack time, you might be interested in children being in their chairs but be unable to keep stopwatches running for all five children at your table. You could instead set a timer to ring every three or four minutes. Each time it rings you record children as being in or out of their seats.

6. If you are in a public school building, you can often enlist the assistance of *older elementary school children* to collect data. Initially the children must be trained either by you or their teacher, but eventually some of them might be able to train subsequent observers. You not only fulfill your own aim of collecting information, but you also provide curricular experiences for the child observers. This activity could be related to social studies (learning to observe and speak objectively about the behavior of others, learning childrearing techniques), or science (making scientific observations and predictions and testing hypotheses).

7. Finally, because recording data is most difficult when you first begin, contrive a reward for yourself until you become more efficient and receive social reinforcements (from supervisors, parents) and uncontrived self-reinforcement (seeing your own success at teaching). You might, for example, give a friend some money or favorite possessions. You can earn these back by showing your friend data you have collected.

DATA COLLECTION TECHNIQUES

Behavior Product Evaluations

Product evaluation refers to measuring the tangible outcome of behavior. The number of worksheets completed, blocks stacked, or toys carried across the room are instances of products of behavior. Products are usually easy to measure and provide a good way to assess behavior change.

1. *Curricular check sheets.* To get more specific information, *date began, date accomplished, level of behavior* (how frequently or quickly or for how long the child does the behavior), *kind of reinforcement used* (task-imbedded reinforcement, contrived social reinforcement, intrinsic reinforcement, schedule of reinforcement).

   Sometimes tasks within a curriculum must be task-analyzed. These task-analysis lists can also be used as check lists. A teacher might, for instance, write out the steps of shoelace tying and check that the child accomplishes each step.

2. *Frequencies of products.* You can record this kind of information on graph paper, labeling the product you are observing on the vertical line and the passage of time on the horizontal line (Figure 11-1).

   When you want to show the effect of different intervention strate-

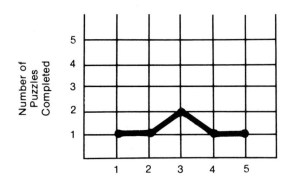

Figure 11-1   *A sample graph showing frequency over time*

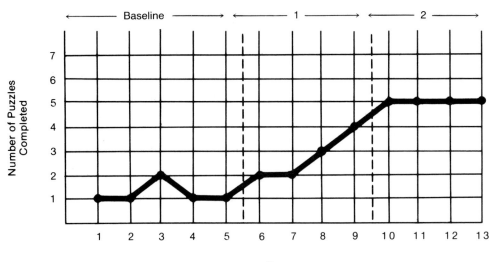

Figure 11-2   *Graph displaying changes in behavior after interventions. (Intervention 1: social reinforcement; Intervention 2: child earns a badge for completing 5 puzzles)*

gies, separate these time periods on the graph by drawing vertical lines. Remember to label and then describe the interventions (Figure 11-2).

Sometimes you want to compare the child's product with some other quality—for example, to compare the number of questions answered to the number of puzzles attempted. You could do this in two ways: you can record the percentage of correct answers, or you can record the number of total answers and the number of correct answers (Figure 11-3).

3. *Rating products*. Some products are more difficult to pinpoint than others. When you check a child's hands after washing, for example, it is

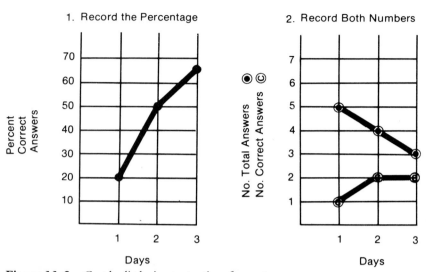

Figure 11-3 *Graphs displaying proportion of correct answers*

difficult to count the number of dirty marks remaining or to assign a number to their intensity. For occasions like this you may prefer to rate the product.

When constructing rating scales, assign a meaning to the individual numbers. To rate handwashing you might assign these meanings:

1 = not attempted
2 = attempted but not done
3 = partially done
4 = almost completely done
5 = completely done

These same numbers and definitions could be used to rate other self-help behaviors such as setting the table, dressing for outside, or eating meals. By mimeographing these rating codes you can use them easily to record several behavior products.

Behavior Process Evaluations

Whereas product evaluation focuses on the outcome of behavior (number of crayons used), process evaluation measures the behavior itself (how often did Billy raise his hand?) where there is no tangible product.

1. *Frequency recordings.* You can record frequency of behavior just as you can products. As you observe and count behavior, it is important to record frequencies, rather than trying to remember how often the behavior occurred. Writing hash marks on a sheet of paper, using a re-

Days

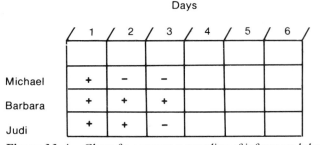

Figure 11-4 *Chart for occurrence recording of infrequent behavior (greeting parents) of several children over a number of days. [(−): no pleasant greeting; (+): pleasant greeting]*

sponse counter (like those used to keep track of the number of people coming through a door), dropping beads into a container, and other simple means can be employed to keep track of frequencies.

Knowing only the frequency of a behavior usually is not enough, however. It is important to know the *amount of time* involved and the *opportunities* for the behavior. "David screamed three times" tells us something, but "David screamed three times in ten minutes" gives us more information. Dividing the frequency by the number of minutes gives us a statement of behavior *rate*. David's *rate* of screaming is three times per ten minutes (or three-tenths per minute). Rates are quite useful, because we do not always observe for the same period of time each day. If David were observed for only five minutes, he might scream only once or twice; nevertheless, his screaming rate could be computed and compared. Opportunities for the behavior in question set the limits on behavior. Counting social contacts or approaches would provide no useful information if there were no other people around with whom to socialize. How many candies are eaten will depend upon the availability of the candy. When opportunities are (more or less) unlimited, we refer to the behavior as a *free operant*; that is, the behavior can occur freely without environmental factors forcing a pause in or cessation of the behavior.

Occurrence recording is a form of frequency recording. Sometimes teachers are interested only in whether or not a behavior has occurred. In fact, many behaviors have an opportunity to occur only once daily. An example is a child greeting his or her parents pleasantly at the end of the school day. Observations of these kinds of behavior need no graphs. A recording form such as the one in Figure 11-4 can be used for noting these infrequently occurring behaviors for several children over a number of days.

At other times, teachers are interested in recording the occurrence of behaviors as they relate to certain environmental variables. For ex-

	snack	free play	language lesson	recess	circle time
1	-	+	+	-	+
2	-	+	+	-	+
3	-	+	+	-	+

(Day)

Figure 11-5   *Chart showing when a particular behavior (thumb sucking) is occurring in relation to several environmental variables. [(+): sucks thumb; (−): does not suck thumb]*

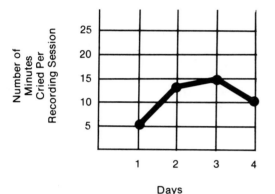

Figure 11-6   *Graph showing duration of a behavior (crying) at each daily recording session*

ample, the occurrence of behaviors may vary with the time of day, classroom activities, or instructor. In these cases, you should construct a slightly more detailed occurrence recording sheet, such as the one shown in Figure 11-5.

In this example, the behavior has many opportunities to occur each day. However, it is not the frequency that is of interest, but rather the occasion. This will reveal possible stimulus control of the behavior. The data in Figure 11-5 suggest that intervention might be attempted first during recess time, because the child does not suck her thumb during this time.

2. *Duration recordings.* When you are interested in the duration or latency of a behavior, you must record passage of time. Such data are easy to collect and record if you use a stopwatch. When you wish to record duration, start the watch when the behavior begins and stop it when it has ended. When the behavior begins again, start the watch. At the end of the recording period, enter the total duration on a graph such as the one shown in Figure 11-6.

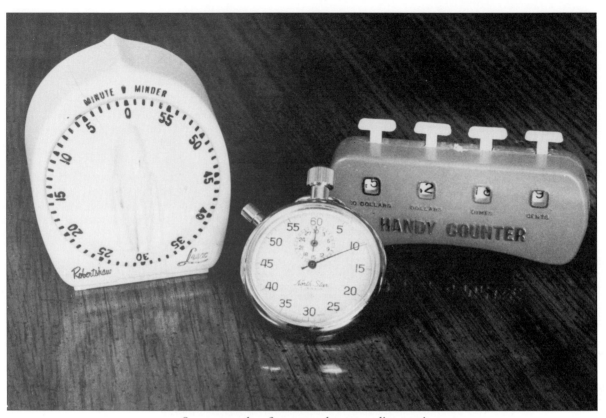

Some examples of common data recording equipment

3. *Latency recordings*. To record latency, start the watch when the stimulus is presented—for example, when you say, "Mary, it's time to pick up the toys." Stop the watch when Mary begins to pick up the toys. Enter the time on the stopwatch on a graph like the one in Figure 11-7.

4. *Intensity recordings*. It is difficult to measure intensity of behaviors without special equipment. However, devices such as sound meters are available and, where expenses allow, teachers do use these. These kinds of data can be recorded in the manner of time recordings.

   Another less-exact way to measure behavior intensity is to measure its effect on the environment. You could count the number of times that a soft-spoken child talks loudly enough to be heard by adults. You could also count the number of times that a child coughs loudly enough to be heard, or speaks so loudly as to be unpleasant, although the criterion of "unpleasant" is obviously subjective (this may be appropriate when subjective reactions are the important effect). Box 11-1 explains why an assistant can be helpful in making observations.

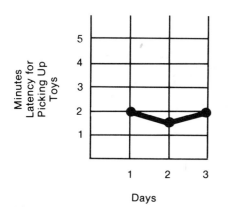

Figure 11-7   *Graph showing latency of a behavior (picking up toys); the number of minutes between the stimulus ("Mary, it's time to pick up the toys") and the behavior is recorded*

Box 11-1   *Two Observers Are Better Than One*

When behavior is observed and recorded, how do we know that the data are accurate? Usually, behaviorists try to get at least two observers to witness and record the same events and then compare the results. The extent to which they agree is a measure of *inter-observer* reliability. When two independent observers produce the same report, we can be much more certain that the behavior being examined is clearly defined and is occurring as reported.

One way to calculate reliability is to divide the number of actual agreements by the total number of opportunities for agreement. Thus,

$$\frac{\text{agreements}}{\text{agreements + disagreements}} = \frac{\text{inter-observer}}{\text{reliability}}$$

Here is an example:

Does Eric pay attention when he is asked to do so? The teacher (being a good behaviorist) knew that "paying attention" is an elusive behavior, so she defined it as making eye contact with the teacher or looking at the target materials during a lesson. She also knew how faulty a single observer can be, so she asked her aide to observe and record Eric paying attention. They decided to observe from 10:00 to 10:10 A.M. for five days. Their results were as follows (A for Attention, N for None):

	1	2	3	4	5
Teacher	A	A	A	N	A
Aide	N	A	A	N	N

Using our formula, we have:

$$\frac{3 \text{ (sessions of agreement)}}{10 \text{ (agreement + disagreement)}} = 30\%$$

This low inter-observer reliability reveals that either the two observers are defining "attention" differently or in some other way are failing to record properly. Low reliability also means we cannot use the data to measure behavior status or change. The teacher discovered that her aide had not credited Eric with paying attention whenever he glanced around the room during a lesson. The teacher did, so long as Eric's main focus was on her or the material. After refining the procedure, the teacher and aide arrived at an 80% reliability level, which could then be used as a reasonable measure of Eric's attention. They subsequently used these reliable observations to monitor Eric's attention before and during treatment.

When Eric took a drug to help his allergies, it was discovered that his concentration or attention to task dropped significantly. Because this drop would interfere with Eric's learning progress, the observation data were used to help the physician adjust the medication until Eric's attention was not substantially reduced.

EVALUATION MATERIALS

A number of useful evaluation devices were mentioned in connection with the techniques you have just read. At this point we review and expand upon these in case you are ready to write a shopping list:

1. Graph paper
2. Mimeographed forms—charts for occurrence recordings, rating scales, and so on
3. Timers—pocket or parking meter timers if you need portability; kitchen timers and egg timers
4. Counters—golf score counters, leather and bead counters, masking tape fastened on a watch band for tally marks
5. Stopwatches—for cumulative timing—combination wristwatch and stopwatch

AN EXTENDED ILLUSTRATION

Mr. Bohn is concerned about the number of fights Ricky is having in his classroom. He first decides to get an accurate count of the frequency of Ricky's fights. Knowing there are little, medium, and big fights, Mr. Bohn defines "fights" as *any* physical attack on another person in the room. The class proceeds as usual; the only difference is that Mr. Bohn counts the frequency of Ricky's fights for five days. His record looks like this:

Day	Number of Fights
Monday	///
Tuesday	/
Wednesday	////
Thursday	//// /
Friday	////

The teacher now must plan a new consequence for the fights. He wants a consequence that will weaken Ricky's fighting behavior. He decides that he should try not only to weaken fighting but also to *strengthen* other behaviors incompatible with fighting. The usual consequence of Ricky's fights is teacher attention. It is hard not to attend to a child who is injuring another pupil! Mr. Bohn, however, realizes that this has to change if Ricky's disturbing behavior is to be decreased. First, he obtains an ordinary kitchen timer. He tells Ricky that she will earn five points every time the timer rings if she has not had a fight since the last time it rang. He first sets the timer for only 15 minutes to make it easy for Ricky to earn points. He then makes the time longer, but occasionally uses short intervals. He tells her that as soon as she has 100 points she may see the special cartoon movies she has been asking for. Note that points can be presented quickly—unlike the movie. The points, then, are a strengthening consequence that can be delivered immediately and consistently. Mr. Bohn believes this procedure may work to strengthen behaviors incompatible with fighting. He now wants to arrange a consequence to weaken fighting. He decides to *charge* points for fighting, just as he is charging points for the cartoon movies. Ricky and the teacher are thus put under a contract; not only does Ricky have to behave in a certain way (refrain from fighting) for her movies, but Mr. Bohn must behave in a certain way (let Ricky see the movies) when Ricky has enough points. This feature should be emphasized, because the point or token system is sometimes thought of as a way to control just the child's behavior. Just as important, the system alters the behavior of the person managing it. Both the teacher and the student are obliged to behave in a certain way to each other's mutual benefit.

Mr. Bohn continues to count the number of Ricky's fights for the next two weeks now that the new consequence is in effect.

The data for the first week of observation and the two weeks on the point system are shown in Table 11-1.

Note that the first week of the new system (days 6 to 10) did not look too promising. In fact, there were more fights on Tuesday of that week than on any previous day. An *increase* of undesirable behavior often occurs when new consequences are initiated. Happily, the third week shows a clear decline in the frequency of fights. Mr. Bohn is quite pleased with his procedures and will probably use this approach often. (Notice that Mr. Bohn's behavior of using this system is strengthened by its outcome.) An easier and better way of recording the results of Mr. Bohn's experiment is to display the data graphically, as shown in Figure 11-8.

Graphs are useful in summarizing data, and provide an easily comprehended capsule description of the statistics of a behavior. They are easy to construct and invaluable to the teacher who wishes to introduce precision into instructional procedures.

Table 11-1 Chart showing frequency of Ricky's fights per day for three weeks of observation

	Observation Only	*Point System in Effect*	
	Days 1–5	*Days 6–10*	*Days 11–15*
Monday	3	4	0
Tuesday	3	7	0
Wednesday	4	3	1
Thursday	6	0	0
Friday	5	0	0

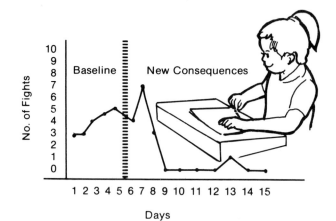

Figure 11-8   *Graphic display of change in Ricky's fighting (adapted from Deno, S. L., Jenkins, J. R., and Neisworth, J. T.* Student motivation and classroom management: a behavioristic approach. *Kalamazoo, Mich.: Behaviordelia, 1977)*

SUMMARY

Behavior evaluation on a day-to-day basis can be useful in selecting programmatic changes. It is useful for measuring inappropriate behaviors, for assessing behaviors about which teachers are uncertain, and for evaluating the effect of educational interventions. Such data also are useful for describing a child's performance to others and for giving the child daily performance feedback. Teachers can measure either behavior products or behavior processes. We suggested several simple techniques and instruments available for data gathering and recording. Using an evaluation-based instructional program, teachers are able to influence child development and provide clear documentation of changes. This specificity is one of the advantages of the behavioral approach; it also permits close scrutiny of *what* is to be learned and whether it *was* learned. No other strategy is as open to close examination of objectives and results—no other approach demands such specificity and accountability.

Review Questions

1. List four occasions on which teachers should collect precise data.
2. Define and give examples of these attributes of a behavior—frequency, intensity, duration, latency.
3. How does sampling make evaluation more efficient?
4. Differentiate between product and process evaluations.
5. Define a behavior rate.
6. List five curricular objectives. For each one state both a product and a process technique that could be used for evaluation.

Suggested Activities

1. State and define a behavior you wish to observe. Share your definition with a classmate who can observe and record with you. If there are discrepancies between your recordings, discuss these and refine your definition until your observations are reliable.

2. Choose an objective to teach a classmate (for example, how to tie a necktie, how to count in another language, how to spell a foreign word, how to an exercise). Determine a precise behavioral evaluation that would be appropriate. Construct a data form. Teach the behavior and enter the data.

3. Use both a product and process evaluation approach to monitor the number of cigarettes smoked by someone you know. What are the advantages and disadvantages of each procedure?

Suggested Readings

Alberto, P. A., and Troutman, A. C. Collecting, graphing data. In Alberto, P. A., and Troutman, A. C. (Eds.), *Applied behavior analysis for teachers*. Columbus, Oh.: Charles E. Merrill, 1982.

Boehm, A. E., and Weinberg, R. A. *The classroom observer: a guide for developing observation skills*. New York: Teachers College Press, 1977.

Cartwright, C. A., and Cartwright, G. P. *Developing observation skills*, 2nd ed. New York: McGraw-Hill, 1984.

Cooper, J. O. *Measuring behavior*. Columbus, Oh.: Charles E. Merrill, 1981.

Gardner, W. I. *Children with learning and behavior problems: a behavior management approach*. Boston, Mass.: Allyn & Bacon, 1978.

Halle, J. W., and Sindelar, P. T. Behavioral observation methodologies for early childhood education. In Mori, A. A., Fewell, R. R., Garwood, S. G., and Neisworth, J. T. (Eds.), *Topics in early childhood special education: managing the preschool environment*. Rockville, Md.: Aspen Systems, 1982.

Neisworth, J. T., Willoughby-Herb, S. J., Bagnato, S. J., Cartwright, C. A., and Laub, K. A. Applying formative and summative evaluation. In Neisworth, J. T., Willoughby-Herb, S. J., Bagnato, S. J., Cartwright, C. A., and Laub, K. A. (Eds.), *Individualized education for preschool exceptional children*. Rockville, Md.: Aspen Systems, 1980.

Ruggles, T. R. Some considerations in the use of teacher implemented observation procedures. In Allen, K. E., and Goetz, E. M. (Eds.), *Early childhood education: special problems, special solutions*. Rockville, Md.: Aspen Systems, 1982.

Stallings, J. A. *Learning to look*. Belmont, Calif.: Wadsworth, 1977.

Willoughby-Herb, S. J., and Neisworth, J. T. Keeping track of child progress. In Willoughby-Herb, S. J., and Neisworth, J. T. (Eds.), *HI-COMP preschool curriculum*. Columbus, Oh.: Charles E. Merrill, 1983.

PART THREE

COGNITIVE-DEVELOPMENTAL THEORY

*P*art Three examines the concepts and applications of cognitive-developmental theory. Chapter 12 introduces the theory by defining *what it is* and *what it is not*. The theory comprises an interacting series of "holisms"—no aspect functions in isolation from the others. The four basic components—intelligence, structure, function, and content—provide a lens through which to examine the growing child. The four factors that influence intellectual development—maturation, direct experience with the physical world, interactions with the social environment, and equilibration—provide another means of examining cognitive growth, which is the focus of cognitive-developmental theory.

Piaget identified stages of growth: sensorimotor, preoperational, concrete operational, and formal operational. Because we are interested in applications to early childhood education, we focus on the preoperational child.

In Chapter 13, we suggest applications. We are most concerned with describing key principles for preschool programs. Our principles focus on integrating curricula, constructing the curricular format, and generating activities. Teachers design a curriculum that facilitates the whole child and ensure that activities meet the needs of each individual. The curriculum framework provides a format within which to develop, use, and evaluate activity plans. Principles for generating curricular activities are derived from the four domains of knowledge. The overall strategy is to arrange the environment to make discovery by the child possible.

In Chapter 14, we stress cognitive-developmental practice in early education. Developmental factors, knowledge areas, and program goals are woven together to design interactive programs for young children. Adult—child and peer group interactions focus on treating children with respect and promoting the child's positive self-image. Free choice, large- and small-group instruction, and block scheduling characterize cognitivist programs. Physical space, equipment, materials, and parent involvement all provide ways of maximizing the child's potential for developmental growth.

Chapter 15 focuses on evaluating cognitive-developmental programs, which requires understanding the rationale for evaluation and the clinical method of assessment. We identify the variety of cognitive schemata that children attain at various intellectual levels and describe developmental changes that occur in cognitive functioning.

A Cognitive-Developmental Approach

*C*ognitive-developmental theory was developed originally by Jean Piaget, a Swiss genetic epistemologist. Piaget studied how learning takes place, and his thoughts and ideas form a relatively complex description of the evolution of human growth. The theory has intertwining concepts and constructs that primarily describe thinking in human beings from infancy through maturity to old age. Much like a mosaic projected within multi-dimensional space, the concepts and constructs are all interrelated with each other. Further, they focus on a "wholeness" of development, or "to-tality." For example, you already know from previous coursework that you can describe cognitive-developmental theory using terms such as "use of the senses," "active involvement," "operational intelligence," "conservation of number or volume," or "sensorimotor growth." Each of these concepts taken individually does not have much meaning; they are not independent theoretical constructs. However, when put together, these concepts form a multidimensional and interactive framework and give a clue to how human beings develop their cognitive repertoires across ages.

The subjects we will examine in this chapter are: (1) Piaget's view on the development of cognitive growth and thinking, and its components; (2) several factors that contribute to intellectual adaptation; (3) stages of growth; and (4) types of knowledge. These subjects, examined in context of the young child from about 2 to 5 years of age, build understanding on how to apply cognitive-developmental ideas to instructions (Chapter 13), design environments (Chapter 14), and evaluate the youngster's growth and learning in preschool (Chapter 15).

COGNITIVE GROWTH AND THINKING

Cognitive-developmental theory, as you might guess from the words them-selves, focuses on intellectual growth. It describes gradual attainment of increasingly more effective thought structures from birth through old age.

It also implies that individuals observe, generalize, apply, and test data against reality (the environment). Cognitive theory takes into account seeing, hearing, touching, smelling, tasting, analyzing, synthesizing, and receiving feedback from the environment. Thus, it is mental action of incorporating processes and manipulating salient aspects of the environment to form and test hypotheses, and to adapt to the outcomes.

From this perspective, intelligence is a coherent system of living and acting operations. Piaget's view of intelligence is an all-encompassing cognitive process of incorporating information into the thought structures, testing the data with past understanding and present feedback, and modifying these structures to fit physical and social environments. From a biological perspective, intelligence becomes biological adaptation at a psychological level. Cognitive-developmental theory as used by Piaget sketches the growth of the individual from the outside in as well as from the inside out. With the emphasis on thinking structures, the preschool youngsters are not viewed by Piaget as simple replicas of the adult. They think very differently from adults and they are less *efficient* and less *logical* in using their thought structures.

For Piaget, cognitive development could be thought of only in terms of an evolution through qualitatively different stages of thought. Piaget believed that the structures of thought through which cognition develops are inherited and species-specific. Although inherited, the underlying intellectual structures change and evolve within and between stages. The material used in building the framework is called operations. An *operation* is the essence of knowledge; it is an internal action that modifies the object of knowledge. Thought is logical—it follows patterns. Accordingly, cognitive development means the presence and growth of logical operations that permit the child to reconstruct, come to know, and understand his or her physical and social (and individual biological) world. While performing operations, the youngster gives up those ideas that are *incorrect* according to new-found thoughts, and replaces them with ideas that fit more accurately into the current framework. Thus, the simple developmental process is made up of conceptually rejecting ideas for others that are presently *correct*. Consequently, the primary goal of cognitive-developmental theory is to investigate the youngster's (rather than the adult's) gradual acquisition

---

Box 12-1   *Aspects of Piaget's Theory of Cognitive Development*

1. The focus of Piaget's theory is evolving cognitive schemata on a continuum of attainment from less to increasingly more abstract thought processes.

2. Structure, function, and content are the three basic components of intelligence. Their theoretical interplay is the key to the growth of thought structures from birth through maturity. Of these components, function alone explains how children make intellectual progress and is of major interest in cognitive-developmental theory.

3. The thrust of cognitive-developmental theory is experiential and at the same time interactional. Youngsters are actively involved with their environment of objects, events, and people. Children react to and act on this environment. Active involvement and cognitive interactions result in the growth of schemata.

4. It is the process of equilibration that is the self-regulator of children's cognitive development. Self-regulation and motivation to interact with the environment are primarily a result of internal, not external, forces residing within, not outside, children. The environment, including adult guidance, can challenge youngsters to discover, invent, solve problems, and develop cognitively.

5. Cognitive discrepancies that occur between children's schemata and experiential encounters result in equilibrated states that form the substance of intellectual growth.

6. The stage networking provides an effective model for cognitive growth.

7. Cognitive structures evolve in the sensorimotor stage and are the roots for all further development. The formal operational stages hinge on the evolution of schemata in the preoperational stage. Your work with young children in the preoperational stage is therefore crucial to their development of cognitive schemata.

8. Children in the preoperational stage come to day-care, nursery-school, kindergarten, and primary-school programs with highly developed and continuously evolving schemata. They challenge and are challenged by objects, events, situations, and people.

9. In constructivism, children actively develop knowledge from their interactional encounters. Constructivism highlights the interrelationship and interactiveness among the constructs and principles fundamental to the development of cognitive systems.

10. Knowledge built from the bedrock of physical objects, social conventions, and object-relations and the way individuals structure this cognitive bedrock encapsulates the interrelationships within cognitive-developmental theory and provides another effective tool in working with young children in classroom settings.

of increasingly more complex, abstract, and effective intellectual structures. Cognitive or intellectual development crystallizes basic conceptualizations that, in turn, become benchmarks for all further thinking.

Piaget's Related Developmental Ideas

In addition, there are several important ideas that relate to the basic definitions of cognitive-developmental theory and intelligence, which further elaborate what Piaget means by intellectual development. They are (1) individual differences, (2) intelligence quotients as determined by normed groups, (3) emotional and personality growth, (4) the three R's, and (5) speeding up developmental growth.

Individual Differences   From a classic Piagetian perspective, intelligence and cognitive-developmental theory do not deal explicitly with individual differences per se. In other words, whether Shanda can and Mark cannot conserve number, or whether one youngster can and another at the same age cannot demonstrate number conservation, is not stressed. Although these differences among individuals in intelligence and cognitive growth do inevitably exist and were initially used to build Piaget's world view, cognitive-developmental theory is applicable to groups rather than specific individuals. In light of individual differences, it is important to point out that Piaget's stages of intellectual growth, one of the cornerstones of cognitive-developmental theory, focus on optimal abilities of thought employed at any of the four stages of development. Thus, the four stages of intellectual development and the cognitive benchmarks in no way depict the mean or average performance or level of cognitive functioning (Ginsburg & Opper, 1979).

IQ   Intelligence from a cognitive-developmental perspective and IQ determined through objective testing and norm-reference groups are not the same thing. The IQ score "is not and cannot be more than a meaningful measure of certain standardized performances directly validated against success and therefore predictive of it" (Furth, 1966, p. 13). However, intelligence from a cognitive-developmental perspective is a system of living and acting operations that is not score- (or norm-group-) specific. Further, IQ essentially defines intelligence by means of a specific score, but it does not provide information about how intelligence develops and to what it leads. In this regard, attaining stages of cognitive development and responding to items on IQ tests are quite different endeavors. IQ test scores give little information about (1) the youngster's stage of cognitive development from an interactionist perspective, (2) characteristics of cognitive structures that are presently used in problem-solving situations, and (3) responses marked wrong on the instruments (that is, why the youngster chooses particular responses that are later marked "incorrect"). From the perspective of cognitive-developmental theory, the IQ is not a valid indicator of the child's level of general intelligence; IQ and general intelligence as viewed from cognitive-developmental theory are separate things.

Emotion and Personality   Cognitive-developmental theory and Piaget's view of intelligence do not emphasize emotional and personality growth of the young child within its framework. This is at first difficult to understand when individuals intuitively believe that emotions and personality are crucial aspects of growth; Freudian and neo-Freudian theories emphasize them. Recall that the thrust of cognitive theory is intellectual growth. Further, even though Piaget realizes both personality and emotional growth contribute to intellectual development of the individual, they are seen as motivational factors of adaptive or cognitive actions. Emotions and personality as factors of growth have many cognitive elements within them and are treated as part of the evolving intellectual system of thought. Thus, emotional and personality growth as separate or related factors basic to cognitive-developmental theory are ignored; their elements that are cognitive in origin become part of the structure of intelligence.

Academic Skills   The meanings of cognitive-developmental theory and intelligence are further clarified by examining the roles of the three R's. The thrust of schooling for the older or nonpreschool child usually focuses on curriculum or academic skills of the three R's (and other subject areas). The thrust of cognitive-developmental programs for preschool children is thinking or active intelligence. Distinguishing between thinking and learning curriculum skills requires at minimum a detailed discussion of the cognitive characteristics of the preschool child, which we will present later in this chapter. For now, it is sufficient to understand that the thinking processes basic to cognitive-developmental theory differ from those learning skills required in subject matter areas. For example, as part of the basic curriculum, young children are told that "ice is cold!" Being told that "ice is cold," according to cognitive-interactionist theory, carries with it little or no understanding of thinking processes. Learning that "ice is cold" in a "telling" manner is meaningless from a cognitive perspective. Developing thinking structures underlying the concept "ice is cold," means that the child sees the ice, picks it up, feels it, smells it, tastes and listens to it, watches it melt, watches it freeze again, cracks and churns it—in short, performs operations on the ice. Only after youngsters have internalized these experiences are they able to meaningfully understand "ice is cold" at their cognitive level.

The basic three R's and other subjects require motivation that is largely extrinsic to the children. However, Piaget believes that the primary motivation to develop thinking structures is intrinsic. For example, the motivation for the children to learn to read, write, and do mathematics usually arises from parents and teachers. The motivation to develop thinking processes is natural to and an intrinsic part of youngsters themselves. Cognitive-developmental theory is not against the three R's or other subject learning. It simply requires us to understand that the motivational elements largely used to learn school subject skills differ from the motivation that is crucial to the development of intelligence and the capacity to think.

Accelerating Development   Some understanding of cognitive-developmental theory and the interactionist view of intelligence usually leads us to ask or think about "speeding up the child's cognitive growth." In Piaget's perspective, the notion of speeding up intellectual growth does not have meaning. Because cognitive development continually evolves and active intelligence grows and expands, the rate at which they develop is optimal. The rate depends on the sum total of past and present experiences and several other factors that contribute to cognitive growth. Also, cognitive growth presupposes active internal motivation, but the notion of increasing the rate of learning implies that motivation is external to the child. Present and future growth, however, occur through internal motivation and with those cognitive structures that are mature. Trying to accelerate the rate of development usually means moving the child beyond her or his present level of understanding through external motivation. The result is usually increased rate rather than increased meaningful learning. When youngsters progress at their own pace and rate through the sequences of cognitive development and use internal motivation, they regulate their own growth and construct cognitive structures necessary for meaningful learning.

Having initially explored Piaget's views of cognitive development and intelligence and explained them in the context of related ideas such as individual differences, intelligence quotient, the basic three R's, and the acceleration of cognitive development, you can better understand Piaget's ideas of intelligence and thinking. Further, when Piaget speaks of intelligence as a totality of all operational thought structures that individuals use within any given stage of their development, intelligence and thinking mesh. Here, intelligence becomes thinking or active functioning of operational thought. Related to intelligence and thinking are several key components of Piaget's theory.

Components of Piaget's Theory

To understand this brief background on what intelligence is and is not from a cognitive perspective, you need to know the components of Piaget's theory. These three basic components of intelligence are structure, function, and content. They are interrelated with cognitive-developmental views of intelligence and thinking.

Structure   *Cognitive structure*, or simply *structure*, refers to organizational properties of intelligence (schemata), which develop through function. Structure determines the nature of behavioral content. As such, it is inferred from the child's particular behaviors or actions (content). However, structures are not inherited. They depend upon the child's history of interaction with previous environments. By schemata, Piaget means the cognitive structures used by individuals to intellectually modify or adapt to their environment. Simplistically, schemata can be described as concepts that assist the child in differentiating among and generalizing across perceived stimuli. Structure means the operations of the child's schemata, which are inferred from his or her particular behaviors. Structures help youngsters interpret stimulus events. We observe the youngsters' particular behavior, and make inferences from their actions, which in turn suggest something about their cognitive structures. Accordingly, structure can be viewed as a metaphor that describes relationships between and among schemata crucial to thinking (Sigel & Cocking, 1977). The relationships or forms of the structure reflect the acquisition of knowledge and the processes used by the child to achieve mental constructions. For example, young children compare the total number of two numerically equal rows of red checkers. Each of the rows of red checkers has four members; both rows are horizontal and parallel to one another and are directly in front of the youngsters. However, the checkers in one row have more distance between them than those in the other row. After counting the checkers in each row, the youngsters are asked to compare the rows numerically. They may say that the rows are unequal and that the row having checkers with more distance between members is greater in number than the row of checkers that is closer together. Here, the adult infers that the children do not yet have a complete concept of *number*. The children's cognitive structure or level of reasoning, in this example, was crucial to their solution to the problem. The observer can describe the children's systems of thinking, reasoning, or logic as representing a state of equilibrium. Because their systems were in equilibrium, the youngsters were basically unaware of their inabilities, individually or jointly, to solve this problem. Further, this interference suggests that the youngsters' schemata for number requires more qualitative growth. Eventually, these youngsters will be able to determine number after their structures have more fully developed and changed. This development and change represents intellectual growth.

Because these children's concepts develop over time to enable them to know number, their structures change with age. Structures serve as mediators, according to Piaget, for they are interposed between function on one hand and the content on the other. Function and content, the remaining basic components of intelligence, are described in the next sections.

Function   The second basic component of intelligence, according to Piaget, is function. Function refers to broad characteristics or attributes of

This boy's organizational skill is an example of intelligence-in-action.

intellectual activity. These attributes are stable as well as continual; they are constant for all individuals and hold true for all ages. Further, function defines the very nature of intellectual action and behavior and is concerned with the way in which the child proceeds in making cognitive advances.

Function is basic to Piaget's theory, for it describes abstract properties of cognitive progress that are characteristic of all individuals. Function as patterns of behavior is the way youngsters go about cognitive progress. The discrete behaviors of the preschooler—for instance, reaching out for, grasping, and throwing an object—or those of the infant—such as bringing food to his or her mouth—fit into the concept of function as patterns of behavior that help the child interact with his or her environment. These attributes of intellectual activity, or *intelligence-in-action*, are what Piaget calls organization and adaptation and the components of adaptation, which are assimilation and accommodation. Assimilation and accommodation are also called functional invariants. These fundamental and invariant components form the intellectual core and make possible emerging cognitive structures through interactions between the individual and environment. Accordingly, function cannot be meaningfully understood without examining the components of the cognitive core—organization and adaptation.

Organization as a fundamental characteristic and adaptation as an invariant attribute of function, as you know, are interrelated processes. Organization is the tendency of all individuals to place patterns of behavior into a system. Organization refers to the cognitive capacity of the individual to order experiential and environmental encounters and thoughts in accord with her or his particular stage of intellectual growth. Every act of intelligence-in-action is an organized process similar to the organized processes of biological digestion, excretion, or reproduction. As intelligence-in-action, the intellectual structure used in encounters implies an organization within which it proceeds. However, organization refers to cognitive systems of order and focuses on relationships among concepts and processes. It operates as a whole or totality in accord with the individual's stage of cognitive development and implies particular stage-dependent properties that are characteristic of all individuals.

A second process of intellectual functioning is adaptation. Adaptation simply refers to the interaction between the individual and the environment in which the complimentary processes of assimilation and accommodation are in the state of equilibrium. This will be discussed in detail later in this chapter.

Adaptation is partial change, because some things remain the same and some things change in the process; according to Forman and Kuchner (1977) adaptation suggests "a continuity of experience and conservation of the past." For example,

> *The infant grasps the newly presented sharp object in a way that is different from the way he used to grasp the familiar round object; yet, in both cases he opens his fingers wide before making contact with the object [p. 26].*

Understanding of past and present experiences is basic to adaptation; it implies a double understanding. Adaptation to future experiential encounters is assured through cognitive acts that coordinate past and present events.

Adaptation and organization can be viewed as the two sides of the coin (function). Adaptation implies an underlying coherence in which organization is produced through adaptation. Adaptive coping is an outward and organization an inward manifestation of the continuous creative interactions between individuals and their environments. Wadsworth (1974) notes that "biological acts are acts of adaptation to the physical environment and organizations of the environment" (p. 9). Viewed as complementary processes that are not separate, "cognitive acts are seen as acts of organization *of* and adaptation *to* the perceived environment" (p. 9). Because cognitive acts cannot be separated from adaptation or organization, Piaget believes that cognitive acts are forms of biological activity. Therefore, "intellectual and biological activity are both parts of the total process by which an [individual] adapts to the environment and organizes experience" (p. 10). Thus, every cognitive act not only presupposes but also involves the functioning characteristics of organization and adaptation.

Content   The third basic component of intelligence is content. Content is observable actions or behaviors that reflect intellectual activity. Examples of cognitive behaviors observed in children include sensorimotor actions, and more conceptual or abstract behaviors such as concrete operational. Content is influenced by specific interactions that the youngsters have with their environment. The content observed will vary depending on the children's environment and the quantity and quality of their interactions with that environment. Content is observed and reflects intellectual activity; for example, when the preschooler asserts that the sun rising in the sky in the morning and setting in the evening follows her or him to and from nursery school. In this example, the behavioral content is sensorimotor because of the relationships the preschooler established between his or her body movement and the movement of the sun. When the child is able to make distance, rate, and time comparisons and to estimate rate given coordination of distance and time, behavioral content that is more conceptual is shown. Thus, behavioral content varies from situation to situation, from age to age, and from child to child. Suggestions for teaching mathematics or science concepts, for example, can be made on the aspects of the growth of number, space, or causality in children (Flavell, 1963). The content component is as important to intelligence as are structure and function. Then too, like structure, content changes with age; and content, structure, and function become the major objectives for study of cognitive development. However, cognitive theory focuses more on examining the role of function and less on the roles of content and structure, because they change with development as a result of interactions between child and environment and with age.

In summarizing the contributions of structure, function, and content, intellectual components constituting intelligence, Flavell (1963) notes that:

> *Function is concerned with the manner in which any organism makes cognitive progress; content refers to the external behavior which tells us that functioning has occurred; and, structure refers to the inferred organizational properties which explain why this content rather than other content has emerged [p. 18].*

Relationships among Components   The following example provides further description and understanding of the relationships of structure to function and content. Preschoolers come in contact with a novel object for the first time. The object is a yellow plastic ring, 3 inches in diameter, which is connected to a string 6 inches long. It resembles part of a fishing pole, with the lure and line but without the pole.

As an aspect of function, the preschoolers begin to explore the plastic ring by looking, touching, and grasping it. They may also swing it around their head. Looking, touching, grasping, and swinging are exploratory accommodations made on the yellow plastic ring and string. Accommodations are one aspect of function. The relationship of function to structure here includes previous interactions the preschoolers have had with similar objects. By virtue of previous object interactions, the preschoolers already possess structures (or schemata) that guide their exploratory accommodations. The new object becomes "assimilated to the concepts of touching, moving, seeing, etc.—concepts which are already part of the child's cognitive organization" (Flavell, 1963, p. 51). Flavell also notes that the actions on the object are accommodations of these concepts (for example, touching, moving) to the physical properties of the ring and assimilations of the ring to the concepts of touching, moving, or seeing. Further, because the youngsters are interacting with the object in a meaningful way and not simply repeating behaviors previously attained, their structures (which in this example are defined through grasping, seeing, holding) become changed themselves as they accommodate to and assimilate the object. The ways in which the youngsters' structures become modified include generalization and variation (Flavell, 1963).

Generalization refers to the fact that structures become generalized in order to assimilate the new object (Flavell, 1963). In this instance, the preschoolers learn that the yellow plastic ring can be swung around their head or grasped around their fingers. In this manner, the structures become changed and now are extended to include this new yellow plastic ring. The preschoolers' cognitive structures become changed "in so far as the structure of the new object necessitates some variation in the way the preschooler swings, grasps, or looks at it" (Flavell, 1963, p. 51). The cognitive structures become generalized to the yellow plastic ring as well as varied as the result of the demands this ring places on these same structures of the child. Here, the preschooler learns actively to "think about what the object is and why the object is not what it is not" (Forman & Kuchner, 1977, p. 163). Accordingly, the youngsters learn that the grasp needed for ringlike objects is somewhat different from other grasps in the past. Further, the preschooler learns that the yellow plastic ring looks as well as feels a little different from other objects previously seen and used (Flavell, 1963). These generalized and varied structures provide a foundation for other present and future accommodations relative to unfamiliar objects these preschoolers interact with in their encounters. "These new accommodations engender further changes in intellectual organization, and so the cycle repeats itself" (Flavell, 1963, p. 51).

The example shows the interactive nature of the relationship of structure to function and content, explains how new information about the environment is gathered, and illustrates the attainment of cognitive progress and intelligence-in-action. The cognitive components of structure, function, and content and their interplay are the cornerstone of intelligence and the keystone of Piaget's theory of cognitive development and cognitive interactionism.

FACTORS INFLUENCING THE COURSE OF COGNITIVE GROWTH

Thus far, we have surveyed Piaget's ideas of intelligence and thinking as well as structure, function, and content and their relations to cognitive development. As you recall, cognitive growth occurs within social, physical, and biological contexts. From birth through maturity, the cognitive structures (schemata) continue to grow and develop as the individual (through her or his constructions based on interactions) assimilates and accommodates in his or her physical and social environments. Thus, there are several factors that influence the course of cognitive development. These factors are global in the sense that they influence the course of thinking in all individuals. Then too, the elements are broad in that they are stage-free factors of Piaget's theory of cognitive development. Generally, you encountered them before in the discussion of intelligence, cognitive development, and the components of intelligence: structure, function, and content. In this context, the factors influencing cognitive development were related but implicit in their descriptions. Further, we will come back to these factors throughout our discussion of the stages of intellectual development and the preoperational characteristics of the young child. At this point, you need to recall that cognitive theory is an interrelated totality—a multidimensional mosaic. Accordingly, the explanation of these factors does not involve entirely new material apart from previous discussions of intelligence, structure, function, and content and their operations within Piaget's cognitive-developmental theory. Rather, the factors give definition to these interrelationships—which are imposed on and operate across the entire developmental continua. Thus, within this global context, the factors influencing cognitive development are: (1) maturation; (2) direct experiences with the physical world; (3) actions with the social environment; and (4) equilibration. In addition, the concept of schemata is explained as developing structures of the child's actions through assimilation and accommodation in his or her environment.

Maturation

Maturation characterizes the development of the biological structures of the child. The contribution of maturation or biological structures to intellectual growth is basic to the development of neurological and endocrine systems in individuals. In accord with Piaget's cognitive-developmental theory, the neurological system refers specifically to the growth of brain tissues. Similarly, the endocrine system means the development of glands. The contributions of the endocrine and neurological systems are specifically defined in cognitive theory. With increased biological growth of brain tissues and endocrine and related physical processes, the child (by virtue of these biological achievements) attains greater and more refined capacities for cognitive development. Further, as the biological processes continue to mature, the youngster is able to make more effective use of physical and social encounters for cognitive development. Maturation can be viewed as a biological unfolding of body parts and their increasing specialization over time, proceeding toward increasingly mature structures. Some of these structures are not seen in the embryonic stages of growth. For Piaget, the maturational process is biological growth as well as specialization and differentiation of biological structures. Here, biological growth is epigenetic because biological growth and specialization of body parts are considered together. However, Piaget unequivocally states that intelligence neither is nor proceeds by maturation. You can assume from previous discussions of cognitive-developmental theory that although the maturational factor in Piaget's theory is biological programming, thought processes and logic are also not innate. Accordingly, the minimal contributions of maturation to cognitive growth are clear for Piaget: "The effect of maturation consists essentially of organizing new possibilities for development; that is, giving access to structures which could not be evolved before these possibilities were offered" (Piaget, 1970, p. 720).

Maturation is the first factor that influences a child's cognitive development.

For Piaget, maturation contributes possibilities for rather than actualizations of cognitive development between which "there must intervene a set of other factors such as . . . [physical] experience and social interaction" (Piaget, 1970, p. 720). "Maturation . . . can do no more than determine the totalities of possibilities and impossibilities at a given stage" (Inhelder & Piaget, 1958, p. 337). Thus, direct experience with the physical world, actions with the social environment, cognitive equilibration, and maturation are indispensable to the course of cognitive development.

Direct Experiences with the Physical World

Direct experience with the physical world, or simply physical experience, is the second factor influencing the course of cognitive development. Physical experiences are motor and sensory actions as well as experiences in problem solving or using reasoning processes (Sigel & Cocking, 1977). The following discussion explains physical experiences as sensory and motor and experiences requiring reasoning processes.

Sensory and motor experiences are based on involvement of the senses and exercise leading to the development of knowledge through the youngster's direct experiences with the physical world. In using sensory and motor actions, the youngster sees, hears, smells, touches, and grasps objects in the environment. In addition, the child with motor actions moves objects from place to place. In using sensory actions of seeing, hearing, tasting, smelling, touching, and coordinated muscle and body movements (kinesthesis), the youngster experiences stimuli of all kinds in the environment and acts on them. This is necessary for the functional invariants of assimilation and accommodation to occur. Through sensory and motor actions and interactions between the child and objects, the child acts on and reacts to the environment. Through this interplay between the child and the environment, cognitive structures (schemata) grow and evolve by assimilation and accommodation.

The second factor that influences a child's cognitive development is direct experience with the physical world.

The role of direct experience with the physical world is important to all individuals at all ages for cognitive growth to occur. However, its role in cognitive growth varies between very young and older children. For instance, quite early in life infants gain direct experience with the physical environment in a direct, observable, and straightforward manner. Their hands grasp and regrasp objects; they "mouth" all types of physical objects. The very young indiscriminately smell, and their eyes focus and explore physical objects. In addition, they make various sounds that are attractive and appealing. At first trial and error, the grasping, regrasping, mouthing, and exploring later become intentional. In addition to using the senses, very young children also employ movement to gain direct experiences on a trial and error basis for cognitive growth. They move their arms, trunk, and other body parts in uncoordinated and coordinated ways. Banging, bumping, pounding, or patting, the infants' movements produce added experiences in their physical world. The interactions within which the infant assimilates and accommodates are primarily sensory and motor and progress from trial and error to intentional acts as age increases.

Older youngsters of seven or eight years of age also gain direct experiences with their physical world. However, these older children's constructions of interactions between themselves and their environment increasingly become more symbolic and intentional. *Symbolic*, in this instance, means that the youngsters do not need to manipulate directly familiar objects to know and recognize the functions these objects serve in their physical world. The children have *internalized* these familiar objects and their functions. Further, they can now mentally represent familiar objects, situations, and people that are not present, not in view, and not in their direct grasp. The children's interactions with the environment are now qualitatively and quantitatively different from those they displayed as infants. For example, two older children were playing a pretend game of fighting bulls. After finding two Y-shaped twigs they began to pretend that the Y twigs were bulls. They placed the twigs end on end and, with one child holding each twig, they played fighting bulls by pushing twigs back and forth to represent charging and ramming animals. Here, the children are showing symbolic actions. Having had previous direct experiences with fighting bulls, they used symbolic processes to show fighting bulls complete with sounds representing the fight. Here, interaction between children and objects based on direct experience with their physical world was symbolic, conceptual, and abstract. The physical objects are manipulated in a more indirect manner than those in the infant's environment. In addition, the children in this example are actively assimilating and to a lesser extent accommodating because they are using twigs *as if* they were bulls without realistic regard to the actual characteristics of the twigs. Here, they were using twigs as bulls and not as twigs, with the intent of playing fighting bulls.

The pretend game may change into a more realistic one that still shows symbolic uses of experiences if the children as a group decide that one bull must win and if rules of fair play are established. The interactions become highly conceptual and are based on active uses of indirect and vicarious experiences. However, assuming the pretend play gives way to the realistic game, the children display more accommodating and less assimilating processes. Regardless of the symbolic quality of the intellectual processes, direct experiences with the physical world are basic to influencing the course of cognitive development. Thus, as children construct interactions based on direct experiences with—and actively assimilate and accommodate to—the physical world, they develop intellectually.

Exercise with sensory and motor experiences with the physical world is also fundamental to developing structures (schemata). According to Piaget, exercise involves actions and reactions of youngsters and objects they manipulate in some fashion. For example, youngsters hold and drop their rattle. They again grasp the rattle, let it drop, and watch as it falls and comes to rest on the blanket. Again and again the same actions of grasping, holding, dropping, and reactions are completed. From these interactions information is acquired and new cognitive structures are developed that are basic to and derived from the exercise. These constant repetitions take place in children regardless of age, and these exercises of action and reaction result in competence or the ability to demonstrate these abilities effectively and behaviorally (Sigel & Cocking, 1977).

Deducing Relationships   Beyond manipulating objects and conceptualizing their particular attributes, there is another major cognitive result of direct experiences with the physical world. This particular cognitive result also influences reasoning or problem-solving processes concerning the validity of experiences; Sigel and Cocking (1977) refer to this particular cognitive aspect as deducing interaction relationships. Manipulating and conceptualizing particular properties of objects assists the growth of cognitive development through interactions resulting in logical deduction. Straight logical deductions are rather clear and straightforward cognitive inferences. Here, new information is gained about experience from interactions and their repetitions based on manipulating objects and abstracting their attributes (that is, singular physical properties and unitary functions). However, deducing interactive relationships refers to inferences made among objects, their attributes, and functions through repeatedly acting on them. When two or more objects produce new information based on how they act and react in this combinatorial setting, deducing interactive relationships, as a reasoning process, evolves. When the same two (or more) objects are used independently, these interactive relationships do not evolve. Instead, logically straightforward deductions of each of the object's attributes are possible. Deducing interactive relationships based on direct experiences with physical objects can also be viewed as higher-order or more conceptually abstract interactions. For example, preschoolers at an easel may use individual colors of blue and yellow to paint their house and parent. Based on direct experience with the physical world, new knowledge and reasoning about the singular attributes of each of the individual colors are made. Here, the children learn about these colors but in rather singular fashion. In addition, if the painting experience is novel, the youngsters come to know how to manipulate a brush and learn about moving paint from its container to the easel without dripping. The new deductions from these experiences concern each of the objects and situations as separate and independent entities. As the preschoolers continue to repeat easel painting with colors of blue and yellow, interesting discoveries are made. For instance, they may mix the colors and create green. They may learn that the order of adding the two together is irrelevant in making green. Combining and ordering of the colors develops new relationships and discoveries for the youngsters. These new relationships among objects conceptually evolve from deducing interactive relationships. In addition, understandings that are produced in this manner are examples of logicomathematical knowledge because "nothing, in the objects [themselves], yields information about their similarities but . . . relationships emerge when the child orders the materials" (Sigel & Cocking, 1977, p. 20). Logicomathematical (and physical) knowledge is explained later in this chapter. Relevant and meaningful knowledge arising from reasoning through deducing interactive relationships involves new actions. Through higher-order interactions among construction activities, new knowledge and reasoning derived from direct experiences with the physical world evolve.

The factor of direct experience with physical objects produces interactive settings in which knowledge through objects and construction activities develops. Like maturation, the factor of direct experience with the physical world assists the construction of schemata and guides the course of cognitive development. In related fashion, the remaining two factors dealing with the social environment and equilibration are also crucial to the growth and progression of cognitive development.

Actions with the Social Environment

The third factor is actions with the social environment. Like direct experiences with physical objects, this factor is based on an interaction that focuses on the child in an active manner. Similar to direct experiences with the physical world, actions with social environment are experiences that are acted on and reacted to by the youngsters. Actions with the social environment are the youngsters' interactions and experiences that occur within their social worlds. The similarities between the second and third factors mean that the course of cognitive structures and logical reasoning is influenced by the youngsters' physical and social experiences.

Social experiences focus on cognitive development of youngsters in social milieux; social institutions and experiences play a leading role in the development of knowledge. In a broad sense, social institutions and experiences transmit socially appropriate ideas that facilitate the child's functioning in society. The medium of social transmission is in part the product of language and education. Social institutions provide additional opportunities to construct cognitive structures through interactions based on these social experiences. The social institutions that play leading roles in influencing the course of cognitive growth include the child's family and its members, adults as significant others, school, religious organizations, and peer groups.

Within a social milieu, ideas between individuals are exchanged; this is social interaction. A social environment is important for the functional components of assimilation and accommodation to occur. With this interplay between youngsters' and others' ideas and feelings, cognitive structures grow by assimilation and accommodation. The development of schemata becomes a product of interactions between youngsters and their social environments.

Social interactions constitute the third influence on cognitive development.

Similar to the roles of direct experiences with the physical world, the role of actions with the social environment is important to all individuals at all ages. However, its role varies between very young and older children. The influence of social worlds on the cognitive development of infants, for example, is observable and straightforward. For the older child, however, the role of the social milieu in influencing the constructions between self and the ideas of other individuals becomes increasingly more symbolic and less directly observable.

Infants act on and react to ideas and stimulus events in their social world. They gain experience in the social world in a less symbolic, more direct way than do older children. For example, infants accept the faces of all people who intrude into their social space—later they can differentiate between the faces of family and nonfamily members. Further, the interactions between faces of family members, their physical movements, pitch, intonation, and rate of communication become the grist that molds the course of the infant's cognitive growth.

Modeling   The role of the actual social environment is directly observable in the toddler. As mother, father, or older sister or brother perform actions, the very young copy them. Modeling is an action basic to the world of social ideas and contributes to cognitive development through exercise and practice at the child's level of functioning. Further, young toddlers and preschoolers, through social interactions with family members and significant others, develop cognitive distinctions between *me* and *you*. For example, the *me* emerges and continues to grow into a socially egocentric individual, and the *me and you* and the *me versus you* are continually practiced through children's social and physical actions. Cognitive egocentric structures permit very young children to know that they are the center of activity. Understanding all occurrences according to their terms, youngsters see everything from their subjective perspectives. As cognitive structures of young children continue to evolve within the world of social ideas, me-versus-you concepts expand into more prosocial ones of competition, then social understanding and acceptance of individual rights of other peers and adults. Here, youngsters display more cognitive sociocentric structures. These permit them to view their own percepts, concepts, and points of view as one of many possible interpretations of reality. In short, very young children with continued and meaningful social experiences over time become more objective and hold increasingly greater world views of reality. These interactions within which very young children assimilate and accommodate operate and evolve; interchanges between individuals become more meaningful and increasingly symbolic.

Older youngsters, 7 or 8 years of age, like very young children, gain experiences within the social world of ideas and use and test them. In turn, this testing promotes reasoning, but the reasoning is more symbolic and less overt. Unlike very young children, older ones have internalized social ideas through parents and other significant adults and peers. Then, too, older youngsters internally represent these social ideas in a more sociocentric—rather than egocentric—manner. Having established, practiced, and repeated me-and-you actions, older children can now cooperate with peers and others in social group settings. The interactions between themselves and the world of social ideas help develop the capacity to take the role of the significant other; they can see and adopt the views of others in the context of ideas and feelings. For instance, several older preschoolers pretend to play house. They discuss and define roles of Mommy, Daddy, Sally, the baby, and Mark, the older brother. As the children begin to assign roles, Greta, who is asked to play baby Sally, says, "I played baby, yesterday. Someone else needs to play the baby." There is momentary silence, as the group members internalize Greta's statement and feelings. Then Frank, assigned by the children to play Daddy, says, "I will be baby this time." The group finishes assigning roles and plays the game. The children, and Frank especially, were able to put themselves in Greta's shoes, understand her feelings, determine what was fair play, and make a judgment based on needs of the other and the group. Their ideas were symbolic and abstract, and had a shared meaning based on social understandings and feelings of and for the other. Further, children in this situation are actively assimilating and accommodating by taking in and modifying social ideas at high conceptual levels. As these children construct cognitive structures derived from actions with the social environments and actively assimilate and accommodate to them, they grow intellectually.

Exercise Play   Exercise or practice plays the same cognitive role in children's interactive social ideas as it does with physical objects. Exercise includes actions on and reactions to social ideas. Older preschoolers role play a significant adult complete with verbal expressions and statements in a pretend episode. The expressions characteristic of the role are repeated and practiced again and again. The youngsters become immersed in a sea of words and ideas that define and refine the significant adult and situation they are playing. Through continued repetition of these roles and use of language, the youngsters acquire competence in these abilities (Sigel & Cocking, 1977). Acquiring competence by stepping into the shoes of significant adults or peers, children come to understand the feelings of the individuals they role play. From this exploration of the children's world of social ideas, new knowledge, in addition, is acquired. Because children act and react to social ideas, improvisation occurs in role play, requiring the youngsters to move beyond what the model actually does and says. In these situations, children create new social ideas and use actions that are not characteristic of this or any known model they have previously observed. In improvising, the social milieux assist youngsters in developing new cognitive structures that arise from this aspect of exercise. Actions with the social environment influences the course of cognitive development through the construction of meaningful interactions and relevant exercise and repetition of these constructions.

Moving from egocentricity to sociocentricity, older preschoolers move beyond physical referents that can be seen or heard to those referents that arise from within their social milieu. Social ideas such as honesty, companionship, and fair play are relatively dependent clusters and constructions arising from interactions within their social milieu. For these constructions and cognitive structures to arise and evolve, the youngster depends on social interactions for the validation of reasoning.

Social interactions that arise in family units, religious organizations, schools, and peer groups, and through media such as television, all contribute to cognitive development. However, they are not independent of the factors of physical interactions or maturation. The interactions develop through assimilating and accommodating and evolve as a whole within a totality. The factors of maturation, direct experience with the physical world, and actions with the social environment, as well as equilibration, influence the course of cognitive development in an interrelated manner.

Equilibration

The fourth factor crucial to the course of cognitive development is equilibration. Because Piagetian concepts are interrelated and picture a totality of intellectual actions, equilibration is also linked with other concepts such as equilibrium and disequilibrium. Equilibration is associated with the cognitive structures of assimilation and accommodation. Further, from a global perspective, it is ultimately linked to the three types of cognition: (1) when assimilation and accommodation are in balance, (2) when assimilation predominates over accommodation, and (3) when accommodation predominates over assimilation (Flavell, 1963). Thus, this section is organized into (1) basic descriptions of the concepts of equilibrium, equilibration, and disequilibrium, (2) explanation of assimilation and accommodation and their relationships with equilibrium, and (3) description of the three types of cognition.

First, the process of equilibration integrates the other three factors of maturation, direct experience with the physical world, and actions with the social environment. As such, equilibration as a set of mental behaviors synthesizes the organizational qualities of cognitive growth. Further, the process of equilibration occurs when there is a balance among these factors. As an internal and self-regulating process, equilibration assists children in attaining increasingly higher levels of equilibrium and is a major keystone of cognitive development. As an internal self-regulating system, it is important for growth along the entire continuum of cognitive development. This self-regulating process operates in children and in all their interactions with their physical and social worlds. Equilibration becomes not only a propellant for cognitive changes but also an explanation for their transitions from stage to stage. Equilibration produces successive and discrete stages, which become organized, operating systems of actions (that is, sensorimotor or concrete operational) whose characteristics as totalities are consistent with and can be explained in equilibrium terms such as mobility (that is, capacity of cognitive movement from lower- to higher-order thought) and stability (that is, capacity of cognitive compensation) (Flavell, 1963).

Second, equilibration gives rise to stages, so it is related to equilibrium and disequilibrium. Equilibration is the process of attaining a state of balance between assimilation and accommodation. In accord with Piaget's theory of cognitive development, this state of balance is active (as opposed to static or restful states in a classical Freudian sense) and refers to the manner in which children act on their environment and gain new knowledge from this activity. Because children are active individuals, they seek to organize, structure, and bring stability to their environment. Because this state of balance is continually and constantly an active one, the children's cognitive system "which has attained a high degree of equilibrium is not at rest" (Flavell, 1963, p. 214). According to Flavell, "the child's cognitive system . . . attempts to deal with environmental events in terms of its structures (i.e., assimilation), as it can modify itself in line with environmental demands (i.e., accommodation). As such, equilibrium, resulting from equilibration, implies activity and a state of relative harmony with the environment" (p. 214).

Disequilibrium   In the process of equilibration, children's cognitive systems go into states of disequilibrium. Disequilibrium exists when the processes of assimilation and accommodation are not in balance with each other. Like equilibrium, disequilibrium occurs between children's present

Equilibrium, which "implies activity and a state of relative harmony," results from equilibration, the fourth influence on cognitive development.

cognitive structures and their experiential encounters. However, unlike equilibrium, disequilibrium occurs when a discrepancy between the two exists. This discrepancy between what the child currently understands (that is, cognitive structures) and the environment (that is, experiential encounters) creates an imbalance in the cognitive structures. Cognitive conflicts are set in motion by the discrepancies between the cognitive structures and experiential encounters. For example, a preschooler at his or her level of cognitive growth comes to understand that all objects float when immersed in water. Of course, the situation is not real or objective to adults. We have come to know that not all objects immersed in water float. This example shows that as adults we come to this encounter with quite differing cognitive structures than the preschooler who understands that all objects in water float. In instances of disequilibrium, children's cognitive systems are not yet stable, and their ways of dealing with the world with respect to a concept are not totally based on objective logic and reasoning.

As a further example of cognitive discrepancy and conflict that could occur between mental structures and experiential encounters, we return to the preschooler who believes that all objects float. As this preschooler continues to encounter objects in water, she or he will come across objects that do not float when immersed. A discrepancy between the preschooler's cognitive structures and experiential encounters occurs and her or his cognitive structures are in a state of imbalance. A change in cognitive structures occurs when these experiential encounters are assimilated to and become accommodated through them. Assimilation and accommodation change existing cognitive structures to new knowledge, such as, "some things float whereas others sink when immersed in water." The preschooler's cognitive structures have been modified through this new information. Thus, equilibration in the process of attaining equilibrium also implies disequilibrium. In turn, disequilibrium provides the necessary cognitive motivation of the child to seek equilibrium and further reach a balance in assimilative and accommodative processes. As the child attains equilibrium through equilibration, the child's cognitive structure moves from disequilibrium to equilibrium (relative to his or her particular interactions with the environment).

In sum, the examples of the preschooler before and after attaining the cognitive structures of "some objects float whereas others sink when placed in water" show two main cognitive aspects: the state of disequilibrium relative to equilibrium, and the movement of cognitive structures from one state to another (or directionality). First, the state of disequilibrium helps explain equilibrium. The individual cannot be in the state of equilibrium and disequilibrium at the same time on the same understanding at the same level of cognitive growth. In this sense, equilibrium becomes a balance between the cognitive structures of assimilation and accommodation. Second, cognitive transition from the state of disequilibrium to equilibrium (and vice versa in cyclical fashion) shows movement of cognitive understanding from lower to higher levels and from stage to stage. Movement, in this sense, shows cognitive structures—a sequence of disequilibrium to equilibrium states across development. More specifically, this movement of cognitive structures into higher forms of equilibrium integrates and incorporates lower states of equilibrium. The result is a more complex totality of cognitive structures. The child integrates this movement (or directionality) of cognitive structure into a new totality, which is assumed to be a *better* equilibrium state than its precursors.

The processes of assimilation and accommodation are related to equilibrium. These two terms will be used again and again throughout these chapters. We have used them in explaining the four factors encouraging intellectual growth. These explanations focused primarily on how assimilation and accommodation operate in the course of cognitive development. Here, the focus is on the definitions of assimilation and accommodation and points to their explicit relationships to equilibrium. Both assimilation and accommodation are derived from biology and are the twin complementary processes that make up adaptation. Both were used in the definitions of adaptation and function earlier in this chapter. Assimilation and accommodation are stable processes and operate throughout the individual's lifetime.

Assimilation, then, is simply the cognitive process used to incorporate, take in, and integrate environmental or stimulus events into presently existing schemata. In other words, youngsters deal with environmental and ex- periential events and constantly integrate these new events into their struc- tures. The process of assimilation permits children to understand these novel stimuli in terms of their own schemata. As an example of assimila- tion, very young preschoolers come across a novel object and incorporate its characteristics into their current schemata; the object could be an orange. To begin incorporating and integrating information on the object into their cognitive structures, the children must act on it. By seeing, touching, tasting, moving, smelling, and hearing, they use their senses to collect these characteristics of the object and begin to fit the orange into their schemata. Information on the object taken into their mental structures may include its roundness, softness, orange color, or sweet taste. As infor- mation on this novel stimulus begins to be incorporated, the cognitive structures themselves sift until one set of schemata could include that ob- ject and its attributes. The data on the orange become integrated into exist- ing cognitive structures, possibly as a round object—orange in color—that is sweet when tasted. As the children have further novel experiences with this object the collection of schemata evolve. In this instance, assimilation can be regarded as the "cognitive process of placing new stimulus events into existing schemata" (Wadsworth, 1974, p. 15). In the example, how- ever, it is important to note that assimilation does contribute to the growth of new cognitive structures but does not modify or change the ex- isting ones. As an example of assimilation processes and their integrating function, Wadsworth (1974) says that "One might compare a schemata to a balloon, and assimilation to putting air into the balloon. The balloon gets larger (assimilative growth) but does not change its shape (develop- ment)" (p. 15). Essentially, assimilation is the twin complementary process of adaptation through which the child functionally organizes his world. The other twin complementary process of adaptation is accommodation.

Modifications   Accommodation as a process is the modification of exist- ing or creation of new structures, which results in development. In other words, in the process of integrating new object characteristics into the mind, the child's cognitive structures are altered. Through the accom- modation process, existing cognitive structures change and new ones de- velop. Children continually adjust their schemata to the idiosyncratic de- mands of their immediate environment. Children accommodate their cognitive functioning to particular characteristics of the stimulus events they are attempting to assimilate (Flavell, 1963). For example, coming across the novel object orange, youngsters accommodate their mental structures to this object and its characteristics. In turn, existing structures change or new structures are developed. The integrated structures develop into the orange schema and the children now readily assimilate and accom- modate this object and similar ones in their environment.

Assimilation, a quantitative change, accounts for growth; accommodation, a qualitative change, accounts for development of cognitive structures. In a state of balance, together they account for equilibrium and intellectual adaptation. Both assimilation and accommodation work as units in all of cognitive thought. Flavell (1963) says that "every assimilation of an object to an organism simultaneously involves an accommodation of the organism to the object; conversely, every accommodation is at the same time an assimilatory modification of the object accommodated to" (p. 46). Operating together they account for all of the growth and development of adaptative and nonadaptative thought.

In addition, equilibration can be viewed as one type of cognition in which assimilation and accommodation are in balance. In this sense, cognitive acts comprise equal amounts of assimilation and accommodation. From this perspective, the functional act of assimilation balancing accommodation is only one of three kinds of cognition (Flavell, 1963). Two other types of cognition do not show the state of balance between assimilative and accommodative processes but represent ones of disequilibrium. The other two operate when the processes of assimilation dominate accommodation and when the processes of accommodation dominate assimilation (Flavell, 1963). These two states of disequilibrium show imbalances between the twin complementary processes. Within any developmental stage, these two types of imbalance occur. According to Piaget, these fluctuations are momentary changes in cognitive development toward more equilibrated thought as age and experiences increase.

When assimilative processes dominate accommodative processes, play, in a general sense, occurs. In play, young children pretend that they are another person, situation, or object as shown through their motoric actions and/or verbal statements. Here, young children pretend they are, for example, Uncle Martin and perhaps play "Uncle Martin going shopping" in dramatic or sociodramatic enactments. The older child and adult also show disequilibrated actions when they daydream and become involved in dreamlike activities. When children show cognitive play, they disregard the dictates of reality and employ egocentric cognitive schemata of objects, people, and situations for their own immediate and subjective goals. Flavell (1963) notes that "in play the primary object is to mold reality to the whim of the cognizer, in other words, to assimilate reality to various schemas with little concern for precise accommodation to that reality" (p. 65).

When accommodative processes dominate assimilative processes, imitation occurs: youngsters copy and model actions of significant adults and peers, and imitate behavioral actions learned through their encounters with objects and situations. In this cognitive activity, children may model and imitate "mother setting the table" while they move plates and spoons around. They become obsessed with placing the silverware on the table in the exact same way as mother. When youngsters show imitation, their cognitive structures focus on an exact replication of previously learned events, situations, objects, and actions. Flavell (1963) notes that in this type of situation, "all energy is focused on taking exact account of the structural niceties of the reality and in imitating and is precisely dovetailing one's schematic repertoire to these details" (p. 65).

In these two additional types of cognitive activity, the primary concerns of children are to adapt reality to themselves in play and to adapt themselves to reality in imitation. Both activities show cognitive structures in disequilibrium because one of the processes remains supreme over the other one. These states of disequilibrium are nonadaptative and can be considered as nondevelopmental in the context of equilibrated or developmental thought. Both are important to children's cognitive progress and their progression from lower- to higher-order thought structures.

Influencing the course of cognitive development, the four factors are: (1) maturation, (2) direct experience with the physical world, (3) actions with the social environment, and (4) equilibration. These factors and their underlying operation in cognitive development also show the interrelations among constructs in cognitive-interactionist theory. These Piagetian constructs, and others that we have discussed previously, are the basis for the stages of intellectual development—the criterion benchmarks of cognitive thought spanning cognitive continua from infancy to maturity.

STAGES OF INTELLECTUAL DEVELOPMENT

Thus far, we have explored several of the interconnected facets of cognitive-developmental theory. These were: (1) Piaget's perspective on cognitive growth and thinking, (2) the basic components of intelligence, and (3) the factors that influence the course of intellectual development. We also surveyed the growth of cognitive structures and relationships existing between these various facets that make cognitive-developmental theory a holistic system.

Related to the structural components and their interlocking constructs is Piaget's notion of *stages*—another key concept that unlocks his cognitive-developmental theory. The idea of stages can be thought of as a framework, with particular stages characterizing cognitive development as the child proceeds from infancy to maturity. The propellants that move cognitive development from one growth level to the other and provide the transitions through the superstructure of stages are the four factors that influence the course of cognitive development. The propellants that move development through the various stages also define each of these levels through constructs such as the components of intelligence (for example, structure and function).

From the perspective of intellectual development, these components, factors, structures, and their interrelationships operate within and between these stages as independent and dependent totalities. The stages focus on cognitive development in dynamically fixed and hierarchically continuous ways. In cognitive-developmental theory, *stage* can have two different meanings.

General Level and Change

First, the term characterizes a general level in the hierarchical sequence of events of cognitive development through which a child moves from infancy to maturity. For example, you might say, "Shanda is in the concrete stage of intellectual development." That statement implies that Shanda has acquired previous cognitive stages and is moving generally to the formal operations one. Second, stage can also mean a particular cognitive process, from within a specific series of cognitive processes, that characterizes attainment and change. For example, you might say that "the stage of conservation of number with physical objects is attained" to describe Shanda's acquisition of this particular cognitive process. Notice that the first definition of stage refers to a global set of cognitive characteristics within a series of broad stages; this is how we will use the term throughout this chapter. The second definition of stage refers to the attainment and change of *specific* cognitive processes. We use the term in this sense in the chapters about the application of developmental theory to preschool classroom settings.

Thus the four stages of development are: sensorimotor, preoperational, concrete operational, and formal operational. All individuals develop these cognitive stages in the same manner but not necessarily at the same rate or speed. For example, all preschoolers will move through the same cognitive stages. However, Michelle, a preschooler, may move through these stages at a faster rate than another preschooler, Anne. The rate at which they move through the stages is variant but development through them is invariant. Related to rate, Piaget has established age ranges for each stage. Because rate is variant, Piaget's age ranges per stage provide relative, not absolute, guidelines for the attainment of cognitive concepts from infancy to maturity. Because our focus is the young child, the sensorimotor, concrete, and formal operational stages of cognitive development will be sketched only briefly; the preoperational stage then will be described in detail.

Sensorimotor, Concrete, and Formal Operational Stages

The sensorimotor, concrete, and formal operational periods are characteristically the first, third, and fourth stages in the cognitive development of the individual. The sensorimotor stage generally encompasses birth to age 2 years; the concrete operational period is from 7 to 11 or 12 years of age. The formal operational stage globally characterizes the range of 11 or 12 through 15 or 16 years of age and upward with subsequent refinement and expansion of the adult's cognitive structures. The major cognitive characteristics attained in the sensorimotor, concrete operational, and formal operational stages are described in the next three sections.

This child is most likely in the sensorimotor stage of development.

Sensorimotor Stage   The first stage of sensorimotor development begins the formal period of intellectual growth. The ongoing development of cognitive structures is the product largely of the four factors that contribute to intellectual growth and the functional invariants of assimilation and accommodation. They result in changes in the child's schemata. The infant in the initial phase of the sensorimotor period shows reflexive behaviors, which are determined largely by heredity; these include sucking, grasping, and crying. Touching the infant's lips and palms of the hand produce sucking and grasping reflexes. These reflexive behaviors are needed for further development. Through assimilation and use of these reflexive behaviors, the infant takes in information from his or her world of physical experiences and practices (or exercises) grasping, sucking, crying, and even bodily movement schemes. By practicing with great variety of stimulus events, the infant begins to discriminate among many different situations in his or her environment. Repetition, practice, and rehearsal of these schemes in many contexts provide the stimulation necessary for these initial differentiations. In addition to assimilation, accommodation swings developmentally into operation and cognitive schemata become modified to the dictates of the infant's environment. Through assimilation, reflexive movements, and accommodation, the actions of sucking, grasping, crying, and body movements evolve from reflexes to cognitive structures. Thus, and from a cognitive perspective, adaptation and organization, as psychological constructs, are central to the cognitive movement from reflexive to highly complex structures.

With continued cognitive growth, the behaviors once reflexive are now learned and, in turn, become modified and practiced for pleasure. New behaviors also are learned and become coordinated, for example, hand–mouth, eye–eye, and eye–object coordinations. Through hand–mouth coordinations, the infant learns to thumb suck. Through discovery, these and other sensorimotor relations become learned by trial and error and then by intention. By following the paths of objects with their eyes and turning their head toward sounds heard, infants acquire the object concept. Through coordinations between eye–object, ear–object, eye–ear–object, and other modalities, infants' behaviors become increasingly adaptive to their environment.

As infants move in their cognitive development from their body to object-discovery outside their own physical body, intention is acquired. First through trial and error, then repetition, infants develop, manipulate, and reproduce novel behaviors and actions on objects that are interesting to them. Grasping, pulling, pounding, and striking behaviors are now repeatedly intentional. Infants in addition can anticipate the positions through which objects will pass; thus, the object concept through assimilative and accommodative processes continues to evolve.

At this level of sensorimotor growth, infants know familiar objects and what to do with them. In addition, they have the motivation to perform specific action schemes with them. For example, having developed the scheme for dealing with the rattle and knowing how to use it in context of the object, infants assimilate the goal of *knowing-and-using* the rattle and the object itself. Here, the *scheme-of-the-goal* (knowing-and-using the rattle), for example, is *shaking-the-rattle* and the scheme functions. At the same time, the infant shows some originality in moving and using the rattle especially when obstacles arise which inhibit the scheme from functioning. For example, an obstacle could be the infant's blanket, which has fallen accidentally over the rattle. The infant with the goal of shaking-the-rattle, in light of the obstacle of the blanket-covering-the-rattle, now employs other schemes learned previously in other situations to accomplish the task. In generalizing from other goal situations to overcome the obstacle the infant tries several schemes. In the course of generalizing (by coordinating the present goal of the scheme with similar past ones), the schemes somewhat change. Through repeated attempts and much active practice, the infant retains the scheme that works best. Two or more schemes become coordinated and the scheme-of-the-goal is activated and functions by removing-the-blanket-and-shaking-the-rattle. Here, the infant puts two previously learned schemes together (removing-the-blanket plus shaking-the-rattle) in a novel manner. The infant not only achieves his or her scheme-of-the-goal but also uses originality by coordinating previously learned behavioral patterns.

At a more advanced level of cognitive development, infants develop ways of accomplishing goals to solve novel problems in their environment other than generalization of previously learned schemes. "When confronted with a problem not solvable by the use of available schemata, the child can be seen to experiment and, through the trial-and-error process, develop new means (schemata)" (Wadsworth, 1974, p. 53). Here, new schemata evolve and novel problems encountered in the environment are solved. With development of totally new action schemes, the infant expands the object concept and other ones. He or she is now able to find objects that are, for example, hidden under blanket one and then hidden under blanket two. The infant searches under blanket one for the rattle. Not being able to find it, he or she quickly goes to blanket two and locates it.

Parallel with the development of new cognitive structures to solve novel problems, "objects beyond the self are for the first time seen as causes of actions" (Wadsworth, 1974, p. 57). With this development of the causality concept, the infant understands and demonstrates that people, situations, and objects can independently affect activities. This is another major cognitive milestone implied by the causality concept.

Near the end of the sensorimotor stage, the child slowly progresses from sensorimotor to representational intelligence; older infants can mentally represent objects in their environment. Further, they can solve new and more complex problems. The experimentation the infant previously used for inventing new means to solve problems now produces faster solutions using representation rather than sensorimotor intelligence. These solutions are generated by representational thought and without physical experimentation. When the infant attains representational or mental thought, the concepts of causality, objects, space, and time further evolve. For example, the infant can now mentally predict cause and effect relations. The schemata for causality and other concepts become more clearly understood and more readily used in discovering solutions to problems.

In sum, the sensorimotor stage contributes many significant aspects of cognitive thought. These include:

- Discrimination abilities among familiar and then novel objects, people, and situations
- Movement of cognitive development from reflexive to more highly complex structures
- Coordinations of eye–eye, hand–mouth, eye–object, and others through trial and error, repetition, and then intention
- Discovery of the body as objects that are independent of his or her own
- Anticipation of movements of his or her body and objects for space, time, and causality
- Solution of novel problems by coordinating two or more previously learned action schemes
- Coordination of action schemes to arrive at solutions to problems
- From very simple to complex cognitive structures to mentally represent objects and generate rather than arrive at solutions through physical or active experimentation

Concrete Operational Stage   The third stage of cognitive growth is the concrete operational stage. The general age approximations for this stage range from 7 or 8 through 11 years. This age range parallels the intermediate grades of the elementary school when the children are in grades four through six. The child in the concrete operational stage displays more abstract logic and higher levels of reasoning than the youngster in the preoperational one. However, the cognitive structures formed in the preoperational and those in sensorimotor stages become the foundations for more advanced development in the concrete operational stage. Further, the work that you do with the child in the preoperational stage assists his or

These German children are probably in the beginning of the concrete operational stage of development.

her achievements in that period as well as provides a foundation for the continued growth of cognitive development in the concrete and formal operational stages.

The system of cognitive thought in the concrete operational stage is integrated, ordered, and coherent. Older children show this as they act on and react to the world around them. Faced with discrepancies between perception of objects in the environment and their cognitive structures (such as, "greater distance over which the same number of objects are placed does not mean greater number"), children in the concrete operational stage focus on salient (number, in this example) rather than superficial aspects (length or distance). They make logical versus perceptual decisions. The concrete operational youngster gives the "decided impression of possessing a solid cognitive bedrock, something flexible and plastic and yet consistent and enduring with which he can structure the present in terms of the past without undue strain and dislocation" (Flavell, 1963, p. 165). Older children avoid the pitfalls of perceptual-boundness and are able to perform all of the intellectual acts and activities that create problems for younger ones. Also, "the concrete operational child behaves in a wide variety of tasks as though a rich and integrated assimilatory organization were functioning in equilibrium or balance with a finely tuned, discriminative, and accommodatory mechanism" (Flavell, 1963, p. 163). The concepts of time, causality, space, and movement become qualitatively refined and further evolve through the continued development of logical thought in this stage.

Further, these cognitive systems of actions are equilibrated units of thought that combine to form additional action systems. They have distinct structural characteristics that become organized into intellectual totalities. Unlike the cognitive systems of action of the preoperational youngster, which fluctuate, are intuitive-based, and are somewhat independent or discrete units, those of concrete operational children become tightly knit. These tightly integrated cognitive systems of action provide the bedrock of more abstract logic and its functional use. These systems, sometimes called operations, mark a significant developmental milestone for the child in the concrete operational stage. Examples of these operations include decentration, conservation, reversibility, classification, and transformation. Each are explained in depth as the precursors of logical thought arising in preoperational development.

Although the child in the concrete operational stage attains these integrated and equilibrated systems of actions, they "are only useful to him in solving problems involving concrete (that is, real, observable) objects and events" (Wadsworth, 1974, p. 90). In other words, for children in this stage to solve problems of reversibility, or decentration, for example, they must go through the medium of using concrete objects. For the most part, concrete operational children do not operate totally with verbal abstract logic. They cannot yet solve problems that are hypothetical and presented in verbal discourse. Accordingly, Wadsworth (1974) views the concrete operational stage as "a transition between prelogical (i.e., preoperational) thought and the completely logical thought of the older child" (p. 90). Adolescents in the formal operational stage have the potential for achieving completely logical thought. They will not need to use observable objects to solve problems of conservation, reversibility, or decentration at the formal operational stages.

Having their foundations in the previous stages, several major and significant accomplishments of the child in the concrete operational stage include:

- Coherence and integration characterizing logical thought structures
- Development and expansion of cognitive systems of action as complex totalities
- Problem solving such as conservation, transformation, or decentration

- Attention to salient rather than superficial characteristics of environmental situations
- High-order problem solving using concrete, real, and observable objects
- Transition between representational thought of the preoperational child and the abstract verbal thought of the formal operational adolescent

Formal Operational Stage   The fourth period in the evolution of cognitive development is the formal operational stage. The cognitive structures that evolve within the sensorimotor as well as the preoperational and concrete operational stages, according to Piaget, are fundamental to and necessary for their continued growth in the formal operational stage. The fact that previous cognitive structures are necessary for later ones shows the interconnectedness of constructs within Piaget's cognitive-interactional theory. The roots of all formal operational thought rest on previous cognitive structures.

To help you understand your work with the young child, we will survey several of the crucial cognitive structures that develop in the formal operational stage. In this stage, adolescents have the necessary cognitive structures to think like adults. The acquisition of these structures presents adolescents with many new possibilities for using, refining, and expanding cognitive schemata for adultlike thought. The assimilative and accommodative processes operating within the sensorimotor period continue throughout this stage (and all of life) to bring about quantitative, and to a lesser extent qualitative, changes in the cognitive schemata. On this point, Wadsworth (1974) says that

> *The structures of intelligence do not improve after this period [the formal operational stage]. . . . Content and function may improve. This is not meant to imply that the use of thought cannot or does not improve after adolescence. The content and function (i.e., use to which thought is put) of thought are free to vary and improve after this period, which in part helps to explain some of the classical differences between adolescent thought and adult thought [p. 101–102].*

Characteristics   In light of the cognitive potential for adult thought, several characteristics of cognitive schemata that evolve in the formal operational stage can be described. They include combinatorial thinking, complex verbal reasoning, and hypothetico-deductive thought.

Combinatorial thinking requires highly complex and abstract cognitive structures and schemes. It refers to the ability to view a problem or situation as a whole (including its subparts) and to develop possible solutions complete with systematic procedures for these solutions. In trying to make the color purple, given three different colors, the adolescent in logical fashion proceeds to develop a systematic plan to solve this problem. For example, to solve the problem of making the color purple, the adolescent could begin by adding: color 1 to color 2, color 1 to color 3, and color 2 to color 3. Through this planned testing and continual pairing of the colors, the problem of making and mixing purple is solved. The adolescent taking on this challenging problem proceeds to solve it by systematically exploring all possible solutions (Wadsworth, 1974).

Complex verbal reasoning is another characteristic of the formal operational stage and also requires adultlike cognitive abilities. It refers to analogies and syllogisms that must be solved verbally using higher-order logic and cognitive structures. For example, the adolescent is given a verbal statement such as, "Henry weighs more than Toby and Henry weighs more than Jane." The verbal problem is to determine who is heaviest of the three. The adolescent uses complex cognitive structures in the form of verbal reasoning to solve it: "Henry is the heaviest of the three individuals."

The hypothetico-deductive thinking, like combinatorial and complex verbal reasoning, is another characteristic of adult thought. In hypothetico-deductive thinking, the adolescent determines through logical analyses premises to solve the problem. The adolescent uses the premises even though they may be contrary to fact to solve the hypothetical problem. For example, problems can begin with the premise that the "moon is made of green cheese." The adolescent conceptualizes this premise even though it is not true and uses it in finding a solution. "The older child can extract the structure of the argument from its content and submit the structure (alone) to logical analyses" (Wadsworth, 1974, p. 105). The adolescent deals with the problem relative to its premises ("moon is green cheese") and solves it with abstract cognitive thought.

The adolescent may not even believe in the premise and may doubt its reality base. But he or she is able to argue successfully its logical conclusion: she or he adopts another perspective and logically deals with it from that perspective.

The roots of the sensorimotor stage provide a basis for the later stages including the concrete and formal operational ones. Several significant accomplishments of the formal operational stage include:

- Development of combinatorial thinking to test problem solutions in a systematic way
- Use of complex verbal reasoning with verbal analogies and syllogisms to solve problems in a logical manner
- Development of systematic reasoning and logical thought
- Ability to solve problems by developing hypothetical premises

Preoperational Stage

The preoperational stage covers the age range of two through seven years and encompasses the nursery school or day-care, kindergarten, and

These children represent the preoperational stage age group.

primary-grade years of the young child. However, recall that the age ranges per stage established by Piaget are general estimates. The rate of cognitive development within and between the stages is variant across individuals. More explanation of this rate characteristic as it relates to the preoperational child is given later in this section.

To understand the significance of preoperational thought and therefore recognize the need for adult flexibility in your work with young children, this section is organized into two parts: general considerations concerning preoperational thought, and specific characteristics of cognitive development (that is, systems of actions or operations) in the preoperational stage.

Initially, several general considerations need to be explained before the specific characteristics of cognitive development in the preoperational stage can be described. The preoperational stage is a precursor to abstract logic.

Prelogic   The prelogic characteristic means essentially that children's thinking in the preoperational stage is imprecise and rather discrete. The youngsters begin to understand relationships in the environment. However, they are not able to work out these relationships in either exact or abstract form. They need to work out relations between objects, situations, or people although they globally understand the concepts. For example, the preoperational child understands that the adult needs to eat more food than a youngster of three or four years because of their size differences and perhaps the differing work requirements between their lifestyles. Even though this and other basic relations are attained, the preoperational youngster does not have the abstract logic to work out these relationships between objects, situations, and people. To continue the example of the relationships between the quantity of food intake and size, the three-year-old child is given eight crackers and asked to show the relation of quantity of food intake between her- or himself and the adult. This preoperational child cannot operationalize the relations in a specific manner by showing with the crackers that the adult might get seven, six, or five of them, whereas the three year old would receive, one, two, or three crackers. Although this youngster shows basic logic by understanding that adults need more food than young children, she or he does not have abstract thought structures to construct these relations of quantity between different-sized individuals. This semilogic or prelogic is an important consideration in working with the young child.

Figurative Thought A second general consideration is figurative thinking. Prelogic and figurative thinking both imply that the cognitive thought structures are representational, basic, and concrete and are not yet operating at the abstract level. Figurative thinking is thought that is reflective and external and tied to the physical actions and activities of the young child (Sigel & Cocking, 1977). Here, relations between situations, people, and events are figurative because they emerge through reflective cognitive schemata and are connected to the child's actions and reactions. Further, preoperational differs from sensorimotor thought in that the former is reflective and internal and the latter is nonreflective and external. Of preoperational thought, Sigel and Cocking (1977) say that, "knowledge is organized in pictorial mental images" (p. 59). The concepts of time, space, causality, and distance, as examples, are connected to schemes of action and reaction that put them into operation. For example, play of the preoperational child rests on pictorial mental images or representational thought that becomes operationalized throughout object actions and reactions. In other words, mental acts, for instance, of time, space, causality, and play are in operation as the child uses objects in his or her environment and acts on and reacts to these tangibles. She or he does not perform these mental acts and activities using abstract thinking or rule-governed behaviors. The pictorial mental images for concepts such as time, space relations, and play arise through acting on and reacting to objects. The cognitive structures, once they are in operation, are reflective. However, these structures are not deliberate or conscious prior to the onset of actions and reactions. The youngster of 2 or 3 years does not deliberately use the rule of behavior, for example, "imitating grandma dialing the telephone." It arises from the child's physical movements that are made on the object—the telephone. As the youngster makes dialing movements in context of the telephone, the pictorial mental image or cognitive schemata of "grandma dialing" emerges and then he or she uses the scheme.

In addition, figurative thinking is also a global aspect of semilogic. In this instance, early preoperational children do not display actions or perform activities using abstract logical and complex thought. They cannot separate cognitive structures or mental images and abstractions of "grandma telephoning" from the telephone and physical movements made on it. The young preoperational child of 3 to 5 years is bound to physical actions and perceptual experiences. Nevertheless, the young preoperational child does show symbolic thought, "as witnessed in this imitative behavior and language, all symbols for previous experiences" (Sigel & Cocking, 1977, p. 59). Older preoperational children of 6 to 7 years begin to develop abstract logic. They act deliberately. In this sense, older preoperational children are better able to identify deliberately action-oriented rules of behavior and go about their activities with more efficiency.

Present-Oriented   The third general consideration is called present-oriented. It is related to semilogic and figurative thinking. Present-oriented means that the young preoperational child of two through four years is bound by, operates in, and is influenced in the present rather than flexibly operating in the past and future, as well as the present. According to Piaget, preoperational children may know and use the terms *tomorrow, today*, or *yesterday*, for example, but they cannot abstractly understand their meanings. Recall from the beginning of this chapter that thought and language are viewed in Piaget's theory as independent of one another. They assist each other in concrete operational and beginning formal operational stages of cognitive development. Therefore, that preoperational children say, "Tomorrow, I go to school!" does not mean that they have meaningfully acquired the cognitive structure that enables them to understand abstractly the concept of time. Further, these children's explanation of *tomorrow* is based on *today*. "These are action-based definitions which are, in fact, not the concept; children are merely using actions to denote or indicate time differences. Thus, to assume that because the children use the word they understand that word, would be erroneous" (Sigel & Cocking, 1977, p. 60). As children progress from the early to the later years of the preoperational stage, they are more likely to view time dimensions flexibly and to meaningfully come to understand them outside of action-oriented definitions.

Irregularities   The final consideration in understanding the child in the preoperational stage is called irregularities (Ginsburg & Opper, 1969). The idea of irregularities applies not only to the preoperational stage but also to all other stages in cognitive-developmental theory. The concept of irregularities gives greater clarification and definition to the preoperational and other stages and provides additional reasons that account for variability in cognitive development between youngsters of the same age within the preoperational stage and among children across different stages of growth.

First, recall that the rate at which children's thought evolves through the stages depends on influential factors that contribute to the course of cognitive growth. For example, the rate of cognitive development varies among Sally, James, and Susan, all age 5 years, and among children across the four stages. This variability shows irregularity in cognitive development. The fact that Sally can and James cannot conserve number at age 5 years and Swiss children (that is, Piaget's "normed" population) as a group demonstrate this operation at age 7 years indicates that the rate of cognitive development from child to child and from group to group can vary considerably. The concept of rate characterized by irregularity is significant for adults working with young children. Thus, adult expectancies in the rate of cognitive growth for children should be individual- rather than group-based.

A second aspect of irregularity clarifies children's expectancies in their rates of cognitive growth. The fact that all children move through the stages is a characteristic that is invariant across groups of children and shows that the course of cognitive development is continuous and in transition from stage to stage. According to Ginsburg and Opper (1969), "the transition is gradual, occurring over a period of time, and the child exhibits many forms of behavior intermediary between . . . stages" (p. 156). Therefore, James may show cognitive schemes, some of which are and some of which are not characteristic of the preoperational stage. "An individual child's behavior takes many forms in addition to those Piaget describes as being typical of the various stages" (Ginsburg & Opper, 1969, p. 156). Thus, from this perspective, adults working with young children in the preoperational stage should expect some cognitive behaviors that are and others that are not typical of actions of youngsters in this age range. The stages are a matrix superimposed over characteristics of individuals within and across periods; they do not include every possible cognitive characteristic. The preoperational stage, for example, includes the most salient characteristics of the young child at this period of growth. The other stages function as grids in the same manner and permit us to view salient cognitive characteristics of young children in meaningful ways along a continuum of development.

The third aspect of irregularity is variability of cognitive behaviors. According to Piaget, a preoperational child may be in stage one in cognitive understanding of the concept of time and in stage three in growth of number conservation. The adult working with 6-year-old Susan, for example, may expect her to show cognitive characteristics at, below, or above the preoperational stage in the development of concepts such as space, causality, time, relations, or classes. Therefore, expecting the child to show characteristics of the preoperational stage of development in all or several areas of concept development is not consistent with Piaget's theory of cognitive interactionism.

The last aspect of irregularity is very close to the third; it is variability of different areas of thought within the same stage of growth. The youngster could be in different areas of thought within the same stage as well as display ". . . different levels of achievement in regard to problems involving similar mental operations" (Ginsburg & Opper, 1969, p. 165). The area of conservation, which is the cognitive capacity to understand that the amount of a substance remains the same regardless of changes in its form or position, provides an example. Sally, a preoperational child age six years, may be able to conserve number but may not be able to conserve mass. She has acquired the capacity of conceptualizing number conservation but is not yet able to schematize the conservation of mass even though the conceptualizations involve the similar cognitive structure of conservation. Therefore, as you work with youngsters in the preoperational stage, you should expect a child to show differences in capacity to solve problems involving the same or similar cognitive operations (Ginsburg & Opper, 1969).

Exploring general aspects of prelogic, figurative thinking, present-orientations, and irregularities within the preoperational stages help you better understand the development of children at the preoperational stage as well as growth as a continuum. In addition, these four main considerations provide a baseline for greater qualitative understanding of the procedures and strategies used to work with youngsters in this important age range of cognitive growth.

Preoperational Characteristics   Characteristics of cognitive growth of the child within the preoperational stage are: egocentrism, nontransformation, centration, irreversibility, nonconservation, identity, and functions.

Egocentrism   Egocentrism, one of the primary cognitive indicators of preoperational thought, is the inability to take on and see a situation, event, or person from another's perspective. Youngsters are cognitively "locked-in" to themselves and see things only from their perspective. Youngsters do not deliberately plan to be egocentric; their thought structures need greater maturity and more peer encounters to actually see situations, events, and people from the other's perspective. Being egocentric, children know unequivocally that everyone thinks the same as they do! When children make a discovery, they essentially make the discovery for all people. Further, youngsters also understand that all individuals think and say the same things as they do. In using language to communicate, preoperational children of three and four years deal with people and events in terms of their thoughts and statements, which they regard as absolute. Children never question their own statements, and their thoughts are the only ones that exist and therefore are real. A three-year-old boy shows the cognitive capacity of egocentrism, for example, when he moves into a chair and trips over one of its legs. The youngster may say, "Bad chair, it tripped me." He may even hit the chair for tripping him. The adult, in turn, tries to explain that the chair did not make him fall—that he accidentally stuck his left foot behind the leg of the chair and tripped himself. However, the child disregards the adult's evidence that he tripped himself because it is in error and his ideas are always correct. Because they are his thoughts and statements, they reign supreme.

As another example of the effects of cognitive egocentrism, a nursery school teacher began to explain the concept of the life cycle to a group of three-year-old children. The life cycle, in this instance, was simply that living things are born and these same living things die. She went on to explain that "cows, pigs, elephants, and bears live and then die." The children apparently assimilated the information and then Jamie exclaimed, "Bears don't die!" The nursery school teacher reexplained the concept differently and focused on "bears." Jamie simply disregarded the evidence and said, "That's not right!" The teacher tried to resolve the issue, but for Jamie it was not an issue and no further explanations or understandings were needed. The children in both of these examples never questioned their own thoughts, expressions, or actions. They assimilated the information, but showed little accommodation to it.

The main cause of moving from cognitive egocentricity to nonegocentricity is the child's peer group.

Related to egocentrism are the cognitive attributes of syncretism and juxtaposition (Ginsburg & Opper, 1969). Syncretism is the cognitive capacity to group a series of unrelated events and connect them together in some illogical fashion. The preschooler who thought he was tripped by the chair connected these unrelated events and responded to the chair by striking it. Juxtaposition is the inability to perceive or see a series of real events as connected and related. This cognitive ability emphasizes seeing events, situations, and people from another's perspective to understand interrelationships between them. The egocentric youngster disregards evidence that is contrary to her or his thoughts and actions, and does not show juxtaposition at the level of cognitive development.

Children 3, 4, and sometimes 5 years old show egocentrism and attributes of syncretism and juxtaposition. Not until youngsters become 6 or 7 years old do they begin to move from egocentrism to nonegocentrism. In the later half of the preoperational stage, children slowly develop the ability to view events, situations, and people from the perspective of the other. The primary cause of moving from cognitive egocentricity to nonegocentricity is the child's peer group. In Piaget's theory, the peer group is significant in influencing cognitive growth of schemes. Children encounter the peer group, and social actions and reactions. They challenge their thoughts, expressions, and actions. Older preoperational children experience peer conflict and begin to accommodate to the beliefs and actions of significant peer others. In accommodating, they question themselves, their thoughts, expressions, and actions and begin to accept contradictory evidence. The youngsters become convinced by examples and the result is a decline in egocentric thinking. Related to egocentrism is the cognitive characteristic of nontransformation.

Nontransformation   Nontransformation is the inability of the child to see a logical connection or relationship between a series of perceptual events that are related. The preoperational child does not have the cognitive maturity to see a series of points as related in beginning and ending fashion. Further, because the youngster does not understand perceptual or cognitive relations between successive points, he or she juxtaposes elements through appeals to physical causality (Flavell, 1963). The preoperational child could conceivably connect a series of unrelated elements and events and group them into a global scheme. The child, in demonstrating nontransformation abilities, or juxtaposition and syncretism, shows transductive reasoning. This type of reasoning goes from specific to specific events within a series of related events. Perceptually focusing on one event then another and treating each as major ones, the child who shows nontransformation draws erroneous conclusions, for the most part, about events and their relations. For example, a nontransformating boy walks along a path from his home to his grandmother's house. He sees a rabbit, which scampers behind a tree. Several seconds later the same child sees the same rabbit but he thinks it is two different animals. In the course of walking to his grandmother's home, he may see the same animal three, four, or five times; each time, he thinks it is a different animal. In addition, the youngster may believe that all of these five rabbits are following him to his grandmother's home. Each rabbit, although the same animal, is treated as a separate, specific, and isolated event; the youngster focuses on these events as discrete and equally important entities.

Because this child is also egocentric, he never questions his line of reasoning used in arriving at the conclusions that there were five rabbits and that they were following him to his grandmother's house. Nontransformation ability is an interesting cognitive capacity to observe in young children. Not understanding that the perceptual elements are intermediary or related between events one and two, the child does not integrate them into relations relative to beginning and ending points.

Nontransformation ability can also be seen, for example, when a child's family visits a nearby friend. Having just gotten into the car and left the house, the youngster asks, "Are we there yet?" Each aspect of the travel becomes a major event which is not connected in leaving and arriving at the friend's home.

Younger children of 3 and 4 years show much nontransformation ability in their daily living and learning. As children progress to 5 and especially 6 and 7 years, nontransformation abilities begin to decrease and transformation capacities increase. Older children of 6 and 7 years, although still in the preoperational stage, can conceptually show through their activities that events are causally related to specific beginning and ending points. Thus, older children, having acquired transformation abilities, arrive at realistic conclusions more often than do younger ones who demonstrate nontransformational schemes.

Centration   Centration is the third characteristic youngsters show in the preoperational stage of intellectual growth. Centration is the cognitive capacity to focus on superficial rather than salient aspects of objects, events, and people. Superficial aspects are the most perceptually striking features to the child. For example, important features of a ball to preoperational children could be its bright red color and its size rather than its critical element of roundness (assuming, of course, that this latter attribute is essential to solving a particular problem or crucial to a specific line of reasoning). Focusing on superficial details, the child ignores the most salient information.

In centration, children assimilate information by acting on and accommodating it by modifying their cognitive structures. Because these youngsters key on superficial features, the assimilating and accommodating that occur lead to distortions in reasoning. For example, in the conservation of mass problem, the youngsters are asked to determine whether two equal amounts of clay are, in fact, equal in mass. After saying that they are equal, one youngster flattens one of the clay masses. The children are questioned again about equality of mass between the round clay and the pancake-shaped clay. A youngster who shows centration says that the two masses are not equal in amount: the pancake-shaped mass has a greater mass than the round one. Even though no amount of substance is removed from either of the masses of clay, the youngster knows that the flat one contains more substance than the round one. In this situation, the preoperational youngster attends to the superficial feature of length rather than the salient one of mass. The child fails to reason that the length of the pancake is not equal to the mass.

In contrast to the younger child, the older one of 5 to 7 years develops the capacity to show decentration. Decentration, the opposite of centration, means that the child can focus on salient rather than superficial features of particular events. Therefore, in the above example, the older preoperational child who shows decentration says that both the flat and round shaped masses of clay are equal in amount. Related to centration is the cognitive attribute of irreversibility.

Irreversibility   Irreversibility is the inability of youngsters to follow a line of reasoning from one point to another and retrace their logic back again to the first point. Preoperational children, in trying to follow a line of reasoning back to its starting point, become perceptually and cognitively lost in the endeavor. For example, boys and girls when added together form a group. The group of children can be separated into disjoint sets of boys and girls. As another example, you can add 9 pennies and 13 pennies and get 22 pennies. You can return to the two original groups of pennies simply with the reverse operation of subtracting 9 (or 13) pennies from the 22 pennies. The actions of retracing logical thought to the original starting point by separating the set of children into the disjoint sets of boys and girls, and by subtracting one set of 9 (or 13) pennies from 22 pennies are impossible for preoperational children. These youngsters cannot abstractly or physically solve problems that require them to reverse their line of reasoning and follow it back to the starting point.

A student in an introductory early childhood course taught by one of the authors once noted in class that the preoperational children he worked with in day care showed reversibility of thought. He explained that children living near the day-care center walked to school and then at the end of the day returned home. This is reversible operation of walking to school and returning home. However, day-care children on further examination were not abstractly thinking about this problem as reversibility. Their going from and returning to home was not a mentally abstract operation. The walking movements were thought of as unidirectional. Walking to school was a different and separate event from returning home—even though the children were retracing their steps and returning to the same end point.

Irreversibility evolves slowly into reversibility in children at 6 and 7 years of age. Older children can acquire operations, for example, when they successfully perform the conservation of mass problem. The concept of reversibility is one of the most important attributes in the evolution of cognitive development as the child matures within the preoperational stage.

Nonconservation   The fifth cognitive characteristic of this stage is nonconservation. Nonconservation is the inability to conceptualize that the amount or quantity of matter remains the same regardless of qualitative changes made on its shape or position (assuming that no amount is removed from this matter). The young preoperational child who is a nonconserver of quantity cannot recognize that amounts among substances remain constant regardless of the number of qualitative dimensions that are altered. The nonconserver focuses on superficial characteristics of matter such as length and appearance, rather than on salient attributes such as number, volume, or mass. Not being able to understand that matter can be conserved in light of qualitative changes made on it implies that young children cannot conserve number, mass, area, weight, and volume (which are the five most common areas of conservation). In turn, the inability to conserve implies that the children's cognitive schemata have not yet matured to enable them to perform these problems. The ability to conserve quantity is a major milestone in the youngster's cognitive achievement from the preoperational stage to more advanced levels of maturity. Thus, this measure of cognitive development is used by Piaget to measure the evolving process of equilibration of cognitive schemata.

Conservation Phases   The movement from nonconservation to conservation (or, in Piaget's terms, "the-coming-into-equilibrium-events") is characteristically a four-phase process. All cognitive milestones in the acquisition of conserving abilities follow this four-step process for number, mass, area, weight, or volume conservation. In step one of the growth of conservation, young children focus on only one dimension of the quantity of matter. For example, they may focus on width but not the crucial variable of number or mass; the children conclude that one quantity of matter has "more" than the other one because they attend to length (over which it lies) rather than the characteristic of number or mass. In phase two, youngsters focus on either the irrelevant or relevant dimension, in this instance, length and number (or mass). However, the children do not cognitively coordinate these dimensions. Instead, they see each one as isolated and separate from one another. Further, these dimensions are attended to in rather successive fashion. For example, in the conservation of number, youngsters in one trial may attend to the number dimension and in the next trial focus on length. But, as they focus on length they forget about number over repeated trials with the same conservation problems.

In step three, the child cognitively understands the dimensions of length, number, or mass, for example, but this awareness is rather heterogene-

---

Box 12-2   Training Conservation Concepts?

In the 1960s, a tremendous number of research studies examined the question: Can preschoolers be trained systematically to conserve, for example, number, mass, or volume? Although this debate over training conservation (or other logical thinking) concepts is not yet settled, it is less heated. Yet the question of training has practical importance, especially in programs for the young child. The responses to this question are at the roots of developmental theory—for it raises a series of related questions about the nature of intellect, performance versus competence, developmental conceptualization versus learning skills, the adult as guider versus trainer, intrinsic versus extrinsic motivation, and so on.

From a purely classical Piagetian perspective, the answer to this question is "no." Some contempo-

rary Piagetians might offer qualifications such as, "It depends on the proper match and the child's current level of operativity!" They might continue by saying, "Those youngsters about to develop conservation might receive a boost into permanent conservation through training, but they would have developed it anyway as a function of their own increasing operativity."

Whether the responses to the question of training are an emphatic no or a no with qualifications, trying to accelerate the rate of development in a training sense is resisted from interactionist perspectives and does not have genuine meaning. Youngsters progress at their own pace through sequences of cognitive development for genuine, meaningful, permanent, and real learning.

ous—"the joint appreciation of both properties within a cognitive act, and hence on (A and B) fields of application" (Flavell, 1963, p. 246). However, in understanding the attributes of length versus number, for example, the child is thrown into conflict. Not knowing which dimensions of length *and* number (or mass) to choose in the number conservation, this conflict results in hesitancy. In stage four, the achievement of recognizing both attributes (that is, A and B as fields of application) is refined and expanded and the young child keys on the relevant dimension required by the conservation of number (or mass) problem. Flavell (1963) notes that in stage four, "there is a shift of conceptual focus from states alone to transformations which lead from state to state" (p. 246). From the point of view of the application of equilibrium, the cognitive repertoire that is now used is "A_1 and B_1 and A_2 and B_2" and so on, which becomes "a logical conjunction of conjunctions" (Flavell, 1963, p. 246). The outcome of this awareness is that youngsters correctly perform the conservation; they have acquired the cognitive schemata to solve this particular conservation problem of number (or mass). Thus, when the fourth level is reached, children perform the conservation problem with no conflict or hesitancy—they have acquired a rigorous concept of conservation.

In the problem of number conservation, usually two arrays of stimulus objects are presented. Each row, for example, may have four red checkers. The rows of checkers are parallel to one another; each checker in the rows is spatially and exactly opposite the others and in one-to-one correspondence. The child is usually asked, "Is there the same number of objects in this row as that row?" As the child confirms the equality, he is asked to spread the checkers in one row further apart. The same question is repeated. After the child responds, he or she is asked, "Why?" or "Show me that one row is equal to (or greater or lesser than) the other row in number." The preoperational child shows nonconservation by indicating that one row has a greater number of checkers in it than the other. The older preoperational child who conserves number says that there are the same number of objects in each of the rows. This latter idea is characteristic of level four cognitive actions.

In the conservation of area problem, the child is usually given two same-sized sheets of green paper, which represent two fields of green grass. She or he also receives two miniature toy cows (of the same shape, type, and color), which are placed on the fields. The youngster is asked a question such as, "Is there the same amount of grass in each field for each cow to eat?" After the child says that there is the same amount of grass in each field, a rectangular piece of wood representing a barn is placed in each of the fields. The question is again repeated and the child confirms that each cow has the same amount of grass to eat in both fields. Now, another rectangular block (of the same type, color, and dimensions as the first pair) is placed in each of the fields. However, in one of the fields the blocks are placed side-by-side or adjacent to one another, and in the other, the barn is placed parallel to but 7 to 8 inches from the other barn. Again, the same question is asked. After the child answers, he or she is asked, "Why?" The young child who shows nonconservation of area says that the cow in one field has less or more grass to eat. The barns spread out appear to the non-conserver to provide the cow with less grass to eat. The child who has achieved stage four in the growth of rigorous conservation of area says that both cows have the same amount of grass to eat in each of the fields.

The conservation of mass paradigm was discussed earlier. The youngster is presented with two equal balls of clay, and is asked to flatten one of them.

The preoperational child of 2 through 4 years cannot conserve number. At age 5 to 7 years, she or he acquires number conservation. For area and mass, the preoperational child of 2 through 6 years usually shows non-conservation of these concepts. However, by age 7 or 8 years (the end of the preoperational stage) the youngster can conserve both area and mass. The other two most common areas of conservation are weight and volume; the child in the preoperational stage on the average cannot conserve either (that is, interior and exterior aspects of volume). The conservation of weight is usually acquired at 9 or 10 years of age; volume is usually mastered at 11 or 12 years. Conservation problems for weight and volume can be constructed using the same paradigm. For conservation of weight, two objects of equal weight are used; for conservation of volume, two equal-sized beakers and one tall cylinder with two equal amounts of water are used.

Identity   The sixth characteristic of the preoperational stage is identity. Identity is a cognitive understanding that quantity and matter can be transferred to other successive states; that is, quantity or matter do not change. For example, in the conservation of mass problem one round-shaped ball is flattened. In modifying the shape of the ball from round to flat, the preoperational child understands that the basic substance does not change. This child recognizes that the shape and hence its appearance look quite different from the original one. However, changing or altering the substance from one state to another does not change its identity. It retains its identity from state to state and change to change. Recognizing that mass, number, or area retains its identity from state to state, a major cognitive milestone is accomplished. Here, children acquire the cognitive schemata to understand that quantity or matter can undergo changes in appearance and physical qualities (such as size, length, distance) and yet retain its identity. Recognizing that matter does not change regardless of appearance, the youngster still may not understand equalities of matter from state to state. In similar fashion, understanding identity from state to state does not mean the children can conserve number, mass, and area. Achieving the concept of identity in this preoperational stage is a major

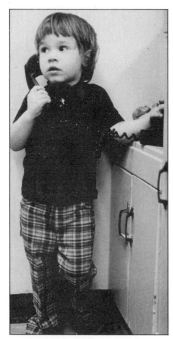

The preoperational child's understanding of functions is limited by maturing cognitive characteristics.

building block for the attainment of conservation of number, mass, and area during this stage and the bedrock for the growth of conservation of volume and weight in the next one.

Function   Function is the seventh and last cognitive attribute. It is defined as the ability to understand and recognize functional relations of objects in the environment. Children of 2 through 7 years react to and act on objects in the environment and can show and express functional relations. Younger preoperational children are more likely to show functional relations between their actions, reactions, and objects; older preoperational children, because they have greater language capacities, can show as well as express these relations.

Further, recognizing functions means understanding that related events can covary. For example, a child strikes a bell; the harder he or she strikes it, the louder the bell rings. A covariation between events exists between increasing striking power and increasing loudness of the bell. Functional relations between events are quite common to the youngster. For example, the larger the milk glass the more milk the child gets. Recognizing variations between pulling a window blind cord and its opening (or closing) is another example of functions. Understanding of functional relations has roots in the sensorimotor stage when the child cognitively determines and intentionally uses specific ways to achieve his or her goals—means–ends relations.

However, the preoperational child's understanding of functions is limited by maturing cognitive characteristics such as egocentrism, irreversibility, and nontransformation. In recalling the example of the window blind, the child recognizes that by pulling on the cord it opens. Through functions, he or she understands the relationship of pulling and opening the blind. However, she or he neither recognizes exactly how or why the pulling is related to opening nor represents these pulling and opening actions on a high abstract cognitive level. The hows and whys behind pulling as a function of the window blind's opening is invariably related to physical mechanics and specifically pulleys and levers. In recalling another example, the youngsters understand that larger glasses provide more milk than smaller ones. They establish a functional relationship between glass size and milk but they cannot abstractly quantify the relationships in the form of fractions or proportions. Thus, the preoperational child's appreciation of the functional relation between glass size and milk is imprecise; that is, the relationship exists but the rationale behind it must await the growth of more complex cognitive structures.

In sum, the cognitive characteristics of the children in the preoperational stage are egocentrism, nontransformation, nonconservation, irreversibility, centration, identity, and functions. They are crucial for adults who work with youngsters to understand. These characteristics must also be taken into account in implementing Piaget's cognitive-developmental theory in classroom settings.

TYPES OF KNOWLEDGE

Thus far we have explained the major principles and constructs underlying Piaget's cognitive-developmental theory. Before understanding how the principles can be applied in the classrooms, we need to describe their interrelationships. More specifically, all of the theoretical constructs and principles thus far explained focus on showing the evolution of cognitive understanding and their interrelationships that shape the course of schemata. These constructs—for example, structure, function, and content—answer questions such as: How does knowledge develop? How does the child obtain this knowledge? The interrelations between the concepts are highlighted further through Piaget's idea of knowledge. He recognizes four types of knowledge: logicomathematical, social, physical, and representational. Knowledge derives from Piaget's notion that individuals interact with and try to make sense of the experiences they encounter. Thus, Piaget's idea of knowledge is constructivist in that individuals react to and act on their world and thereby construct it out of their interaction. Accordingly, children do not receive knowledge solely from stimulus events outside themselves, nor are they born with it in a maturationist sense of heredity. The types of knowledge focus on the various sources that the child actually uses to construct them. They are related to the four factors that influence the course of cognitive development, the three components of intelligence, and the bedrock elements basic to the stages of growth. Each of the types of knowledge are described in this remaining section of this chapter. The types of knowledge will be especially significant as you learn about implementing Piaget's cognitive-developmental theory with youngsters in classroom settings.

Logicomathematical knowledge is the individual's organization of the relationships among objects in the environment. Constructing such relationships is an internal cognitive act. With this type of knowledge, children receive feedback about the correctness of their predictions. For example, youngsters conceptualize relations of classification by color, size, shape, number, and shared relations between objects. Piaget focuses his writings on describing how individuals construct logicomathematical knowledge from nonlogical (that is, perceptual) to logical.

Social knowledge is culturally determined; it is based on children's construction of understandings concerning their social milieu. Their social milieu varies from society to society and is arbitrary and relative given a particular society. For instance, social knowledge in our society consists of knowing the names of the days of the week, the months of the year, delineated units of clock time, and numerous other social conventions that assist us in functioning. Bilingual children's social knowledge includes constructing understandings of social conventions in two cultures, for example Greek *and* English or Spanish *and* English. Youngsters also construct social knowledge relating to behavior, character, moral decisions, ethics, and other crucial aspects of conduct.

Physical knowledge implies the construction of concepts about objects that evolves from feedback youngsters receive from objects in their world. Hard, soft, rough, smooth, sharp, rolling, bouncing, square, and numerous other concepts are all examples of physical knowledge. Physical knowledge essentially encompasses rather specific characteristics of (but not the social names for) objects and the feedback about them that assists the construction of knowledge. Physical knowledge is based on the correctness of children's predictions about their physical world.

Representational knowledge is related to logicomathematical, social, and physical knowledge and refers to the way youngsters structure all knowledge in representing reality. From a constructivist position, representational knowledge is based on children's acting on and reacting to concrete objects and social situations, and on their active construction of mental images to represent these social and physical experiences and object relationships. The three levels of representational knowledge are: (1) index—recognizing whole objects from just their parts, (2) symbol—forming mental images to represent objects not physically present, and (3) sign—using abstract signs for objects that bear no relationship to them.

Logicomathematical, social, physical, and representational knowledge show the kinds of understanding that evolve from a constructivist perspective. These same four areas of knowledge show the relationship of Piaget's constructs and principles and become organizers in showing you the *whats* and *hows* of planning the classroom environment.

SUMMARY

This chapter described selected principles and constructs of Piaget's cognitive-developmental theory: (1) view of intelligence and its components, (2) factors influencing the course of cognitive development, and (3) stages of cognitive development and types of knowledge.

The cognitive-developmental theory views intelligence as the attainment of increasingly effective thought structures from birth to maturity. As such, intelligence is a coherent system of living and acting operations. Accordingly, intelligence is not the same as IQ or academic skills. The components of intelligence are structure, function, and content. Structures are neither totally inherited nor external to the child; they depend on the child's history of interaction with previous environments. Function is broad attributes of intellectual activity; content refers to observable actions or behaviors that reflect intellectual activities and acts. The interactive nature of structure, function, and content describes how new information is gathered about the environment and beautifully illustrates intelligence in action. The factors of maturation, direct experience with the physical world, interactions with the social environment, and equilibration are primary to the course of cognitive development. The four stages of development are sensorimotor, preoperational, concrete operational, and formal operational. Each stage has major cognitive characteristics that emerge and grow within the individual. In rather additive fashion, these stages as abstractions become tools for understanding the child age 2 through 7 years. They also highlight the contributions within other stages to knowledge—logicomathematical, social, physical, and representational. These classifications of knowledge emphasize that Piaget's theory is constructivist; constructivism explains what knowledge is, how it develops, and how it is attained in individuals. It is essentially the capstone that describes a holistic perspective and explains the interrelated totalities of thought set against an active, interactive, and evolutionary framework. The types of knowledge also serve as a functional tool to assist the adult in working with young children in the preoperational stage.

Each of the key principles and constructs of cognitive-developmental theory explained in this chapter becomes an element in a mosaic; these principles together illustrate operation of thought structures in the young child. They unfold through application to children, classroom settings, and evaluation of cognitive growth.

Review Questions

1. Tell why token and social reinforcement systems for shaping the child's behavior are not relevant in explaining the origins and development of knowledge from cognitive-developmental perspectives.
2. Describe the relationships between Piaget's view of intelligence and skill learning, for example, in the three R's.
3. Provide a definition of maturation from a cognitive-developmental perspective and tell how the definition is congruent with this orientation.
4. Explain the interrelations between assimilation and accommodation at the preoperational and sensorimotor levels, and give examples for each of these interrelations.
5. Identify the four factors that contribute to the course of cognitive development and explain their contributions and interrelationships.
6. Describe the types of knowledge and kinds of conservation, and give examples of each.

Suggested Activities

1. Chart the number of sensorimotor responses an infant shows in a 5-minute period as he or she responds to and acts on his or her environment.
2. Build a *feel box*. Take a small shoe box and cut a hole in one of the sides for children to insert their hands to feel objects they cannot see. Ask a child to feel, and then describe the object and its uses. Then, ask her or him to name the object.

Determine the roles of direct experiencing with physical objects in assisting the youngsters in conceptualizing attributes of tangibles in the feel box.

3. Identify a 3-year-old who is egocentric and one who is less so. Construct a situation in which they have to cooperate to some degree to accomplish a task. Write down the oral dialogue and classify it into egocentric and less-egocentric speech. Identify the characteristics of each using the results of your classification.

4. Determine whether a 6-year-old child has attained a rigorous state of equilibrium as you introduce him or her to cognitive conflict with the conservation of area problem.

5. Try out a successive displacement problem with 2-, 3-, and 4-year-old children. Describe and explain differences in responses among the children.

6. Work with a preoperational child of 3 or 4 years and one of 5 or 6 years and see if they can demonstrate the cognitive characteristics of transformation. Record the successes and problems observed in demonstrating the transformational capacity in each of these youngsters.

Suggested Readings

Furth, H. G. *Thinking without language: psychological implications of deafness.* New York: Free Press, 1966.

Furth, H. G. *Piaget and knowledge: theoretical foundations.* Englewood Cliffs, N.J.: Prentice-Hall, 1970.

Furth, H. G. Two aspects in ontogeny: development and learning. In Reese, H. W. (Ed.), *Advances in child development and behavior*, vol. 9. New York: Academic Press, 1974.

Kamii, C., and Derman, L. The Englemann approach to teaching logical thinking: findings from the administration of some Piagetian tasks. In Green, D. R., Ford, M. D., and Flamer, G. B. (Eds.), *Measurement and Piaget.* New York: McGraw-Hill, 1971.

Langer, J. *Theories of development.* New York: Holt, Rinehart & Winston, 1969.

Piaget, J. *The psychology of intelligence.* London: Routledge & Kegan Paul, 1950.

Piaget, J. *The child's conception of number.* London: Routledge & Kegan Paul, 1952.

Piaget, J. *The construction of reality in the child.* New York: Basic Books, 1954.

Piaget, J. *Play, dreams, and imitation in childhood.* New York: Norton, 1965.

Piaget, J. *The child's conception of physical causality.* Totowanda, New Jersey: Littlefield, Adams, 1969a.

Piaget, J. *The child's conception of time.* London: Routledge & Kegan Paul, 1969b.

Piaget, J. *To understand is to invent.* New York: Grossman, 1973.

Piaget, J. Piaget's theory. In Mussen, P. (Ed.), *Carmichael's manual of child psychology*, vol. 1. New York: Wiley, 1970.

Piaget, J., and Inhelder, B. *The child's conception of space.* New York: Norton, 1967.

Piaget, J., and Inhelder, B. *Mental imagery in the child.* New York: Basic Books, 1971.

Applications of the Cognitive-Developmental Perspective to Instruction

$\mathcal{Y}$ou have read about cognitive-developmental theory. In Chapter 12 you learned about the basic factors that contribute to the child's cognitive development. Within each of the four stages of cognitive growth, specific cognitive abilities evolve and develop. Further, these specific abilities are the steps through which the young child's cognitive development proceeds in an orderly, systematic, and hierarchical fashion.

This chapter identifies, in some detail, key principles derived from the cognitive-developmental approach for instructional programming in preschools. Instructional programming, in a Piagetian sense, is broadly defined as: (1) the curriculum—the ways in which activities or experiences are presented to the child, (2) the curricular format—the procedures the adult uses in lesson planning, and (3) the curricular areas—the grouping of knowledge into developmentally derived categories for purposes of instruction.

In the first section of this chapter, we look at curriculum integration. You will see that the three major goals for a cognitive-developmental program are: (1) psychomotor development, (2) socioemotional development, and (3) cognitive development. Although these goals are separable, you must remember that within a Piagetian framework a child's development proceeds as a whole. Accordingly, the youngster's growth is stimulated in all areas simultaneously.

The second section, which looks at instructional programming, proposes a curriculum framework using activity plans and evaluation procedures. We describe the format for developing activity plans for your own use, and also make suggestions about the integration of various curricular activities.

In the third section, we show how the four types of cognitive knowledge (physical, logicomathematical, social, and representational) can be used to generate activities. Although each area is described individually, the youngster develops in all areas at the same time. Therefore, the curriculum, like the curricular format, also should be viewed as an integrated whole. It is presented here as separate areas of knowledge only to outline a system through which you can master the concepts of a Piagetian approach to early childhood. As you develop skill in diagnosing and interpreting children's responses to situations, you will become more flexible in the use of the proposed curricular areas of knowledge.

INTEGRATING THE CURRICULUM

The most important component of the curriculum is the teacher. In Piagetian classrooms, teachers have two roles. On the one hand, they must design a set of experiences that will facilitate development of the whole child in general. On the other hand, they must make sure that when the activities are carried out, they meet the needs of the individual children who participate in them.

This dual role means that teachers must be conscientious about planning, implementing, and evaluating the curriculum. In planning for a well-balanced curriculum, teachers will use many different kinds of activities to guide development in a particular area. Also, many different areas of growth will be stimulated by a single activity. In actually carrying out specific activities, Piagetian teachers will have in mind the various structures and abilities preschool children are developing. Just as important, they will be carefully listening to and watching individual children to see how they can make best use of a particular experience. Finally, evaluation of the curriculum means looking at how effectively teachers have combined specific activities balanced across areas and days with spontaneous learning in unplanned activities to promote the development of all children in the classroom.

Learning How to Present Activities

It takes time for one to gain the skills necessary to integrate the curriculum. Start with the parts and build them up into an interrelated whole. At all times keep in mind that the ultimate goal is to be able to interact with each child on an individual basis and provide the experiences that best match the child's development level. Working with this child is far more important than any specific skill, activity, plan, or curriculum. Integrating the curriculum and curricular experiences with the child rests on your ability to incorporate cognitive-developmental concepts into different curricula and in a meaningful way. In a Piagetian sense, you cannot depend on any one curriculum or activity or activity plan for purposes of integration. Means of integrating curriculum experiences in meaningful ways with children emerge from the activities and in what they do and say. The experi-

Cooking activities can help children learn the physical properties of food and mixtures, the names of foods, and seriation techniques, among other things.

enced teacher knows that the youngsters and the curriculum must each be treated as *complete* entities. To focus on any one part exclusively is to lose that wholeness that makes each child a special individual.

Free Play   In free play situations, you turn play into meaningful cognitive experiences. Here, integrating the curriculum depends on your teaching ability and more specifically on your own capacity to observe and diagnose as well as provide follow-up experiences that extend cognitive thought processes. In the capacity of a skillful teacher, you observe the youngsters' activities, and (1) provide information for their use (social knowledge), (2) provide materials and objects through which they can represent their experiences (representational knowledge), and (3) ask questions to help them focus their attention on important attributes of objects (physical knowledge) and relationships (logicomathematical knowledge). The experiences that traditionally occur in early childhood programs can be used to promote cognitive development in all curriculum areas. For example, unit blocks come in different sizes and shapes and can be seriated and classified. The children learn the properties of wood, for example, "hard" and "smooth" and can match blocks in one-to-one correspondence. In addition, the youngsters learn the names for shapes, such as square and rectangle, and for the things they build, for example, towers and roads. As the children construct, they make representations of reality and engage in sociodramatic play. Further, youngsters cooperate and share with other peers in building projects and in taking different roles.

Cooking activities can be used as a basis for integrating the curriculum. Cooking activities are opportunities for children to learn the physical properties of food and mixtures (for example, changing and dissolving). They learn the names for the foods and for the actions they perform (avocado, blending). They use time seriation in following directions, one-to-one correspondence in putting things in cups or bowls, and classification in separating foods for different purposes. They use their representational knowledge to interpret the pictures on the recipe card.

Another common activity in preschools that helps to promote cognitive development in all curriculum areas is playing grocery store, which allows the children to role play the storekeeper and the customer. They can classify the products in the store; for example, cans—here, boxes—there. They seriate boxes and cans by ordering them by size, and form a one-to-one correspondence between items purchased and pieces of play money. The customers can make grocery lists, copying letters from the products they want onto a piece of paper.

Structured Settings   In a more structured sense, integration of curriculum is also meaningful to the development of the whole child. The following series of steps are suggested for developing and practicing these important skills:

1. Concentrate first on learning how to present an activity that deals specifically with only one knowledge area. The activity plan has its greatest value here. The activity plan is hierarchically organized from simple to complex and from concrete to abstract. Accordingly, the activity plan is designed as a reminder of the growth sequences the child goes through in development.

2. Use the same materials for different knowledge areas at different times. For example, use cans and straws for a number concepts activity on Monday, for classification on Tuesday, and for seriation on Wednesday. This helps you recognize ways to use the same materials to teach different concepts.

3. Use the same materials for two different curriculum areas at the same activity but with different children. If you use silverware, one child can be seriating the spoons and ordering them by size while another is classifying which are metal and which are plastic. This makes you familiar with the procedures for both curriculum areas, because you switch rapidly back and forth between them when working with different children.

4. Use three or more different curriculum areas in the same activity at the same time. With this step, you start to move away from directed discovery activities planned to promote different curriculum areas toward those that are multipurpose and able to be carried out in many ways. Your full teaching ability is called on here to follow the interests of each child and to match your questions to that particular child's developmental level.

As you become more skilled in observation and a better diagnostician of children, you will find numerous opportunities throughout the day to help them extend their cognitive abilities.

Methods for Presenting Activities

From a cognitive-developmental perspective, there are three ways in which teaching can be planned:

Exploring the growing cognitive self.

Free Discovery   Children are exposed to an environment that is rich in materials and opportunities for exploration and discovery. They are allowed to follow their own inclinations, sort through materials, and choose their own activities. For example, the classroom would contain objects such as balance scales and other measuring devices that the children would be allowed to explore freely and use in their own way.

Prompted Discovery   You can markedly increase children's chances of discovery by structuring the environment and including specific props and materials. The environment is prepared by placing within it specific objects that serve your particular goals of discovery. For example, you could put out blocks of various sizes with the balance scale and encourage the children to try different ways of using them.

Directed Discovery   Here, you help children focus on relevant attributes of objects and situations. To use this method of presenting activities effectively, you ask questions and pose problems for children to solve. At the balance scale, for example, you ask, "What would happen if you put a block in this pan?" or, "How could you make the two sides the same?"

In each area of knowledge, all three levels of presenting activities for discovery can be employed. You can use the methods sequentially or simultaneously within the same activity. Although most activities can be presented at the free or prompted discovery levels, you may use directed discovery in presenting learning activities in the different content areas or as explicit ways of evaluating children and activities.

In the remainder of this chapter, the framework of a cognitive-developmental curriculum is described. To assist you in learning the teaching skills necessary for a Piagetian approach to early childhood education, we will present each area of cognitive knowledge. In each we include: (1) instructions for presenting an activity in the directed discovery mode, (2) a sample activity plan for directed discovery, (3) ways to present activities using free or prompted discovery, and (4) a sample plan showing how prompted or free discovery can be used to extend activities in that knowledge area to other items during the day or to other types of activities.

CURRICULUM FRAMEWORK

The cognitive-developmental curriculum provides a framework from which activity plans and evaluation procedures can be constructed. First, a general format for the cognitive knowledge area is presented. Then, each knowledge area will be explained and samples of activity plans given. Finally, some suggestions are made for integrating parts of the curriculum into a coherent whole.

Box 13-1   Let's Play . . .

In applying cognitive-developmental perspectives to instruction, free play and adult-guided play activities are ideal. Recall that in make-believe play, children actively represent objects, things, and situations, and this is one of the ways they structure their physical, logical, and social knowledge. In addition to make-believe, the other forms necessary for symbol development are: imitation (use of the body without props for representation), onomatopoeia (use of sounds for representation), three-dimensional models (construction of three-dimensional representations), and two-dimensional models (drawings or pictures of objects). *Let's play* . . . permits the youngsters to use each of these five forms and is a substantive part of cognitive-developmental programming for young children.

Examples of *Let's play* . . . with each of these forms of symbol development follow. For make-believe, youngsters individually or in groups can engage in playing:

- House or other familiar family situations in which they enact these episodes
- Familiar children's fantasy stories (*Three Little Pigs*) and real ones (*Story of Airplanes*) as themes

For imitation without props, children can play by modeling:

- Movements of favorite animals (elephant's walk, kangaroo's hop) with their bodies
- Physical actions of television heroes and

heroines or story characters with their body movements and coordinations

With onomatopoeia, children play by making:

- Sounds of animals, people, and objects in dramatic and sociodramatic play
- Noises and sounds of trees and leaves blowing in the wind, thunder on a rainy afternoon, and other living nonhuman things

For three-dimensional models, youngsters play as they use:

- Clay to fashion objects, things, events, and situations
- Blocks, Tinker Toys, and other construction materials to represent objects, situations, and events

With two-dimensional forms, youngsters play as they make:

- Drawings using crayons, fingerpaints, and regular paints to show settings and situations; they then talk about the pictures
- Cut-outs of figures and objects, which they paste on construction paper and discuss

Therefore, ample amounts of instructional time should be devoted to play employing make-believe, imitating, onomatopoeia, and two- and three-dimensional models.

For additional ideas with children on *Let's play* . . . , see: Yawkey, T. D., and Pellegrini, A. D. (Eds.), *Child's play and play therapy*. Lancaster, Pennsylvania: Technomics Publishing, 1984.

Activity Plans

For each type of knowledge area, plans are developed and used as guides in presenting the activity. Activity plans are used to guide you in planning, preparing, and presenting instructional activities, and to guide you in presenting an activity someone else has prepared.

The activity plan becomes a learning device to develop your teaching and diagnostic skills. Filling in the parts of the activity plan in detail aids in planning the activity and identifying all of the materials needed. Each step of the activity plan matches an objective, and you can check the level of difficulty between the step and the objective. During the activity, the plan serves as a memory aid, helping you recall what step comes next and what kinds of questions to ask. The adult experienced in working with young children may just use the outline of an activity plan or none at all. Finally, the activity plan serves to ensure a balance in emphasis between the areas of knowledge.

An activity plan that is prepared for use by another person or for use at a future time must be more detailed than one that will just be used to jog your own memory. Materials and steps must be described explicitly to ensure that another person can understand and follow them. Remember, the activity plan should be an aid in planning, preparing, and presenting activities, not simply a chore to be done the same way each time.

Objectives

The objectives of the activity deserve special mention because they can be misinterpreted easily. The goal of all cognitively-oriented activities is to develop the child's thinking processes. Accordingly, cognitive processes such as decision making, problem solving, and generalizing are the important outcomes; behaviors like one-to-one correspondence, sequencing objects by color, or oral counting are not the true goals. Of course, it is possible to know what processes are going on in the child's mind only by observing behaviors that are guided by these cognitive processes. Hence, objectives are stated in terms of observable behaviors. However, behaviors are the goals of the activity only to the extent that they reflect the cognitive processes underlying them.

The objectives are stated in the order of easiest to most difficult. A child is not expected to master every objective for every activity. Instead, children are expected to function at their own developmental level. Your task is to help expand their intellectual abilities to different content areas. Thus, the objectives should be appropriate for children at all levels of development.

Activity Plan Format

For easy use, the activity plan is divided into seven sections: (1) heading, (2) general information, (3) objectives, (4) materials, (5) presentation, (6) extensions, and (7) evaluation. These sections comprising the format of the activity plan are shown in Table 13-1.

Heading   The heading gives information about what is contained in the entire activity plan. The *type* of activity tells what the main goal area of the activity is. This can be social knowledge, physical knowledge, classification, seriation, or number concepts. The *title* is the name of the specific activity described in the plan.

General Information   This section contains information that is used in planning activities. For *time*, write down either the amount of time it

Table 13-1   The Format of an Activity Plan

Type:
Title:

1. General Information
   A. Time:
   B. Place:
   C. Children:
2. Objectives
   A.
   B.
   C.
   D.
   E.
3. Materials
   A. Set per child:
   B. Common materials:
4. Presentation
   A. Introduction:
   B. Procedure:
      1.
      2.
      3.
      4.
      5.
5. Extensions
6. Evaluation
   A. Observation cards:
   B. Comments and suggestions:

would take for a child to complete the activity or the time period during the day which is most suitable for the activity (for example, free choice time or snack time). For *place*, state the location in the room that would be a good setting for the activity. Often the description is as simple as "any floor or table area." However, some activities need special facilities; these should be described here (for example, any table near an electrical outlet). For *children*, write down the number of children that can be best accommodated by the activity.

Objectives   The objectives describe the specific behaviors children should show as evidence of their thinking processes. The objectives are listed in theoretical sequence from the easiest (or the ones that the child is expected to develop first) to the most difficult (or the ones that the child demonstrates last).

Materials   List all the materials necessary to conduct the activity. Under *set per child* identify the set of materials needed by one youngster to complete the activity. Be sure to include in the description the size, shape, number, color, and materials from which they are made—when these characteristics are important to the activity (for example, hard wood, rough sandpaper). A poor description of materials for a classification activity is "a set of blocks." However, a better description is "a set of nine blocks consisting of three squares, three circles, and three triangles with one of each shape red, one blue, and one green." Under *common materials* include those things you need for the activity and those that the children share (for example, sponge and paper towels or stapler and scissors).

It is important that the materials be described specifically because the nature of the materials often determines whether or not children are able to do the activity. For example, children may be able to seriate a set of sticks that are 1 in., 3 in., 5 in., and 7 in. long but not a set of sticks 3 in., 3¼ in., 3½ in., and 3¾ in. They may be able to classify plastic flowers but not flowers made out of construction paper and popsicle sticks. In general, youngsters show more advanced performance using objects with which they are most familiar.

Presentation   The *presentation* lists suggestions for the introduction and implementation of the activity. The *introduction* sets the tone for the activity and explains the reason for doing it with the child. Although it need not be memorized or read verbatim, a direct quote is listed so you will have a clear idea of the first few words to use in introducing the activity ["Hi, (child's name), I took all the silverware out of this tray. Now, I'm trying to put it back. Would you like to help me?"]. A good motivating introduction captures the child's interest.

Under *procedure*, list the steps to be followed in presenting the activity.

There should be at least one step for each objective, and the steps should be listed in the sequence of easiest to most difficult. In a more detailed activity plan, each step could also include samples of specific questions you might ask ("Can you find all the blocks that are the same and put them on this shelf?"). These questions need not be memorized or read verbatim but are included as a guide.

Extensions   Suggestions for *extensions* should be included as an aid to seeing different ways to present the same activity to different children or at various times of the year. There are four basic ways in which an activity may be extended and varied: changing the presentation method, using different materials, extending the activity within the knowledge area, and extending the activity to another knowledge area.

Evaluation   Information from observation cards provides feedback on children and activities. Under *observation cards*, list the observation card or cards that are most appropriate for this activity. Leave a space for *comments*. Here, you can give reactions and suggestions for improvement or variation after completing the activity.

Conducting an Activity

After planning the activity, you are now ready to conduct it. Although there are many different plans depending on the types of activities, there are certain principles that are common to conducting all types of activities.

In general, before the children perform the activity make sure that all necessary materials are displayed where children can easily get to them. The materials should be attractive and arranged to invite participation by the children. Rather than piling materials in the center of a table, group them so that each youngster has a complete set. Next, carefully observe how the youngsters act on and react to the situation. In turn, use the information gained from the observation as cues in asking questions, expanding the activity, and in extending the children's thinking process.

Introduction   As children arrive to perform an activity, smile and greet them by name. Then, begin to introduce the activity. You could use one of the following introductions:

1. *Story format.* Either a traditional story, such as "The Three Bears," or a made-up story, like taking a walk through the park, could be used.
2. *Game format.* Guessing games, bean toss games, and games in which the child follows directions on a spinner are popular.
3. *Task format.* The child is given a job to do, such as putting away the silverware or making a bouquet of flowers.

4. *Surprise format.* You may try to surprise the child or introduce elements of novelty to maintain attention and interest. As other children arrive at the activity, you may introduce the activity or have a child already there tell the others how it is done.

Procedure Before you attempt any teaching, the children should be allowed some time for exploration. This is very important, for it provides the youngsters the time to familiarize themselves with new objects or reacquaint themselves with old ones. It is unreasonable to expect a child to use a new toy or material in an adult-guided activity without first assimilating some of its interesting characteristics. The child should be encouraged to explore freely and manipulate the item to discover its properties.

As the children actively participate in performing the activity, use the activity plan as a guide, not as a set of rules. Encourage the children to manipulate the materials themselves rather than doing it for them. Respond to children's questions and promote interactions between children. This procedure will enable you to respond to individual children and their different ability levels, attention spans, and interests rather than treating them as a group. In addition, you should ask questions that promote logical thinking by the child. These questions are sequenced according to the objectives of the activity, and in general they require more than a yes, no, or one-word answer. Throughout the activity, observe what they say and do with the materials and how they answer your questions. However, because it is more important to observe the children and help them focus on relevant aspects of the activity, defer recording your observations until you have some free time after the activity.

As children begin to leave the activity, make sure that it reaches some kind of closure. Here, reaching closure means completing a craft project, replacing pieces of a puzzle, or simply gathering up the materials used in the activity. After closure, evaluate the activity while it is still fresh in your mind. Add comments and suggestions to the activity plan for future reference.

Evaluation Evaluation and diagnosis are important parts of the instructional role. All teachers observe their children and make informal judgments about their progress and interests. However, these observations are likely to be incomplete, affected by the teacher's ability to remember every detail, and colored by intervening activities. Developing a systematic method of collecting information can help you: (1) evaluate activities by providing information about their levels of difficulty and interest, (2) determine at what developmental level the child is operating for various activities, and (3) plan future activities that are both interesting and at the appropriate developmental level. In addition, having the observation card at the activity reminds you of the major objectives and their sequence of development for that activity.

Evaluation Format

Corresponding to each knowledge area is an evaluation card (see Table 13-2). This can be a 5-in. × 8-in. index card on which the objectives for the activity are written. In the upper left and right corners, there are spaces for the *title* of the activity, primary *knowledge area, date,* and your *name.* Across the top of the card are the *objectives*, listed in order, for this knowledge area. Prior to the section labeled *objectives*, there are two columns entitled *observes* and *explores materials*. The categories of observing or exploring are filled in when the youngster is not directly involved with the activity. For example, if the youngster is watching the activity or the children performing it, the *observes* column is used to note his or her actions. However, if he or she is manipulating the materials in random fashion or playing with them in a personal way, the *explores materials* column is used. In classifying actions as observing or exploring, you should not feel that the child is not gaining anything from the activity simply because that child is not showing any observable behaviors that you can interpret as meeting the objectives of the activity plan.

As children come to the activity, write their names in the *child's name* column. Then, as children proceed through the activity, put a check (√) beside their name and under each objective that they accomplish. If they attempt the behavior described in an objective but do not accomplish it, you can put a minus (−) beside the children's name under that objective. Under *comments*, write additional information about the children's performance. Helpful comments for all areas of knowledge include: (1) a child's

Table 13-2   The Format of an Evaluation Card

(Knowledge Area) / (Activity Title)	Observes	Explores Materials	Objectives						Date: _____ / Teacher: _____
Child's Name									Comments
1. Henry Jones									
2. Maria Reynaldo									
3. Angelo de Pinta									
4. Suzie Walsh									
5. Pamela Brown									

level of interest and participation ("wasn't interested"; "left before I could ask a question"; "was very involved in the activity"), and (2) how readily the child was able to complete the activity ("completed without peer help"; "completion took 10 minutes"). These comments are useful for evaluating the knowledge areas.

CURRICULUM AREAS

The curriculum of cognitive knowledge is divided into four areas: physical, logicomathematical, social, and representational knowledge. Logicomathematical knowledge is further subdivided into classification, seriation, and number concepts. In each of these curriculum areas, the general strategy is to arrange the environment to make discovery possible by the child.

Physical Knowledge

Physical knowledge is feedback youngsters receive from objects in the physical environment. By acting upon this, they learn that objects act and react in regular and consistent ways. For example, yellow and blue make

---

Box 13-2   Piagetian Curriculum Areas

The curriculum areas are grouped into physical, logicomathematical, social, and representational knowledge. Briefly, physical knowledge is feedback children receive from objects and things in the physical environment; logicomathematical knowledge is based on relations among objects (classification, seriation); social knowledge is derived from feedback from people; representational knowledge is the way youngsters structure the initial three knowledge areas to represent reality.

We attempted to show that any knowledge concept can be used to set the stage for development of concepts in the other three areas. In a classical Piagetian sense, concepts in these areas are threaded together and, with guided discovery, growth can occur in all the developmental areas.

Using this integrated approach, we can show with the concept of colors how true integration works. Teaching preschoolers to understand the color concept "purple" could include, for example:

- Mixing paints to make the color purple (physical knowledge)
- Finding and matching purple objects in the environment (logicomathematical)
- Identifying feelings associated with the color purple (social)
- Putting on a purple robe as might be used by a favorite king or queen and enacting a fantasy story about that character (representational)

This same integration across knowledge areas can be used for developing each concept in curricula using either subject areas (reading, mathematics) or social living and holiday areas (family, transportation, animals, Halloween). The preschool teacher who strives to integrate knowledge areas for understanding of concepts realizes the benefits of using cognitive-interactionist psychology to encourage meaningful and permanent learning.

When children act on objects in different ways and observe the results, they learn to predict the effects the actions will have.

green when a child mixes them, when you mix them, or when other children mix them; when a child mixes paint or colored water or crayons; when a child mixes them on Tuesday or on Friday. By acting on objects in different ways (folding, dropping, squeezing, breaking, pulling, squashing) and observing the results of their own actions, children predict the effects actions will have on them. Based on consistency of and feedback from the object itself (yellow and blue always make green), youngsters begin to structure their physical knowledge.

Objectives   At the same time children are learning about the properties of objects, they are also learning a scientific process—a method for learning more about the world. The purpose of physical knowledge activities is not to teach children correct predictions, but to encourage them to think about possible outcomes and the variety of actions they can perform to test their ideas. This process is reflected in three short-term, activity-specific objectives:

1. The child will *predict* what changes will occur as a result of his or her actions.
2. The child will *test* her or his prediction.
3. The child will *state the outcome* of the experiment.

Two long-term objectives become apparent over time and across activities rather than at one time and within one particular activity:

1. The child will *increase the repertoire of actions* he or she uses to explore the properties of objects. For example, many different actions can be used to transform paint. These include painting with brushes, string, sponges, and fingers, mixing to form new colors, and beating to change the texture.
2. The child uses her or his repertoire of actions to *explore increasingly less familiar objects* as well as familiar objects. Encouraging the child to verbalize his or her predictions and the results of his actions help you understand the child's mental processes. However, the child's telling you is not an end in itself.

Your role in physical knowledge is to prepare the environment and encourage children's experimentation. Further, you do not have to correct errors because the physical world will usually do it for you in a more convincing manner. For example, if children say that a cork will sink, simply suggest that they test their prediction. Asking questions encourages the child to predict possible outcomes, test predictions, and verbalize results.

Materials   Science curriculum materials for developing physical knowledge are limited to those in which change is readily observable and repeatable. Appropriate materials are those that deal with objects that change (a seed becomes a plant), that can be made to change (mixing yellow and blue makes green), or that change other objects (a magnifying glass makes ob-

Some things float, and some things sink . . .

jects look bigger). Activities from the following four areas should be considered: (1) biology (the child's own body, plants, and growing), (2) physics (i.e., heat; light—shadows and prisms; sound—loud and soft; musical instruments; magnets; gravity; weights—scales; machines—using levers, gears, and pulleys), (3) chemistry (cooking and making mixtures), and (4) using equipment (hot plate, scales, magnets, magnifying glass).

Presentation   First show the children the materials and allow them to explore and become familiar with them. If needed, help children with labels for objects and their properties (dry, hot, cold).

1. Encourage children to *make predictions* about the possible results of their actions on the materials. Your questions, in all cases, should go from the very general (which allows the most freedom to explore alternatives) to the more specific (which helps focus on relevant and salient properties of the materials). Examples of questions that flow from the general to the specific are, "What can you do with the objects? . . . What else?" to "What will happen if you mix yellow and blue paint?" and "How do we make this ice cube melt?" It is important that children make a prediction. It does not necessarily have to be a correct one. If the prediction is not correct, they will soon find out when they test it in the environment.

2. Encourage children to perform actions on the objects to *test their predictions* ("How can we find out if the cork will sink?" and "Let's see what will happen when you mix yellow and blue paint."). It is very important that children act on the objects themselves. Children learn through their own activities. Watching the adult give a demonstration does not

have the same learning potential as having children do the experiment themselves.

3. Ask children to *state the outcome* of the experiment after they have tested their prediction. This verbal statement helps children focus their observations and gives you clues to their thinking. Again, the questions should start with the more general and become more specific if the child needs help. For example, "How did you make the paint turn green?" "What happened to the cotton ball in the water?" "Did the marble sink or float?"

Table 13-3 shows an example of a completed activity plan for curricula in the area of physical knowledge; the content is magnification of textures.

Extensions   Learning about physical knowledge does not need to be limited to directed discovery activities. Understanding about physical knowledge can be extended to other times and at other activities. Throughout the entire day, children have opportunities to learn about the properties of the world around them. For example, in the playground they may observe snow melting on the sidewalk. Further, you help children focus their observation by having them bring some snowflakes inside to see what happens to them in a warm room. Also, ask children questions that encourage predicting and testing possible outcomes with different kinds of actions. For example, "What will happen if the snow is put under a light, or in the refrigerator?" After predicting, the youngsters test their predictions.

Physical knowledge activities are easily extended to other knowledge areas by using prompted and free discovery:

1. *Social knowledge*. Children should be encouraged to use appropriate terms in describing objects and their actions upon them. Examples: rough, smooth, dissolve, stir, attract.
2. *Classification*. Children should not be expected to know why their actions result in a particular outcome. However, they can be guided by the adult to classify and arrange objects according to their similarities and differences. Examples include objects that float and objects that sink, and objects that are attracted by a magnet and objects that are not.
3. *Seriation*. Many physical knowledge activities, especially cooking, involve following a recipe. During and after the activity, children can describe the steps taken; ask, "What came first . . . second . . . and last?"
4. *Number concepts*. Most physical knowledge activities also involve measurement and one-to-one correspondence. For example, youngsters match the number of cups of flour that go into the bowl with the same number of pictures of cups on a recipe card.

There are many ways to connect different areas of knowledge in one activity. For example, a representational activity, such as easel painting with

Table 13-3   An Activity Plan for Physical Knowledge Using Magnification of Textures

PHYSICAL KNOWLEDGE
Magnification—Textures

General Information
Time: free choice time
Place: any table or floor area
Children: 1–5

Objectives
A. Given assorted objects and a magnifying glass, the child will predict how the objects will look when seen through the glass
B. Given the objects and the glass, the child will look at the objects through the glass
C. The child will state the difference in each object's appearance when seen through the glass

Materials
Set per child: Magnifying glass
Common materials: assorted objects with different textures, such as nylon net, wood scraps, fabrics, leaves, pipecleaners, pictures

Presentation
Introduction: "Hi _____. This is a magnifying glass. Today we're going to look at some things through this magnifying glass. How do you think this will look through the glass?"
Procedure: 1. Ask the child to predict how the object will change in appearance when looked at through the glass
2. Encourage the child to look at objects through the glass
3. Ask the child to state the change he or she sees

Extensions
A. Physical knowledge: Encourage the child to move the magnifying glass up and down and state the results. Let the child find different objects in the room to look at through the glass
B. Social knowledge: Encourage the child to use the terms *big, bigger, large, larger, little, small, smaller, rough, smooth,* in describing the appearance of the objects
C. Classification: The child can sort the materials according to how they look through the magnifying glass, e.g., rough or smooth

Evaluation
Observation card: physical knowledge
Comments and suggestions:

reds and blues, sets the scene for the child to discover the physical knowledge that mixing them makes purple. Table 13-4 shows an example of an activity plan connecting the areas of physical knowledge and representation.

Evaluation   Throughout the activity, the children's actions are observed. In turn, these actions are recorded on a physical knowledge observation card by a check (√) under each objective met or by a minus (−) for those

Table 13-4   Extending Physical Knowledge in the Area of Representation

ART
Easel Painting with Red and Blue
Symbol, Sign

1. Area: Art; number of children: 1–6.
2. Objectives: To allow children to represent their experiences through two-dimensional pictures (symbols).
3. Materials: easels, large newsprint, easel brushes, smocks, paint in two colors (blue and red).
4. Directions: Children use brushes to paint pictures or designs to represent their experiences at the symbol or sign level.
5. Note: Using just two colors of paint will allow the child to mix them to form a new color. Be alert for this. Asking children to describe their pictures and the colors in them may help the children to notice color changes.

that are not achieved. In addition, the appropriate box is checked each time the youngster performs the action. Thus, for example, the box under *predicts outcome* could contain one or more checks. Useful comments would be: (1) what children predicted, (2) how they tested their predictions, and (3) how much help they received from the teacher. An observation card showing assessment items and statements is illustrated in Table 13-5.

Logicomathematical Knowledge

Logicomathematical knowledge differs from physical knowledge in that the former is not dependent upon the physical properties of the objects involved. Rather, logicomathematical knowledge is based upon the relationships between objects. In physical knowledge, feedback about the correctness of a child's predictions comes from the physical environment. However, in logicomathematical knowledge, feedback comes from children's own logical way of thinking. Do not correct mistakes. Telling or showing children that they are wrong doesn't convince them. Children must construct their own knowledge by acting on objects and reversing their actions, putting objects together in different ways, and performing other logical operations. Providing children with many opportunities and experiences to structure their own knowledge gives more relevant feedback.

It is important for children to develop their logicomathematical thought processes so that they can deal with the world in an orderly and efficient way. Just think how confusing a supermarket would be if everything was mixed together instead of classified into dairy, meat, and other groupings. By generalizing their experiences, children do not have to figure out a new way of dealing with each new situation they meet. Instead, they handle new situations and problems by applying their reasoning abilities. Once they learn that touching a hot stove burns, they can generalize this knowl-

Table 13-5   Evaluation of Children's Actions in Physical Knowledge Using an Observation Card

Physical Knowledge (Knowledge Area) Mixing Colors: (blue and yellow paint) (Activity Title)	Observes	Explores Materials	Predicts Outcome	Test	Verbalizes Outcome			Date: April 16 Teacher: Ms. Denise
Child's Name								Comments
1. Ellen Samuels		√	√	√	−			No trouble
2. Mark Beatrice			√	√	√			Had no idea what would occur.
3. Angelo Gomez	√							Did not want to get hands "messy."
4. Shanda Smith			√	√	−			Predicted "red." Does not know label for "green."
5. Lisa Shupkinsky		√	√	√				Just wanted to paint a picture.

edge to other hot things without first burning themselves on irons and toasters, too.

There are three major categories within logicomathematical knowledge. They are: (1) classification, (2) seriation, and (3) number concepts.

Classification

Classification is the ability to group things according to their likenesses and differences. When children first begin to classify, they form interesting designs, pictures, and logical patterns (a red triangle, a blue triangle, a blue circle) instead of forming groups. They may start classifying by one characteristic but become distracted by other characteristics of the objects and quickly lose their intended purpose. As children start classifying objects into groups by trial and error, they can first classify only objects that are almost identical (red squares and blue squares). Gradually, they are able to classify objects that are similar or share only one common characteristic (red square, red circle, red triangle versus blue square, blue circle, blue triangle). Having placed the objects in groups, however, they find it difficult to think of other ways to classify them. When children reach a more advanced stage of cognitive development, they use a deliberate method for finding similarities among objects. They are able to shift their method of classifying and can also categorize by two characteristics simultaneously. They understand class inclusion; for example, girls and boys are members of disjoint classes, but both belong to a class of children.

Objectives The objectives for classification activities are not the same as their final products. Rather, objectives emphasize the development of the processes of: (1) inventing a method for classifying and using it consistently, (2) giving an explanation for why objects are grouped in a certain way, (3) regrouping objects in many different ways by shifting the method of classifying, and (4) thinking independently rather than depending on others' judgments. Thus, the objectives for classification are:

1. Children will *classify* a group of objects in their own way.
2. Children will give an *explanation* for the way they classified the objects; a verbal explanation can be used to determine whether youngsters have classified intentionally or accidentally.
3. Children will demonstrate *another classification* by grouping the objects in a different way than their earlier classification.
4. Children will give an *explanation* for their new way of classifying.
5. Children will do a *multiple classification* by grouping objects by two common properties simultaneously. (For example, forming four classes consisting of red squares, red circles, blue squares, and blue circles.)
6. Children will give an *explanation* of how the objects are alike in two ways.

Materials The materials for a classification activity must have at least two characteristics by which they can be classified. However, materials that have many characteristics may be distracting to the child. Before the children arrive at the activity, you should sort the materials into sets for individual children. Each set must be able to be classified in at least two ways. For example, it is frustrating to children to try to classify a set of materials when they have inadvertently gotten all green teddy bears. Four to six objects in a set may be sufficient for preschoolers to classify. More objects could be confusing.

Presentation The presentation of these activities is important. When children arrive at the activity, they should explore the materials freely. After children become familiar with the materials, help them focus on the ways in which they can be classified. The adult's questions and strategies should start with the most general, allowing children the most freedom of choice, and progress to the more specific. Some examples of questions that help children focus on relevant characteristics include: "Look at these colors and shapes. Can you tell me what the colors and shapes are?" "How are these two items the same?" "How are the items different from one another?" "What does this object feel like?" By naming the characteristics of these objects, children show whether they have the necessary vocabulary to be able to give an explanation for their ways of classifying.

1. Encourage children to classify objects after they have identified the properties. Some examples of suggestions that can assist youngsters in classifying include: "Put the flowers that go together in the vase." "Put all the silverware that is alike in some way together in this pile." "Can you find any way that these clothes are alike? Let's put them over here." These directions should encourage but not tell children how to classify. (An example of telling a child how to classify is, "Put all the red beads over here and all the blue beads over there.") Telling how to classify takes the initiative from children. Discovering how to classify gives children the initiative and helps them construct knowledge by determining their own way of grouping.

   If children are having difficulty classifying, there are several strategies that you can use to guide discovery. One is to provide containers for each class of objects; clothes can be classified into baskets or silverware into trays, pieces of construction paper or cardboard boxes can be pretend garages for toy cars and trucks. A second strategy is simply to hold or point to one object and have children find another one like it. You should use noncuing questions, such as, "Can you find another one like this one?" or "Show me another block that's the same as this one." Noncuing questions help children pick out common properties. After they have found one object that goes with the initial one, ask them to find a third one that is like both of the first two. A third strategy should be used when the children leave out some objects in the set. It encourages them to reexamine the unclassified objects. As examples, you can ask: "Does this bead belong in this cup?" "Where does this bead belong?" Further, try to put an object in the wrong set—for instance, "Should I put this bead here?"

2. Ask youngsters to explain their system of grouping after they have classified all the objects. Some examples include: "How did you know the silverware goes in the tray?" "Why did you put these clothes in this basket?" "How are all these flowers alike?" Children often have trouble giving a reason why they have grouped objects in a certain way, even if it is obvious to you. You can encourage children's reasoning by holding up two objects from the same class and asking how they are alike. Or, hold up two objects from different classes and ask how they are different. Another helpful strategy is to pick up an object, place it in the wrong pile, and ask, "Can I put this one here? Or, does it belong somewhere else? . . . Why?"

3. Give youngsters opportunities to classify objects in various other ways. Examples of questions to guide and extend classification systems include: "Can you put the clothes in the baskets in a new way?" "Is there

another way to put the silverware back in the tray?" "Last time you put together all the flowers that were the same color. How else can you put them together?" When children are encouraged to discover other ways of classifying, combine the groups after their first classification. This procedure enables the youngsters to refocus on the problem of grouping in novel ways. After they have classified objects in additional ways, ask for explanations.

4. Encourage as many different classifications as possible and again ask for explanations of them. Multiple classifications or grouping objects simultaneously on the bases of two characteristics show high levels of thinking. You should observe for this type of categorizing.

Table 13-6 illustrates a complete activity plan for classification in logico-mathematical knowledge.

Extensions   Classification abilities can be extended through activities occurring at many times during the day. Also, they can be developed through many activities. When playing grocery store, the youngsters put similar items together in bags or on shelves. In the kitchen area, certain foods go together in parts of the refrigerator. When cleaning up the unit blocks, put shapes that are common together on the same shelf. Practicing classification skills at many different times and in many different settings develops the ability to reason logically. You can assist the process by helping children focus on the similarities and differences among the objects they use. You can prompt children to see classification possibilities, but make sure that the materials are classifiable. For example, materials available at common pretend activities, such as shopping at the grocery store, provide ideal settings for classifying. Soda cans and cereal boxes and other materials can be classified by type, color, and size. In Table 13-7, classification abilities are extended through the grocery store play activity.

Within a directed discovery mode, matrix classification is possible; it is more difficult than classifying by one property alone. A matrix with missing parts is set up for children to complete. For example, a two-by-two matrix is set up with the top row having a red circle and red square and the bottom row having one blue circle. The children fill in the missing blank in the bottom row by choosing a blue triangle, blue square, or yellow square. In order to fill in the blank and complete the bottom row, two properties must be held in mind at the same time—the square for the column and blue for the row (Figure 13-1). Matrices may be varied by increasing their size (two-by-three and three-by-three). With each size increase, matrix classification activities increase in level of difficulty.

Classification activities also can be extended to other areas of knowledge:

1. *Social knowledge*. Children should learn the names for the characteristics of objects they classify. For example, characteristics and properties include: soft, rough, color, and bumpy. Understanding

Table 13-6   An Activity Plan for Classification in Logicomathematical
Knowledge

CLASSIFICATION
Silverware

General Information
Time: free choice time
Place: any floor or table area
Children: 1–4

Objectives
A. Given materials and directions by the teacher, the child will classify the
silverware by own criterion
B. The child will give a verbal explanation for his or her classification in A
C. The child will classify the silverware by a different criterion
D. The child will give a verbal explanation for her or his classification in C

Materials
Set per child: Assorted silverware—knives, forks, and spoons—all of which
may be of different colors, sizes, shapes, or materials. One silverware tray.

Presentation
Introduction: "Hi _____. Do I have a job for you! Today we have to clean
out this silverware tray and make it nice and neat. Let's look at the silverware closely and see which ones might go together."
Procedure:
1. Encourage the child to classify the silverware
2. After the child has made his or her groupings, ask for a verbal explanation
3. Ask the child to classify the silverware in a different way
4. Ask the child to give verbal explanation for her or his additional classification
5. Encourage the child to do as many additional classifications as he or she
can; ask for a verbal rationale after each one

Extensions
A. Social knowledge: Encourage the child to use the proper term, e.g., *fork,
spoon, knife, plastic, metal*
B. Seriation: If the silverware is in different sizes, it can be seriated
C. Number concepts: The child can set the table, establishing a one-to-one
correspondence between each place setting and each piece of silverware
(social knowledge is also involved here in learning the standard way to set
a table)

Evaluation
Observation card: classification
Comments and suggestions:

and recognizing that objects are members of classes is also basic to
social knowledge. Examples are: shapes, animals, and tools.

2. *Seriation.* Objects that are classified by size or other attributes
along one dimension also can be seriated. For example, three
classes of juice cans are small, medium, and large; these in turn
can be seriated by size.

Table 13-7   Extending Children's Classification Abilities in Logicomathematical Knowledge

SOCIODRAMATIC
Grocery Store
Index, Symbol, Sign

1. Area: any area; number of children: 2–8
2. Objectives: to allow children to represent a trip to the grocery store using indices, symbols, and signs
3. Materials: paper and pencils, shopping bags, soda cans (be sure to have several of each kind [Pepsi, Coke, RC Cola]), cereal boxes of different kinds (Cheerios, Wheaties, Froot Loops), blocks, plastic fruit
4. Directions:
   a. At the index level, children can use cereal boxes, cans, and so on as grocery items.
   b. At the symbol level, children can use blocks to represent boxes (make-believe); play the roles of customer and cashier (imitation).
   c. At the sign level, children can make grocery lists by copying the names on the boxes to stand for those items.
5. Note: Look for children classifying items such as cereal boxes or soda cans by type, or groceries according to their type (e.g., cereal, fruit, beverages).

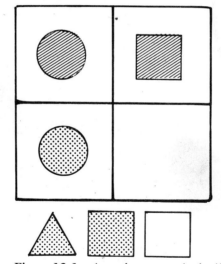

Figure 13-1   *A two-by-two matrix classification*

3. *Number concepts.* Concepts such as one-to-one correspondence between items of two sets are basic to understanding numbers. Youngsters can develop one-to-one correspondence if they have already classified objects into two sets—for instance, cups and saucers from a set of dishware.
4. *Physical knowledge.* Many classification activities also provide the

opportunity to learn about the physical properties of objects—
for example, things that sink and things that float.

Evaluation Throughout the activity, the observation card can be used to
record the child's actions. In addition to the column for each objective,
there is also a column headed *attempts to classify*. This category is used
when children try to group the objects but do not form consistent classes.
They may, for example, be forming pictures or patterns. In this instance,
helpful comments might include: (1) how many objects the child is able to
classify, (2) what property or properties were used in making classes, and
(3) what explanations were given for the classifications. Table 13-8 shows
an evaluation card for children's classification activities.

Seriation

Seriation is the process of ordering objects or events by degree of difference. It involves establishing relations between objects by arranging them
in some logical order along the dimension on which they differ. Seriation
is a logicomathematical process. Children receive feedback about the correctness of their series from their own logical thinking and not from the

Table 13-8 Assessment of Children's Classification Abilities Using an Evaluation Card

Logicomathematical Knowledge/Classification (Knowledge Area) Silverware (Activity Title)	Observes	Explores Materials	Attempts to Classify	Classifies	Classifies and Verbal Rationale	Additional Classification	Additional Classification and Verbal Rationale	Multiple Classification	Multiple Classification and Verbal Rationale	Date: January 23 / Teacher: Mr. Sam
Child's Name										Comments
1. Lucy Johns				√	−					Did not know names for silverware.
2. Rey Columbus				√	√	√	√			(1) silver/plastic (2) knife/spoon
3. Sally Martin	√									Just wanted to watch.
4. Jonathan Georgian				√	√	√	√	√	√	Consistent classifications
5. Gary Duvall		√√								Held spoons and put into mouth.

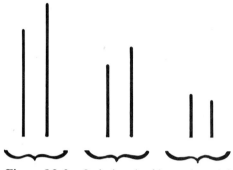

Figure 13-2   *Seriating six objects using trial and error (brackets indicate the comparisons performed during ordering)*

adult. The development of seriation is important because it helps children bring order to their world by seeing the relationships between objects. For example, money can be seriated according to its value, clothes in a store by size, and children in a family by birth order and by height. Through classification children become aware of similarities and differences between objects and situations. Through seriation, they see that these similarities and differences can vary by degree.

Children who are just developing the ability to seriate must first be able to compare two objects on a given dimension. These comparisons may be in terms of opposite pairs such as big–little, rough–smooth, or hot–cold. Although young preoperational children can identify the endpoints of a series, they have difficulty in placing the objects between the endpoints. When given more than two objects to seriate, they proceed randomly by ordering pairs of objects or reordering the series in trial and error fashion. Figure 13-2 shows the outcome of seriating by trial and error; the brackets indicate the comparisons performed by the child in ordering the set of six objects.

Older youngsters make individual comparisons between pairs of objects rather than seeing the series as a whole. As children's seriation ability develops, they can seriate larger subsets of objects. The older preoperational child can seriate up to ten items by trial and error.

Once the series is complete, the child considers it a finished product and has difficulty inserting a new item into that series. When children reach the concrete operational stage, they can make many comparisons in forming and reforming the series. They understand the concept that the middle object of a series of three can be simultaneously larger than the first item and smaller than the third. Concrete operational children are also able to establish serial correspondence: they can match the items in two seriated sets so that the smallest (or lightest or softest) item in one set corresponds to the smallest (or lightest or softest) item in the other set; the second smallest item in one set to the second smallest item in the other set, and so forth.

Objectives   As in classification, the objective of presenting seriation activities is not to create the final product of a seriated set of objects. Rather, the goal is the development of thought processes. Some of these thought processes include: (1) ordering objects or situations along a dimension, (2) giving a verbal explanation for why objects are ordered in a certain way, (3) understanding that an object's position in a series is relative to the other objects in that series, and (4) thinking independently rather than depending on others' judgments.

Based on these goals for seriation, the following are objectives:

1. Children will *find the endpoints* of a set of nonseriated objects.
2. Children will *seriate* objects along the dimension on which they differ.
3. Children will give an *explanation* for their seriation.
4. Children will *insert an additional item* into a completed series.
5. Children will establish *serial correspondence* between two sets.
6. Children will give an *explanation* for their serial correspondence.

Materials   Any materials that can be ordered along a dimension are appropriate for seriation activities. Some of these dimensions are size, color, shape, shade, texture, weight, volume, and time. Time seriation involves ordering events—first, second, last. The child may be able to seriate objects with gross differences (1 lb, 2 lb, 3 lb, or 4 lb) but not those with more subtle differences (1 oz, 2 oz, 3 oz, or 4 oz). Thus, you should begin seriation with materials having differences that can be distinguished and recognized easily. In addition, materials that are identical except for the dimension along which they vary are the easiest to seriate—for example, small, medium, and large teddy bears. However, materials that show a variety of characteristics may also be used as long as they vary in a serial order along one dimension—for example, a small stuffed dog, a medium-sized doll, and a large teddy bear.

Presentation   The presentation starts with a set of at least five objects of which the child is given only four. In that way, one item is held aside to be inserted later. The child still has one more object to seriate after finding the endpoints.

1. Ask the children to find the endpoints of the series of objects after they have had time to explore the materials. Then place the materials a short distance apart so they can fit between them. You can say, "Find the object that is the smallest in size." "Which one is the heaviest?" "Show me the roughest one." Youngsters who show problems learning words that describe dimensional attributes should be given them constructively. With additional practice in using words for these dimensional attributes in seriating, the problems of remembering and pronouncing them and understanding their meanings vanish. Words describing se-

lected dimensional attributes of objects can be learned. For example, short, tall, shorter, and taller are ideal for use and practice with the dimensional attribute of height.

2. Encourage youngsters to seriate the remaining items after they establish the endpoints in the series. Examples of questions to ask at this point are: "Where do the rest of the objects fit in the row?" "Can you put the objects in a row so they go from the shortest to the tallest?" "Can you put the materials in a row so they go from heaviest to lightest?" Mistakes in constructing a series should not be corrected. Instead, you can structure additional activities that help focus attention on relationships between objects. In structuring situations aimed at correcting inappropriate actions, you can either reduce the number of items to be seriated or increase the amount of difference between the objects.

   Seriating objects by length creates problems. Preschoolers most often seriate objects by length by focusing on the tops of the items. They may disregard the bottoms of the items and where they fall. If this situation occurs, establish a baseline along which they can line up the items. Masking tape can easily serve as a baseline in these activities.

3. Ask for a verbal explanation after the series is constructed. Examples of questions that challenge youngsters to explain their actions are: "How did you decide to put them like that?" "How do you know the objects go like that?" "Why did you put them that way?" If children show any difficulty in giving reasons for their seriation, you can move one item to a new place in the series and then ask, "Could I take this one out and put it in here? Why (or why not)?"

4. The child is given the remaining item in the set that was held aside while she or he seriated the four objects. Ask her or him to put it in its proper place in the series. Examples of questions include: "Where does this object belong?" "Can we put this object in with the rest so they still go from heaviest to lightest?" "Can you put this one in with the rest so they still go in a row that starts with the littlest and then gets bigger and bigger all the way up to the biggest?" It may be helpful to give the youngster a reason for not having given him or her the item with the rest of the set. For example, "This object was under the table. I wonder where it belongs in the line."

5. For serial correspondence, give children another set of objects that corresponds to the first set in number and dimension. However, this set should be in mixed order. The youngster is asked to seriate the objects in the second set so that each object in that set corresponds to an object in the first series. Examples of some guiding questions include: "Can you put the cars in a row so the row of cars and the row of boxes are alike?" "Here are some balls to go in the boxes. Let's see if you can put each ball in the box that fits it best." "Can you put each ball in a box so the smallest ball goes in the smallest box, the biggest ball goes in the

Where do they fit in the row?

biggest box, and every other ball goes in its box?" It is helpful if the two sets have some kind of logical connection, such as cars and their garages or salt and pepper shakers. Initially, if you use objects that are connected or related in some logical manner, children find serial correspondence easier to understand.

6. Finally, ask for an explanation of the serial correspondence. If the children have difficulty in verbalizing, switch two of the items and ask "Could I take this ball out of this box and put it in this one? Why (or why not)?"

In Table 13-9, à complete activity plan is illustrated for the activity of seriation using cars and garages in the logicomathematical area.

Extensions   The area of seriation can be extended easily by spreading out or pushing together one of the two series so the series no longer correspond spatially. Then, you can point to an item in one series and ask which item in the other series corresponds to it. This is more difficult for the child than just establishing serial correspondence. Another popular game is for children to cover their eyes while the series is mixed up. They then try to fix the order of the items.

Seriation activities also can be extended to other areas:

1. *Social knowledge.* The children are given the names for the endpoints and for the dimensions with which they are working (for example, "weight," "tall," "short").
2. *Classification.* Seriation materials can be used easily for classification. The items being seriated need not be identical in every way

Table 13-9   A Seriation Activity Plan Using Cars and Garages

SERIATION
Cars and Garages

General Information
Time: free choice time
Place: any table or floor area
Children: 1–6

Objectives
A. Given a set of four toy cars, the child will find the largest and the smallest
B. Given completion of A, the child will arrange the cars from large to small
C. Given completion of B, the child will give a verbal explanation for his or her series
D. Given one more car, the child will insert it at the proper point in the series
E. Given five garages, varying in size, the child will arrange the garages from large to small corresponding to the five seriated cars
F. The child will give a verbal explanation for her or his serial correspondence

Materials
Set per child: 5 toy cars, seriated by size
                         5 boxes (garages) corresponding in size to the cars

Presentation
Introduction: "Hi _____. My friend, Jack, parks cars. Today he wants to park some of these cars, but he is very busy. Would you like to help him?
Procedure:
1. Give each child a set of four cars and ask him or her to find the biggest and the smallest
2. Ask the child to seriate the cars
3. Ask the child for a verbal explanation for her or his seriation
4. Give the child the fifth car and ask him or her to add it to the series
5. Ask the child to find and arrange the garages so that they go with the cars
6. Ask the child for a verbal explanation for her or his serial correspondence

Extensions
A. Seriation: Try switching two cars and have the child correct the mistake
B. Social knowledge: Help the child learn the labels for the colors of the cars and garages
C. Classification: Cars can be classified by type or color
D. Number concepts: One-to-one correspondence can be established between cars and garages, ignoring their sizes

Evaluation
Observation card: seriation
Comments and suggestions:

except the dimension along which they vary. A series of boxes could be of two or three different colors; after or before the seriation activities, the boxes could be classified by color.

3. *Number concepts.* Serial correspondence materials can be used for one-to-one correspondence if variations in each series are ignored. The child learns that two series of the same length that are

Table 13-10   Extending Logicomathematical Knowledge through a Large Group Activity

LARGE GROUP ACTIVITY
Seriating Children

1. Area: any area; number of children: 2–8
2. Objectives: to allow children to practice their seriation abilities in a group. To allow children to model and imitate seriation; to allow children to act cooperatively
3. Materials: none
4. Directions: The teacher selects four volunteers of varying height and asks them to seriate themselves by size. The rest of the class can give directions and feedback to help them. After the four children are seriated, select a fifth child to be added to the line. He or she may find his or her own position or the class may help him or her. Repeat the procedure with another group of children.

put in serial correspondence always have the same number of objects in each series.

4. *Physical knowledge.* Time seriation and physical knowledge are combined in many cooking and art activities that follow recipes.

There are numerous opportunities throughout the day for children to develop seriation abilities. Blocks come in various sizes and lengths. Building a tower, for example, provides built-in feedback about the correctness of the seriation. In the kitchen area, all cups, spoons, and dishes come in various sizes. Children can be encouraged to talk about what they have done during the day in a time series of first, second . . . last. At snack time, the children can compare the levels of juice in their cups. During large group times, the entire class can participate in a seriation activity. Table 13-10 shows a group activity for children seriating themselves.

Evaluation   Throughout the activity, use the observation card to record the children's actions. In addition to the columns corresponding to the objectives for seriation, there is a column for *partial seriation*. Check this box if the child seriates at least three, but not all, of the items correctly. Examples of helpful points to include in the *comments* are: (1) the number of items correctly seriated, (2) where the child placed the item inserted later (if he or she did so incorrectly), and (3) what explanations the child gave for their placement. A completed observation card showing the evaluation of a seriation activity is shown in Table 13-11.

Number Concepts

Children must master three basic processes before they can develop a mature understanding of the concept of number. One-to-one correspondence is a process in which children establish two sets containing equal number

Table 13-11   An Observation Card for Assessing Seriation

Logicomathematical Knowledge/Seriation (Knowledge Area) — Blocks (Activity Title) — Child's Name	Observes	Explores Materials	Finds Endpoints	Does Partial Seriation	Completes Seriation	Completes Seriation and Rationale	Adds Item to Complete Series	Does Serial Correspondence	Completes Serial Correspondence and Rationale	Date: September 26 Teacher: Ms. Beatrice — Comments
1. Gary Duvall			✓		✓	✓	✓			Seriated 6 blocks.
2. Susan Whin			✓		✓	✓	—			Added to end of series.
3. John Van Der Koiij	✓									Built a garage.
4. Vic Miller			✓	✓						Could only do 3.
5. Margo Ellis			✓		✓	✓	✓	✓	✓	
6. Mark Constantine			✓		✓	✓				Said "small, bigger, bigger, bigger, biggest!"

of objects and then match each element of the first set to an element in the second set. For example, if asked to get enough napkins for all the children at a snack table, a child might count the number of children and then count out the same number of napkins. However, young children often cannot count objects. Even if they can recite the numbers in order, when counting things they often skip one or count one more than once. Another strategy the youngster can use to get the correct number of napkins is to put one napkin in front of each child, establishing a one-to-one correspondence between children and napkins.

The process of reversibility like one-to-one correspondence is nurtured and encouraged in a cognitive-oriented program. It evolves in preschoolers as they continue to interact with their physical and social worlds. Reversibility is the conceptual ability to follow a line of reasoning from beginning to ending points and to retrace the steps back to its initial starting point. From the perspective of number, children demonstrate reversibility when they can join two sets of objects into a single set, determine its numerical quantity, and divide or separate it into the former two sets. Thus, for example, two cars can be joined with three cars, and this set equals five cars. In turn, the set of five cars is separated and put back into two sets containing three and two cars.

Finally, conservation of number is shown when children understand that the number of objects remains the same even when the spatial arrangement of those objects is changed. Thus, there are still eight pieces of candy if they are arranged in a straight line, a circle, or a pile. From a cognitive-developmental perspective, the very young child first thinks of number as "a lot" or "a little." As long as the difference between two sets of objects is large, he or she can tell which has more. When shown six cups in a row with five saucers in a row spaced farther apart, the child may say that there are just as many cups as saucers; the child is focusing on only the length of the rows, not on the number of items in each row. An older preoperational child can establish one-to-one correspondence between the two sets, putting one cup on each saucer. However, she or he cannot always conserve. When the cups are spread out to take up more room than the saucers, he or she insists that there are more cups.

When children reach the concrete operations stage, they realize that any change in the spatial arrangement of the objects can be reversed. They know that the number of objects does not change unless some objects have been added or removed. This understanding of number is necessary for children to be able to solve simple addition and subtraction problems with concrete sets of objects.

Objectives   The objective of activities focusing on number concepts is to encourage the processes of: (1) one-to-one correspondence, (2) reversibility, (3) conservation of number, and (4) thinking independently rather than depending on others' judgments. The objectives for an early childhood program are:

1. Children will *establish one-to-one correspondence* between the items in two sets.
2. Children will give an *explanation* for why the two sets have the same number of objects.
3. Children will *state that the two sets are still equal* when the sets are no longer in one-to-one correspondence.
4. Children will give an *explanation* for stating that the two sets are still equal.

Materials   The materials needed for number concept activities are two sets of objects that can be matched one to one. There may be some logical connection between the items of the two sets (cups and saucers, soda cans and straws, heads and hats) or no obvious relationship between the two sets (a set of blocks and mixed objects). However, sets with logical connections are the easier of the two for the child to correspond.

Presentation   In the presentation, youngsters should be allowed an opportunity to explore freely, manipulate, and become familiar with the materials prior to using the four strategies that follow.

1. Give children one set of six objects, and place another set of eight objects in a pile on the table. Then ask them to make the two sets equal by establishing one-to-one correspondence. Some helpful questions and statements include: "Can you find enough straws for all the cans?" "Let's put one cup on each saucer." "Each of these cars needs a garage." The children should start with only three or four objects and work up to more. If they have difficulty establishing one-to-one correspondence, ask questions that challenge their thinking: "Is there one straw in each can?" "Does each saucer have a cup on it?" Children will often deal with leftover items by matching two for one. For example, if children who do not understand one-to-one correspondence are given five soda cans and six straws, they will usually put one straw in each can and two straws in the remaining can.

2. Inquire whether the two sets the children created are the same in number after they establish one-to-one correspondence. Then ask, "Why are (or aren't) they equal in number?" "Are there enough straws for each can? How do you know?" "Does each garage have a car?" "Are there the same number of cups as saucers? Why or why not?" As explanations, youngsters may say that for each object in the first set there is an object in the second set, or count the members of each set to determine numerical equality. However, make sure that you remove the extra items from in front of the children or they may include these items in their judgments.

3. Have the youngsters spread out or bunch together one of the sets after they agree that the two sets are equal in number. With the two sets no longer in visual one-to-one correspondence, ask the children if the sets are still equal in number. If possible, give a reason for moving the items ("Let's wash all the cups"). Then ask, for example: "Are there still the same number of cars as garages?" "Now is there one straw for each can?" "Are there still enough cups for all the saucers?" If children do not understand that there still are the same number of objects in both sets, you will need to have them reestablish one-to-one correspondence between the two sets. However, as one-to-one correspondence is reestablished, this time only slightly spread out or bunch up one of the rows. Again, inquire about their numerical equality. This procedure can be repeated a number of times and the amount of space taken up between members in one or both sets can be increased gradually.

4. Ask for an explanation after youngsters state unequivocally that the sets are equal in number even when not in one-to-one correspondence. Examples of lead questions include: "How do you know there will be

enough cars for each garage?" "Why do you think there is the same number of straws as cans?" "How can you tell there's still one cup for each saucer?" Children will probably answer the "why" question by counting the members of each set and stating that they are still the same, stating that nothing was added to or taken away from either set, or reestablishing one-to-one correspondence between the two sets. In the third type of explanation, youngsters may demonstrate their rationale nonverbally by simply performing the correspondence over again as you watch. If children have difficulty giving an explanation, they can be encouraged to show the equality of the sets. To initiate the process, you might say "How can you make them the same again?"

Table 13-12 illustrates instructional procedures for these number concepts using various objects.

Extensions   There are several ways to extend number concepts within the area of number. The spatial arrangement of two sets can be altered or changed in various ways. The adult, or more preferably the children, can rearrange the sets into piles, lines, or circles. The children then can be asked if the two sets are equal in number. A second way of extending number concepts is to add or remove an item from one of the sets. Both sets can be spread out so they take up the same amount of room. In similar fashion, questions are asked to determine whether the sets are equal in number. In turn, youngsters are asked to explain why the sets are (or are not) equal in number.

Number concept activities can also be extended to other areas:

1. *Social knowledge*. Children can be encouraged to use correct names in referring to the characteristics of groups of objects (sets, members, or elements; separate and join).
2. *Classification*. Many number concepts can also be classified, either by sets (salt shakers and pepper shakers) or, if the objects within one set are not identical, by their characteristics (color).
3. *Seriation*. Number concept materials that vary in size dimensions may also be used for seriation and serial correspondence.
4. *Physical knowledge*. Recipe cards are useful for matching, for example, three cups of flour on the recipe card, represented by pictures of three cups, with three cups of real flour (in this example, number concepts and physical knowledge are combined).

There are many opportunities throughout the day for children to practice number skills: setting the table at snack time, playing store and exchanging one piece of play money for each item, planting one seed in each pot, and putting one cherry in each cup when making jello. Extending number concepts of one-to-one correspondence using a snack activity is illustrated in Table 13-13.

Table 13-12   An Activity Plan for Number Concepts in the
Logicomathematical Area

NUMBER CONCEPTS
Cans and Straws

General Information
Time: free choice time
Place: any floor or table area
Children: 1–6

Objective
A. Given the cans and straws and directions by the teacher, the child will match one can to one straw using one-to-one correspondence
B. The child will give a verbal explanation for his or her arrangement in A
C. Given an equal number of straws and cans differing in spatial arrangement, the child will state the straws and cans are still equal
D. Given completion of C, the child will give a verbal explanation for her or his decision that the cans and the straws are equal

Materials
Set per child: 6 soda cans, 8 straws

Presentation
Introduction: "Hi _____. Today we're going to pretend that we're going to a soda fountain to get a can of soda. You can choose your own flavor of soda and get a straw to drink it with. What flavors do your friends want?"
Procedure:
1. Give the child five cans and eight straws and ask him or her to place them in one-to-one correspondence
2. Ask the child if the cans and straws are equal in number and why
3. While the child is watching, change the spatial arrangement of the cans by spreading them out or bunching them together; ask if the straws and cans are still equal in number
4. Ask the child for a verbal explanation for this decision

Extensions
A. Number concepts: Given an unequal number of cans and straws in an equal spatial arrangement, ask the child if there is still the same number of cans as straws
B. Social knowledge: Children can learn the names of the letters on the cans
C. Classification: Soda cans can be classified as to type (Pepsi, Coke, Dr. Pepper)
D. Seriation: Straws can be cut to different sizes to seriate and place in the cans

Evaluation
Observation card: number concepts
Comments and suggestions:

Table 13-13   Extending Logicomathematical Knowledge with a One-to-One Correspondence Activity

SNACK ACTIVITY
One-to-One Correspondence

1. Area: table; number of children: 2–6
2. Objectives: to allow children to establish one-to-one correspondence between children, napkins, cups, and crackers
3. Materials: paper cups, napkins, at least one cracker for each child
4. Directions: Put crackers, napkins, and cups in the center of the table. Allow one child to pass out the napkins, one the cups, and one the crackers. This should be done one at a time, not with all three children passing things out at once. Other children will provide feedback about whether or not they have received their napkin, cup, or especially their cracker.

Evaluation   Throughout the activity, use the observation card to structure your observation. It identifies important actions performed by the children in the activity. In addition to a column for each objective, there is a column *attempts one-to-one correspondence*. Check this category if children try to establish one-to-one correspondence but fail. They may, for example, make the two rows equal spatially (a row of three saucers as long as a row of four cups). Comments that provide clues to children's development in this activity include the number of objects matched in one-to-one correspondence, and the type of explanation given. In Table 13-14, children's actions showing their level of cognitive growth of one-to-one correspondence are entered on the observation card.

Social Knowledge

Social knowledge refers to the culturally determined knowledge that is derived from feedback from people. In receiving feedback from people, youngsters hear and see the reactions to things they say and do of parents, caregivers, other significant adults, older and younger children, and peers. This feedback assists developing and learning. Accordingly, social knowledge includes: (1) identifying emotions, (2) recognizing others' feelings and rights, (3) recognizing the child's own printed or spoken name and those of others, (4) naming the physical properties of objects (for example, color, shape, size, texture), (5) giving numerical and letter symbols, and (6) learning standards of social conduct and behavior (the limits to and consequences of behavior at home or at school). Much of social knowledge is arbitrary in the sense that there is no reason that certain names are attached to objects or properties; they are applied by social convention. For example, an apple could be described as "rojo," "rouge," or "red," depend-

Table 13-14   An Observation Card Recording Abilities in One-to-One Correspondence for Logicomathematical Knowledge

Logicomathematical Knowledge/Number (Knowledge Area) Cups and Saucers (Activity Title)	Observation	Exploration	Attempts One-to-One Correspondence	Establishes One-to-One Correspondence	Verbally Explains Equality with One-to-One Correspondence	States Two Sets Equal Without One-to-One Correspondence	Verbally Explains Equality Without One-to-One Correspondence	Date: April 7 Teacher: Mr. Steve
Child's Name								Comments
1. Jerry Lusky			√	√	√	√		Said didn't take any away
2. Andy Kamaii			√	—				Because I said so
3. Julie Smith			√	√				Matched 20
4. Sandy Reagan	√√							Watched Julie perform activity

ing on what language you are using. In contrast, physical and logico-mathematical knowledge is the same for all cultures. Because social knowledge is structured from feedback from other people, reinforcing right answers, correcting mistakes, and telling right answers are appropriate in this area.

The curricula of traditional preschool programs are often made up of primarily social knowledge. This type of knowledge is developed in a cumulative fashion, with children increasing their vocabulary and knowledge of social conventions as they get older.

Objectives   The objective of teaching social knowledge is that children be able to communicate with, understand, and get along with others in their environment. When naming is involved in social knowledge, it is taught by meeting the following objectives:

1. Children will *match* an object to an identical or similar one which is shown to them.
2. Children will *find* (point to, pick up) an object with particular attributes (color, shape, texture) when *given verbal directions* to do so.

3. Children will provide the correct *verbal label* or *name* for these attributes when asked to do so.
4. Children will *match a number symbol* to a particular number of objects (or the reverse); this objective applies only to number symbols.

Materials   Any materials can be used for social knowledge providing they reflect the properties of, for example, color, shape, size, texture, number symbols, letters, names, telephone numbers, or addresses. The materials should unambiguously represent the characteristics of the objects. For example, if working with colors, "blue-green" should be avoided.

Presentation   As usual in the presentation of activities, the child is initially given a chance to become familiar with the materials. In turn, several procedures follow:

1. Ask children to find another object that is similar or identical to the one you first select. Use statements such as "Can you find a flower that is the same color as this one? Where is it?" "Pick out a shape that looks like this one. Where is another piece of material that looks like this one?" It is easiest for children to match objects that are identical in all respects. It is most difficult to match objects that are not alike except for one common property. When children are just learning the names for properties, the object and its relevant characteristic can be pointed out by the adult. For instance, in teaching the name for the color *red*, you can find a red object, such as a flower. You should label the property by saying, "Here is a red flower! Can you find another red one?" In this manner, the child links the name of the property to its visual cue.

2. Have children find a particular object after providing only its name: "Can you find a triangle?" "Show me something smooth." "Where is a red flower?" When you use this procedure, be extremely careful not to point to a similar object, or the child may simply match it.

3. Select an object and ask children to name it. For instance, you might say: "What color is this one?" "I forget what shape this is. Can you tell me?" "How does this one feel?" Watch carefully to see if children have difficulty in trying to find a particular object from your directions. If they do, you will need to use the previous procedure of naming the object and having them find a match for it.

4. When you work with number symbols, select a specific number of objects and ask children to find the numeral that corresponds to that quantity of items. For example, questions that guide children in this procedure are: "How many flowers are there?" "Can you put that numeral beside them?" A variation is to select a numeral and ask the child to find that quantity of objects: "What number is this one? Can you find five

beads?" "Put this number of cans over here." If children are having difficulty with naming and counting, you should give the name for the numeral and show them the counting routine for that many items.

A complete activity plan in the area of social knowledge is featured in Table 13-15. It emphasizes color by using coloring books.

Extensions   Extending social knowledge is straightforward because preschool classrooms are filled with opportunities for children to increase their social knowledge. The child is surrounded by a physical environment made up of shapes, colors, textures, numbers, letters, and other tangibles and by a social environment composed of people. You can use many opportunities to help children learn the names of the things in the environment. In addition, carefully observe the various properties of the materials being used in the activities. You will be able to incorporate easily several other types of social knowledge into the same activity. For example, in an activity designed to promote peer interaction, children can also learn about colors. Table 13-16 illustrates a sample activity plan for encouraging peer interaction routines among preschoolers. As a second area basic to social knowledge, naming color properties of objects can also be learned.

Social knowledge activities can also be extended to other areas of knowledge.

1. *Classification*. Objects and materials used in social knowledge can often be classified according to that content area—for instance, shape and color.
2. *Seriation*. Often social knowledge materials also can be seriated by size, color, texture, or number of objects—for example, dominoes by number of dots.
3. *Number concepts*. Many social knowledge activities include sets of objects that can be matched in one-to-one correspondence.
4. *Physical knowledge*. Names for properties or characteristics of objects are also important parts of physical knowledge activities, such as being able to say that some things *float* and others *sink*.

Evaluation   Observation cards for social knowledge are used in a slightly different way than those for physical or logicomathematical knowledge. Knowledge of specific content areas (such as color and shape) rather than process is important. Generalizing across content areas is not possible. Accordingly, each area requires a separate observation card. Instead of objectives, the columns across the top of the card are filled in with the specific words or concepts being taught; see the sample observation card in Table 13-17.

The content area (for example, color) is printed in the upper left corner of the card. The objectives are reflected in a numerical code printed along

Table 13-15   An Activity Plan in Social Knowledge Emphasizing Instruction in Color

SOCIAL KNOWLEDGE
Color—Color Books

General Information
Time: free choice time
Place: any table area
Children: 1–6

Objectives
A. Given a picture of a certain color and directions, the child will match it to another picture of the same color
B. Given verbal directions to find a specific color, the child will find that color
C. When asked, the child will name the color of the picture

Materials
Set per child: 5 pieces of newsprint folded in half and stapled along the spine to form a booklet
Common materials: glue and gluebrushes, scissors, pictures of objects of different colors cut from magazines, and extra magazines

Presentation
Introduction: "Hi _____. Today we are going to make color books. Here are some pictures that have different colors in them. What picture would you like to start with?"
Procedure:
1. Have the child select a picture and glue it in his or her book
2. Ask the child to find another picture that is the same color as the first and glue it in her or his book
3. Ask the child to find a picture of a specific color
4. Ask the child to name the colors of the pictures in his or her book

Extensions
A. Social knowledge: Books can be made for other areas of social knowledge (e.g., numbers, shapes, textures, feelings)
B. Classification: Children can classify pictures by putting all of the ones that are the same on one page (e.g., by color, object in the picture, type of activity pictured)
C. Seriation: Pictures can be seriated by color shade
D. Number concepts: Children can form one-to-one correspondence between pictures and pages in the book

Evaluation
Observation card: social knowledge—color
Comments and suggestions:

Table 13-16   Extending Social Knowledge by a Peer Interaction Activity

PEER INTERACTION ACTIVITY
Balloon Man

1. Area: small table(s); number of children: 2, 4, 6, or 8
2. Objectives: to allow children to work cooperatively; to teach the names of colors
3. Materials: picture of a man holding balloons, colored balloons cut in half like jigsaw pieces so only the same colors will fit together (see picture), glue, and brushes

4. Directions: Children work in pairs. One child selects half a balloon, and the other child must find a matching half. Both children then glue their pieces onto the balloon-man picture to make a complete balloon. Children can take turns selecting balloon halves and can indicate the correct color to the other child either by showing it so he or she can match it, or by naming the color for the other child to find.

the bottom of each card for reference. The numerical code is 0 for observing and exploring material, 1 for matching appropriately, 2 for performing actions from verbal direction, 3 for verbally labeling names, and 4 for matching symbols with the number of objects. Thus, as the youngster meets an objective for a certain concept, the number corresponding to that objective is printed in the box opposite her or his name. In addition, the numerals for codes 1 to 4 can also appear with or without circles around them, meaning a child has or has not met the objective. For example, if the child has found a yellow car at the adult's request, a 2 should be placed in the box under the column *yellow* for that child. If, however, the youngster was unable to find a yellow car, the numeral would be written as ②, indicating that she had the opportunity to meet the objective but failed. In

Table 13-17   Adapting the Observation Card for the Social Knowledge Area Using Color as Content

Social Knowledge (Knowledge Area) Color Bingo (Activity Title)	Red	Yellow	Blue	Orange	Green	Purple	Black	White	Brown	Date: Oct. 20 Teacher: Mr. Frank
Child's Name				Coding*						Comments
1. Katherine Rish	1,2,3	1,2,3	1,2,3	1,2,③	1,2,③	1,2,③				
2. Sandy Reagan	1,②	1,②	1,②							Doesn't know colors.
3. Shana White	1,2,3	1,2,3	1,2,③	1,2,3	1,2,3	1,2,③				Confuses blue and purple.
4. Andy Kamaii	0									Just watched.
5. Pamela Brown	3	3	3	3	3	3				Named all the colors right away.

*Coding Key: 0 for observing or exploring; 1 for matching; 2 for finding from verbal direction; and 3 for labeling verbally. Numerals not enclosed and enclosed by circles (e.g., 2 or ②) show whether the child succeeded or failed to meet the objective.

comments, the particular concepts that seemed difficult for the child can be noted. The observation card in Table 13-17 shows the various procedures for evaluating the content product of "color" in the social knowledge area.

Representational Knowledge

Classically speaking, Piaget regards representational knowledge as a level rather than an area of knowledge. For emphasis and consistency, we refer to it as an area. Representational knowledge refers to the way children structure their physical, logical, and social knowledge to represent reality. To develop representations of reality, children must start from a base of active experience with concrete objects and events. They take the information they receive from their environment and actively construct mental images to represent experience.

Even knowledge of objects that are seen directly must be constructed by the preschooler, because each object is seen from only one particular point of view at a time. The youngster must mentally put these points of view together to form a whole object. The ability to construct mentally whole objects when seeing the objects develops into the ability to form mental images of objects that are absent. There are three levels of representation: index, symbol, and sign.

At the index level, the child recognizes the whole object from just a part of the object or a mark or sound made by it. For example, the child can recognize a dog by seeing only its head, seeing its pawprints, hearing the dog's bark, or feeling its fur. At the symbol level, the child begins to form mental images to represent objects that are not physically present. The child actively represents these objects through some medium. There are five types of symbols:

1. *Make-believe*: the use of objects to symbolize or represent other objects (a broom becomes a horse).
2. *Imitation*: the child's use of his or her body to represent directly other objects without the use of props (the child gallops around pretending to ride a horse).
3. *Onomatopoeia*: the use of sounds to represent objects (making the sound of a siren to stand for a fire engine).
4. *Three-dimensional models*: construction and recognition of objects through toys or three-dimensional representations (a garage built out of blocks).
5. *Two-dimensional drawings*: construction and recognition of objects in pictures (a drawing of a car).

At the sign level, the child uses abstract signs that bear no resemblance to the object being represented. Both written and spoken language are examples of representation at the sign level.

Objectives   The objective of representational activities in a preschool program is to strengthen the mental images the child has at the symbol level to make written and spoken language more meaningful. Therefore, the objective is to have the child actively represent objects and experiences through indices, five types of symbols, and signs.

Materials   Materials at all three levels of representation—index, symbol, and sign—should be used to help children form mental images. At the index level, children need much direct experience with concrete objects, places, and events. This can be accomplished by: (1) taking children on field trips into the community to have first-hand experiences with different places and occupations, (2) bringing things into the classroom such as animals, special guests, or interesting objects, and (3) allowing children to be actively involved with objects in their environment. In this way, children gain experience in the construction of a whole object through seeing, smelling, feeling, hearing, and even tasting just a part of it.

At the symbol level, activities have been divided into four categories according to the medium being used. They are:

1. *Art activities*, such as easel painting, drawing, and fingerpainting, allow children to construct their own symbols as two-dimensional representations.

2. *Craft activities* involve the construction of three-dimensional models by changing, cutting, pasting, and manipulating materials such as paper, clay, and pipe cleaners.

3. *Construction activities* also allow children to construct three-dimensional models by building with individual units that do not change, such as blocks, Tinker Toys, or Lincoln Logs.

4. *Sociodramatic play* allows children to use imitation, make-believe, and onomatopoeia to represent experiences. In playing house, children imitate familiar people in their life by playing the roles of mother, father, or baby. They use props in their play, making believe that a block is the telephone. Also, they use onomatopoeia to represent parts of their environment, such as the baby crying or the car driving away.

At the sign level, language is stressed. However, it is important that children have rich and detailed mental images for the words they are using. Therefore, the learning of language must be accompanied by many experiences with objects at both the index and symbol levels of representation.

Presentation   Representational activity plans are written in a different format than activities in the other three areas of knowledge. Five- by eight-inch index cards are used for the plans. They can be filed for easy reference.

1. Format. At the top of the index card is a heading consisting of (1) the type of activity (for example, art, craft, construction, or sociodramatic), (2) the title of the activity, and (3) the level of representation. The other sections in the activity plan are items of general information: (1) area of the room, (2) number of children, (3) objectives, (4) materials, and (5) directions for carrying out the activity. Table 13-18 shows the vari-

Table 13-18   Extending Representational Knowledge through a Sociodramatic Activity

SOCIODRAMATIC ACTIVITY
The Hospital
Index, Symbol

1. Area: any area; number of children: 2–8

2. Objectives: To allow the children to represent their experiences in a visit to the health center using indices and symbols (imitation, make-believe, and onomatopoeia).

3. Materials: white shirts, stethoscopes, bandaids, gauze, doctors' and nurses' hats, tongue depressors. Stuffed animals may be used as patients.

4. Directions:
   a. At the index level, the children can use the props as a doctor or nurse would.
   b. At the symbol level, the child can imitate the roles of doctor, nurse, and patient; use make-believe with the props (e.g., using a stick for a needle), and use onomatopoeia to represent the sounds of the hospital.

ous parts of the activity plan for the area of representational knowledge and examples of instructional content using a sociodramatic activity at the index and symbol levels.

2. Presentation. For representational activities, the general teaching strategy is to go from very specific and concrete experiences with objects and events to progressively more abstract representations of those experiences. Several specific procedures follow.

   a. Provide many concrete experiences with real objects to strengthen representational abilities at the index level. Field trips are an excellent way to provide this necessary experience. Representational abilities at the index level also develop by playing guessing games. For example, games that emphasize recognizing objects by seeing only their parts or several of their selected attributes are ideal. Some examples of games include: "I see a leg. I wonder what is on the other end of that leg." "Listen carefully. I hear 'bark-bark'! What is it?" "I wonder what made this footprint!"

   b. Next, provide many different opportunities that can represent experiences at the symbol level after the youngster constructs concrete images of objects from first-hand experiences with them. At the symbol level using imitation, an example is "Show me what a doctor does." Using make-believe, say "Let's pretend this stick is a horse." An example of employing onomatopoeia is "What does a monkey sound like?" For three-dimensional models, use examples such as "Can you make something with your clay that we saw today?" For two-dimensional pictures, a simple example is "How about drawing a picture about our field trip." After a field trip to the fire station, for example, the preschoolers should play fire station, make fire hats, and draw or paint pictures of the members of the fire company. In this manner, children become able to represent their concrete experiences in increasingly more abstract ways.

   c. Begin to use representations at the sign levels, after the preschooler has had many, many experiences in representing objects at the index and symbol levels. For example, youngsters can use letters to write their name on their work products. Also, nametags can be hung on a board at the end of each day so that the next morning children can select the one that belongs to them. Here you can inquire, for instance, "Which one of those says Michelle?" Gestural signs can be made to stand for objects or actions. This not only is a sound practice that encourages representations but also is a superb teaching strategy, for it substitutes nonverbal for verbal communication. A game using gestural signs standing for objects or actions is "When I clap my hands, jump up."

Teaching strategies for representation vary with the type of activity. Some arts and crafts activities have a definite purpose, such as making a bus. In this type of activity, you help the child create a product; this is also more adult directed than other activities in which children are able to express their creativity and construct their own images of reality. In activities such as fingerpainting, drawing, or block building, you act as a resource person and allow the child to determine the direction of the activity. Most activities are neither all directed nor all open-ended. It is best to strike a balance between taking over the activity and remaining completely outside of it. For example, in sociodramatic play you can play a customer in a store if the children suggest and welcome it. However, it would be inappropriate to assign the youngsters' roles. Then, too, when the children model clay, you could participate in the activity, but to suggest that the children fashion their objects like that of another youngster would be over-directive.

In this type of painting activity, the child is allowed to determine the activity's direction.

Extensions   Extending representational knowledge is not difficult, because representational knowledge is involved in everything the child does throughout the day. The materials used in physical, logical, and social knowledge activities can be at any of the three levels of representation. Children can classify real silverware or pictures of silverware. They can seriate real shoes, dolls' shoes, or drawings of shoes. In social and physical knowledge, children can label the properties of real objects. In social knowledge, they can also work at the sign level with letters and numbers. Thus, children have many chances to expand their representational abilities at many times and in many activities.

Evaluation   Observation cards can be used during representational activities or at other times during the day to check types and levels of representation that the youngsters perform. If the child specifically uses a given type of representation, a check mark is placed in the box. In addition, a minus symbol is placed in the box if he or she does not use the suggested type of representation. Example comments record what original objects the child is representing, how full or detailed the representation is, and how well integrated the three levels of representation are. An observation card for a kitchen activity is illustrated in Table 13-19.

SUMMARY

The curriculum of the cognitive-developmental program is organized around four areas of cognitive knowledge: (1) physical, (2) logico-mathematical, (3) social, and (4) representational. For each area, we discussed objectives, materials, presentation, extensions, and evaluation. Although the types of activities, adult strategies, and methods of evaluation vary with the type of knowledge, the ultimate goal is to coordinate these different approaches into an integrated curriculum focusing on all areas of

Table 13-19   Evaluating Representational Knowledge Using an Observation Card

Representational Knowledge (Knowledge Area) / Kitchen (Activity Title) / Child's Name	Observes	Explores Materials	Index — Part of the Object	Index — Sound Made By the Object	Index — Mark Made By the Object	Symbol — Imitation	Symbol — Make-believe	Symbol — Onomatopoeia	Sign — Three-Dimensional Models	Sign — Two-Dimensional Pictures	Sign — Written Words	Other Signs	Date: May 5 Teacher: Ms. Paula Comments
1. Pamela Brown		✓											Manipulated dishes
2. Jerry Lusky						✓		✓					Washed dishes and "yelled at kids"
3. Katherine Rich						✓	✓						Cooked a block for dinner (meatloaf)
4. Shanda White			✓	—	—								

the child's development. The teacher is the most important element in observing, evaluating, and providing experiences that meet each child at her or his own developmental level.

Review Questions

1. List three cognitive processes that are essential prerequisites for the understanding of numbers.
2. Explain the meaning of "integration of areas of knowledge" in preschool programming.
3. Describe a minimum of four major concepts that compose each of the four main areas of knowledge.
4. Identify a minimum of four strategies that can be used by the adult to guide and structure learning activities in cognitive-oriented preschool programs.
5. List the adult strategies for presenting activities to preschoolers in the area of physical knowledge.
6. Tell why extending knowledge to other times and other activities is not only necessary but also basic to cognitive-oriented preschool programs.

Suggested Activities

1. Observe a group of preschoolers in sociodramatic play. Jot down the ways in which they use the symbols of make-believe, imitation, and onomatopoeia.

2. Identify one preschooler who can and one who cannot demonstrate one-to-one correspondence. Ask the preschooler who can to instruct the other in performing one-to-one correspondence using saucers and cups.
3. Direct a preschooler to draw a picture of his or her house, mother or father, and her- or himself. After he or she has completed the two-dimensional drawing, ask her or him to tell you about the picture. Note the level of descriptive language used in the child's explanation.
4. Construct a preschool activity in matching objects; use one instructional routine appropriate to free discovery and another for guided discovery.
5. Using the two ways of extending number concepts to other times and activities described in the chapter, write an activity plan for each and use it with a group of preschoolers. Observe the differences in the children's actions and evaluate their progress using the observation card.
6. Develop and try out an activity plan and instructional strategies that extend number concepts through social knowledge.

Suggested Readings

Croft, D. S., and Hess, R. D. *An activities handbook for teachers of young children.* New York: Houghton Mifflin, 1980.

Evans, E. D. *Contemporary influences in early childhood education,* 2nd ed. New York: Holt, Rinehart & Winston, 1975.

Fraisse, P., and Piaget, S. (Eds.). *Experimental psychology: its scope and method,* vol. 7. New York: Basic Books, 1963.

Furth, H. G. *Piaget for teachers.* Englewood Cliffs, N.J.: Prentice-Hall, 1970.

Hess, R. D., and Croft, D. S. *Teachers of young children,* 2nd ed. New York: Houghton Mifflin, 1975.

Hildebrand, V. *Guiding young children,* 2nd ed. New York: Macmillan, 1980.

Piaget, J. *The child's conception of movement and speed.* New York: Ballantine, 1971.

Pratt, C. *I learn from children.* New York: Cornerstone Library Press, 1970.

Singer, S. L. (Ed.). *The child's world of make-believe.* New York: Academic Press, 1973.

Taylor, B. *A child goes forth.* Provo, Utah: Brigham Young University Press, 1975.

Chapter 14

Designing the Interactive Environment

Now that you understand cognitive-developmental theory and the physical, logicomathematical, social, and representational knowledge areas, it is time to derive a number of principles for designing preschool programs. Essentially, the four areas of knowledge, viewed as the core of cognitive development, are largely the focal point of cognitive preschool programs. There are a number of related adult strategies necessary for planning, designing, and implementing sound preschool programs.

In this chapter, we will explain relationships between the four knowledge areas for planning and for adult strategies. Both are used to design and implement sound cognitive preschool programs. Taken together these planning and adult strategies make up the typical day in a cognitive program. The elements for planning, designing, and implementing cognitive programs include: (1) factors, areas, and program goals, (2) characteristics of the preoperational child, (3) adult and child interaction, (4) activity periods and scheduling, (5) physical environments, and (6) parent involvement.

First, we describe the relationships among the factors contributing to intellectual development, knowledge areas of cognitive development, and goals of a cognitive preschool program. These relationships form the core of planning programs described in Chapter 15 and are based on the knowledge areas outlined in Chapter 13. Second, we investigate how designing and implementing cognitive programs requires recognizing the characteristics of intellectual growth at the preschool age; the success of cognitive preschool programs rests on gearing them to these cognitive characteristics. Third, we show that adult and child interactions highlight the *whats* and *hows* of integrating appropriate activities in light of the individual child's level of development. The principles derived from developmental theory for adult and child interaction explain why certain types of activities and methods are used. Fourth, we use activity periods and scheduling to describe essential mechanics of program planning and design that take place at different levels (daily, weekly, or long-term planning). We will describe examples of planning the activity periods and schedules. Fifth, we will suggest ways to plan the physical environment of the program, including principles of arrangement and sample materials used with young children. Sixth, we show that parent involvement is as effective as the planning that goes into it.

Thus, the six program elements are the additional aspects that encourage development and learning in an interactive environment. Each of them has specific principles derived from cognitive-developmental theory that adults can use to design and implement preschool programs.

DEVELOPMENTAL FACTORS, KNOWLEDGE AREAS, AND PROGRAM GOALS

Translating theories of development into congruent, workable, and exciting programs and interactive environments for young children can be a difficult task. Theories can lose something in the process of translation. Or, programs can get so tied up in the intricacies of the theory that they be-

---

Box 14-1   *Title VII Projecto PIAGET: A Hispanic Preschool Model*

Projecto PIAGET is a model preschool program for 5-year-old Hispanic children with limited English proficiency and cognitive deficits; it also includes their parents. It has been operating since 1981 in the Bethlehem, Pennsylvania Area School District with assistance from The Pennsylvania State University. PIAGET stands for *Promoting Intellectual Adaptation Given Experiential Transforming*; the program is funded by the U.S. Department of Education. This preschool model is derived from cognitive-developmental theory, and the interactive environments in centers, classrooms, and homes stress the four knowledge areas of cognitive development. The adults working with these children use 21 Piagetian-derived strategies in guiding growth.

Hispanic preschoolers are assessed, and those who have limited English language proficiency are enrolled. Through Piagetian-derived strategies plus a curriculum that stresses English and Spanish language growth through discovery activities, youngsters increase their communication in English,

which enables them to succeed better in their public school years.

The results obtained with these Hispanic PIAGET preschoolers and their parents from 1981 to 1984, relative to comparison groups of Hispanic youngsters and parents not enrolled, provide support for designing and using interactive environments based on cognitive-developmental theory. For example, there were significant increases for PIAGET children on product and process measures of cognition, socioemotional growth, English language development, and English reading readiness. Results also show significant increases for parents in self-concept, ability to work with their own children in home settings, and perception of their youngsters' cognitive and language growth.

Designing interactive environments based on cognitive-developmental theory that are successful, at least from measures of process and product, is not only possible—it has been done.

come very rigid and may forfeit their appeal to children and adults who work with them. It is important to be able to apply ideas inherent in the theoretical orientation to specifics of planning for programs and learning environments. Therefore developmental factors, knowledge areas, and program goals are salient to formulate a program for young children from a cognitive perspective. It is important to point out the relationships of developmental factors to applications that are relevant to program planning.

Developmental Factors and Knowledge Areas

This discussion highlights the relationships between the four factors that contribute to cognitive growth and the four knowledge areas. The factors principally focus on the child, and the knowledge areas focus on curricular adaptations to preschool programs. However, you must again realize that they are integrated with and integral to one another; they are bound together by the commonalities of cognitive processes in development. As you will recall, the factors explain the origin and evolution of cognitive development in human beings. Accordingly, growth proceeds via the factors of maturation, direct experiences with the physical environment, social transmission, and equilibration. Preschool programs must include opportunities for development through each of these four processes. The four knowledge areas describe the types of intellectual growth that form the core for the evolution of thought. Both focus on cognition and the individual. The four factors are translated into program planning through the four knowledge areas.

1. *Physical knowledge*: uses physical experience and equilibration
2. *Logicomathematical knowledge*: uses maturation, experience, and equilibration
3. *Social knowledge*: uses social transmission and equilibration
4. *Representational knowledge*: uses maturation, experience, social transmission, and equilibration

Without understanding this initial relationship between developmental factors and knowledge areas, you cannot identify the goals for preschool programs.

Program Goals

The four knowledge areas with the four factors of development become sets of goals for cognitive-developmental preschools. Two areas of general developmental growth also are important as goals. These are socioemotional and psychomotor development. These two general areas and the

Table 14-1   The Three Major Goals for Cognitive-Developmental Preschool Programs

---

   I. *Socioemotional development.* The development of inter- and intrapersonal skills.
  II. *Psychomotor development.* The development of large and small muscles, and eye–hand coordination.
 III. *Cognitive development.* The development of thought processes and the symbolization of knowledge. Objectives of this goal are realized through four knowledge areas:
    A. Logical knowledge
        1. Logicomathematical knowledge
           a. classification
           b. seriation
           c. number concepts
        2. Spatiotemporal relationships
    B. Physical knowledge
    C. Social knowledge
    D. Representational knowledge

---

cognitive one form the three major goals for cognitive preschool programs. These three major goals, in turn, facilitate designing, organizing, and implementing program development and day-to-day activity. A detailed description of each appears in Table 14-1.

Implementing these three goals is a major part of program design. Further, implementing these program goals into classroom practice emphasizes their interrelatedness. Socioemotional development may occur through social knowledge activities that are directed at cognitive development. The names for emotions (sad, happy, angry) or the names of the children in the class are labels that are learned through social knowledge. They are also important for the development of inter- and intrapersonal skills, an objective of socioemotional development. Psychomotor development may be a part of a physical knowledge activity, such as discussing properties of weight by lifting light and heavy objects such as a feather, block, bicycle, table, and cup. It could be part of a logicomathematical activity, such as a bean bag game in which children classify differently shaped and colored bean bags by throwing them into piles. These interrelationships highlight the principle that development and learning occur as a unified process.

CHARACTERISTICS OF THE PREOPERATIONAL CHILD

Early childhood programs must be geared to the specific development characteristics and individual processes of the preoperational child. This key factor forms the second major set of principles that have relevance to programming, planning, designing, and implementing.

Active Learner

The preoperational child learns by actively manipulating, experiencing, and acting on his or her environment. This includes not only motor activity but also mental activity such as questioning and manipulating things through thinking. Knowledge is constructed by children themselves through interaction with their environment, and so direct instruction is not especially relevant. Instead, opportunities must be provided for children to structure their own knowledge. The construction, the *process*, is what is important, not the *product*. This is a vital aspect in developing a curriculum and implementing a schedule.

For children to actively construct their own knowledge, they must have opportunities to manipulate, explore, initiate, and choose. Examples include activities in which children can touch, probe, and experiment (but not activities with delicate or complex materials that only the adult can manipulate and understand). Activities where children can get directly involved are also crucial. Let them try to work out problems by themselves, such as making green fingerpaint by mixing up blue and yellow fingerpaint. You must provide many opportunities for them to initiate and choose their own activities. You act more as a resource person than as an instructor for most activities, and children are encouraged to decide for themselves in what activities to participate.

Concrete Level of Thinking

Preoperational children think at a concrete level. Although they are capable of forming mental images, they need to experience and work with objects and events to be able to formulate concepts and develop representations of their world. This means that activities should include concrete materials, events, and new experiences.

Use objects that children can manipulate to see their properties. Try to use as many objects from real life as possible (for example, use real silverware instead of toy silverware). Also, use materials that can withstand the strain of repeated and extensive manipulations. Employ real-life experiences from which children can develop mental images. Include many events that children will experience in their daily world. Activities in the classroom can focus on such experiences as shopping at the grocery, going to the doctor, visiting the shoe store; these can be supplemented by field trips.

New experiences also need to be included at the concrete level. A train ride, for example, is a new experience for most young children. It might be hard to understand what it is like to ride a train just by talking about it, but going to the train station, seeing the trains and conductors and perhaps even taking a short ride makes the experience very real. Such concrete ex-

Developing the ability to predict occurrences may mean gooey hands and messes.

periences become content for representation. The children can act out the roles of conductor and passengers, build trains out of blocks, paint pictures of trains, and even make sounds like a train.

Different Developmental Levels

Within the preoperational stage, children progress at different rates and thus will not all be at the same developmental level at the same time. Programs must provide a wide range of activities to meet the developmental needs of individual children. Your observations of children and inferences about their developmental levels will be an invaluable aid in individualizing programs. Some activities have multiple levels, and children can choose at which level to perform. Gear activities to varying developmental levels by designing them to appeal to children for different reasons. For example, a parquetry block activity will include several different levels of classification; while one child is classifying by one property such as color, another might be grouping by size or shape. When working with numbers or letters, some children may be able to find and name the letters in their name, or find the number that represents their age, whereas others may be able only to match letters or numbers with identical ones.

Children should be able to choose their own activities. A variety of activities encouraging free choice is optimal. Children will choose activities at their cognitive level that meet their own interests. For example, some children enjoy cooking experiences. Others like to get their hands gooey, others like to see the process of making food. Some want to predict what will happen when certain ingredients are mixed together. The reasons for choosing bead stringing also may be varied. One child may enjoy the concentration and eye–hand coordination required. Another might like to make the longest string of beads possible.

Development through Massed Experience

Preoperational children need many, many experiences to facilitate their development. It is only after they are able to generalize about a concept that they incorporate it into their cognitive structures. Therefore, it is important to promote generalization by providing a wide variety of activities and experiences as well as individual and group settings.

Program goals can be promoted in a range of approaches. For example, learning the names for different colors is an objective of social knowledge in the goal area of cognitive development. But colors need not be learned only during certain periods of the day. The color red can be applied to the apple that is eaten during snack time, the fire engine seen on the field trip, the book that is read during small group, the robin in the tree on the playground, Jim's shoes, and the beads that are strung during free play. The child and adult can talk about colors, sing about them, paint with them, and mix them. You can also provide a variety of activities and experiences if you recognize that children need some continuity over a period of time. Although new ideas and experiences are important, the inclusion of some old and familiar activities provides a sense of regularity and consistency and also a feeling of competence as children become confident in their ability to perform certain actions. It is a good idea to include at least one or two activities each day that children are already familiar with. It might be a favorite game, or a construction activity, or tracing letters and numbers with crayons. In addition, you can provide the link between new concepts by introducing them in different activities. You might say, "The fire engine is red. Does anyone remember what else we have seen today that was red?" Children can then volunteer that they worked with red paint, ate red apples, and so on. Or you might point out that these are a big doll and a little doll, just like the big blocks and little blocks in the block area.

Provide opportunities for children to interact in a variety of individual and group settings. Some activities work well with groups of children, whereas others are more suited for an individual child. Consider, for example, a cooking activity in which many youngsters participate, as opposed to an activity such as identifying letters in a child's name, which would be difficult to conduct with many children at the same time. There are times when preschoolers like to be in a group and other times when they like and need to be alone. Group experiences also provide variety. Group experiences not only are good for singing, game playing, and sharing, but also promote the acquisition of rules for interactions in group settings (for example, taking turns).

Development through Cognitive Conflict

As you will recall, development occurs as children experience a discrepancy between the way they think things are, and the way those things are in the environment. For example, youngsters may think that everything floats in water. If they try to float a variety of objects, they will see that the cork does float, but the rock does not. They reorganize their knowledge about floating from "all things float" to "some things do float but others do not." Or, David may think that Shanda is getting more juice because Shanda has a tall thin cup whereas David has a small, wide one. By pouring the juice from Shanda's cup into David's and then back, David will see that a tall, thin container will hold the same amount as a short, wide one. Programs can help promote cognitive conflict by including objectives in activities that are at a higher level than the child's own structures. This induces a discrepancy between the child's level of thought and the actual situation.

In program planning, cognitive conflict can be brought about in two ways. First, activities should include varying objectives so that children at different levels can experience cognitive conflict. Question and provide motivation for the child to attempt these higher objectives. For instance, you might pose a problem to the child. "Amy, I need to find the letter B, but I don't know what it looks like. Can you help me find it?" Or, when a child is grouping objects, ask him if there is another way he could group those same objects. For example, you might say, "David, can you put all the blue ducks together and all the yellow ducks together?"

Second, peer interaction will also help promote cognitive conflict as it encourages the reduction of egocentrism. The child's peers may see things differently than he or she does, causing the child to realize that his or her point of view is not the only point of view. For instance, a child may seriate a row of blocks from the smallest to the biggest, but may have several blocks out of order. Another youngster may see this and rearrange the order of the blocks so that they are seriated correctly.

ADULT–CHILD AND PEER INTERACTION

Interaction is the third aspect that is crucial to designing and implementing preschool programs based on cognitive-developmental theory. Any interaction between two individuals will involve some sort of interpersonal communication, whether it is verbal or nonverbal. Such interactions involve the ability to communicate, to take the role of another person and see his or her perspective, and to make inferences about others. Many of these skills depend on cognitive abilities (for example, decentration), but many also involve social capacities as well. Interactions that promote the acquisition of a certain type of knowledge—for example, social knowledge—will necessarily involve an interplay between teacher and child, child and child, or teacher and group. Cognitive interactions are one type of interpersonal interaction. In this section we will examine interpersonal interactions in the classroom, emphasizing the goal area of socioemotional development.

We will describe several types of interpersonal interactions. There are the general characteristics of adult interaction with children at the individual, small group, or large group levels. The relation between teacher and child may at times involve some sort of prevention, discipline, or management on the part of the teacher. This is a very real concern of all preschool educators. We will outline the relationship that classroom management has to cognitive-developmental theory and suggest some practical techniques for handling specific behavioral problems and discipline. We will then examine peer interactions. As mentioned before, peers have an important role in cognitive-developmental theory and therefore in cognitive preschool programs. This role is described as well as ways in which you can promote different types of peer interactions in classroom settings.

Adult Interaction

Knowledge of cognitive theory, especially the characteristics of preoperational thinking, will help you become more sensitive to the needs of the child. You must also become skilled at interacting with children. Some may contend that good teachers who interact well with children come to this ability naturally. Although this may be true in some cases, many interpersonal interaction skills can be learned. Once learned, these skills can help to develop a good relationship between teacher and child. Certain principles of interpersonal interaction encompass and include the following actions: respecting youngsters, promoting their self-image and creativity, and managing their behaviors.

Treat Children with Respect   You must treat children with respect, recognizing and being attentive to their needs as individuals. This is consistent with cognitive-developmental theory, which emphasizes respect for children's mental abilities. Treating others as one would like to be treated involves the developmental concepts of decentration and coordination among people. The individual must consider not only how he or she feels about and views the situation, but also others' viewpoints and feelings. He or she must coordinate his or her perspective with the perspectives of others. It is essential that adults do not impose their own thinking and way of seeing things on children, but rather have respect for children's abilities. This extends into the area of socioemotional development. *Acknowledging feelings* and *being honest* are two related actions that can show that you respect the child. Treating children with respect means acknowledging their feelings. Children, unfortunately, are sometimes treated as small playthings, or as miniature adults who as yet have no feelings or emotions. But anyone who has lived or worked with young children knows that children do have feelings and can easily be hurt. They also have ideas that are important and need to be listened to. To acknowledge feelings first, listen to children. By listening to their thoughts or their fears, you show children that they are okay and worth listening to, which helps them to develop a positive self-concept. Also, the child will in turn respect you and be more likely to cooperate. For example, sitting down and listening to Beth tell you of a nightmare she had last night shows not only that you care but also that you understand her fear. It also allows you to understand why she is cranky and uncooperative today. In this manner, both teacher and child benefit from this interaction. By listening and responding to children's feelings, you are also providing a model for their interactions with peers and other adults.

Treating youngsters with respect means reacting to them honestly. Experienced preschool teachers note that the child truly shares and is autonomous when a spirit of cooperation and mutual respect exists. Although children may not know the words to express the feelings, they can sense dishonesty and mistrust. Part of acknowledging feelings is letting them know your feelings. You may tell a child that you are angry as long as the child knows why you are angry. In turn, demonstrate your anger in an acceptable manner that provides a model for a possible way in which the child can express anger. For instance, you might say: "It makes me angry and it hurts when you pull my hair. I know that it is hard to wait, but if you want to ask me something, Sally, you will need to wait until I'm done talking with Beatrice."

Promote a Positive Self-Image   Feelings of well-being, self-confidence, and competence stem from the child's self-image. If children (or adults, for that matter) feel good about themselves, they will be more willing to trust their own knowledge and abilities instead of continually looking to others for acknowledgement and guidance. This helps to develop a feeling of autonomy, which is important not only in cognitive but also in socio-emotional realms. There are several strategies that can help to promote a positive self-image.

First, encourage children to make their own choices. Children not only become accountable for their actions, but also learn how to cooperate with others and develop their own system of rules of conduct. For example, in free choice activities, the child's own decision is what motivates her or him to participate in certain activities. If Lisa becomes involved in the fishing game and does not get a chance at the cooking activity, this is her decision. Perhaps next time, she will regulate her time more carefully so that she has an opportunity to participate in more than one activity.

Second, use children's names when speaking to them. The youngster becomes an individual person and not just one child in many when the

---

Box 14-2   *Improving Preschoolers' Self-Concepts*

As explained in the text, *self-concept* refers to a global entity or configuration of the self and can be observed in what children do and say and how they do and say things. Projecto PIAGET, a Hispanic preschool model for increasing English language development, attempts to improve the self-concept of its Hispanic youngsters.

Relative to the objective of self-concept, Projecto PIAGET—through its classroom components—enhances four areas of self concept: body self (or body image), cognitive self, social self, and self-esteem (Samuels, 1977). Examples of activities for enhancing self-concept of preschoolers in each of the four growth areas follow (Thompson & Yawkey, 1984, pp. 19–21):

For developing sound body self:

- Sing songs containing children's names
- Use photographs and drawings of the human form for cutting out pieces which the children could assemble

For enhancing cognitive self:

- Read to the children
- Encourage imagination and language development by having youngsters enact and retell stories

For improving social self:

- Arrange play activities to take place based on sharing of objects among adults (including parents as well as teachers) and children
- Have the children exchange identity with their teachers (and parents) and then have them explain what happened while they were role-playing the other person

For increasing positive self-esteem:

- Say more positive than negative things about children and their behavior
- Have each of the youngsters make a *ME* book to include family, pets, and (vacation) trips, all of which can be shared with other youngsters

Improving preschoolers' self concepts, whether in Projecto PIAGET or in your own cognitive-interactionist classroom, meshes nicely with ongoing developmental activities and experiences and provides an integrated approach.

Samuels, J. *Enhancing self-concept in early childhood.* New York: Human Science Press, 1971.
Thompson, C. T., and Yawkey, T. D. Improving self-concept in young bilingual children: an example from Projecto P.I.A.G.E.T. *Bilingual Journal* 8:18–23, 36, 1984.

teacher takes the time to address him or her by name. Other children learn names faster when they hear them being used and thus are able to individualize and address children properly. Using the child's name also shows that the teacher has taken time and attention to view the child personally. Accordingly, one way in which to help children learn the names of others is to use name games at circle or large group times. This might be a guessing game in which the teacher names a child and the others have to point to him or her. Or names can be rhythmically clapped out and children stand up when their name is called.

Third, include activities and opportunities throughout the day in which children can learn about themselves. These include looking in the mirror, talking about feelings and emotions, identifying parts of the body and types of clothing, and, as just mentioned, getting to know other children and being able to view oneself as one child with a name, yet also as the member of a group of many individual children.

Encourage curiosity . . .

Encourage Curiosity and Creativity   The child learns through doing, in relation not only to cognitive skills, but to social-cognitive skills as well. By encouraging curiosity and creativity, you encourage active exploration. Interpersonal relationships expand and develop as children become curious about others in their social world. While being nondirective, you should provide opportunities for curious explanation and creative development by accepting children's ideas and challenging them with questions to further stimulate creativity. For example, the model for physical knowledge involves critical thinking and problem solving, and accepts and encourages curiosity. If you mix blue and yellow paint together and then explain how these colors make green, children may attribute this to teacher magic. However, if you make colors available and ask the children what they think will happen if they mix them together, their curiosity and creativity will stimulate them to solve the problem. This same process extends to interpersonal interactions; children can adapt and use the same problem approach to resolve differences in conflict situations, as we will describe.

Management and Prevention Techniques   As related to classroom interaction, cognitive-developmental theory does not focus on the areas of discipline and management. Yet certain explanations for ways in which to manage the classroom, prevent disruptions, and solve individual disputes and problems can be found within the fundamental principles of cognitive theory.

One important principle encompasses the relationship between adult and child. We have stated that teachers should treat children with respect, part of which consists of honesty and acknowledgement of feelings. We have also said that this relationship should promote a positive self-image and encourage independence. Such an interpersonal relationship emphasizes equality, trust, and confidence, and cannot exist if the teacher wields and exercises a great deal of power over the child. Experienced preschool teachers understand that cooperation on the part of the child, because of mutual respect, is certainly different than cooperation based on an obedience–authority relationship.

Along with this recognition goes the principle of giving children the freedom of making and being responsible for their own choices. We stressed the importance of having children choose their own activities. It is also crucial for children to make choices regarding their behavior. They are responsible not only for their choices, but also for the consequences of those choices. Children can choose to cooperate with others. Or, they may choose not to. However, it is what results from this conscious choice, rather than an arbitrary restriction imposed by the teacher, that helps children to see their behavior and start to conduct their own rules of conduct.

Strategies for Disciplining   As discipline and behavioral problems arise, there are several effective strategies consistent with cognitive theory that you may wish to employ. An example of a typical problem and a suggestion for how to deal with this problem is presented with each strategy. These interpersonal interaction strategies include: arbitration, rationales, cause and effect, and adult as model.

First, when disputes between children occur, you can suggest arbitration to resolve the conflict. This involves discussing the problem, hearing both sides, and then jointly reaching a solution. Children find their own solutions to problems in this manner. Here, you serve as a model and guide, and possibly suggest solutions to the problem if children are having trouble reaching a solution themselves. You need not impose your authority and will on the youngsters. In using arbitration, you show them that you respect their abilities to find a solution. In addition, this strategy encourages freedom of choice as the children together decide on a way to resolve their conflict. For example, David and Zoraida are fighting over a tricycle and are pushing each other and yelling. Each claims that they were there first. If arbitration is used, the solution is meaningful for cognitive growth. First, remove the tricycle (or other objects of dispute) so that the children can no longer physically fight over it. Then listen to each child's version of what happened. Ask them if they can figure out a way to solve the problem. For example, "What do you think you could do so that both of you can have a turn riding the tricycle?" David and Zoraida discuss what they could do as the adult listens. They finally reach a solution. Zoraida will ride the tricycle for a while as David plays with blocks, and then David will take a turn while Zoraida paints.

A second approach is to provide rationales. For example, two children knock over another child's carefully constructed block tower. A possible solution is: "Tracey and John, David has spent a long time building his tower. When you knock it down, it makes him sad and angry and ruins the tower. You'll need to help him rebuild the tower so that we can all enjoy it again."

Attending to the child's version of what happened . . .

As another example, Mary is crayoning on the table top. You may solve the problem by saying, "Mary, when you color on the table, it makes the table dirty and then it is hard for us to eat on it or do other activities. I'll show you where the sponge is so you can wipe it off."

Cause-and-effect strategies are a natural continuation of rationales. Once children have acted, and you have established a rationale, tell them the effect, such as when the child deliberately breaks something. The natural consequence is that he or she will no longer be able to play with the object because it is broken. Other consequences are externally imposed. However, they should have a consistent and logical relationship to the problem. Depriving Dan of his snack because he knocked over someone's blocks is an arbitrary punishment! It bears absolutely no relation to the problem. But having Dan help rebuild the blocks, and sending him to another activity if he continues to disrupt the block area, makes more sense. Suppose that Mary, who previously crayoned on the table, refuses to wipe the marks off. The solution is to state: "Mary, you have to wipe off the table because the crayon marks will ruin the table. If you will not wipe the marks off, then you will have to go to another activity where we are not using crayons."

The fourth strategy is to model specific actions to avert or solve problems and conflicts. One example is to ignore minor misbehavior that may be an attention-getting device in the first place, such as name calling and making faces. In other situations, by expressing feelings and sharing concern and understanding, you can provide a model for the child who is having difficulty expressing her- or himself. For example, Jason is sitting in a corner of the room, crying. He won't tell anyone what is wrong. Instead of repeatedly asking what is wrong, you might reflect how he is feeling as a way to open up discussion. You might say, "You are sad and feeling lonely. Sometimes people feel that way when they are afraid of something or when they miss someone." Jason looks relieved and proceeds to tell you that his mother has gone into the hospital to have a baby and he misses her very much. You discuss this with Jason. Finally, after discussion, Jason decides to go back to an activity.

Peer Interaction

Peer interaction serves an important function in a preschool program. Through interactions with other youngsters, children learn a great deal about social relationships. They must be able to decenter—that is, to see more than one aspect of a situation. If children are egocentric and cannot understand others' viewpoints, they may have difficulty interacting with others. They may want their own way and not be able to cooperate. The desire and need for good social relationships can do much to increase decentration and develop cooperation and sharing. Because peer interactions serve developmental purposes, even those that might be considered stressful should be promoted. Shortly, we will discuss why such stressful interactions are beneficial, and the ways in which to encourage peer interaction. First, we will look at the role of peers in the three goal areas of the program.

Peers and Cognitive Development   Peers contribute to and facilitate cognitive development through interactions within the different knowledge areas. Remember that preoperational children are quite egocentric in actions and perceptions. Children may think that everyone sees blocks on the table, for example, in exactly the same manner as they do, even though others may be sitting and viewing the blocks from different perspectives. Children may ask for something by saying "Give me that," instead of "Give me the red block," and expect others to know what they are asking for. Peers may not be as understanding and patient with the egocentric child as an adult can; whereas an adult may be willing to interpret the child's egocentric actions or communications, peers may demand that the child explain her- or himself. Thus, peers help to reduce egocentrism through their unwillingness to accept and cater to the egocentric child. This promotes cognitive development in two ways:

1. It forces children to realize that everyone does not see things in the same way that they do.
2. It forces a reorganization of knowledge on the part of preschoolers so that they can communicate effectively with others.

Peer interaction also facilitates decentration, which is vital to many of the knowledge areas within cognitive development. For example, two youngsters are classifying a group of multicolored and multishaped beads by different criteria. Anita is grouping by color and Brian by shape. For Anita to understand Brian's grouping, she will have to decenter—that is, shift her focus from one aspect of the beads to another. Decentering will help her to see that the beads are not only of different colors but also of different shapes.

Cognitive conflict is promoted by peer interaction. Children will ask questions of other youngsters that cause a discrepancy between present cognitive structures and the situation being experienced. Once again, decentration and the reduction of egocentrism cause a reorganization of knowledge and may help to extend the child's developmental level, or even expand to the next level. For instance, in a logical knowledge activity involving classification, one child may be able to classify by only one criterion, such as color, whereas another youngster can classify according to multiple criteria, color and size. To understand this child's classification, the first child will have to extend his or her cognitive structures to include the concept of multiple classification.

Peers and Socioemotional Development   In the goal area of socioemotional development, peer interaction is obviously important. Adults working with young children should encourage interactions with peers as one dimension of interpersonal interactions. Through relationships with peers, children learn that others have feelings and rights just as they do. They develop a sense of justice and a code of morality as they interact with others and determine what is and is not fair. They also learn that they must share with their peers. Peers do much to promote a positive self-image through their acceptance of other children, and their acknowledgement and admiration for other children's capabilities. Peers support and often defend the members of their group. It is through interactions with others of their own age that children learn what it is like to be a member of a group, and how to communicate effectively with others.

The reduction of egocentrism and centration are involved in socioemotional as well as cognitive development. The youngster that cannot see others' viewpoints or can concentrate on only one aspect of a situation will not be very popular when it comes to group projects such as block building or sociodramatic play.

Peers and Psychomotor Development   Finally, peer relationships can encourage psychomotor development. Large muscle activities such as running, climbing, swinging, and tumbling are a lot more fun when there is someone with whom to do them. The eye–hand coordination required in cutting, writing, or bead stringing may not seem as frustrating when the child is sitting and talking with friends while engaged in these activities.

Stressful Interactions with Peers   Many of the interactions just mentioned are stressful for the young child because they may involve a certain

Developing coordination also means having fun.

amount of tension and even conflict. This stress can yield positive benefits. The reduction of egocentrism and centration and the creation of cognitive conflict may come about through stressful interactions, and may help to extend knowledge and promote cognitive development. Similarly, interactions within the socioemotional realm that are stressful and emotionally charged help the child learn intra- and interpersonal skills. For example, children who constantly interrupt the large group activities may suffer the wrath of peers. They see that they must cooperate and that the needs of the group may often supersede their own individual needs. Also, even though the development of psychomotor skills should not be encouraged or forced (because other children are skilled in certain areas), the excitement and friendship that is naturally a part of group activities may provide motivation for children who are unsure of themselves. For instance, if climbing on the jungle gym is part of an outdoor game of explorers, Mark, who is somewhat afraid of climbing, may be more inclined to join in if he is expected to and encouraged by others. Any stressful situation may be useful and beneficial provided no physical harm is involved. Arguments should not be allowed to continue if they include any type of physical violence.

Types of Peer Interactions   Peer interactions can occur at several different levels and within a variety of activities and situations. The types of peer interactions are one to one, small group, and large group. First, one-to-one interactions are probably the most prevalent. Reading together in the book area, painting at an easel, or washing hands in the bathroom are ex-

Group activities may provide motivation for children who are unsure of them-selves—for example, climbing on the jungle gym.

amples of individual peer interactions that occur frequently throughout the day. Similarly, children will strike up intense individual friendships that involve interaction on the playground and within activities—although these friendships may be short in duration.

Second, small group interactions may be spontaneous, as when groups of children work together on construction projects or play games out of doors. However, these children may be working separately and thus would not be interactive as a group. Large group interactions are ideal for learn-ing rules for interactions in groups. There are also more planned interac-tions, such as circle or group time and field trips.

Adults' Role in Promoting Peer Interactions   The teacher's role in peer interactions is once again that of a facilitator. You structure the environ-ment so that peer interactions are more likely to occur. You should try not to intervene in these interactions unless it is necessary, such as when two children are arguing. In this situation, try arbitration to help them work out their arguments. There are several ways in which you can promote peer interactions:

1. Plan a variety of activities that will involve peer interactions at dif-ferent levels (one to one, small group, and large group).
2. Plan activities for group time that involve peer interaction. Most games and activities require cooperation among peers. For in-stance, the *Farmer in the Dell* song game requires that children

join hands, move in a circle, and listen to the words and the actions of children in the middle. When you play *Simon Says*, use a child rather than a teacher as Simon.

3. Plan cooperative projects that require children to work together. For instance, a social knowledge activity about shapes might consist of children matching two pieces of a construction paper balloon (that are of different colors) to "mend" the balloon. Children can work together at these activities with minimal assistance from the teacher.

4. Be nondirective during representational activities and outdoor play. As children work and play together, interactions between peers will be plentiful and spontaneous. Avoid interfering with and directing these interactions.

5. Enlist the help of children to tell newcomers about an activity or to assist others. For instance, if children are making butter, one of them could explain to the child entering the activity what is going on and what to do. In the same vein, children can help each other with things that normally require adult assistance, such as cutting, pasting, and cleaning up spills.

ACTIVITY PERIODS AND SCHEDULING

The daily schedule of any program usually is made up of a number of different activity periods that have certain focuses, such as story time or art time. The specific schedule will vary depending on special needs of individual programs. In a program based on cognitive-developmental theory, the goals of the program will be reflected in the content and type of activity periods which compose the daily schedule. One goal area may be especially emphasized in a particular activity period, such as the goal of cognitive development during free choice period. However, remember that all goal areas can be incorporated in all types of activities. For example, snack time can encompass objectives in socioemotional development, because the children are interacting with each other and with adults, and psychomotor growth for eye–hand coordination is required to pour a glass of juice; it also can promote cognitive development through one-to-one correspondence between the number of napkins the child is passing out and the number of chairs at a table. Similarly, activities that implement the goal area of cognitive development, such as a classification activity in which children group blocks, can also realize socioemotional development in that it is a cooperative project: youngsters must share the blocks. As we outline the various activity periods, we will illustrate integration of goal areas.

Besides attending to the goal areas, remember that principles such as the child's learning through activity and the importance of peers in development must somehow be integrated into activity periods and specific experiences. Some examples of how these principles can be put into action will be given in the following sections.

Free Choice

Free choice periods involve a variety of activities from which children may select the ones in which they want to participate. During this time, activities based on the objectives, for example, of logicomathematical, physical, and social knowledge are selected and set up by the teacher. Children are then able to choose their own activities from among these areas. Several options should be provided. The number of options depends on such things as the size of the room, the types of activity areas, and the number of adults and children. Representational activities may also be available during this time and may even be a part of another activity plan. This free choice period should last long enough so that children have a chance to try most of the activities, but not so long that they become bored and restless. One hour is usually a good length. In a short session or half-day program, this free choice period may be best at the beginning of the morning or afternoon, when children are alert and fresh. In a full-day program, several free choice periods can be interspersed throughout the day.

Free choice activities may involve several goal areas. As previously mentioned, the goals of socioemotional and psychomotor development easily become a part of cognitive activities. Activities that are *child-directed* require the youngsters to direct and initiate their own activities, and the adult usually does not participate. In addition, child-directed activities require the youngsters to be self-sufficient and to work well with peers with or without the adult's supervision. Peer interaction, recognizing other persons, and developing a positive self-image naturally fit into a wide variety of activities and interactions, although they can be made a specific part of an activity. These socioemotional goals are evidenced particularly in social knowledge activities such as recognizing emotions. Recognizing emotions is important to the social emotional goal objective of developing a positive self-image. Other examples follow:

1. Using large muscles for psychomotor development is important to cognitive activities. For instance, hopscotch not only involves jumping and throwing, but also requires that the children recognize and attach labels to numbers. The child can also arrange a series of large blocks from smallest to biggest and then use them to climb on.

2. Utilizing eye–hand coordination is involved in all activities that use scissors and glue as well as pencils and other drawing materials. Tracing letters involves social knowledge. Cutting out shapes

and gluing them into a collage is a classification activity. While stringing macaroni for a necklace, the child can identify and group different colors together.

3. Creativity, confidence, and curiosity are all socioemotional objectives that come naturally within free choice activities that focus on cognitive development. Curiosity about the physical world can be fostered through a cooking activity such as making gelatin. Confidence comes from being able to do something well, such as writing names or finding all the red beads in the pile on the table.

The idea of children as active learners is strongly emphasized during this period. They participate in making the gelatin. They jump through hopscotch as they recognize and learn about numbers. Children not only manipulate and explore their environment, but make their own choices as to the activities in which they participate. For instance, Reynaldo likes to string macaroni and work with blocks. He decides to string macaroni first and then go to the block area. Cognitive conflict occurs through the activities themselves, by your questions, the structuring of the environment, and interactions with peers. As Beatrice cuts out shapes to glue onto construction paper, you ask her to tell you about the shapes, and also why she is grouping them in a certain manner. Here, you challenge Beatrice by holding up a different shape and asking what pile it would go into on her paper. A wide variety of individualization within activities will not only meet the needs of children at different developmental levels but will also provide the generalization that comes through massed experience. Classification is a part of the block activity. It is also part of collages, macaroni stringing, and even making gelatin by grouping cooking utensils together. Each activity also involves the concepts of large and small, and includes labels for different colors.

Large Groups   A large group or circle time is an opportunity for the class to meet as a group. Children learn what it is like to be a member of a group and adhere to the rules that govern groups. Activities include singing, fingerplays, exercises, games, creative movement, dramatic presentations, stories, films or other media, and special guests. This is also a time to discuss the day or special events such as field trips. Large groups should be of fairly short duration, approximately 15 minutes to ½ hour, so that interest runs high and participation is strong.

Whereas large group times are especially conducive to the objectives of socioemotional and psychomotor development, certain activities can also be introduced that fall within the goal of cognitive development. For example, a game can involve classifying properties of youngsters by color of their clothes, age, and hair or seriating them by height. Guessing games are good vehicles for social knowledge such as names of objects, colors, and children, as are classroom guests who share new ideas—for instance,

Psychomotor development can be stimulated during large or small group activities.

about musical instruments. Physical knowledge activities can involve group participation, such as making butter with each child having his or her own small container of cream to shake.

Small Groups   Smaller groups of children and adults get together for quieter and more individualized group interactions. This is an ideal time for reading stories, engaging in logicomathematical activities, or playing quiet games. Small group activities also are a time when children can relate personal experiences to a group without encountering the disruptions and impatience of a larger group. In a half-day program, small groups can occur once and last from 15 minutes to ½ hour. A longer program may have several of these small group periods. Children acquire a sense of belonging by knowing which group is theirs. They also learn consistency by being part of this group over an extended period of time. On the other hand, if you vary the composition of the group from time to time, you can promote peer interaction.

All three program goal areas can be realized during small group activities. Psychomotor development through creative movement is encouraged after reading a story about animals. Children can act out, for instance, the various movements of elephants, horses, or other animals. As exercises, these movements add some excitement and a chance to stretch. Working with dot-to-dot pictures of numbers and letters is a social knowledge activity. Planting a seed together involves physical knowledge. Relationships with peers and adults, cooperation, and respect are very important during small group time, because one child can easily disrupt the activities of the others.

Teachers and peers can promote cognitive conflict during small group activities through questions, guessing games, puzzles, or stories. Bringing in objects to examine during this time, such as nature objects or a family pet, gives children opportunities to manipulate concrete materials.

Representational Activities   During this time, children structure knowledge from the physical and social world and develop active representations of this knowledge. Representational activities may be of a varied range and usually encompass such traditional activities as: arts, crafts, construction, and sociodramatic play. These representations may be at the level of indices, symbols, or signs. As you will recall, they may also be in the form of imitation, make-believe, onomatopoeia, two-dimensional representation, or three-dimensional models. During representational activities, remember that you can assume nondirective roles so that the child invents representations on his or her own. Of course, it may be necessary for you to explain the activity, and help with putting on smocks and even guide certain psychomotor actions such as cutting with scissors. Adults may also be needed as customers for shoe stores, restaurants, or other make-believe activities. Representational activities can last ½ to 1 hour. Children may become very involved with their projects, and some may require more time than others. If needed, these activities may be combined within the free choice period.

Representational activities especially lend themselves to the goal areas of socioemotional and psychomotor development. For instance, producing a puppet show involves a certain amount of motor coordination as well as cooperation. Easel painting, clay modeling, and paper chain making necessitate eye–hand coordination and sharing of materials. Although the goal area of cognitive development is not emphasized as much during representational activities as it is during free choice, it is also a natural part of these activities. The donut man in sociodramatic play lines up his boxes from small to large. Children must know the colors of paints to ask for them to use at the easels. Talking about how finger paints feel requires social knowledge labels for textures—for example, *gooey* or *sticky*.

Other principles of cognitive theory also are evidenced during this period. Building with Lincoln Logs or playing dress up, along with the teacher in a nondirective role, helps children to construct their own knowledge. Construction games and sociodramatic play also require peer interaction in which particular desires of the individual child must give way to the demands of the group. Thus, the egocentric child will have to realize the viewpoints of others if he or she is to participate.

Outdoor Play   Outdoor play is a time for children to exercise their muscles. Outdoor equipment should be easily available, with plenty of space for running, climbing, riding bicycles, playing games, swinging, and sand play. You should assume a nondirective role during this time. However, be present and alert for reasons of safety! At least one ½-hour period should be allotted for outdoor play in half-day programs; plan two or more periods for full-day programs.

Because of your nondirective role, this is not a good time for the implementation of cognitive goals that require a formalized lesson. However, informal questioning (for example, comparing different colored leaves and different sized rocks) can encourage cognitive objectives. Of course, psychomotor growth occurs during this time, as does socioemotional development in the spontaneous interactions with peers.

Snacks and Meals   Enough time should be allowed so that snacks and meals can be unhurried and pleasant for both adults and children. Children should be encouraged to serve themselves and care for the rights of others by sharing. Informal conversation can be a means for more individual contact between teachers and children, and logicomathematical activities can be a natural part of the snack experience. For instance, children match one napkin for each chair at the table, one cookie for each child, and one cup for each child. Talking about new or unusual snacks involves social knowledge labels, and may even involve physical knowledge as children relate how they made the snack during a cooking activity. Pouring juice without spilling involves muscle control and eye–hand coordination. A half-day program might have one snack. A full-day program should probably have two snacks and lunch, depending on the hours of the program.

Rest   Full-day programs need a rest or nap period. Half-day programs might encourage resting through the use of quiet activities during small group time.

Optional Activities   Special activities such as field trips, guest visits, films, or special cooking experiences may be planned throughout the year. Parents should be notified in advance of these activities. They should take place early in the day while children are alert and less likely to become restless.

Sample Schedules

A schedule for half-day programs with two teachers is shown in Table 14-2. One for half-day programs with more than two adults appears in Table 14-3. Last, a schedule for a full-day program with two or more teachers is illustrated in Table 14-4. These are just some of many possible scheduling patterns. Different programs have different requirements and may have to adapt these or develop new schedules to fit their needs. The

Table 14-2   A Sample Schedule for a Half-Day Program with Two Teachers

8:30 to 9:15 A.M.	Free Choice 1. Classification: bean sorting 2. Physical knowledge: making jello (one teacher) 3. Social knowledge: hopscotch 4. Social knowledge, representation: tracing and coloring letters 5. Seriation: felt family (one teacher)
9:15 to 9:30	Large group time
9:30 to 9:45	Wash-up and snacks
9:45 to 10:00	Small group time (one teacher with each group)
10:00 to 10:30	Outdoor play
10:30 to 10:55	Representational activities 1. Construction: unit blocks 2. Art: easel painting (one teacher) 3. Craft: stringing macaroni necklaces (one teacher) 4. Sociodramatic play: kitchen
10:55 to 11:00	Clean-up, preparation to go home

Table 14-3   A Sample Schedule for a Half-Day Program with More Than Two Adults

8:30 to 9:15 A.M.	Free choice 1. Classification: bean sorting 2. Physical knowledge: making jello (one teacher) 3. Number concept: soda cans and straws (one teacher) 4. Seriation, construction: making stairs from blocks (one teacher) 5. Classification, social knowledge: shapes, collages (one teacher)
9:15 to 9:30	Large group time
9:30 to 9:45	Wash-up and snacks
9:45 to 10:00	Small group time (one teacher with each group)
10:00 to 10:30	Outdoor play
10:30 to 10:55	Representational activities 1. Construction: unit blocks (one teacher) 2. Art: easel painting (one teacher) 3. Craft: stringing macaroni necklaces (one teacher) 4. Craft: clay 5. Sociodramatic play: store (one teacher)
10:55 to 11:00	Clean-up, preparation to go home

Table 14-4   A Sample Schedule for a Full-Day Program with Two or More Adults

8:00 to 9:15 A.M.	Free choice
9:15 to 9:45	Large group time
9:45 to 10:15	Outdoor play or field trips
10:15 to 10:30	Wash-up and snacks
10:30 to 11:30	Free choice and representational activities
11:30 to 12:00	Clean-up and small group time
12:00 to 12:30 P.M.	Lunch
12:30 to 12:45	Small group time
12:45 to 1:45	Nap
1:45 to 2:15	Outdoor play
2:15 to 2:30	Wash-up and snacks
2:30 to 3:30	Representational activities, free choice, preparation to go home

number of teachers in a program can make quite a difference in types of activities and the sequencing of activities. For example, the scheduling pattern for a program having two teachers and 20 children (Table 14-2) can be adapted to include representational activities with the free choice period. Also, cognitive activities that are child-directed should be used, such as bead stringing, indoor hopscotch, or bean sorting. Other activities that do not require supervision such as puzzles, tracing, or sociodramatic play can be included with some that need only nominal supervision—for instance construction, drawing, and painting. Two teachers could supervise the entire room while remaining at cognitive-oriented activities that involve adult–child interactions.

Some Mechanics for Planning

Developing programmatic goals from theoretical principles gives a clear direction and structure to planning. The various activity periods and scheduling patterns provide the framework within which to weave these goals and principles. These basic ingredients, however, do not make program planning a cut-and-dried formula that can be plugged in any time and any place. Not only do the particular needs of children and the particular requirements of programs have to be considered, but also the consequences of planning over time should be taken into account. If planning is done with little regard to overall long-term effects and long-range developmental goals, then even carefully mapped-out schedules may not be as valuable and effective as they could be.

Two areas will be considered. One concerns the broad, overall mechanics, or the *hows*, of program planning; the way to form content, provide themes and give unity to planning. The other is specifics of planning at different levels: short- and long-term planning.

How to Plan   One of the first things that should be taken into account when planning is how the content of the program reflects the overall goals of the program—that is, cognitive, socioemotional, and psychomotor development. These goals in themselves are somewhat content free. The goals are very broad, basic goals that may be actualized in a variety of ways. This is because goals focus on *abilities* in the cognitive and social domain, which do not depend on specific activities to be realized. For example, classification is a type of logicomathematical ability that falls within the goal of cognitive development. The content and activities through which the child's classification ability is facilitated can vary. They can be, for instance, grouping pots and pans in the child's kitchen just as well as a carefully constructed classification activity. That a child knows the difference between large, blue beads and small, red beads is not important to this activity. However, it is important that he or she can identify and group objects according to different properties.

It is necessary, however, to consider content when you plan the daily activities. Daily activities acquire some commonality as they are planned around a particular theme or idea. This helps you structure the environment by providing a framework around which to plan activities. The follow-through in the activity also provides motivation, excitement, and interest for children. A week that focuses on animals provides motivation as children classify toy animals, label animals and animal sounds, sing about animals in large group, and even bring in their pets from home. Experiences are generalized as children see a variety of animals and use them in different forms (for example, drawing pictures or making sounds).

Theme Approach   One method of choosing content is through a theme approach. One of the biggest aids in planning and developing a schedule that has continuity is to base ideas on a unifying theme. This gives a common idea or event to plan around and draws the day, week, or month together while it serves as a focal point for children and teachers. A theme can be a way for the child to generalize and relate knowledge. For example, children may have done a seriation activity with pumpkins during Halloween. They also seriated snow figures in the winter and flowers and rabbits in the spring. They have gone shopping for pumpkins with parents, where they saw different sized pumpkins. They see that no matter what objects they use, they can place objects along a dimension according to certain criteria (smallest to largest, thinnest to widest). It is not so important that they can seriate pumpkins or rabbits, but their concept of seriation *is* important. Thus, children begin to generalize knowledge and concepts.

Themes can be organized around many different ideas, holidays, and events. Several possible suggestions are:

1. Community helpers and careers
2. Transportation

3. Animals
4. Seasons, nature, environment
5. Family
6. Circus
7. Special days, such as Valentine's Day, Thanksgiving, the first day of Spring, and Halloween.

For example, the theme of special days is selected. In turn, Halloween is chosen. Using the knowledge area of cognition, for instance, the content can be identified. In Table 14-5, the various processes and content are shown for Halloween.

Common Experiences of Children   Another way in which to choose content for a program in relation to goal areas is to consider the topics relevant to the child's world. Several types of knowledge important for the preschool child are:

1. Body parts
2. Food
3. Clothing
4. Vehicles
5. Toys
6. Colors
7. Size
8. Shapes
9. Animals
10. Plants

Table 14-5   Identifying Content and Processes in the Cognitive Knowledge Area for the Theme *Halloween As a Special Day*

1. Social knowledge
   a. The color orange
   b. The color black
   c. Fall vegetables
2. Physical knowledge
   a. Making a jack-o'-lantern
   b. Making a pumpkin pie
3. Representational knowledge
   a. Playing a jack-o'-lantern
   b. Drawing a jack-o'-lantern
4. Logicomathematical knowledge
   a. Classification: grouping multicolored felt pumpkins
   b. Seriation: seriating real pumpkins
   c. Number concept: witches and broomsticks or cats and whiskers (on paper or cardboard)

Table 14-6   Procedures for Incorporating the Topic of *Plants* into the Cognitive Knowledge Area

1. Social knowledge
   a. Learning the names of different types of plants and trees
   b. Learning the parts of a plant
2. Physical knowledge
   a. Planting seeds
   b. Sprouting beans
3. Representational knowledge
   a. Playing gardener
   b. Drawing pictures of plants
   c. Making clay pots for plants
4. Logicomathematical knowledge
   a. Classification (different types of seeds)
   b. Seriation (plants and gardening utensils along different size dimensions)
   c. Number concepts
      1. Putting one seed in one pot
      2. Matching watering cans to plant pots

Select one or several topics. You can then incorporate these topics into the various areas. For example, Table 14-6 illustrates the procedure for incorporating *plants* into the cognitive knowledge area.

Incidental Topics   Besides considering topics important and relevant to the child's world, examine other areas that are of interest and provide good experiences. This type of content might be considered somewhat incidental, but it is still valuable. Some possible topics are:

1. A child's or teacher's trip to the beach, the mountains, or another country
2. A child's new kittens
3. A guest gymnast, musician, or magician
4. A sudden snowstorm
5. Ethnic goods

Levels of Planning   The suggestions given on how to plan are helpful when schedules are being made at the daily, weekly, monthly, or even yearly level. Activities must be varied, balanced, interesting, and able to meet goals and objectives not only within one activity period, but throughout the entire day or week as well. Such long-range planning can get rather complicated. However, by selecting goals and implementing them through content in the form of themes, and noting activities that meet these requirements, you can design a more unified schedule. To aid such planning, we present several working forms. At first you may need to actually fill in such forms each time you plan. Later, the forms may serve only as a reminder of things to keep in mind when planning.

Weekly Planning   When making up plans on a daily or weekly basis, the first thing to determine is what goals will be implemented and the type of theme or content to be used. This will help to tie together the week or day. Activities can be chosen on the basis of how they help to meet the goals or emphasize the theme (not all activities will do so). This will help organize the week and point out potential weak spots, such as a day on which only socioemotional goals are emphasized, or an overemphasis on cognitive goals throughout the week.

Table 14-7 shows a weekly goals sheet. The objectives within the three goal areas are filled in the left column. For instance, one cognitive goal is recognizing shapes. It is instituted throughout the week in different ways. On Monday, there is a shapes–collage activity. On Wednesday, the children play a guessing game about shapes and sing a song about them during the large group. On Friday, they paint with sponges cut out into various shapes. This form would be used by the person who plans the weekly ac-

Table 14-7   A Sample Format for a Weekly Goals Sheet

	Days of the Week				
Goal areas	*Monday*	*Tuesday*	*Wednesday*	*Thursday*	*Friday*
Cognitive knowledge	Shapes—collages Ordering—blocks by size	One-to-one correspondence—saucers and cups	Shapes—guessing game using labeling Shapes—songs	Socio-dramatic—play using theme of *The Three Bears*	Shapes—sponge painting
Socioemotional knowledge	Sharing—interpersonal skills in talking about experiences	Helping—putting on dress-up clothes Being a friend—qualities of a friend	Cooperating—assignment of members of groups to tasks	Listening—qualities of a good listener	Feelings—seeing and talking about pictures, showing emotion
Psychomotor knowledge	Body coordination—rocking boats	Dynamic balance—hopping and walking balance beam	Fine motor—cutouts using scissors and glue	Body coordination—skipping and galloping	Gross motor—indoor climbing apparatus Static balance—standing on one leg at a time

Table 14-8   A Sample Daily Schedule Form for a Half-Day Program

Day of Week:	Monday		
Theme of Week:	Halloween (Special Events)		
Planner for Week:	Ms. Beatrice		
Room Manager:	Ms. Pearl		

Period	Title of activity	Objectives	Teacher
9:00– 9:45 A.M.	Jack-o'-lantern collage	Construct collage with paper sheets and paints	Ms. Smith
10:15–10:45	Building trains and roads	Order randomly, then by size	Ms. Trudy
10:45–11:15	Shopping in east mall	Talking about field trip in small group fashion	Mr. Tom
11:15–11:45	Riding in a rowboat	Practice and refine forward, backward movements of trunk of body	Mr. John

tivities; it may be a teacher or the director, depending on the type of program. If you plan a week with little regard to implementing goals and then attempt to fit the content back into the different goal areas, there is a strong possibility that you will have a poorly planned week. It is important to first determine goals from theory and then decide on content.

Daily Planning   After deciding on the goals for the week, and the content used to implement them, you must complete a schedule for each day. A daily schedule should list: (1) the day of the week, (2) the theme for the week, (3) who is planning the week, and (4) who is the room manager. The format for the daily schedule is shown in Table 14-8. The type of activity and its objectives are listed for each activity period. In addition, the teacher in charge of the activity and the location of activity in the room are given. This helps the planner in determining where to put certain activities.

In conjunction with the daily schedule form, the planner should also fill out a checklist, which is helpful in making sure the activities encompass a range of processes and activities—for instance, how is the activity being accomplished (cooking, experimentation, manipulation) and what are the types of materials used (real, two-dimensional, three-dimensional). It may be helpful to fill this out *before* completing the daily schedule form to see how well-balanced the day is and determine if any changes need to be made. A sample daily checklist form is illustrated in Table 14-9.

After filling in the name of the activity, add three different areas of each activity: objectives, materials, and process. Within each area are several categories that the activity fulfills. For example, the shapes collage can meet the objectives of both a social knowledge and a classification activity. It uses two-dimensional and three-dimensional materials (pieces of paper, pieces

Table 14-9   A Sample Daily Checklist Form for a Half-Day Program

Planner for Week: Ms. Beatrice					
Day of Week: Monday					
Title of Activity	Objectives	Check (√)	Processes	Check (√)	Materials
Jack-o'-lantern collage	Construct collage		cooking experimentation (discovering) touching smelling		paper paints crayons blocks
Building trains and roads	Order randomly then by size		moving seeing generalizing recognizing transforming problem solving defining		nesting sets puzzles see-saw jungle gym sand/water scissors
Shopping in east mall	Talk about field trip in small groups		talking rehearsing constructing seriating		rocking boats stringing sets dress-up clothes toy sets (cars, trucks) Lincoln Logs
Riding in a rowboat	Practice and refine forward and backward movements of trunk of body				

of string, small objects). It employs the manipulative process and it is also a take-home activity. Each one of these would thus be checked (see Table 14-9). Checklists may be made for representational activities and other activity periods as well; only a free choice checklist is illustrated.

Finally, an overview of the week will give a clear picture of what the week will be like. The weekly schedule need not be as specific as the daily schedule. Write down the name of each activity within each period of the day. Table 14-10 suggests a format for developing a weekly overview.

Long-term Planning   The beginning of the month, the term, or the year is a good time to determine what is to be accomplished over this longer stretch of time. Children undoubtedly change as the year moves along, and planning should reflect an understanding of these changes. Once again, a good perception of the child's developmental level will be an invaluable aid in making these long-range plans and deciding the focus of cognitive abili-

Table 14-10   A Sample Weekly Overview Form for a Half-Day Program

WEEKLY OVERVIEW FORM (Half-Day Program)		
Day of the Week	Activity Periods	Name of the Activity
Monday	9:00– 9:45 A.M. 10:15–10:45 10:45–11:15 11:15–11:45	Jack-o'-lantern collage Building trains and roads Shopping in east mall Riding in a rowboat
Tuesday	8:30– 9:00 A.M. 9:00–10:00 10:40–11:40 11:40–12:00 noon	One-to-one correspondence Playing house A friend Dynamic balance
Wednesday	8:15– 8:45 A.M. 9:15– 9:30 10:10–10:30 11:15–11:45	Shapes—game Shapes—song Group cooperation Fine motor—scissors and glue
Thursday	8:30– 9:30 A.M. 10:00–11:20 10:20–10:45	Playing *The Three Bears* A good listener Skipping and galloping
Friday	9:00– 9:45 A.M. 10:30–10:50 10:50–11:20 11:20–11:45	Shapes—painting Feelings—emotion Climbing indoors Static balance

ties. For example, whereas children may not know the names of certain colors in September, by April most children will. Social knowledge objectives should take this into account. You might start out in the fall using primary colors, and in the winter begin to use secondary colors. Classification would focus primarily on single classification in the fall, but some children might be capable of multiple classification by the winter or spring. More emphasis should be placed on social knowledge objectives in the beginning of the year. These are somewhat easier to structure than logical knowledge and supply the labels and symbols that may be needed in other knowledge areas. For example, if a child does not know the names of colors or the dimensional attributes of an object, he or she may have a harder time classifying or seriating. Also, at the beginning of the year shorter activities should be emphasized while children become acquainted with the program and develop longer attention spans.

Social and Physical Developmental Changes in the Child   Besides cognitive goals, you should determine how goals in the socioemotional and psychomotor areas of development change. When children first start in the preschool program, they may not have developed their interpersonal skills.

As the year goes by and they learn to interact with others and care for others' rights, activities can include more cooperative and group projects. For instance, to play *The Farmer in the Dell* in a larger group, children must be able to take turns and realize that they cannot be the farmer every time the game is played. Such an activity may have to wait until children are more capable of sharing. Physical development will also change during the year, with children becoming more skilled and adept, particularly in activities involving eye–hand coordination. Children may at first have trouble cutting with scissors, especially if they have not used them at home. However, as they use them more often in the program, they will be able to cut out more complicated shapes.

PHYSICAL ENVIRONMENTS

The physical environment of a preschool program and center is related to cognitive-developmental theory. The same principles applicable to program planning also have relevance to the physical environment and the equipment and materials of the classroom.

Physical Space

Once again, the most important applicability of theory to planning is the view of the child as an active learner. If the child needs opportunities to manipulate, experiment, touch, and explore, then the classroom must provide him or her with these opportunities. The layout of the room must be such that children can move about freely, see what is happening in other parts of the room, and feel safe and comfortable. Many things can be used to stimulate the child's thinking. Bulletin boards, mobiles, pictures, nature exhibits, selected pets, and artwork displays are all examples.

Interaction between children can be encouraged by the environment. Areas where several children can work together should be included. On the other hand, children do need to be alone at times. A quiet corner such as the library is ideal. Obviously, these quiet areas should not be near the noisier ones such as the large group area or places where children do art work. Activity areas can be multipurpose. For example, the art area is not used solely for art work but also for small table games and cooking. This provides more flexibility to the physical environment. Further, areas can be arranged so all quiet activities are at one end of the room.

Children can be encouraged to work and learn by themselves if the physical environment is supportive. For example, a sink that is within the child's reach will be helpful in getting children to clean up their own spills. A bathroom with child-sized fixtures will encourage independence in wash-

Bathrooms should have child-size fixtures to encourage independence in washing and toileting.

ing and toileting. Lockers for each child will foster responsibility for personal possessions, as well as being a source of pride in knowing they each have their own special place.

Equipment and Materials

Objects that are used within the planned environment should reflect theoretical principles. Again, it is important that children manipulate, taste, touch, and squeeze or use other forms of actual involvement with the materials. This means that objects must be sturdy, safe, exciting, and colorful. Equipment should promote peer interaction by including materials that require cooperation and joint efforts. At the same time, there should be enough materials so that children do not have to share continuously all materials. Concrete experiences can be provided by including real objects in the classroom, especially objects that the child may not have encountered elsewhere. A piano, small animals, and a full-length mirror are some examples.

Equipment should be multipurposeful so that it can be used in different goal areas. This emphasizes the point that goal areas are content free; the beads can be used for a classification activity on Monday, a social knowledge experiment about sinking and floating on Friday. A built-in advantage of multipurpose equipment is that it can help cut costs: equipment can be kept at a minimum. Using the same materials in a variety of situations also helps to generalize knowledge.

Multiple sets of the same equipment are a good idea. Not only does it allow each child at an activity to have a set, but it can encourage different uses of the same materials at one time. While one child is classifying one set of felt rabbits according to color, another is seriating a set of rabbits by size. Materials that have several features encourage classification and seriation. A set of identical green rabbits would be hard to group or seriate. But green, red, and blue rabbits that come in several sizes have different features that are optimal for classification and seriation. On the other hand, too many properties can be distracting. Seven multicolor rabbits of different texture, shape, and size would be too confusing.

Materials should encompass the different levels of representation. Some children may need to work with materials at the index or symbol levels, whereas other children will work at the sign level. For example, very young children may be able to represent the concept of dog only through hearing a dog bark; records of animal sounds would be good for them to listen to. Other children may be able to conceptualize a dog through pictures in books or by imitating a dog in sociodramatic play. Still others may be able to see the word dog and know the object for which it stands.

Equipment can come from a variety of resources. It can be commercially purchased, it can be teacher- or parent-made, it can represent the latest in materials or it can be very traditional. All have advantages and disadvantages and all have a place in an early childhood program. Commercial materials may be sturdier and more easily duplicated than teacher-made materials, yet they can also be prohibitively expensive. Teacher-made materials can be modeled after commercially popular equipment and be much less expensive. However, they require a lot of time and patience. For instance, a hopscotch board can be made out of a large sheet of plastic or cardboard. Macaroni can be dyed and used for stringing instead of expensive beads. Innovative materials can help bring new ideas into the classroom, but on the other hand, they may not interest the child. An elaborate science kit that explores the properties of buoyancy may seem interesting to you, but the child may be more eager to try floating common objects found around the room in a pail of water. Traditional materials may seem terribly old fashioned, but they have proven to be interesting to children and do not represent a passing fad. A set of good, sturdy unit blocks will be used in myriad activities, and children will never tire of them. Thus it seems that all types of materials have a place in an early childhood program. The ratio of commercial to home-made or new to traditional will depend largely on monetary and other resources of the program.

When you buy or make materials for the cognitive-oriented program, it may be helpful to ask yourself several questions. These can help determine whether the materials are adequate and suitable for an activity in particular and the program in general:

1. Do the materials seem to complement and enhance the activity? Do they meet the needs of the activity? Do they have enough features to classify or seriate?
2. Would the materials attract a young child to the activity? Are they interesting? Are the materials colorful, eye-catching, and unique?
3. Do the materials match the child's developmental and conceptual level? Can children at varying developmental levels use these same materials? Do they reflect the different levels of representation?
4. Are the materials versatile? Can they be used for more than one activity? Are the materials flexible enough to be used across a broad range of activities, such as classification, number concept, social knowledge?
5. Are the materials safe for young children? Are they made well, with no sharp points or rough edges? Will they break easily? Do they contain too many small, dangerous parts?
6. Are the materials sturdy enough for frequent use and active manipulation? Will the materials last throughout the year or will they need to be replaced constantly? Are they made of delicate materials, easily torn?
7. Would the materials be easy to replace? Will it be difficult to order replacement parts or can the materials be repaired right in the classroom?

PARENT INVOLVEMENT

Parent involvement means that parents are partners with adult caregivers in the preschools in maximizing the child's potential for developmental growth. Although parent involvement in the preschools has existed since the 1920s movement of the parent cooperative nursery schools, the significant contributions parents have made to designing and implementing programs have occurred in the later quarter of this century. Further, forms of parent involvement are common to almost all of the different theory-derived programs in contemporary early childhood education. However, parent involvement serves especially important functions in designing and implementing preschool programs based on cognitive-developmental theory.

The first and overriding goal of parent involvement in preschools is to facilitate cognitive development as well as growth processes of the child as a whole being. This goal is the same for both teachers and parents. It brings together both home and school with common objectives and interests. Further, cognitive theory and research on childrearing show that parents have a profound influence on their child's development. Parents who are informed about child growth and who use principles in childrearing make sound decisions concerning their youngsters that markedly maximize the potential for development in the formative preschool years. Thus, derived from cognitive theory is the principle that parents of all income levels are directly and centrally involved with their child's development and with the school and home environments that help shape it.

Beyond this initial goal of parent involvement there are several others important to planning and implementing programs. Effectively listening to parents, dealing with their feelings, and providing them with support help you to strengthen your preschool program and facilitate the youngsters' growth in both school and home settings.

A third goal is to provide parents with information and to work with them in using the principles derived from cognitive-developmental theory. In other words, the same principles that *you* use, such as those dealing with adult–child interaction, preparation of physical environments, and characteristics of the preoperational child, can also be effectively shown to parents. The fundamental goal of all involvement programs is training parents to prepare them to work with children in preschool (and home) settings. The sessions for training parents under your guidance provide an added dividend. Both teachers and parents working in the preschool will show consistency in using principles that are common to cognitive programs.

A fourth goal is to provide you with an extra pair of hands to work with children. To help you handle all the children's needs effectively and provide for their individual growth, parents become invaluable resources to you and the preschool program.

A fifth goal of parent involvement in cognitive preschool programs is to help parents set realistic growth targets and better understand the problems of their children.

The five major goals can be implemented through program participation, home visits, letters and news media, group meetings, and parent–teacher conferences. Each of the means of involving parents in programs increases the avenues of communication between home and school and maximizes the developmental potential of young children.

Program Participation

Cognitive-oriented programs for children involve parents on advisory and governing boards charged with administering the program, and in directly working with children in classroom settings. Parents need to be trained for either role. Set up training sessions. Show parents their responsibilities and how to perform them as members of advisory and governing boards.

Parental involvement in the preschool helps teachers effectively provide for each child's individual growth.

Where parent functioning goes beyond custodial caregiving, tremendous opportunities occur for maximizing cognitive growth and meeting other goals of parent involvement.

Home Visits

Another way of implementing the goals of parent involvement is through home visits. Meeting with the parents in the home environment and conducting an interactive discussion in a nonthreatening manner can give you greater insights into the development of the child. You gain an understanding of the home environment, ways in which the parent and child interact, and feelings, problems, and concerns of the parent. Home visits also enable you to work with parents in home settings in showing them how to use adult caregiving principles and common materials effectively in the home in assisting their child's development and learning. In addition, home visits enable you to share information with parents about their child and the preschool program. Ultimately, a rich relationship between home and school can develop as an outcome of home visits.

Letters and News Media

In conjunction with involving parents in the program, using letters is extremely effective (personal notes, invitations, newsletters, and newspaper articles). Send them home to the parents with the child. Personal notes to the parents could be written about their youngster's specific accomplishments of the day (for example, matching squares and circles in logico-mathematical knowledge, role playing a character in representational knowledge) as well as her or his general progress in the program. Invitations to attend group meetings and to participate in the program are also key pieces of information sent home. In addition, some programs have written monthly newsletters for parents. Clippings reproduced from newsletters or from other sources of information concerning school activities, developmental caregiving routines, or other topics can be used. Letters and news media provide parents with a communication channel that facilitates parent involvement in the preschool program.

Group Meetings

Implementing parent involvement also means sharing relevant information about aspects of child development and the program. By attending group meetings based on common interests of the parents—such as goals of the program, children's behavior and misbehavior, communications with the child, and growth of self-concept—parents learn more about the program and their youngsters. In addition to parent discussion, some preschools use films, role-playing episodes, and lectures to share salient information with parents. Study groups on a particular topic may arise from group meetings. Group meetings may also be purely social, where parents come together for fellowship over coffee or tea or a potluck supper. Whether sharing information about aspects of the program or in fellowship at social gatherings, parents and teachers enjoy opportunities to become more acquainted with one another over their common interest in preschoolers.

Parent–Teacher Conferences

Although effective, parent–teacher conferences must be used in conjunction with other methods of implementing parent involvement within cognitive programs. Parent–teacher conferences are a most effective vehicle for sharing and gathering information about the child and the goals of the program. They can be scheduled regularly by the parent or the teacher. They are used by the teacher not solely for reporting information about the child. Rather, they are used as a forum to listen to parents as well as to exchange ideas about the youngsters and program in an interactive fashion. You will need to plan for these conferences by thinking through the several items to be discussed and preparing specific items highlighting the child's accomplishments (concrete examples of work products, anecdotal notes, activity plans).

SUMMARY

This chapter examined selected aspects of planning, designing, and implementing programs. First, the factors involved in development are implemented through the goal areas of cognitive, socioemotional, and psychomotor development. Second, the developmental characteristics of the preoperational child are considered, such as that these children are active learners. Third, adult and child interactions in preschool classrooms are developed from a knowledge of cognitive theory and from interpersonal skills. Fourth, activity periods must reflect the three goals of cognitive-developmental theory. The format used for short- and long-term planning is crucial in implementing programs in a consistent manner. We discussed the mechanics of program planning. Fifth, the environment should be designed in accord with programmatic principles and cognitive-developmental theory. Sixth, the ways parents are involved in preschools can facilitate the operation of a preschool program.

All these significant aspects, as well as those key procedures for planning in the cognitive knowledge area described in Chapter 13, become the guideposts for designing and implementing cognitive-oriented preschool programs. Taken together they provide necessary information for you to adapt cognitive-developmental theory to teaching groups of young children.

Review Questions

1. Tell why the activity periods must reflect the goals of the preschool program.
2. Give a minimum of three examples to show how materials and play objects in the preschool encompass different levels of representation.
3. List the major characteristics of cognitive development of the preschool child, and generalizing from these characteristics, describe a minimum of three principles adults could put into action in working with youngsters of this age.
4. Tell how you select themes and topics for preschool activities using implications from cognitive theory.
5. State how the adult actions of treating children with respect and promoting a positive self-image encourage cognitive development in a preschool program.
6. Describe the use of the daily checklists, and tell how it differs from the weekly overview.

Suggested Activities

1. Generate a list of possible topics that you think are important for preschoolers to know. Then, ask several young children to identify topics about which they would like to know. Compare your list and the children's lists.
2. Develop schedules for half- and full-day programs and compare them on number of activities used and times at which they are held.
3. Interview a preschool teacher and ask him or her to identify several social and physical developmental changes that have occurred in a child over the past three to four months.

4. Gather a set of materials and tangibles using the criteria for equipment selection. Explain why you would include these items in your preschool center.
5. After observing the layout of the physical environment in a preschool classroom, change it around by moving tables, chairs, and other items. Observe for any differences or changes in the children's behavior as they use this preschool classroom.
6. Develop and implement an activity with youngsters based on one of the goal areas for preschool programs and show how it can be used to encourage growth in the social as well as the logicomathematical knowledge domains.

Suggested Readings

Cartwright, C. A., and Cartwright, G. P. *Developing observation skills.* New York: McGraw-Hill, 1974.

Davis, D., Davis, M., Hansen, H., and Hansen, R. *Playway: education for reality.* Minneapolis: Winston Press, 1973.

Forman, G. E., and Kuschner, D. S. *The child's construction of knowledge: Piaget for teaching children.* Monterey, Calif.: Brooks/Cole, 1977.

Frost, J. L., and Kissinger, J. B. *The young child and the educative process.* New York: Holt, Rinehart & Winston, 1976.

Furth, H. G., and Wachs, H. *Piaget's theory in practice: thinking goes to school.* New York: Oxford University Press, 1974.

Morrison, G. S. *Parent involvement in the home, school, and community.* Columbus, Ohio: Charles E. Merrill, 1978.

Proshansky, H. M., Ittelson, W. H., and Rivlin, L. G. (Eds.). *Environmental psychology: man and his physical setting*. New York: Holt, Rinehart & Winston, 1970.

Stanley, J. C. (Ed.). *Preschool programs for the disadvantaged*. Baltimore: Johns Hopkins University Press, 1972.

Taylor, B. S. *A child goes forth*. Provo, Utah: Brigham Young University Press, 1975.

Werner, P. H., and Burton, E. C. *Learning through movement: teaching cognitive content through physical activities*. St. Louis, Mo.: Mosby, 1979.

Chapter 15

Evaluating Intellectual Growth

T. S. Eliot believes that time present is composed of time past, and time future is composed of time present plus time past. Similar to T. S. Eliot's ideas of achievement are those of assessment from a cognitive-developmental perspective. Common to both are the idea of additivity of experiences and demonstration of their attainment. Because present levels of cognitive development are rooted in the bedrock of past attainment, the present and past levels of intellectual achievement provide a base for future levels. Within this developmental perspective, evolution of intellectual attainment becomes an assessment of cognitive processes that rest on the child's attaining and knowing about self, social conventions, including individuals, objects and object-relations. Further, assessment of the child's intellectual processes rests on: (1) the principles of cognitive-developmental theory, (2) their applications to instruction, and (3) the design of instructional environments. In other words, evaluation methodology used in assessing cognitive processes from a cognitive-developmental perspective must be consistent with its constructs. Thus, the major determinants of the *whats* of assessment (methodological problem specifications), the *hows* of evaluation (strategies), and related instrumentation are not intuitively determined by the teacher or paraprofessional but by the cognitive-developmental world view. There must be consistency between what is done and what is evaluated in cognitive-developmental programs for young children.

This chapter is organized into several sections: (1) the rationale for our approach to evaluation of children, (2) the clinical method of evaluation, and (3) the use of the clinical method in cognitive-developmental assessment.

RATIONALE FOR COGNITIVE-DEVELOPMENTAL EVALUATION

Working with and evaluating young children are linked together within the cognitive-developmental world view. The main ideas of evaluation that show interrelationships among the principles of cognitive-developmental theory are: focus in evaluating, equilibration, developmental changes, stimulus materials, and situational and instructional generality.

Cognitive Content

The focus of evaluation is to identify the cognitive schemata that children show at various intellectual levels. This mode of assessment is to use observations and questions based on children's actions and reactions with objects (physical knowledge), social conventions (social knowledge), and, more important, object-relations (logicomathematical knowledge). Assessing children's thinking is the key. The correctness of the child's answers in an interview is not important. This may be difficult to understand, because we have a school system that is based on a hierarchy of correct answers to questions over time. Remember that evaluation focuses on determining the level of evolving thought structures, not on whether the child is able to solve a conservation of mass problem. Correct and incorrect answers are equally important; they indicate the child's cognitive schemata. We are not saying that standardized tests, developmental and diagnostic instruments, or teacher-prepared tests (given largely in primary grade programs) are wrong and should be eliminated. Their purpose is different—they compare the child's level of achievement with a normed group on the basis of

---

Box 15-1   *Yes, Virginia (and Virgil), There Is a . . . Process (and Product) Evaluation of Intellectual Growth*

Programs based on cognitive-developmental theory, contrary to some beliefs, intuitions, or criticisms, can be evaluated. Commercial tests for young children are readily available in each of the four knowledge domains in cognitivist programs. A review of these commercial tests is available in Burros (1970).*

In addition to the commercial tests, you can easily develop your own. The development and use of observation cards was explained in Chapter 14. Also, try behavioral checklists, conservation fluency, and videotaping as other examples of process and product measures.

To create a behavioral checklist, identify a list of competencies for each of the knowledge domains. As the child shows the competence, place a check alongside it and describe the setting (for example, doll corner/pretend play) in which it is shown. To describe a child's conservation fluency develop three columns: (a) shows conservation, (b) sometimes shows conservation, and (c) does not yet show conservation. Check one of the columns as the child performs for each conservation problem.

You can also videotape 10-minute segments of the child's actions (for example, a dramatic play episode). Then view the tape and score it on a number of dimensions, such as number of pretend actions with objects, frequency of language usage, types of objects played with.

Evaluation of the children's competencies documents the effectiveness of your cognitive-developmental program. The strategies for evaluation are unlimited.

*Burros, O. K. (Ed.). *The seventh mental measurements yearbook*. Highland Park, N.J.: Gryphon Press, 1970.

Right and wrong answers are equally important.

whether the answers are right or wrong. Recall Piaget's view of intelligence versus the concept of IQ. Intelligence is a set of structures in operation that show the qualitative and quantitative degree of thought employed by the child as she or he acts on and reacts to the environment; the IQ measure indicates whether the youngster is below, equal to, or above a normed group in specific skill achievement. Thus, for cognitivists, the observation and interview are used in evaluation to identify and determine the individual's level of thinking using correct as well as incorrect responses. It is not to determine the child's standing using a quantitative figure based on group-normed comparisons. More explanation of evaluative observation and interviews and of how this type of assessment works in cognitive-developmental programs is given elsewhere in this chapter.

Cognitive Processes

The concept of equilibration is related to the purpose of assessment. The primary focus of evaluation rests on determining degrees of cognitive functioning, so the degree of equilibration and range of application are assigned primary status. Whether the child shows certain motor actions, specific perceptual skills, or language labeling is not of primary concern.

Equilibration processes are self-regulating mechanisms that explain why and how youngsters move (or do not move) from one level of equilibrium to another. By observing and interviewing youngsters, the adult determines the children's developmental level as they respond to cognitive discrepancies by using their processes of equilibration. Placing children in situations that demand equilibration determines whether they can resolve conflict by logical methods and whether they have the capacity to integrate two or more cognitive schemata to solve the problem. As they resolve the conflict through coordination of cognitive schemata, equilibration occurs. Children show adaptive actions and thus their cognitive level of attainment.

For example, Chuck is presented with our conservation of number problem. The rows of four objects are parallel; all of the elements in the rows are opposite one another. As the adult interviews Chuck about the equality in the number of objects between the rows, he must make finer and finer distinctions in the equilibration as he spreads out the four objects in one of the rows so that they extend over a greater distance than those in the other row. The conflict between number and length requires that Chuck invent a legitimate method of cognizing this discrepancy, which is central to this activity. As Chuck invents his solution, he must coordinate his thought structures. Chuck is aware that although the endpoints of one row of objects go beyond those of the other row, there is more space between the objects in that row relative to the other row. Here, he compensates for length by equality of number. We note that Chuck has attained the cognitive level of the acquisition of number conservation. To determine that it is rigorous (permanent) number conservation, we must repeatedly observe Chuck solving the number conservation problem using different types and different quantities of objects. Thus, by observing, interviewing, inducing conflict, and noting equilibration to a number of situations, we determine the stability of and consequently the level of children's cognitive thought.

If a child fails to invent logical methods and coordinate two or more cognitive schemata to solve this problem, we know that the child has not attained the level of thinking that shows conservation of number; his or her equilibration process is not stable enough to distinguish between the schemata of length and number, recognize the conflict, and resolve it.

Equilibration processes are crucial to evaluation, for they show whether children can invent strategies through internal-cognitive regulation, imitation, and activity to solve problems involving compromises such as those in conservation of number or mass. Equilibration relative to evaluation means "that you get out of an encounter exactly what you put into it; and active engagement with data, involving a certain intracognitive [conflict] . . . is what leads to stable and quasi-permanent structural change" (Flavell, 1963, p. 418).

Criteria for Change

The concept of developmental changes also is a part of the rationale for evaluating the child's achievements. Seeing developmental changes that occur in cognitive functioning over time is important in working with young children. Determining exactly what is a developmental change has a great deal of importance in cognitive-developmental theory.

Developmental changes in cognitive functioning show reversibility and culminate in greater intellectual organization. The child's cognitive growth history is a record of previous evaluation. Increasing capacities to show reversibility and organizational functioning suggest that the child has acquired a greater propensity for equilibration and for developing more complex thought structures, the functioning of which is relatively independent of perceptual discrepancies in the environment.

For example, Mark is evaluated at the beginning of school and his level of thought structures can be determined by conservation of mass problems. The results of this evaluation over a number of instances show that Mark does not yet possess cognitive schemata for attaining rigorous conservation of mass. However, with increased opportunities for acting and reacting to differing amounts of mass, Mark achieves reversibility and greater cognitive organization and can solve environmental discrepancies between mass and length. In realizing that length is a superficial dimension, Mark attains the concept of rigorous conservation of mass. Repeated trials using different types and sizes of objects demonstrate Mark's developmental change.

Mark's developmental change had two underlying characteristics. First, his cognitive system showed increasingly structured actions relative to conservation of mass over time. Second, his cognitive system moved through a series of changes that resulted in a permanent modification in his structures and their operations. The cognitive changes in reversibility and organizational functioning show movement from preexisting to defined or permanent structures and operations and are regarded as valid developmental changes. When you evaluate the child's level of thinking, developmental changes are significant milestones in the growth of defined cognitive structures. Developmental changes should be a part of their cognitive growth record.

Generality

We mentioned object, situational, and instructional generality in our discussion of equilibration. Determining whether the child attains permanent number conservation depends on repeated assessments using different types and quantities of objects—that is, on the child's ability to generalize from one problem to another.

The purpose of evaluation is to note the child's level of thinking over time and to show a progression to greater levels of abstraction. Unlike behaviorists, cognitivists are not concerned with evaluation of children

merely to determine the accuracy of their responses; we assess thought processes and do not assume that these are basically identical in all pre-operational children from two through seven years of age. Our focus is developmental change and, consequently, evaluation in one or two specific testing situations does not suffice.

Evaluation thus determines developmental changes and progression of thinking through object, situational, and instructional generality, not specificity. In our number conservation example, not only should the objects be varied, but the number of objects used per row also should be changed. In addition, the situation used in the evaluation must vary. We can change the array into circles; we can also clump the objects together in a pile.

In addition to changing the types and number of objects, the instructional strategies for the problem can be modified. In number conservation, the instructional strategy, for example, "Is there the same number of objects in this row as in that row?" can be used. To achieve degrees of instructional generality, the initial question can be changed while continuing to focus on assessing number conservation. Examples are: "Is there a greater number of objects in one array than the other?" "Is there a lesser number of objects in one array than the other?" "Is the number of objects in this array greater than, lesser than, or the same as in the other array?"

Object, situational, and instructional generality in assessment provide a valid picture of the levels of logical thinking and developmental changes in young children. This rationale suggests that evaluation in cognitive-developmental theory focuses on levels of thought processes within the same mental operation across object, situational, and instructional generalities. The child in the preoperational stage shows (or does not show) logical thought relative to number, mass, and area conservation or subject-matter problems, regardless of the objects, situations, and instructional strategies used in the evaluation.

THE CLINICAL METHOD AS A PROCEDURE FOR EVALUATION

The clinical method of evaluating consists of observing and interviewing the child. We will describe this method and its major characteristics.

In providing a broad description of the clinical method, Ginsburg and Opper (1979) note:

> *By the use of suitable probing questions that attempt to reveal the underlying reasons for a child's initial statement or judgment, by presenting countersuggestions to the child's arguments, and by providing conflict situations, the teacher who employs this method can discover a great deal about the child's cognitive functioning [p. 113].*

In addition, the clinical method of evaluating gives the child the freedom to move from thought sequence to thought sequence in a natural manner that is in accord with his or her level of thinking. The problems posed through the countersuggestions and cognitive discrepancies become highly meaningful to the child. The clinical method provides an ongoing and connected set of responses that are directly interpretable and highly focused on intellectual functioning. These ongoing series of responses result as the adult follows the child's line of thinking step by step. The value of the clinical method lies in *tracking* the child's thoughts. The adult moves with the child's logic to observe the variety of intellectual processes the child uses.

Characteristics of the Clinical Method

The clinical method has four characteristics: (1) adults' questions are based on concrete objects, (2) children's responses to the questions are made in conjunction with objects, (3) contradictions are presented to children, and (4) adults' statements and questions must be flexible (Ginsburg & Opper, 1979). We will explain each of these characteristics.

Use of Concrete Objects for Questions   The questions used in assessing young children in the clinical method are based on concrete objects placed before the child. Children act on and react to objects to solve the problems posed. As youngsters become involved with the materials using senses of seeing, touching, hearing, and smelling, they have greater opportunities of solving the problem; they are able to develop. Remember that direct experience with objects is one of the factors that contribute to growth and provide a medium for the preoperational child to develop schemata to operationalize and solve the problem. Associating the adult's questions directly with the objects used in the problem produces a more valid assessment.

For example, you ask "Is there the same amount of grass for this cow in pasture one to eat as for that cow in pasture two?" The associated objects would be two miniature cows, two green sheets of construction paper representing grassy pastures, and two blocks representing miniature barns. However, these objects are used with the question about equality in amounts of grass among cows and pastures with barns. Here, there is a direct and observable parallel between the adult's questions and the objects used by the child in helping him or her to answer the questions and solve the problems.

The clinical method of assessment is also used in subject matter (rather than conservation) areas to evaluate levels of thinking. In assessing for the subject matter concept of matching objects, for example, you ask the child to match pictures of five different farm animals to another set of pictures showing five farm animals, four of which are the same. The youngster finds a pair for each of the pictures except the last items in the set (because they are not the same animals).

In the clinical method, assessment questions are based on the use of concrete objects.

Use of Objects for Responses   The second characteristic of the clinical method is that the child's responses to your questions are also made in conjunction with objects. Having the child solve the problem without objects would require a heavy reliance on verbal answers. The Piagetian perspective, however, emphasizes that cognition arises before language and that children may possess the necessary thought structures to solve the problem but lack the language to express their solutions abstractly. Thus, objects are better than language in assisting the child's thought processes. More specifically, the child's manipulations of the objects while he or she tries to solve a problem are better indicators of the child's level of thought processes than abstract verbal statements. This approach produces a valid assessment of mental processes.

The thought processes of the preoperational child are still primitive. Accordingly, thought processes that operate effectively at this relatively primitive level occur while his or her language system is still poorly developed. Thus, the clinical method requires the child to use objects and sensory movements rather than verbal statements to solve problems. By using questions, observing the child's sensory movements made with the objects, and listening to what the child says as he or she acts and reacts to the objects and problems, we are better able to recognize that child's current levels of thinking and determine developmental and organizational thought structures and changes.

As children think about and answer the adult's questions, the objects enable them to find cognitive solutions at their level of thinking. In fact, the adult guides children to use the objects in accord with the problem. For example, in the conservation of area problem, you ask about the amounts of grass each cow has to eat in the pastures. In guiding the child in setting up the objects for the problem, you can say, "These are 'pretend' areas of grass. Place each cow in the grass so that it can eat." With this introduction, you guide the child in manipulating and thereby representing the objects in a cognitive manner. In addition, this ensures that the youngster's responses to your questions or statements are made in conjunction with acting on and conceptualizing objects.

Use a similar introduction with subject matter problems. In the problem of matching farm animals, ask the children to pick up the initial set of five animals and describe each of them. Hand the second set of five pictures to the children and have them describe these as well. Then have the children spread out the pictures on the table (make sure that each picture is kept within its respective set). Now ask the youngsters if they can match the second with the first set of pictures. The youngsters thus have the opportunity to respond to your questions in conjunction with acting on and reacting to the objects.

Use of Contradiction   The third characteristic of the clinical method for assessing thinking processes is presenting contradictions or discrepancies to children. This means questioning and making statements to them based on their responses. This is also called using countersuggestions or counterarguments. According to Ginsburg and Opper (1979), it involves "presenting the child with a point of view that contradicts his own, and asking him what he thinks of the opposing view" (p. 114). In our conservation of area problem, the child must first affirm that the two cows have the same amount of grass to eat in the pastures with the barns placed side by side. Given the child's affirmation, you need to pursue her or his line of thinking or reasoning to determine the permanence of her or his concept of conservation of area. You provide a counterargument to test further her or his level of cognitive processes. An example of a discrepancy is to move the two barns apart and repeat the same question. A second but related reason for providing a counterargument is to ensure that the child is not simply giving the answer that she or he believes the adult wants to hear. Distinguishing between children's answers based on what they think you want to hear and those based on their level of thinking is basic to the clinical method. Only by determining children's real answers to the problems can you assess effectively their cognitive progress and developmental changes.

You can ask the child to alter or modify the problem. For instance, you can ask him or her to spread the barns apart in one of the pastures. This provides a further opportunity to assess the child's authenticity of thinking. After he or she has separated the barns in one pasture, again ask the child whether the cows have equal amounts of grass to eat. The youngster who possesses some stability of cognitive processes in number conservation indicates both cows still have the same amount of grass to eat. Of

The clinical method of evaluation also involves the use of open-ended questions to allow a wide range of responses.

course, additional conservation of area problems should be given to test object, situational, and instructional generality. However, if the youngster says that the cows do not have the same amount of grass to eat, then he or she does not possess stable cognitive structures for area conservation.

The same idea of cognitive discrepancy or countersuggestion can be used with subject matter problems. In the example of matching farm animals, for instance, the countersuggestion is built into the problem. As the child matches the four animals in each set that pair exactly with one another, he or she comes across the fifth picture in one set and the dissimilar last picture in the other. For example, as a countersuggestion, you can ask, "Is this a picture of the same animal as that one?" The child affirms or disaffirms the countersuggestion and you further ask, "Why?" The child now has the opportunity to use objects to respond to your question.

Use of Open Questions The chain of questioning and responding evolves as the adult interprets and responds to the child's answers. For example, sound questions that are open-ended can begin with "why" or "how" and provide the youngsters with ample room for responding. The adult and child become partners. The adult initially leads in setting up the problem and providing the objects. However, from that point on the child's responses shape further questions. The adult provides guidance and cues rather than direction. Asking preestablished questions would not be sufficiently flexible.

Ginsburg and Opper (1969) compare the clinical method to Socratic questioning: "In a group or individual setting, a skillful teacher does not simply ask questions which require the recall of correct answers; even more importantly, he asks provocative questions that stimulate the pupil to think, and to become aware of underlying causes" (p. 236). Open-ended questions and the Socratic method are both based on *why* and other probing questions to situations. "In addition, teachers need to adapt the level and pace of their questions to the understanding of pupils; teachers need to be able to listen and observe in order to understand the meaning of a response" (Ginsburg & Opper, 1969, p. 236).

Flexibility means asking questions based on the child's lines of thinking and being sensitive in your interpretation of the child's replies.

Using the Clinical Method

You can see the importance of assessing the child's level of cognitive structures. Because the clinical method requires that questions emerge from the interview, there can be no standardization of questions or content. Nonetheless, there are three levels of assessment that are broad guidelines to assist you in understanding and using this tool. These levels at minimum show how you can initiate the clinical interviewing cycle. Although explained as separate and ordered units, the levels actually overlap. They serve only as guidelines to help you understand what this tool is and how it can be used. They are observation, challenge by questioning, and contradictory situations and use of "why" and other probing questions. We will explain each of these.

Observation   In observation, the overriding objective is to have the child act on and react to the objects used in the problem situations. The materials are laid out in front of the child, who is encouraged to manipulate them to understand what they are and how they are used. The adult does not guide but simply watches the child. You observe what the child does with the objects and how he or she uses them. For example, are the objects stacked, rolled, or pounded? Are they used as pretend garages or as monsters? You also take careful note of what the youngster says as he or she moves and uses the objects. The child's responses are behavioral data that provide you with cues on what to say and when to begin the questioning process.

Questioning   After youngsters have a chance to familiarize themselves with objects, guide them to set up the problem situations. Then challenging by question begins. For the conservation of number problem, the first question focuses on determining whether the child understands equality when the arrays are of equal length. In this manner, the child works from the known to the unknown, from the concrete to the abstract, and from the simple to the complex. After the child responds to the initial question by saying, "Yes (or no), they are (are not) the same," you might ask, "*Why* are (or aren't) they the same?" Or, "Show me that they are (or aren't) the same." In almost all instances, children acknowledge that there are the same number of objects in the equal-length arrays. If they do, you can proceed to level three of the clinical method.

Contradictory Situations   At level three, cognitive discrepancy is presented and probing questions are used to further reveal the youngster's line of reasoning. The arrays in the conservation problems are modified. The questions that focus on equality are again used. As the child conceptualizes the new arrays and understands the question, he or she states either that they still are or are not equal in number. Once again, you ask "Why?" A whole series of additional questions and associated changes in the arrays can evolve. The child who has attained levels of cognitive thinking to solve the conservation of number problem resists the countersuggestions presented in level three. The youngster moves beyond the cognitive discrepancy by establishing equality of number in new transformational arrays. If

---

Box 15-2   Evaluating Children's Make-Believe—(But, How Can We?— It Is Play.)

Assessing a youngster's quality and quantity of make-believe is not only possible—it is a must in any cognitive-interactionist classroom. By evaluating make-believe, you get an idea of the qualitative level of the youngster's pretend abilities, and how the growth of his or her representational thinking is progressing. You also understand whether children have developed make-believe schemata for representing objects, actions, and situations. Assessing the nature and quantity of make-believe should not be ignored or left to chance, because it too is a necessary component in the youngster's growth of cognitive development.

First, to evaluate this concept, you can ask children to show a reality response and then a fantasy response to the same question. For example, you might say that you are going to ask them to do some things and that you do not want them to use words. Ask them, "Please use your body to show how you (or others) would normally do this." Say, "Show how a person_____(sweeps the floor, opens a door, peels a banana, takes off a sweater)." After they have made reality responses, ask the youngsters to use their bodies to show how a make-believe giant (or tooth fairy, or other fictional characters) would do that. Repeat the examples and see whether there is a difference between children's responses. Repeat and prompt as necessary to achieve differences.

Second, in evaluating make-believe, you might ask children to show how they feel by using words and body actions to the following emotion traits. For example, say, "Pretend you are_____(happy, worried, sad, excited)." When you observe the children's responses to these examples and other "Pretend you are_____" statements, make sure that you accept each of their responses and reassure them that it is okay to be—and to show that they are—*worried, sad,* or *excited.*

Evaluating the quality and quantity of make-believe provides an additional insight into the growth of symbol and cognitive development. For this assessment, you do not need any written tests or instructor's manuals—and there is nothing to correct. You simply need some situations and actions and a record of how the young child performed on each question.

the youngster does not resist the countersuggestion, you can pursue his or her line of reasoning by going back to level two or remaining at level three with continued questioning at the same level of difficulty. In addition, you can try different objects to determine whether the child has attained the levels of reasoning to solve the discrepancy in some form at level three. The adult-questioning–child-responding chain can be continued in any direction you desire in order to reveal this child's levels of thought processes. Introducing cognitive discrepancies through transformations of objects is used in subject matter areas as well as for mental operations such as classification and seriation.

The clinical method is an effective tool for adults to use in working with young children. The fact that questions based on objects unfold as the child responds to them makes the clinical method an ideal form of evaluation in cognitive-developmental programs.

SUMMARY

This chapter provided an overview of assessment in cognitive-developmental programs, and explained the uses of the clinical method for assessing the young child's thinking. Evaluating the child's levels of thinking and developmental changes is of primary concern. Comparisons are made over time between assessments of the individual child. The focus of evaluation is to identify the individual's level of thinking rather than to draw comparisons to normed groups.

The clinical method has four characteristics: (1) the adult's questions are based on concrete objects, (2) the child's responses are made in conjunction with objects, (3) contradictions are presented to the child, and (4) the adult's statements and questions to the child are flexible. The three levels that serve as evaluation guidelines are observation, challenge by questioning, and contradictory situations. The clinical method is an effective procedure to assess the youngster's level of thinking. Its flexibility permits you to determine the stability and authenticity of children's thought structures.

Review Questions

1. Explain why the clinical method does not use only language to evaluate children.
2. State the purpose of the clinical method and tell why it is consistent with cognitive-developmental theory.
3. Define the concept of *flexibility* as one of the characteristics of the clinical method and give two examples of this attribute.
4. Describe four differences between level two, challenge by questioning, and level three, contradictory situations.
5. Discuss the adult-questioning–child-answering

cycle and give two examples of this sequence in a conservation of number problem.

6. Distinguish between the purposes of standardized tests and the cognitive-developmental assessment of children in the preoperational stage.

Suggested Activities

1. Use the clinical method and the same conservation of number problem with two 5-year-old children. In one instance use objects, and in the other do not use objects. Compare the differences between the children's approach to solving the problem.
2. Observe a preoperational youngster as he or she manipulates objects and write down what he or she does and says.
3. Use "Why?" and "How do you know?" questions to assess two preschoolers of the same age for the subject matter concept of matching. Record their levels of thinking.
4. Try assessing two young children's understanding of time and, particularly, the concepts of *before* and *after*.
5. Use pennies and then checkers as objects to evaluate a 6-year-old's number conservation using the clinical method. Note whether different stimuli make a difference in the child's ability to conserve.

Suggested Readings

Almy, M. *Logical thinking in the second grade*. New York: Teachers College Press, 1970.

Bloom, D. S. *Stability and change in human characteristics*. New York: Wiley, 1964.

Cohen, D. H., and Stern, V. *Observing and recording the behavior of young children*. New York: Teachers College Press, 1974.

Deasey, D. *Education under six*. London: Croom Helm, 1978.

Gordon, I. J. (Ed.). *Early childhood education*. Chicago: University of Chicago Press, 1972.

Hechinger, F. M. (Ed.). *Pre-school education today*. New York: Doubleday, 1966.

Maccoby, E., and Zellner, M. *Experiments in primary education: aspects of Project Follow-Through*. New York: Harcourt Brace Jovanovich, 1970.

Moore, S. G., and Kilmer, S. *Contemporary preschool education: a program for young children*. New York: Wiley, 1973.

Wohlwill, J. F. Methodology and research strategy in the study of developmental change. In Goulet, L. R., and Baltes, P. B. (Eds.), *Life-span developmental psychology: theory and research*. New York: Academic Press, 1970.

Yawkey, T. D. (Ed.). *The self-concept of the young child*. Provo, Utah: Brigham Young University, 1980.

PART FOUR

EPILOG

*I*n Chapters 5 through 15 you examined in detail both operant and cognitive-developmental theory and their application to early childhood education. This was a lot of material, covering both the abstract and the concrete aspects of program development. In Chapter 16, we provide some of the highlights of the history and the future of early childhood education.

As old as humankind, early childhood education is today an exciting and expanding field. More and more children are entering formal early-education and child-care programs. This increase is reflected both in absolute numbers and in the relative percentages of the total population of the age groups involved. In part, this expansion reflects major societal and economic changes; in part it reflects an increasing awareness of the importance of the early childhood period for future growth and development. Also, the increases are a reflection of changes in the definition of early childhood education itself. As we have presented it, early childhood education involves any programmatic effort in which an agent, operating within a context, uses some means, according to some plan, to bring about desired changes in behavior of infants and young children. Within this broad definitional framework, there are many planned early childhood education programs; many more can exist if we are creative enough to design and evaluate them and if the broad determinants of early childhood programs and policies are right.

Thus the form and content of early childhood programs, as we know them now, are not permanent. Both are subject to change. The change may be gradual and evolutionary, or, if the circumstances are right, it may be rapid and revolutionary.

It is hard to predict what the changes will be with any exactness. But, as we saw in the early chapters of this book, the changes that do occur will be a result of decision making at many levels. A study of the progress of the kindergarten, preschool, day-care, compensatory-education, and family-based program movement provides us with clear indications of how macro-environmental cultural patterns expressed through the economic, political, and social systems influence such decisions. These large-scale factors particularly influence the resources available for early childhood programs and the values that are expressed in their design, delivery, and content. Within the United States and other western developed countries, the macrosystem determinants of decision making have led to a highly diversified array of early childhood services, operating side by side and at times in competition with each other.

The openness of the resources and value systems also has led to diversity of the content of early childhood education programs.

In the United States particularly, a great number of content variations has emerged. The alternative curriculum models that have been developed are based on decisions about the meaning of theory and research as interpreted by each group developing models. Most of the current models can be sorted into one of the three major streams of educational thought: the maturationist-socialization, cultural-training or behaviorist, or the cognitive-developmental stream. We have emphasized the behaviorist and cognitive-developmental approaches in this book, but all three are respected positions. Neither research nor practical experience points to one best model or approach for all children in all situations.

Indeed, what is important about the models approach is not the strength of our beliefs, but rather our willingness to test beliefs through empirical research, evaluation, and systematic analysis of our own experience.

Early Childhood Education Today and Tomorrow

*T*he central theme of this book has been the notion that real people in real situations base their day-to-day early childhood education decisions on a theory. Our decision-making process is greatly improved if our theory base is consistent and coherent, and if the practices we derive from that base are subjected to continuous evaluation. What each of us does in the classroom says a great deal about what we believe about development and learning. Conversely, what we say about development and learning should influence what we do in the classroom. What you do will reflect what you believe.

Table 16-1 reviews the essential assumptions about children, learning, and development of the three major theoretical perspectives. Rather than reviewing the central principles and tenets of each position, we thought we might take a more personal approach. In the next section, we further introduce ourselves to you.

A CONVERSATION

One evening, we were sitting around the fire, having just reviewed each other's chapters. Our conversation went something like this.

Peters: Tom, what is the primary goal of your program?

Yawkey: The primary goal, pure and simple, is intellectual development. However, remember that in Piagetian thought social, motor, and other developmental areas are subsets of the cognitive domain.

Peters: Jack, how would you answer that?

Neisworth: Easy. The primary goal of a behavioral preschool is repertoire expansion, especially the repertoire of skills that produce self-management and accomplishment. Further, the goal is to teach means-and-ends relationships in self- and social behavior. Children must learn how

Table 16-1   Assumptions of Three Theories *

	Cognitive-Developmental Theory	Cultural-Training or Behaviorist Theory	Maturationist-Socialization Theory
Children	Active	Active and passive	Adaptive
	Qualitatively unlike adults in thought	Qualitatively like adults in learning	Qualitatively unlike adults in emotions
Development	Occurs in surges	Quantitative—gradual repertoire expansion	Occurs in stages as a result of conflict resolution
	Predetermined biological sequence modified by experience	Reciprocal operation of environment and child	Predetermined genetically programmed sequence in a supporting environment
Learning	Motivation from within	Motivation from the environment	Internal and external based on conflict
	Based on sensory education	Based on language, overt and covert verbal labeling	Based on social experience
	Stage-dependent	Cumulative and continuous	Progressive stages that may be reversible in adverse circumstances
	Based on massive general type of experience	Based on specific training	Natural unfolding
	Process approach	Product approach	Individual expression/process
	Irreversible (invariant)	Reversible	Reversible under adverse circumstances—premature demands may stagnate development

* Adapted from Verma and Peters (1975) and Elliott (1972).

their behavior influences their attainments and problems and how their behavior builds or weakens cooperation, friendships, and other social relationships.

One final point. An important goal is to use *means* that are themselves *ends*. By use of positive social reinforcement, we not only use means that shape specific child behaviors, but also model strategies that we wish the child to imitate.

Peters: Jack, Tom, if you had to pick one thing that would distinguish a behavioral or cognitive-developmental program from all others, what would it be? What would an observer look for as the hallmark of your program?

Neisworth: Well, Don, the most salient feature of a behavioral program is its emphasis on arranging and assessing antecedents and consequences of child behavior. By engineering the environmental circumstances, behaviorists often are able to shape behavior toward preselected objectives. Using data-based feedback, adjustments in prompts, and reinforcers or punishments, they can create powerful arrangements to build developmentally progressive behavior. Behavioral programs may differ topographically—they often look different from one another or use different materials and activities—but they are functionally the same. All must collect data on the influence of what comes before and after behavior. Data-based contingency management is the hallmark, and there is usually some system for continual data collection. Moreover, the staff have an obvious concern for delivering immediate and systematic reinforcement, either verbally or in a more tangible form.

Yawkey: I think the hallmark of a cognitive-developmental program lies in its integration. Integration is a Piagetian principle of working through a series of "holisms" for the development of the whole child while ensuring that the needs of individual children are met. For example, in our program for preschoolers in Bethlehem, Pennsylvania (Yawkey, 1982, 1984; Yawkey & Diantoniis, 1984), different kinds of activities are designed for different knowledge areas and the staff use their skills to guide the development of the whole child. We provide opportunities for dramatic play and communication among children, not to teach a single skill or group of skills, but rather to allow children to explore experience and to provide an opportunity for the staff to guide and extend experiences to incorporate social knowledge, physical knowledge, and representation. Assuming the children's interaction centers on their doll's birthday, the teacher might observe the children and extend the learning opportunity by asking, "How many candles should we put on Dolly's birthday cake?" The teacher, by providing a small cardboard box for the children to use as a cake, provides additional representational opportunities for extending the children's thoughts and actions. Finally, as the children's interest wanes, the teacher might redirect their attention to physical attributes and relationships—the round eyes of the doll and the correspondence of children and candles. "Are there the same number of candles as there are children? How can we tell?"

This integration for the whole child is not always easy to observe. The experienced teacher in the naturally flowing momentum of the cognitive-developmental program makes the teaching strategies subtle. When it is done well, it is beautiful. You need to watch closely to see how the teacher observes each child, gauges his or her interests, and responds to those interests with just the right question for a child's developmental level. The teacher and the child work together to produce an integrated learning experience.

Peters: You both mention individualization and consider it an important issue for early childhood education. From your perspective, what is the heart of individualization? How would we see it in your classroom?

Yawkey: Well, first, let me say what individualization is not. From a cognitive-developmental perspective, individualization does not mean giving the child repeated exposure to the same or a slightly less difficult task to enable him or her to perform the criterion, nor does it mean having the children practice the task until they learn how to perform it to the satisfaction of some arbitrary adult-derived criterion. Nor, for that matter, does it have to do with having all children of the same age perform conservation of number at the same chronological age.

Individualization for a cognitive-developmentalist is a process involving determining a particular child's level of thinking, attempting to understand the child's thought processes, and providing opportunities that guide and challenge that child at his or her level. In this sense, individualization relates to the question you asked earlier on the hallmark of the cognitivist program. The teacher observes the children's actions and reactions to objects and events and then, through questions or actions, helps to increase the meaningfulness for the child. The teacher looks on children's answers to questions, whether correct or incorrect, as important indicators of the children's level of thinking—critical keys in planning the *match* between the children's thinking and the next activity. Because knowledge and understanding for the child are constructed by the child her- or himself, the *process* of knowledge building, rather than the *product*, is what is important.

You could simply put out lots of materials and equipment, provide lots of opportunities for manipulation, and leave the individualization up to the children. However, guidance is necessary, and guidance requires astute observation, inferences about the child's thinking, and the creation of opportunities for developmentally enhancing choices. When working with groups of children, the teacher must select activities that meet the different levels of the children involved.

Peters: Tom's original comments sounded like a bit of a poke at behavioral approaches to individualization. Within the behaviorist tradition, is individualization simply different levels of practice or different pacing of instruction?

Neisworth: No. Within behavioral programs, every child is treated as an individual with specific and personal objectives, "custom-fitted" prompts and consequences, and single-subject evaluation. Individualization requires tailoring objectives, materials, and techniques to each child, based on individual data. For the behaviorist, the unit of importance *is* the individual case. How the group is doing is of interest to the teacher, but the group is made up of individuals. Each child must have an individual educational/development plan and evaluation. The whole point is to make individualization systematic rather than accidental.

Peters: It is nice to have individualized programs, but it is group management that new teachers seem particularly concerned about. Sometimes, this is called *discipline*. Jack, what are the foremost concerns in group management and discipline from your perspective?

Neisworth: Discipline should be positive whenever possible. Prosocial behavior is shaped and reinforced, whereas antisocial behavior is treated with nonrewarding consequences. By accentuating the positive, the need to punish becomes diminished and aversive tactics are rarely used—and indeed are more effective because of their infrequency. When punishment must be employed, the teacher should precede the aversive consequences with a consistent signal such as a countdown. Such actions become a conditioned preaversive stimulus that is in itself effective for reducing the unwanted behavior. This is a positive, mild, and socially appropriate way to discipline.

Prominent features of a behavioral approach to child discipline include these qualities:

- It accentuates the positive through differential reinforcement
- It is consistent
- It is preemptive: it includes a prepared environment where prompts and activities are prearranged to maximize acceptable behavior and constructively engage each child
- It is premeditated: what is OK or not OK and the consequences of each are laid out and understood as part of the planned environment

Peters: Tom, how about group management and discipline?

Yawkey: As a former day-care, nursery-school, and kindergarten teacher, I know the concerns that new teachers have about discipline and group management. Cognitive-developmental theory has not examined group management. However, group management and discipline fall primarily in the domain of social knowledge—the area that is arbitrary and external to the child. The teacher models, provides rationales, and presents cause-and-effect statements for the child.

Some traditional group-management procedures are more appropriate than others. Because one of the program's goals is to help the child to decenter, discipline procedures that honestly acknowledge feelings are useful. It is perfectly acceptable for the teacher *or* the child to say, "I feel tired . . . or sad . . . or mad . . . or happy today." Such statements promote trust, confidence, and equality while making the child aware of others' points of view. Similarly, arbitration procedures enhance the child's understanding of alternative perspectives, cause-and-effect relationships, and reciprocity. Finally, strategies that challenge children to make decisions and live with the consequences help children to develop their own rules of discipline and conduct.

Peters: Jack, we know you are an enthusiastic behaviorist, but is there some aspect of theory or practice that would recommend to teachers and parents a behavioral program above and beyond other approaches?

Neisworth: Yes. More than any other quality, a behavioral approach is preferable to other approaches because it is a natural-science approach, in which empirical findings are accumulated to permit general principles to be inferred. Behavior theory does not change during each generation, or get thrown away when a new theory bandwagon passes by. The behavioral approach is built on scientifically verifiable functional relationships between child behavior and the environment. Our information is not as grand and exciting as that of some other schools of thought, but it is solid and encourages steady development. It is consistent, systematic, and fully accountable; it is subject to disproof and self-correction—and that, after all, is science.

Peters: How about you Tom? Is there some aspect of cognitive-developmental theory or practice that recommends it above others?

Yawkey: It is the holistic nature of the theory and its naturalness that recommend it above all others. The theory places young children's natural play in a central position. It is fairly easy for teachers and parents to use this approach as a vehicle for maximizing children's potential for representational and logical thinking.

Peters: Does either of you think it takes a particular kind of person to be a good teacher in your program?

Neisworth: It is not easy to be a good teacher in any program. A good behavioral teacher can be shaped by the program situation. How easy it is for the teacher will depend on his or her teaching repertoire and the prevailing training and maintenance contingencies in the program.

Yawkey: To be a good cognitive-developmental teacher requires a thorough knowledge of Piagetian theory. The teacher should have practiced the applications of this theoretical approach under the guidance and supervision of a master teacher in a preschool setting. The teacher must develop expertise in the clinical method—observing and adapting to each child's cognitive level. Immersion in theory and participation in skilled practice will provide the teacher with the essential deep respect for the children with whom he or she works. The cognitive-developmental teacher also needs patience—the willingness to wait and watch as the child's thought processes become challenged and evolve. Patience also means believing that the processes are far more important than the products. It may take tomorrow or a hundred tomorrows for developmental experiences to culminate in meaningful cognitive growth.

Patience and understanding are difficult for a "new" teacher. We tend to expect children to understand concepts when they are first introduced rather than waiting, observing, and guiding.

A day-care director under whom I once worked used to make well-intended statements about new teachers. One day, three of us were guiding the children's experiences and activities. After observing us and the children's responses, the director shared something special and meaningful with us. She said that it had taken her 22 years of teaching experience to arrive at the effective procedure we had used that morning—and we had learned it by applying theory and some practice! The point I am making is that a good theory (and cognitive-developmental theory is the best) will serve a teacher well in the first year or the twenty-second year of teaching. That's why we've written this book, isn't it?

Peters: You are right, Tom. Now, I'd like to change the pace and ask a more speculative question. In the early chapters of this book, we placed early childhood education in a larger social and historical context. We looked at the origins and trends in the kindergarten, nursery-school, day-care, compensatory-education, and home-based program movements. We also tried to incorporate a cross-national perspective and to show how social, economic, political, and technological changes affect the development of early childhood programs and policies. What I would like to discuss now is: What will be the most likely and important changes in the field of early childhood education?

Neisworth: Well, in the short haul, say the next ten years, I believe the major change will be in the area of individualization and technology. Early childhood education will become more technology-assisted and more individualized. Social demands that each child be treated as an individual and the rapidly emerging technology together make a hi-tech, individualized program desirable and feasible. The large supplier industry of early education is already moving that way. Obviously, a behavioral approach is well suited to technology; teaching machines, automated response monitoring, computer programming, and electronic games are all "naturals" for a behavioral model. With these technological advances, early education for the "normal" child will more and more resemble early special education with its individual educational programs and diagnostic–prescriptive teaching model.

Peters: Clearly, technology will have its role, and indeed the introduction of computers into the preschool already is occurring rapidly—though sometimes without much thought to its appropriateness. This is more consistent with a behavioral approach than with the cognitive-developmental approach, at least as it is being used currently. The cognitive-developmental approach—with its emphasis on manipulation of a wide range of materials, extensive individual choice, and emphasis on social interaction and dramatic play—sees the computer and current software offerings as too narrow and constraining. Further, the logic of programming is an adult logic that is inconsistent with the preoperational thought of the preschool years. The preschool use of computers may well be an area in which the clearest distinctions in theory and practice are drawn during the coming decades.

It occurs to me that another area where a sharp distinction will be made is in the area of home-based early education. What do you think?

Neisworth: I agree. Within the next 25 years, I see a shift in the setting for intervention—a shift that is already well under way. When advanced telecommunication is available in homes and neighborhoods, much of what we now call formal early childhood education will take place in the child's home. Parent education and training programs, also available via television and computer software and communications, will make the child's own home the best place for development. Early educators will have new roles as parent educators, child evaluators, trouble-shooters, and specialists in certain areas of development—for example, communications, motor, and social skills.

Peters: That projection assumes, of course, that the parents are in the home to take the responsibility. It is true that business and industry are diversifying and moving into the information age—potentially allowing workers to work from their homes rather than in a central location. The corporate sector of the economy also is developing broader family-oriented policies—maternity and paternity leave, split-time arrangements, and the like—but it still appears that most children will need care outside of their homes. What do you think, Tom?

Yawkey: No doubt single-parent households, dual-worker families, and alternative-family forms will continue to increase over the next decades. These social changes will put additional pressures on early education to supplement the care provided for children, whether in extended nursery schools, day-care centers, or the like. The field will grow in all sectors as a result. The greatest growth is likely to be in the area of infant care. We will need more full-day programs and more infant programs.

Neisworth: I agree that early education will be provided to younger and younger children, with infant programs being increasingly available to both nonhandicapped and handicapped youngsters.

Peters: The increase in demand for child-care arrangements is likely to produce greater diversity in the field. Although the commercial, for-profit day-care field will grow rapidly, so too will some "old" forms of child care. For example, the demand for nannies—live-in trained child-care workers—has increased recently. The few schools training such people in the United States and Britain have been unable to keep up with the demand. This form of child care for the more affluent, high-tech, two-worker family will show a marked increase in the years to come. The nanny's pay and working conditions often are excellent, and the child's quality of care is good. The executive mother who hires a nanny has a relatively clear conscience, and in fact having a nanny is a status symbol for these upwardly mobile, young, professional families. The nanny system fits well with Naisbitt's (1984) idea of the balance of high technology and high human contact—high-tech/high-touch, as he puts it.

Yawkey: I think that the early childhood education field will see real progress in salaries and working conditions for teachers over the next decade. Currently, the salaries of day-care and nursery-school personnel are shamefully low compared to other professions. As a day-care teacher, for instance, I can recall making $1.64 an hour, beginning my day at 7:00 A.M. and ending it at 5:00 P.M. Today, even with the federal minimum wage, the pay is markedly low. Over the next ten years, the salary must increase if we are to attract the qualified people needed in the growing early childhood education field.

Peters: The increased demand should increase salaries—but only if the movement toward professionalism in the field is successful. Credentialing and licensing requirements will have to be maintained and improved; program accreditation is essential, as are a number of other efforts designed to increase respect for the work of caring for and teaching young children.

Neisworth: The increased use of technology, the accountability afforded by behavioral approaches, and the scientific basis of behaviorism will all help in that regard.

Yawkey: We also will need to move toward a system of tax-dollar support for early education programs. Targeted federal programs and income-tax deductions for child care are not enough. Publicly funded preschool programs already exist in California and New York. I see these increasing over the next 20 years. However, we need to provide safeguards so this does not become just an extension of the public schools to younger children. Preschool children have different needs, and programs designed to meet those needs must be far more comprehensive than those currently found in public schools.

Neisworth: I agree that the programs should be comprehensive. Indeed, over the next 25 years, I see early education becoming even more multi-disciplinary than it is now. In particular, I see a much closer relation with the biological health fields. Dietary, biochemical, and technological means will become increasingly available for enhancing and directing development. Social and biological engineering will come together at some point. I hope we will see a corresponding development in our means to control ourselves and our culture—or all will be lost.

Peters: Yes, it would be nice to have some assurance that we will all be here to evaluate our projections for the next several decades. I have one prediction on which I think we can all agree. There will be a continued reliance on research to provide some direction to the field of early childhood education.

There has been a closer relation between theory and practice in this field than in most other human-service fields. We have benefited from that relationship, and so have the children and parents. We all have benefited from the diversity that is early childhood education. There is no reason to expect a marked departure from that position in the future. Because theory, research, and practice work together closely, we shall continue to see growth, progress, and diversity in the field of early childhood education.

Review Questions

1. Briefly list the major differences that distinguish a cognitive-developmental program from a behavioral program.
2. Each of the authors expressed what he considered to be the requirements for being a good teacher. What characteristics do you think are essential? What kind of a program would you prefer? What personal characteristics do you have that you believe would match with your program choice?
3. Outline the major procedures used for group management in the cognitive-developmental program. How do they differ from those in more traditional programs you have observed?
4. How might new high technology be used in the early childhood education field?
5. Given current economic and social trends, what are the most likely sources of fiscal support for early childhood education over the next several decades?

Suggested Activities

1. Retake the Teacher Belief Inventory (Box 3-2, p. 58) and compare your scores to those you obtained in the beginning of the course.

2. Discuss changes in your beliefs with others in your class or with coworkers. Try to decide what made you change. Do you think you now have more congruence between your beliefs and behavior?
3. Read *Megatrends* or similar publications concerning the future directions of society. Discuss how these changes are likely to affect your personal and professional life.
4. Discuss the future of the nursery-school, day-care, and home-based program movement in the United States. Do you see any new movements on the horizon?
5. Convince a friend who is not studying or employed in early childhood education that it is a field worthy of more public and professional recognition, better pay, and public support.

Suggested Reading

Peters, D. L., and Klein, E. The education of young children: perspectives on possible futures. *Theory Into Practice* 20:141–147, 1981.

References

Alberto, P. A., and Troutman, A. C. *Applied behavior analysis for teachers*. Columbus, Ohio: Charles E. Merrill, 1982.

Alford, R. D. (Ed.). *Home oriented preschool education: curriculum planning and guide*. Charleston, W. Va.: Appalachia Educational Laboratory, 1972.

Allen, K. E. *Mainstreaming in early childhood education*. Albany, N.Y.: Delmar, 1980.

Allen, K. E. Curriculum models for successful mainstreaming. *Topics in Early Childhood Special Education, 1* (1981), 45–55.

Allen, K. E., and Goetz, E. M. *Early childhood education — special problems, special solutions*. Rockville, Md.: Aspen Systems, 1982.

Ambron, S. Casual models in early education research. In Kilmer, S. (Ed.), *Advances in early education and day care*, vol. 2. Greenwich, Conn.: JAI Press, 1980.

Andrews, S. R., Blumenthal, J. M., Bache, W. L., and Weiner, G. *The New Orleans model: parents as early childhood educators*. Paper presented at the biennial meeting of the Society for Research in Child Development, Denver, Col.: 1975.

Apollini, T., and Tremblay, A. Peer modeling between toddlers. *Child Study Journal, 8* (1978), 243–253.

Arnheim, R. *Visual thinking*. Berkeley: University of California Press, 1971.

Axelrod, S. *Behavior modification for the classroom teacher*, 2nd ed. New York: McGraw-Hill, 1983.

Azrin, N., and Besalel, V. *How to use overcorrection*. Lawrence, Kans.: H & H Enterprises, 1980.

Baer, D. M., and Roberts, R. R. *How to plan for generalization*. Lawrence, Kans.: H & H Enterprises, 1981.

Bagnato, S. J., and Neisworth, J. T. *Linking developmental assessment and curricula: prescriptions for early intervention*. Rockville, Md.: Aspen Systems, 1981.

Batshaw, M. L., and Perret, Y. M. *Children with handicaps: a medical primer*. Baltimore: Paul H. Brookes, 1981.

Becker, W. C. *Parents are teachers: a child management program*. Champaign, Ill.: Research Press, 1971.

Beller, E. K. Research on organized programs of early education. In Travers, R. (Ed.), *Second handbook of research on teaching*. Chicago: Rand McNally, 1973.

Beller, E., Zimmie, J., and Aitken, L. *Levels of play in different nursery settings*. Paper presented at the meeting of the International Congress for Applied Psychology, Liege, Belgium, 1971.

Belsky, J. Early human experience: a family perspective. *Developmental Psychology, 17* (1981), 3–23.

Belsky, J., and Steinberg, L. The effects of day care: a critical review. *Child Development, 49* (1978), 929–949.

Bereiter, C., and Engelmann, S. *Teaching disadvantaged children in the preschool*. Englewood Cliffs, N.J.: Prentice-Hall, 1966.

Berger, E. H. *Parents as partners in education — the school and home working together*. St. Louis, Mo.: Mosby, 1981.

Bijou, S. W., and Baerm, D. M. *Behavior analysis of child development*. Englewood Cliffs, N.J.: Prentice-Hall, 1978.

Bissell, J. S. *Implementation of planned variation in Head Start*. Washington, D.C.: Office of Child Development, 1971.

Bloom, B., Hastings, J., and Madaus, G. (Eds.). *Handbook on formative and summative evaluation of student learning*. New York: McGraw-Hill, 1971.

Borstein, P. H., and Queuillon, R. P. The effects of a

self-instructional package on overactive preschool boys. *Journal of Applied Behavior Analysis, 5* (1972), 443–454.

Bowlby, J. *Maternal care and mental health.* Geneva: World Health Organization, 1951.

Braun, S., and Edwards, E. *History and theory of early childhood education.* Washington, Ohio: Charles A. Jones, 1972.

Bronfenbrenner, U. *Two worlds of childhood: U.S. and U.S.S.R.* New York: Russel Sage Foundation, 1970.

Bronfenbrenner, U. *Is early intervention effective?* DHEW Publication No. (OHD) 76-30025. Washington, D.C.: U.S. Department of Health, Education, and Welfare, 1975.

Bronfenbrenner, U. *The ecology of human development.* Cambridge, Mass.: Harvard University Press, 1979.

Brophy, J. F., and Evertson, C. M. *Learning from teaching: a developmental perspective.* Boston: Allyn & Bacon, 1976.

Caldwell, B., and Freyer, M. Day care and early education. In Spodek, B. (Ed.), *Handbook of research in early childhood education.* New York: Free Press, 1982.

Carew, J. V., Chan, I., and Halfar, C. *Observing intelligence in young children: eight case studies.* Englewood Cliffs, N.J.: Prentice-Hall, 1976.

Casto, G., White, K., and Taylor, C. An early intervention research institute: studies of the efficacy and cost effectiveness of early intervention at Utah State. *Journal of the Division of Early Childhood, 7* (1983), 5–17.

Chou, S., and Elmore, P. *Early childhood information unit: resource manual and program descriptions.* New York: Educational Products Information Exchange, 1973.

Cohen, A. S., Peters, D. L., and Willis, S. L. The effects of early childhood education student teaching on program preferences, beliefs and behaviors. *Journal of Educational Research, 70*(1) (1976), 15–20.

Cole, J., Welch, K., Yawkey, T. D., and Sucher, F. *Crossties: a discovery program for young children.* Oklahoma City: Economy Company Educational Publishers, 1978.

Colvin, R. W., and Zaffiro, E. M. (Eds.). *Preschool education: a handbook for training of early childhood educators.* New York: Springer, 1974.

Connell, D. B., Layzer, J. I., and Goodson, B. *National study of day care for infants: findings and implications.* Cambridge, Mass.: ABT Associates, 1979.

Cook, R. E., and Armbruster, V. B. *Adapting early childhood curricula: suggestions for meeting special needs.* St. Louis, Mo.: Mosby, 1983.

Cooper, A. Y., and Holt, W. J. Development of social skills and the management of common problems. In Allen, K. E., and Goetz, E. M. (Eds.), *Early childhood education: special problems, special solutions.* Rockville, Md.: Aspen Systems, 1982.

Corcoran, G. B. *Language experience for nursery and kindergarten years.* Itasca, Ill.: F. E. Peacock, 1976.

Corey, J. R., and Shamow, J. The effects of fading on the acquisition and retention of oral reading. *Journal of Applied Behavior Analysis, 5* (1972), 311–315.

Craighead, L. W., Brownell, K. D., and Noran, J. J. Behavioral interventions for weight reduction and smoking cessation. In Craighead, W. E., Kazdin, A. E., and Mahoney, M. J. (Eds.), *Behavior modification principles, issues and applications.* Boston, Mass.: Houghton-Mifflin, 1981.

Dawkins, R. *The extended phenotype: the gene as the unit of selection.* San Francisco: W. H. Freeman, 1982.

Day, M. C., and Parker, R. K. *The preschool in action*, 2nd ed. Boston: Allyn & Bacon, 1977.

Deno, S. L., Jenkins, J. R., and Neisworth, J. T. *Student motivation and classroom management: a behavioristic approach.* Kalamazoo, Mich.: Behaviordelia, 1977.

DeVries, R. Theory in educational practice. In Colvin, R., and Zaffiro, E. (Eds.), *Preschool education: a handbook for the training of early childhood educators.* New York: Springer, 1974.

Dewey, J. My pedagogic creed, 1897. As reprinted in R. Ulich (Ed.), *Three thousand years of educational wisdom.* Cambridge, Mass.: Harvard University Press, 1954.

Dorry, G. W., and Zeaman, D. Teaching a simple reading vocabulary to retarded children: effectiveness of fading and nonfading procedures. *American Journal of Mental Deficiency, 79* (1975), 711–716.

Dreyer, A., and Rigler, D. Cognitive performance in Montessori and nursery school children. *Journal of Educational Research, 62* (1969), 411–416.

Dudzinski, D., and Peters, D. L. Home-based program: a growing alternative. *Child Care Quarterly, 6*(1) (1977), 61–71.

Dunkin, M., and Biddle, B. *The study of teaching.* New York: Holt, Rinehart & Winston, 1974.

Elliott, D. L. *Early childhood education: how to select and evaluate materials.* New York: Educational Products Information Exchange Institute, 1972.

Engelmann, S., and Bruner, E. C. *DISTAR reading.* Chicago: Science Research Associates, 1969.

Engelmann, S., and Carnine, D. *Distar arithmetic.* Chicago: Science Research Associates, 1969.

Engelmann, S., Osborn, J., and Engelmann, T. *Distar language.* Chicago: Science Research Associates, 1969.

Erikson, E. *Childhood and society.* New York: Norton, 1963.

Etzel, B. C., and LeBlanc, J. M. The simplest treatment alternative: the law of parsimony applied to choosing appropriate instructional control and errorless learning procedures for the difficult-to-teach child. *Journal of Autism and Developmental Disorders, 9* (1979), 361–382.

Evans, E. *Contemporary influences in early childhood education,* 2nd ed. New York: Holt, Rinehart & Winston, 1975.

Evans, E. Curriculum models and early childhood education. In Spodek, B., (Ed.), *Handbook of research in early childhood education.* New York: The Free Press, 1982.

Evans, J. *Working with parents of handicapped children.* Reston, Va.: Council for Exceptional Children, 1979.

Fein, G., and Clarke-Stewart, A. *Day care in context.* New York: Wiley, 1973.

Fein, G., and Schwartz, P. Developmental theories in early education. In Spodek, B. (Ed.), *Handbook of research in early childhood education.* New York: The Free Press, 1982.

Ferster, C. B., and Culbertson, S. A. *Behavioral principles.* Englewood Cliffs, N.J.: Prentice-Hall, 1982.

Ferster, C. B., and Skinner, B. F. *Schedules of reinforcement.* New York: Appleton-Century-Crofts, 1957.

Flanders, N. *Analyzing teacher behavior.* Reading, Mass.: Addison-Wesley, 1970.

Flavell, J. H. *The development psychology of Jean Piaget.* New York: D. Van Nostrand, 1963.

Forman, G. E., and Kuchner, D. S. *The child's construction of knowledge: Piaget for teaching children.* Monterey, Calif.: Brooks/Cole, 1977.

Forrester, B. J. *Parents as educational change agents for infants: competencies not credentials.* Paper presented at the annual meeting of the Council on Exceptional Children, Washington, D.C., 1972.

Fosburg, S. *Design of the national day care home study.*

Paper presented at the annual meeting of the American Educational Research Association, Boston, 1980.

Fowler, W. *Daycare and its effects on child development.* Toronto, Canada: The Ontario Institute for Studies in Education Press, 1978.

Fraiberg, S. H. *The magic years: understanding and handling the problems of early childhood.* New York: Scribner, 1959.

Frank, L. The beginnings of child development and family life education in the twentieth century. *Merrill-Palmer Quarterly, 8*(4) (1962), 7–28.

Freud, S. *Psychoanalysis for teachers and parents.* Boston: Emerson Books, 1935.

Frost, J., and Klein, B. *Children's play and playgrounds.* Boston: Allyn & Bacon, 1979.

Furth, H. G. *Piaget and knowledge: theoretical foundations.* Englewood Cliffs, N.J.: Prentice-Hall, 1960.

Furth, H. G., and Wachs, H. *Thinking goes to school— Piaget's theory in practice.* New York: Oxford University Press, 1975.

Gesell, A. *The preschool child: from the standpoint of public hygiene and education.* Boston: Houghton-Mifflin, 1923.

Ginsburg, H., and Opper, S. *Piaget's theory of intellectual development.* Englewood Cliffs, N.J.: Prentice-Hall, 1969.

Glass, R. M., Christiansen, J., and Christiansen, J. L. *Teaching exceptional students in the regular classroom.* Boston: Little, Brown, 1982.

Goetz, E. M. Behavior principles and techniques. In Allen, K. E., and Goetz, E. M. (Eds.), *Early childhood education.* Rockville, Md.: Aspen Systems, 1982.

Goldfarb, W. The effects of early institutional care on adolescent personality. *Journal of Experimental Education, 12* (1943), 106–129.

Good, T., Biddle, B., and Brophy, J. *Teachers make a difference.* New York: Holt, Rinehart & Winston, 1970.

Goodwin, W., and Driscoll, L. *Handbook for measurement and evaluation in early childhood education.* San Francisco: Jossey-Bass, 1980.

Gordon, I. *Early child stimulation through parent education* (final report). Washington, D.C.: U.S. Department of Health, Education, and Welfare; Children's Bureau, 1971.

Gordon, I. An instructional theory approach to the analyses of selected early childhood programs. In Gordon, I. (Ed.), *Early childhood education*. Chicago: National Society for the Study of Education, 1972.

Gordon, I., and Jester, R. E. Techniques of observing teaching in early childhood. In Travers, R., (Ed.), *Second handbook of research on teaching*. Chicago: Rand McNally, 1973.

Gray, S., and Klaus, R. The early training project: a seventh year report. *Child Development, 41* (1970), 909–924.

Grotberg, E. *Project Head Start: review of research 1965–1969*. Washington, D.C.: Office of Economic Opportunity, 1969.

Guralnick, M. J. (Ed.). *Early intervention and the integration of handicapped and nonhandicapped children*. Baltimore, Md.: University Park Press, 1978.

Hall, R. V., and Hall, R. C. *How to use planned ignoring (extinction)*. Lawrence, Kans.: H & H Enterprises, 1980a.

Hall, R. V., and Hall, R. C. *How to use time out*. Lawrence, Kans.: H & H Enterprises, 1980b.

Hall, R. V., and Hall, R. C. *How to negotiate a behavioral contract*. Austin, Texas: Pro-Ed, 1982.

Harrell, J., and Ridley, C. Substitute child care, maternal employment and the quality of mother-child interaction. *Journal of Marriage and the Family, 37* (1975), 556–564.

Hart, B. So that teachers can teach: assigning roles and responsibilities. In Mori, A. A., Fewell, R. R., Garwood, S. G., and Neisworth, J. T. (Eds.), *Topics in early childhood special education, 2* (1) (1982), 1–8.

Heinicke, C., Friedman, D., Prescott, E., Puncel, C., and Sale, J. The organization of day care: considerations relating to the mental health of child and family. *American Journal of Orthopsychiatry, 43* (1973), 8–22.

Hellmoth, J. (Ed.). *Disadvantaged child: compensatory education, a national debate*, vol. 3. New York: Brunner/Mazel, 1970.

Hendrick, S. *Total learning for the whole child*. St. Louis, Mo.: Mosby, 1980.

Herron, M. A toy can be more than a plaything. *American Education, 8* (1972), 21–23.

Herron, R. E., and Sutton-Smith, B. *Child's play*. New York: Wiley, 1971.

Heward, W. L., Dardig, J. C., and Rossett, A. *Working with parents of handicapped children*. Columbus, Ohio: Charles E. Merrill, 1979.

Hildebrand, V. Families and child care: a global ecosystem perspective. In Kostelnik, M., Raben, A., Phenice, L., and Soderman, A. (Eds.), *Child nurturance*, vol. 2. New York: Plenum Press, 1982.

Hofferth, S. Daycare in the next decade: 1980–1990. *Journal of Marriage and the Family, 41* (1979), 649–658.

Hoffman, D. *Parent participation in preschool day care*. Atlanta, Ga.: Southeastern Education Laboratory, 1971.

Honig, A. Parent involvement in early childhood education. In Spodek, B. (Ed.), *Handbook of research in early childhood education*. New York: Free Press, 1982.

Hundert, J. Stimulus generalization after training an autistic deaf boy in manual signs. *Education and Treatment of Children, 4*(4) (1981), 329–337.

Huxley, A. *Brave new world*. London: Chatto and Windus, 1958.

Inhelder, B., and Piaget, J. *The growth of logical thinking from childhood to adolescence* (A. Parsons and S. Pribram, Trans.). New York: Basic Books, 1958.

Johnson, B. Marital and family characteristics of the labor force: March, 1979. *Monthly Labor Review, 103* (1980), 48–52.

Kadushin, A. Child welfare strategies for the coming years: an overview. In *Child welfare strategy for the coming years* (OHDS 78-30158). Washington, D.C.: U.S. Department of Health, Education, and Welfare. 1978.

Kagan, J. The effect of day care on the infant. In *Policy issues in day care: summaries of 21 papers*. Washington, D.C.: U.S. Department of Health, Education, and Welfare, Office of the Assistant Secretary for Planning and Evaluation, 1978.

Kamerman, S., and Kahn, A. *Social services in the United States*. Philadelphia: Temple University Press, 1976.

Kamii, C. Evaluation of learning in preschool education. In Bloom, B., Hastings, J., and Madaus, G. (Eds.), *Handbook on formative and summative evaluation of student learning*. New York: McGraw-Hill, 1971.

Kamii, C., and DeVries, R. Piaget for early education. In Day, M. C., and Parker, R. K. (Eds.), *The preschool in action* (2nd ed.). Boston: Allyn & Bacon, 1977.

Kamii, C., and DeVries, R. *Physical knowledge in preschool education.* Englewood Cliffs, N.J.: Prentice-Hall, 1978.

Karnes, M. B., Hodgins, A. S., Teska, J. A., and Kirk, S. A. *Investigations of classroom and at home interventions* (final report). Washington, D.C.: U.S. Department of Health, Education, and Welfare; Bureau of Research, 1969.

Karnes, M. B., and Teska, J. A. Toward successful parent involvement in programs for handicapped children. In Gallagher, J. J. (Ed.), *New directions for exceptional children: parents and families of handicapped children.* San Francisco, Calif.: Jossey-Bass, 1980.

Katz, L. *Policy formation and early childhood pedagogy.* Paper presented at the annual meeting of the American Educational Research Association, Chicago, 1974.

Kazdin, A. E. *Behavior modification in applied settings*, rev. ed. Homewood, Ill.: Dorsey Press, 1980.

Kazdin, A. E. The token economy: a decade later. *Journal of Applied Behavioral Analysis, 15*(3) (1982), 431–445.

Kessen, W. *The child.* New York: Wiley, 1965.

Kohlberg, L. Early education: a cognitive-developmental view. *Child Development, 39* (1968), 1013–1062.

Krasner, L., and Krasner, M. Token economies and other planned environments. In Thoresen, C. E. (Ed.), *Behavior modification in education: the seventy-second yearbook of the national society for the study of education, part 1.* Chicago: University of Chicago Press, 1972.

Kroth, R. L., and Simpson, R. L. *Parent conferences as a teaching strategy.* Denver, Col.: Love Publishing, 1977.

Lally, J. R., and Honig, A. S. The family development research program. In Parker, R. K., (Ed.), *Preschool in action*, 2nd ed. Boston: Allyn & Bacon, 1975.

Landreth, C. *Preschool learning and teaching.* New York: Harper & Row, 1972.

LeBlanc, J. M. Instructing difficult-to-teach children. In Allen, K. E., and Goetz, E. M. (Eds.), *Early childhood education—special problems, special solutions.* Rockville, Md.: Aspen Systems, 1982.

Levitt, E., and Cohen, S. Educating parents of children with special needs. In Baruth, L. and Burrgra, M. (Eds.), *Counseling parents of exceptional children.* Guilford, Conn.: Special Learning, 1979.

Loda, F. The health of children in group day care. In Elardo, R., and Pagan, B. (Eds.), *Perspectives on infant day care.* Little Rock, Ark.: Southern Association on Children Under Six, 1976.

Lomax, E. M. *Science and patterns of child care.* San Francisco: W. H. Freeman, 1978.

Long, F., Peters, D. L., and Garduque, L. Continuity between home and day care: a model for defining relevant dimensions of child care. In Sigel, I. (Ed.), *Advances in applied developmental psychology.* Norwood, N.J.: Ablex, 1984.

Lorton, S. W., and Walley, B. L. *Introduction to early childhood education.* New York: D. Van Nostrand, 1979.

Maccoby, E., and Zellner, M. *Experiments in primary education: aspects of Project Follow-Through.* New York: Harcourt, 1970.

Mager, R. *Preparing objectives for programmed instruction.* San Francisco: Fearon, 1962.

Malott, R., Tillema, M., and Glenn, S. *Behavior analysis and behavior modification: an introduction.* Kalamazoo, Mich.: Behaviordelia, 1978.

Marion, M. *Guidance of young children.* St. Louis, Mo.: Mosby, 1981.

McKusick, V. A. *Mendelian inheritance in man.* Baltimore: The Johns Hopkins University Press, 1976.

Meyers, E. S., Ball, H. H., and Crutchfield, M. *The kindergarten teacher's handbook.* Los Angeles: Grammercy Press, 1973.

Miller, L. K. *Principles of everyday behavior analysis.* Monterey, Calif.: Brooks/Cole, 1980.

Miller, L., and Dyer, J. Four preschool programs: their dimensions and effects. *Monograph of the Society for Research in Child Development*, Serial #162, vol. 40 (1975), 5–6.

Miller, W. H. *Systematic parent training: procedures, cases, and issues.* Champaign, Ill.: Research Press, 1975.

Mori, A. A., and Neisworth, J. T. Curricula in early childhood special education: some generic and special considerations. *Topics in Early Childhood Special Education, 2* (1983), 1–8.

Naisbitt, J. *Megatrends.* New York: Warner Books, 1984.

Neisworth, J. T., Kurtz, D., Ross, A., and Madle, R. A. Naturalistic assessment of neurological diagnoses and pharmacological intervention. *Journal of Learning Disabilities, 9* (1976), 24–25.

Neisworth, J. T., and Smith, R. M. Approaches to explaining retarded behavior. In *Guiding the retarded to success: basic behavior principles and practices.* Austin, Texas: Pro-Ed, 1984.

Neisworth, J. T., Willoughby-Herb, S. J., Bagnato, S. J., Cartwright, C. A., and Laub, K. W. *Individualized education for preschool exceptional children*. Rockville, Md.: Aspen Systems, 1980.

Parker, R. Theory in early education curricula. In Colvin, R., and Zaffiro, E. (Eds.), *Preschool education: a handbook for the training of early childhood educators*. New York: Springer, 1974.

Peters, D. L. *Day care homes: a Pennsylvania profile* (CHSD Report No. 18). University Park, Penn.: Pennsylvania State University, 1972.

Peters, D. L. Early childhood education: an overview and evaluation. In Hom, H., and Robinson, P. (Eds.), *Psychological processes in early education*. New York: Academic Press, 1977.

Peters, D. L. Social science and social policy and the care of young children. *Journal of Applied Developmental Psychology*, *1* (1980), 7–27.

Peters, D. L., and Beker, J. (Eds.). *Day care: problems, process, prospects*. New York: Human Sciences Press, 1975.

Peters, D. L., and Belsky, J. The day care movement: past, present and future. In Kostelnik, M., Rabin, A., Phence, L., and Soderman, A. (Eds.), *Child nurturance*, vol. 2. New York: Plenum, 1982.

Peters, D. L., Burgess, J. L., and McConnell, H. *COMPARENT: a training program for parents*. University Park, Penn.: Pennsylvania State University, 1979.

Peters, D. L., and Klein, E. The education of young children: Perspectives on possible futures. *Theory Into Practice*, *20*(2) (1981), 141–147.

Peters, D. L., and Koppel, F. Day care: an overview. *Child and Youth Services*, 1(4) (1977), 1–11.

Peters, D. L., and Willis, S. L. *Early childhood*. Monterey, Calif.: Brooks/Cole, 1978.

Piaget, J. *Play, dreams, and imitation in childhood*. New York: Norton, 1962.

Piaget, J. *The language and thought of the child*. New York: New American Library, 1974.

Powell, D. R. *The interface between families and child care programs*. Detroit: Merrill-Palmer Institute, 1977.

Powell, D. R. Correlates of parent–teacher communication frequency and diversity. *The Journal of Educational Research*, *71* (1978), 333–341.(a)

Powell, D. R. The interpersonal relationship between parents and caregivers in day care settings. *American Journal of Orthopsychiatry*, *48* (1978), 680–689.(b)

Powell, D. R. Family-environment relations and early childrearing: the role of social networks and neighborhoods. *Journal of Research and Development in Education*, *13* (1979), 1–11.

Powell, D. R. Toward a socio-ecological perspective of relations between parents and childcare programs. In Kilmer, S. (Ed.), *Advances in early education and day care*, vol. 1. Greenwich, Conn.: JAI Press, 1980.

Premack, D. Reversibility of the reinforcement relation. *Science*, *136* (1962), 255–267.

Raben, A. Supplementary parenting in the Kibbutz childrearing system. In Kostelnik, M., Raben, A., Phenice, L., and Soderman, A. (Eds.), *Child nurturance*, vol. 2. New York: Plenum, 1982.

Rabin-Bickelman, E., and Marholin, D., II. Programming generalization of treatment effects: S stimulus control procedure. *Journal of Behavioral Therapy and Experimental Psychiatry*, *9* (1978), 277–281.

Ramey, C. T., and Bryant, D. M. Evidence for prevention of developmental retardation during infancy. *Journal of the Division for Early Childhood*, *5* (1982), 73–78.

Rhine, W. R. (Ed.). *Making schools more effective: new directions for follow-through*. New York: Academic Press, 1981.

Robinson, C. C., and Robinson, J. H. Sensorimotor functions and cognitive development. In Snell, M. E. (Ed.), *Systematic instruction of the moderately and severely handicapped*. Columbus, Ohio: Charles E. Merrill, 1983.

Robinson, M. E. *The parent–child development centers: an experimental R&D strategy*. Paper presented at the biennial meeting of the Society for Research in Child Development, Denver, Col.: 1975.

Robinson, N., and Robinson, H. A cross-cultural view of early education. In Gordon, I. (Ed.), *Early childhood education*. Chicago: University of Chicago Press, 1972.

Robinson, N., Robinson, H., Darling, M., and Holm, G. *A world of children*. Monterey, Calif.: Brooks/Cole, 1979.

Rodes, T., and Moore, J. *National child care consumer study: American consumer attitudes and opinions on child care*. Arlington, Va.: Kappa Systems, 1975.

Rose, T. L., Koorland, M. A., and Epstein, M. H. A review of applied behavior analysis interventions with learning disabled children. *Education and Treatment of Children*, *5*(1) (1982), 41–58.

Ross, A. O. *Child behavior therapy: principles, procedures and empirical basis*. New York: Wiley, 1981.

Rowbury, T. Preacademic skills for the reluctant learner. In Allen, K. E., and Goetz, E. M. (Eds.), *Early childhood education*. Rockville, Md.: Aspen Systems, 1982.

Rowen, B., Byrne, S., and Winter, L. *The learning match: a developmental guide to teaching young children*. Englewood Cliffs, N.J.: Prentice-Hall, 1980.

Ruopp, R., Travers, J., Glantz, F., and Coelen, C. *Children at the center*, vol. 1, Final Report of the National Day Care Study. Cambridge, Mass.: ABT Associates, 1979.

Rutherford, R. B., and Edgar, E. *Teachers and parents: a guide to interaction and cooperation*. Boston: Allyn & Bacon, 1979.

Ryan, S. *A report on longitudinal evaluations of preschool programs*, vol. 1. Washington, D.C.: Office of Child Development, 1974.

Safford, P. L. *Teaching young children with special needs*. St. Louis, Mo.: Mosby, 1978.

Sanford, A. *Learning accomplishment profile*. Winston-Salem, N.C.: Kaplan School Supply, 1978.

Sciarra, D. S., and Dorsey, H. G. *Developing and administering a child care center*. New York: Houghton Mifflin, 1979.

Sears, P. S., and Dowley, E. Research on teaching in the nursery school. In Gage, N. L., (Ed.), *Handbook of research on teaching*. Chicago: Rand McNally, 1963.

Shearer, D. Parents as educators. In Maybanks, S., and Bryce, M. (Eds.), *Home-based services for children and families*. Springfield, Ill.: Charles C Thomas, 1979.

Shearer, M. S., and Shearer, D. E. The Portage project: a model for early childhood education. *Exceptional Children*, 39 (1972), 210–217.

Sigel, I. E., and Cocking, R. R. *Cognitive development from childhood to adolescence: a constructivist perspective*. New York: Holt, Rinehart & Winston, 1977.

Singer, S. *Human genetics: an introduction to the principles of heredity*. San Francisco: W. H. Freeman, 1978.

Skinner, B. F. *The technology of teaching*. New York: Appleton-Century-Crofts, 1968.

Skinner, B. F. *Contingencies of reinforcement: a theoretical analysis*. New York: Appleton-Century-Crofts, 1969.

Skinner, B. F. *About behaviorism*. New York: Alfred A. Knopf, 1974.

Smith, D. D., and Lavitt, T. C. The differential effects of reinforcement contingencies on arithmetic performance. *Journal of Learning Disabilities*, 9 (1976), 32–40.

Snell, M., and Smith, D. Developing the IEP: selecting and assessing skills. In Snell, M. E. (Ed.), *Systematic instruction of the moderately and severely handicapped*, 2nd ed. Columbus, Ohio: Charles E. Merrill, 1983a.

Snell, M., and Smith, D. Implementing and monitoring the IEP: intervention strategies. In Snell, M. E. (Ed.), *Systematic instruction of the moderately and severely handicapped*, 2nd ed. Columbus, Ohio: Charles E. Merrill, 1983b.

Soar, R., and Soar, R. An empirical analysis of selected Follow-through programs. In Gordon, I. (Ed.), *Early childhood education*. Chicago: National Society for the Study of Education, 1972.

Spitz, R. A. Hospitalism: an inquiry into the genesis of psychiatric conditions in early childhood. *Psychoanalytic Study of the Child*, 1 (1945), 53–74.

Stallings, J. Implementation and child effects of teaching practices in Follow-through classrooms. *Monograph of the Society for Research in Child Development*, Serial #163, 40 (1975), 7–8.

Steinberg, L., and Green, C. *How parents may mediate the effect of day care*. Paper presented at the biennial meeting of the Society for Research in Child Development, San Francisco, 1979.

Stokes, T. F., and Baer, D. M. An implicit technology of generalization. *Journal of Applied Behavior Analysis*, 10 (1977), 349–368.

Suchman, L. *Evaluative research*. San Francisco: Sage, 1967.

Tanner, D., and Tanner, L. N. *Curriculum development*. New York: MacMillan, 1975.

Taylor, B. S. *When I do, I learn*. Provo, Utah: Brigham Young University, 1974.

Thomas, A., Chess, S., and Birch, H. G. *Behavioral individuality in early childhood*. New York: New York University Press, 1971.

Touchette, C. E. Mental retardation: an introduction to the analysis and remediation of behavioral deficiency. In Marholin, D. (Ed.), *Child behavior therapy*. New York: Gardner Press, 1978.

Travers, J., and Ruopp, R. *National day care study: preliminary findings and their implications: 31 January, 1978*. Cambridge, Mass.: ABT Associates, 1978.

Ulich, R. *History of educational thought*. New York: American Book Co., 1950.

Ulich, R. *Three thousand years of educational thought*. Cambridge, Mass.: Harvard University Press, 1954.

Van Houten, R. *How to use reprimands*. Lawrence, Kans.: H&H Enterprises, 1980.

Verma, S., and Peters, D. L. Day care teacher practices and beliefs. *The Alberta Journal of Educational Research*, *21*(1) (1975), 46–55.

Wadsworth, B. J. *Piaget's theory of cognitive development*. New York: McKay, 1974.

Walsh, H. M. *Introducing the young child to the social world*. New York: Macmillan, 1980.

Weikart, D., Deloria, D., Lawson, S., and Wiegerink, R. *Longitudinal results of the Ypsilanti preschool project*. Ypsilanti, Mich.: High/Scope Educational Research Foundation, 1970.

Willoughby-Herb, S. J., and Neisworth, J. T. *HICOMP curriculum*. Columbus, Ohio: Charles E. Merrill, 1983.

Wohlwill, J. F. The age variable in psychological research. Psychological Review, *77*(1) (1970), 49–64.

Wolfensberger, W. *The principle of normalization in human services*. Toronto: National Institute on Mental Retardation, 1972.

Wright, H. F. Observational child study. In Mussen, P. H. (Ed.), *Handbook of research methods in child study*. New York: Wiley, 1960.

Yawkey, T. D. *Project P.I.A.G.E.T.: bilingual–Hispanic Title VII demonstration kindergarten model—results of the first project year, 1981–1982* (vol. 1, final technical report No. 135 submitted to the Office of Bi-

lingual and Minority Languages Affairs, U.S. Department of Education, mimeographed). University Park, Penn.: Pennsylvania State University, 1982.

Yawkey, T. D. *Project P.I.A.G.E.T.: bilingual–Hispanic Title VII demonstration kindergarten model—results of the second project year, 1983–1984* (vol. 1, final technical report No. 165 submitted to the Office of Bilingual Education and Minority Languages Affairs, U.S. Department of Education, mimeographed). University Park, Penn.: The Pennsylvania State University, 1984.

Yawkey, T. D., Askov, E. N., Dupuis, M. M., Cartwright, C. A., Fairchild, S. H., and Yawkey, M. L. *Language arts for the young child*. Itasca, Ill.: Peacock, 1981.

Yawkey, T. D., and Diantoniis, J. M. *Effects of dramatic play as a basis of parent instructional model for home intervention programming for Hispanic parents of preschool children: findings from project years 1981–1982 and 1982–1983*. Research paper presented at the tenth annual meeting of The Association for the Anthropological Study of Play, Clemson, S.C., 1984.

Zigler, E., and Lang, M. Head Start: looking toward the future. *Young Children*, *38*(6) (1983), 3–6.

Zigler, E., and Valentine, J. (Eds.). *Project Head Start: a legacy of the war on poverty*. New York: Free Press, 1979.

Zimiles, H. Psychodynamic theory of development. In Spodek, B. (Ed.), *Handbook of research in early childhood education*. New York: Free Press, 1982.

INDEX

PHOTO CREDITS